Diaspora

An Introduction

Jana Evans Braziel

Blackwell
Publishing

BLACKWELL PUBLISHING
350 Main Street, Malden, MA 02148–5020, USA
9600 Garsington Road, Oxford OX4 2DQ, UK
550 Swanston Street, Carlton, Victoria 3053, Australia

The right of Jana Evans Braziel to be identified as the author of this work has been asserted in accordance with the UK Copyright, Designs, and Patents Act 1988.

Designations used by companies to distinguish their products are often claimed as trademarks. All brand names and product names used in this book are trade names, service marks, trademarks, or registered trademarks of their respective owners. The publisher is not associated with any product or vendor mentioned in this book.

This publication is designed to provide accurate and authoritative information in regard to the subject matter covered. It is sold on the understanding that the publisher is not engaged in rendering professional services. If professional advice or other expert assistance is required, the services of a competent professional should be sought.

First published 2008 by Blackwell Publishing Ltd

1   2008

Library of Congress Cataloging-in-Publication Data

Braziel, Jana Evans, 1967–
    Diaspora : an introduction / Jana Evans Braziel.
        p.   cm.
    Includes bibliographical references and index.
    ISBN 978-1-4051-5339-3 (hardcover : alk. paper) – ISBN 978-1-4051-5340-9 (pbk. : alk. paper) 1. Emigration and immigration–Social aspects. 2. Globalization. I. Title.

JV6035.B73 2007
304.8–dc22

                                    2007024731

ISBN-13: 978-1-4051-5339-3 (hardback)
ISBN-13: 978-1-4051-5340-9 (paperback)

A catalogue record for this title is available from the British Library.

Set in 10 on 12.5 pt Sabon
by SNP Best-set Typesetter Ltd, Hong Kong
Printed and bound in Singapore
by Utopia Press Pte Ltd

The publisher's policy is to use permanent paper from mills that operate a sustainable forestry policy, and which has been manufactured from pulp processed using acid-free and elementary chlorine-free practices. Furthermore, the publisher ensures that the text paper and cover board used have met acceptable environmental accreditation standards.

For further information on
Blackwell Publishing, visit our website at
www.blackwellpublishing.com

Diaspora

For Zalman and Charles,
orphans, brothers, loggers, diasporas

Contents

Acknowledgments

For my family, Jessi, Maddie, Dylan, and especially Jim Braziel, who no doubt suffered greatly during the writing of this manuscript, I can only evoke the words of Emmanuel Levinas who soberly wrote, "*there is no debt* in regard to the other, for what is due is unpayable: one is never free of it." I do, however, owe other debts – finite and infinite, intellectual and emotional. For research funding, I owe an intellectual debt of gratitude to the Taft Center for the Humanities, the McMicken College of Arts and Sciences, and the Department of English at the University of Cincinnati. With immense gratitude, I acknowledge and express my thanks to Jayne Fargnoli, the most amazing editor, and her wonderful assistants, Ken Provencher and Margot A. Morse. I also thank Jack Messenger, copy-editor extraordinaire! Thanks to exacting, yet supportive professors and mentors: Nancy Felson, Ron Bogue, Sarah Spence, Robbie Schwartzald, Lisa Henderson, Anne Ferguson, Cathy Portuges, and Elizabeth Petroff. Thanks also to colleagues at the University of Wisconsin-La Crosse: Susan Crutchfield, Don LaCosse, Sonia Schrag, Terry Beck, and Joe Young. I am also grateful to colleagues in the Five Colleges of western Massachusetts, especially to Nate Therien, Lorna Peterson, Dale Peterson, Judy Frank, Barry O'Connell, Andrea Rushing, Rhonda Cobham-Sander, Jeff Ferguson, Rowland Abiodun, and Leah Hewitt. For intellectual support and friendship, I am equally indebted to all of my colleagues at the University of Cincinnati, but especially to Karen Gould, Lee Person, Jon Kamholtz, Russel Durst, Jonathan Alexander, Michelle Gibson, Deb Meem, Stan Corkin, Maria Romagnoli, Jim Schiff, Jay Twomey, Julia Carlson, Laura Micciche, Gary Weissman, Michael Griffith, Nicola Mason, Brock Clarke, Joanie Mackowski, Tamar Heller, John Bryan, Sharon Dean, Beth Ash, Lisa Hoagland, Jenny Wohlfarth, Tom LeClair, and Kathy Rentz. For generously loaning his books on Mexico and guiding me across the border, thanks to Dan LaBotz. Friends to whom I am immeasurably grateful: Julie Gerk-Hernandez, Madhu Sinha, Susan Vesio-Steinkamp, Kirk Boyle, Sarah Domet, Suzanne Warren, Annelie Klein, Neil Hartlen, Dawn Pittman Baker (*in memoriam*), and my siblings Julie Crawford,

Dawn Kyle, and Ron Evans. Julie, you are rock and foundation and love, and I am grateful to you (both of you!) And, of course, express and heartfelt gratitude to my parents Ronald and Judy Evans and their parents, my beloved grandparents: Ralph and Leona Evans; Leroy and Winnie Clements. For kindness, love, friendship, and guidance, I say in closing: *you* are the *raison d'être*!

– faith, thought, meaning. *brulé zen!*

Thank you all!

Preface
Between Homelands and Homelessness? New Diasporas, Global Refugees

International migrants, those residing outside of their country of birth, totaled 154 million in 1990. By the year 2000, the United Nations estimated that there were 175 million immigrants worldwide; and by 2006, that figure totaled 200 million international migrants. Of these numbers, a significant proportion are those legally designated and politically labeled as "illegal aliens" (those who have crossed international borders and entered into a country illegally), or undocumented workers (those living and working in a country illegally): in the United States alone, there were an estimated 2.5 million "illegals" in 1989, and the number had escalated to an estimated 8.5 million in 2000.[1] By most recent scholarly estimates, the number of "illegal" immigrants in the US now totals approximately 11.5 million people. Globally, refugees also comprise a significant proportion of total international migrants: in 1990, there were approximately 15 million refugees worldwide, and by 2000, there were approximately 21.5 million refugees and an additional 30 million internally displaced persons (IDPs), although this number seems modest and must be contextualized within a "refugee crisis" since the 1990s and the declining number of post-Cold War nation-states granting refuge.[2]

International migrants, uprooted from family, friends, and nation-state, dispersed from their homelands, and scattered across the globe in one or more countries of adoption, form vibrant diasporic communities. These phenomena – international migration, diasporas, and diasporic politics – are the subjects of this book. International migrations and transnational diasporas are also, in many ways, the twin faces of late capitalism or global capitalism: these intertwined phenomena manifest the lived experiences, human complications, and ideological contradictions of the era. Foreign-exchange students, professors, corporate executive officers, financial managers, nuclear physicists, physicians, nurses, electric and electronic engineers, contractors, carpenters, mid-level managers, agricultural farm workers, textile manufacturers, maids and other domestic workers, cooks, dishwashers, and garbage collectors, the global economy in all its messy sprawl and multinational efficiency, or inefficiency as the reality may be, requires the migration and relocation of diverse workers – some highly literate and skilled, others uneducated with low-level skills, but no less vital to the machinations of global capitalism and its interlocking systems of multinational production and transnational monetary flows.

Migrations and diasporas are thus part of global capitalism: the international divisions of labor; the transnationalizations of production and finance; the consolidation of the "international" monetary fund; the regulation of world trade in goods and services; and the interstitial relations of development and international (or "world bank") lending have all led to massive displacements in human capital – some voluntary, some not – as people migrate to work, or flee violence and political repression, and as developing countries strategically export labor and import multinational corporations, or ground national economic development policies within a three-pronged strategy of exported labor, returned diasporic remittances, and imported multinational corporations. Migratory flows and diasporic communities are both produced by the discordant flows of globalization, even as they are productive of its disjunctures and cultural cacophony. Power may be productive, as Michel Foucault taught us; but it is not always in control of what it produces. In other words, global capitalism may produce diasporas, but diasporas also "write back" to power. Global traffic is not one-way; nor is it simply two-laned; its traffic moves through multiply striated vectors and cross-wired flows of myriad exchanges.[3]

Since the early 1980s, with the administrations of US President Ronald Reagan and UK Prime Minister Margaret Thatcher during the late and waning years of the Cold War, marked by economic excess, huge national deficits, proliferation of nuclear armament production, and an escalation of the US-USSR "arms race" ending in a final fiscal blow to communism by the US and the overdeveloped first-world countries which outspent the Soviets and bankrupted their union, neoconservatism has spread across the globe, though promulgated by international neoliberal economic policies in the service of geopolitical neocons. The fall of the Berlin Wall on November 9, 1989, and the subsequent national reunification of the Bundesrepublik Deutschland (BDR) and the Deutsche Demokratische Republik (DDR) in October 1990, and the concomitant collapse of communism in the world's second Superpower and the dissolution of the Soviet Union in 1991 – all led to a preemptory celebration of global capitalism in the West with capitalist cheerleaders like Francis Fukuyama lauding the transcendence of capital and "The End of History": this "new" moment of global capital was not, for all its basking in the aura of the "new," new at all. Global capitalism was decades-long in the international making, a post-World War II phenomenon, and a worldwide strategic plan for international economic development. Spill out from the end of the Cold War and the so-called "death" of communism has been manifold: the early 1990s saw the absolute end to Soviet support for small states in the "third world" (as US-designated); the outbreak of ethnic conflicts in newly independent states (NISs) formerly part of the Soviet Union; the secondary geopolitical dissolution of socialist or Marxist states, which were formerly supported by the USSR; a global refugee crisis as people fled inter-ethnic violence and genocidal pogroms of "ethnic cleansing"; economic liberalization in Russia (a system of graduated capitalist transformation called *Perestroika* and greater political transparency known as *Glasnost* under Mikhail Gorbachev) and in other communist states, particularly in China and in Cuba, both of which experienced influxes of US dollars and other capitalist currencies; the expansive power of transnational or multinational corporations (in place since the late 1960s to early 1970s, but with their structural roots in the Bretton Woods conference of 1944); the post-communist signing of multilateral trade agreements, such as the North American Free Trade Agreement (NAFTA), and the formation of the World Trade Organization (WTO) from the remnants of the General Agreement on Tariffs and Trades (GATT) in 1944; and the creation of regional trade agreements, such as the Caribbean Community (Caricom) and the European Community, or the European Union (EU). The period also witnessed a rapid increase in international migration (and global diasporic communities) of capitalists, corporate executives, mid-level managers, students, engineers, computer scientists, and other high-skilled migrants, and the creation of global diasporic communities supported by transnational relations; sustained through financial remittances, telecommunications, and digital and cybertechnologies, and prior to September 11, 2001, the ease and relatively inexpensive cost of international airfare for those with cultural capital to burn. That being said, another fact remains true of this time period: international migrants without cultural capital, and especially those lacking in monetary capital, continued to cross international borders illegally (often smuggled across geopolitical borders in unheated semi trucks, huddled in the backs of minivans, or sewn into the seats, perilously adrift in small boats tossed on waves crossing the Atlantic, or treacherously racing daylight and immigration authorities across the Adriatic sea in high-speed motorboats – to reference only a few of the most egregious and widely media publicized examples).

Two important factors impacted global migratory patterns during the 1970s and 1980s: first, as a consequence of the internationalization of financial capital and globalized modes of multinational production beginning in the 1970s, which led to the greater flexibility and increased mobility of capital and multinational corporate sites of production, certain types of economic migration, particularly economic migrants seeking jobs in garment manufacturing and textiles production, declined as multinational corporations moved from former first-world production sites located within developed national economies throughout Mexico, the Caribbean, Central America, the Asian Pacific, and South Asia. Out-sourcing began to replace the influx of economic migrants, in manufacturing at least. Other forms of economic migration persisted, particularly in the areas of service-sector employment with economic migrants leaving Mexico, Guatemala, the Philippines, Jamaica, South Africa, Nigeria, and elsewhere to seek employment in construction, hotel and restaurant service, domestic labor (particularly as maids, nannies, or *au pairs*), nursing, and sex trade workers. While economic migrants in construction and hotel/restaurant positions are directly addressed in chapter one, economic migrants seeking work as maids, nannies, nurses, and sex work are addressed in chapter two, which focuses on issues related to gender and diaspora, since the migrant workers in these areas have been predominantly women from developing countries.

Second, global migratory patterns – beginning in the 1980s, but remaining a dominant pattern throughout the 1990s and even into the first decade of the twenty-first century – have been directly impacted by international shifts in immigration policies related to refugees, and shifts in the foreign policy equation of sovereignty, military intervention (often rhetorically coded as "peace-keeping forces" even by the United Nations), and the plights of IDPs within the fragile, metastable, and often volatilely breaking-down borders of nation-states (as was the case in the former Yugoslavia). In the 1980s and 1990s, regional, national, and international regulatory bodies – such as NATO, the US, and the UN – inaugurated a pattern of military intervention in war-torn countries precisely to pre-emptively prevent the mass exodus of refugees. Before we begin our extended discussions of diasporas and diasporic communities, therefore, I think it both warranted and crucial to reflect for a moment on the post-Cold War "refugee crisis."

While the notion of refuge within a sovereignty, or sovereign state (particularly for individuals fleeing religious persecution) dates to the late seventeenth century in Europe (from the Edict of Nantes and the Edict of Potsdam), and while "The Right of Asylum" may be documented as early as 1725, it is not until the early twentieth century that political protection and statutes dedicated to the legal guarantee of the rights of refugees emerged as part of the international agenda, first within the League of Nations and subsequently within the United Nations.[4] Early twentieth-century refugees included Russian refugees fleeing the country during the Bolshevik (or "October") Revolution of 1917, European refugees fleeing fascist, totalitarian regimes in Italy, Spain, and Germany during the 1930s, and Jewish refugees seeking political asylum from Nazi Germany and Nazi-occupied territories in Western and Eastern Europe during the mid-1930s to mid-1940s, though shockingly few were granted refugee status and conferred political asylum; and 6 million Jewish Europeans were systematically killed in modernity's most pervasive mass genocide, the *Shoah* or Holocaust.

As Claudia Tazreiter avers in her comparative study, subsequent to the fall of the Berlin Wall in 1989 and the economic collapse of the Soviet Union in the early 1990s, post-Cold War immigration politics and legal shifts globally have tended to regard both asylees and even refugees as "illegals" – whose very entry into a country through illegal means or mechanisms (fraudulent paperwork; black market purchased identity documents, such as passports; covert passage across borders and ports of entry) marks them as criminalized "aliens"[5] – and this phenomenon cannot be adequately examined without a sustained analysis of "global human smuggling," or the trafficking in and transportation of migrants.[6] This abrupt post-Cold War shift in international refugee politics followed decades of refugee-friendly policies (beginning in the wake of World War II and in the aftermath of the Holocaust and continuing, though too often selectively applied to those fleeing communist states, throughout the Cold War) in Europe, the UK, the US, Canada, Australia, and New Zealand, albeit fueled by anti-communist, pro-capitalist sentiments that were the engine of Cold War international politics. In other words, "illegal aliens," because legally undocumented, were thus politically classified and juridically-administratively subject to detention and deportation procedures through no other requisite criminal act than that of their "illegal" entry into the host country: in effect, these individuals are criminalized, barred permanent refuge, and subject to often severe legal and material repercussions regardless of the motivating factors (hunger, even starvation; famine; poverty; under-employment; political dissidence; religious persecution; racial violence, "ethnic cleansing," or genocidal pogroms) that may have initially led to their illegal entry into the country in which they ultimately hoped to find political asylum or refuge. While "illegal aliens" are often regarded by the public citizenry as economic migrants – and thus also as "undocumented workers" – migrants classified as "illegal aliens" are often individuals who might (under other circumstances, with "proper" documentation, and during periods in which the public citizenry is more sympathetic to the plights of oppressed minorities in other countries) be classified as refugees. As Tazreiter trenchantly notes, "there are millions of people around the world who are displaced, [but] only a relatively small number are afforded the substantive protection of refugee status."[7]

One impact of the 1989 fall of the Berlin Wall and the presumed "death" of communism following the collapse of the Soviet Union has been not only a significant increase of refugees fleeing former "bloc" countries of the USSR in Eastern Europe, but also, and troublingly, the privileging of these refugees over "third world" (and particularly African) refugees during the 1990s, even those seeking refuge from war-torn and ethnic pogroms in countries of Africa, such as Rwanda, Liberia, Uganda, Sierra Leone, and most recently, Sudan and Chad. Regrettably, "[s]ince the early 1990s the recognition rates of asylum determination processes have declined in many Western states."[8] Increasingly, receiving countries are redefining refugee "rights" (residency, employment, education, instruction in language acquisition) as "resources," and in the wake of the Washington Consensus agenda stipulating privatization of state utilities and reductions in state-funded welfare spending on public resources, rights-turned-resources are too frequently eliminated as legislative priorities (as in Proposition 187 in California).[9] This phenomenon has thus been accurately called the "refugee crisis" of the 1990s, though we are still in its wake in the early years of the twenty-first century; and those international migrants most deleteriously impacted by the terrorist events of September 11, 2001, as discussed in this book's concluding "Postface," have been, overwhelmingly, political refugees.

The global refugee crisis of the 1990s, moreover, was not merely the consequence of increasing numbers of people fleeing "ethnic cleansing" in Bosnia, genocidal warfare in Rwanda, and civil warfare in newly independent states in Eastern Europe, Central and South Asia, and in parts of sub-Saharan, western, and the eastern Horn of Africa, such as in the Congo, Sierra Leone, Liberia, Uganda, Somalia, and Eritrea, as well as in Rwanda; it was also a direct (and indefensible) consequence of increasingly restrictive refugee policies among the overdeveloped countries of Europe, North America, and the Asian Pacific. As the number of refugees (blacker, browner, poorer, and Muslim) increased worldwide, so too did the doors to asylum seem to slam shut. And scholars have, regrettably, noted the implicit, if not explicit, racism grounding political asylum and refugee

laws internationally. No longer refugees fleeing Gulag prisons in despotic communist states, like Russia, Cuba, or China, refugees of the 1990s were Haitians,
Afghans, Sri Lankans, Tibetans, Kashmiri, Iraqis, Hutus, Tutsis, Liberians,
Kosovars, Bosnians, Herzegovinians, fleeing small despotic regimes, militia violence, and inter-ethnic and religious strife in small states without economic power
or ideological and symbolic significance, or what Pierre Bordieu refers to as
"cultural capital": too often they were arrested and detained while their asylum
applications were reviewed, denied refuge, and ultimately deported back to war-
torn countries and imperiled circumstances.

Precisely because international migrants and scattered diaspora communities
remain negatively inflected, partially structured, and even, at times, perilously
impacted by the flows of global capitalism, nationalism, and extra-territorial
forms of transnational imperialisms, we issue a political-materialist caveat against
premature celebrations of poly-*scaped* transnational exchanges, the presumed
death of nationalism, and hybrid forms of diasporic productions: as Fredric
Jameson might intimate, such celebrations operate according to a still predictable
"cultural logic" of global capitalism and are grounded upon the equally presumed, yet no less problematic, death of Marxisms: we must then remain vigilant
and cognizant of the myriad ways in which nationalisms are alive and well (and
even imperialist and militaristic), forcibly remaining active policing mechanisms
that regulate the flows of people, capital, finance, and military arms across
borders. In other words, transnationalism does not and has not brought an end
to nationalism or a death to the nation-state, and certainly not to the self-defined
"one indispensable nation": the United States of America. Nor has the presumed
"triumph" of capital led to the ineluctable passing away of Marxist resistances,
or materialist-based forms of diasporic resistances. Caveats issued, let us
proceed.

Diaspora: An Introduction is, as the title suggests, intended as a critical introduction to diaspora and the field of diasporic studies. The book analyzes patterns
of diasporic movement (economic migration, political asylum, and global capital
or "corporate" mobility) and the myriad issues impacting various diasporic communities globally. It also highlights key issues (labor, gender, sexuality, race,
transnational activism, global capitalism) that are significant to contemporary
discussions of diaspora or diasporic studies. Structurally, the book is organized
around key themes – with chapters, for example, on labor and economic migration, gender and diasporas, queer diasporas, race and diasporas, transnational
activism and diasporic "arts of resistance," as well as the dark recesses or nefarious mechanisms of international migrations and arrested flows: immigrant detentions, transnational military prisons, and the global trafficking in human subjects
– but it also forwards a specific thesis that is interwoven throughout the book:
that diasporas write counter-globalization narratives to the "master" narratives
of nationalisms, imperialisms, and global capitalism. Additionally, the book also
examines the fractured politics of national borders and the often arduous journey
involved in crossing borders, as well as tensions surrounding terrorism, homeland
security, immigrant detention practices, and legal discourses authorizing detention of "enemy combatants." The introduction to the book thus overviews
important migration patterns and defines key terms within the field of diasporic

studies. Chapter one examines diasporic workers in the "new global economy" and probes the interlocking issues of labor, immigration, legal documentation, illegal (or undocumented) workers, diasporic remittances, and economically driven migration patterns, such as agricultural migrant labor, housing or construction work, and other service-sector forms of employment (particularly in hotels and restaurants). In the second chapter, we survey major migratory patterns that have gendered parameters, examining the economic migration of service laborers and focusing primarily on domestic workers and registered nurses. Chapter three examines one of the many contradictions of global capitalism, the international sex industry, and "global traffic" – namely, the coexistence, often intermingled, of voluntary sex worker diasporas, migrant smuggling, human trafficking of laborers, and the involuntary sexual trafficking in women and children. The fourth chapter discusses the globalization of sexual politics, which has moved simultaneously in two directions: the queering of diasporic communities and the diasporization of queer communities. It also addresses issues of sexual persecution, international refugee law, and political asylum cases to protect queer minorities. The fifth chapter tackles the vexing and often volatile social problematics of race, immigration, and debates about citizenship, particularly in France, the US, and Australia, examining diasporic subjects who are racialized along two dominant patterns: those barred entry for implicit racial reasons; and those racially targeted as outsiders within the nation-state. The chapter focuses on the racist discrimination against Haitian refugees in the US, Southeast Asians in Australia, and Maghrebis living and working in France. As a public intellectual and humanities scholar, I have become increasingly interested in what some scholars have referred to as the "globalization of dissent" (Arundhati Roy), "transnational grassroots movements for social justice" (Glick Schiller and Fouron), and "cosmopolitical activism" (Gilroy). In the sixth chapter, we thus focus on diasporic activist forms of mobilization and everyday practices of resistance to oppression. The chapter sketches out the malleable and living contours of diasporas and political dissent. It also explores the interrelations of homeland and diasporic forms of cultural production – from film and television to visual arts, music, or street arts (murals, graffiti, street theater) – as arts of resistance. The "Postface" addresses the diasporic shifts within international migratory patterns post-9/11 with the onset of the "War on Terror," wars in Afghanistan and Iraq, continued terrorist attacks in Madrid, Bali, London, Istanbul, and elsewhere. Examining shifts (and fierce legal debates) in international law around issues of asylum, detention, and immigrant (and citizen) surveillance, we will strive to understand how these geopolitical and legal realignments may further impact diasporic communities, global migration patterns, and worldwide debates about citizenship, nationality, and political belonging.

Questions for Reflection and Discussion

- How may we understand and interpret international laws about political asylum and refuge within the contexts of World War II and the Cold War?

- How have geopolitical and geo-economic shifts since 1989 impacted the post-Cold War period?
- What impact have these shifts played in altering patterns of international migrations and diasporas?
- What causes led to a "refugee crisis" beginning in the 1990s?

Additional Research

Thinking through writing

Read one or more of the following essays on post-Cold War (post-1989) global shifts, reflect on the questions enumerated below, and then select one of the essays to analyze in a short essay of your own:

Barber, Benjamin. "Jihad vs. McWorld." *Atlantic Monthly* 269.3 (March 1992): 53–65. www.theatlantic.com/politics/foreign/barberf.htm.

Bush, George H. W. "Address before a Joint Session of Congress on the Persian Gulf Crisis and the Federal Budget Deficit." *Weekly Compilation of Presidential Documents* 26.37 (September 17, 1990): 1358–1363. www.bushlibrary.tamu.edu/research/papers/1990/90091101.html.

Fukuyama, Francis. "The End of History?" *The National Interest* 16 (Summer 1989): 3–18. www.marion.ohio-state.edu/fac/vsteffel/web597/Fukuyama_history.pdf.

Huntington, Samuel P. "The Clash of Civilizations?" *Foreign Affairs* 72.3 (Summer 1993). www.alamut.com/subj/economics/misc/clash.html.

Questions to consider about secondary readings

After reading the essay(s), reflect on the questions enumerated below.

George H. W. Bush, "Address before a Joint Session of Congress on the Persian Gulf Crisis and the Federal Budget Deficit"
- How does Bush rhetorically structure his "New World Order" speech? What rhetorical devices are deployed and to what effect? How does he directly appeal to audience on a general and an individual level?
- *Paragraph 7:* How does Bush conceptualize what he describes as a "New World Order"? How and why does he deploy birth imagery to describe this order?
- How does the rhetorical argument shift from security threat to "economic interests"?
- How and why does Bush simultaneously deploy hyperbole and understatement (*paragraph 9*)?
- *"Finally, let no one even contemplate profiteering from this crisis. We will not have it."* Is this statement ironic or non-ironic? What are the problems of interpreting it ironically and of interpreting it non-ironically?
- How does the speech chart shifts from Cold War enemies, the USSR, to the Middle East?
- What is the effect of the closing emotional appeal?

Francis Fukuyama, "The End of History?"

- What does Fukuyama mean by "the end of man" and "the last man"? How are these ideas embedded within Hegelian and Marxian ideas about historical progress?
- What are the viable or potential critiques of this teleological, linear conceptualization of history?
- How does Fukuyama predicate his argument about "the end of man" on the "unfolding of modern natural science"?
- How does he see science as dictating "a universal evolution in the direction of capitalism"?
- How does Fukuyama's argument ignore how colonialism bolstered the expansion of capital, and how both colonialism and capitalism are predicated on fundamental social and political forms of institutionalized inequities or inequalities?
- How does this "logic of modern science" reify national science and natural histories that have always already been predicated on racialized, hierarchical, and unequal foundations?
- Is the Hegelian master-slave dialectic one that Fukuyama privileges as "ideal" or as "actual"? That is, does Fukuyama interpret it as a projected model or an explanatory one?
- How and why does Fukuyama contrast Hegel with Anglo-American discourses of the "rights of man"?
- Can there even be reciprocity "between states" when there are structurally unequal relations among states with respect to production, labor, and consumption, or even with respect to differentials of sovereignty?

Benjamin Barber, "Jihad vs. McWorld"

- What are the presuppositions undergirding Barber's depictions of the "two possible political futures"? How can those premises be challenged?
- Barber theorizes that factions arise from ethnic nationalisms or tribalisms. How might factionalism emerge concomitantly with (or even as a result of) the forces of colonialism, imperialism, and global capitalism?
- "*What is the power of the Pentagon compared with Disneyland?*" What are the ideological implications of Barber's statement? What are the "blindspots" within this statement? Do you agree or disagree with Barber's pronouncement?
- Are the world's actors global or local? What does Barber suggest? Do you agree or disagree? Why or why not?
- What are the implications or ideological assumptions embedded within Barber's generic deployment of the Islamic term "Jihad"?
- "*This mania has left the post-Cold War world smoldering with hot wars.*" How are these wars the consequences of colonialism, nationalism, imperialism, and global capitalism?
- "*The nation-state would play a diminished role, and sovereignty would lose some of its political potency.*" How would this idea be implemented or actualized? How would the idea be equally actualized geopolitically? What would

be the geopolitical implications and material consequences of a loss of sovereignty, and for whom?

Samuel Huntington, "The Clash of Civilizations?"
- What does Huntington describe as the emergent or "next pattern of conflict"? Do you find his description of the emergent "world order" persuasive? Why or why not?
- How and why does Huntington revise nationalism and the nation-state with "civilizations"? What are the consequences of this revision?
- What are possible, viable critiques of Huntington's notions about "civilizations"?
- Does Huntington reify age-old and stereotypical ideals about religious, continental, or cultural differences? Why does he theorize the inevitability of "conflict" or "clash" among "civilizations"? And what does that presumed ineluctability reveal about Huntington's presuppositions and conclusions?
- How does Huntington's theorization of the "clash of civilizations" "between Islam and the West" rest on monolithic, homogenizing conceptualizations of both? How is the idea grounded within a rhetoric of "crusades"?
- Why does Huntington believe in the inevitable clash between "the West and the Rest"?
- What are the consequences of this rhetorical positioning of empire? How does it obscure material issues motivating military and economic incursions?

Introducing Diaspora:
Key Terms

Outlining the historical roots and contemporary routes of international migration, this book offers an examination of diasporas, the dispersal of human migratory populations from their homelands. We will place diasporas and diasporic communities within several important historical and contemporary frames. Within this introduction, those historical frames include the Jewish diaspora, the African diaspora, and the post-abolition migrations to the Americas driven by the need to replace slave labor with low-wage paid labor; within the larger framework of the book, as already prefaced, we more specifically examine twentieth and twenty-first century forms of international migration, focusing on the period since the late Cold War. In this introduction, we first trace the emergence of the concept of *diaspora* as a defining element of Jewish dispersal from Jerusalem; then, we examine how the transatlantic slave trade and the Middle Passage created an African diaspora in the Americas, drawing parallels to the Jewish diaspora; and finally, as a third pre-twentieth century historical moment, we study late nineteenth-century migrations, comparing the impacts of post-emancipation migrations to the Americas (North America, South America, Central America, and the Caribbean) and European colonial expansion in the nineteenth century and its impact on later waves of twentieth-century postcolonial migrations, particularly to Britain and France. Throughout the book, we will contextualize contemporary diasporas within the geopolitical shifts of the twentieth and twenty-first centuries as already briefly outlined in the Preface.

In this introduction, we thus overview important migration patterns and define key terms and categories within the field of diasporic studies. As a historical term with ancient Greek roots etymologically, *diaspora* as a concept first emerged from the Septuagint and midrashic rabbinical writings to describe the Jewish diaspora, or dispersal from the "homeland" and those living in exile from Judea or Jerusalem. The word *diaspora* has also been aptly applied to modern diasporas to discuss the Middle Passage, the transatlantic slave trade, and the dispersal of peoples of African origins throughout the so-called New World or the Americas. Other "victim" diasporas include the Armenian diaspora following genocide in Turkey under the Ottoman Empire (Cohen 1997). Yet it is important to remember that these early historical diasporas, though symbolically important, have multiple, scattered postmodern correlates. A critical difficulty thus entails asking and answering this question: how to pay critical intellectual attention to the symbolic and structural imports of both the Jewish diaspora and the African diaspora within the field of diasporic studies without singularly reifying those earlier historical dispersals in ways that render them static and eclipse the myriad fragmenting forms of historical migratory trajectories within each of those larger rubrics throughout the late nineteenth and the entire twentieth centuries? Or to be more concrete, how to talk about the definitive structuring elements that the "Jewish diaspora" and the "African diaspora" have had on notions of *diaspora* without eliding the particularities of Jewish Italian refugees moving from Italy under Mussolini into São Paulo, Brazil and the specificities of Jamaican expatriates arriving in London in the early 1950s?

Looking to these earlier historical models of diaspora (Jewish, African, post-abolition labor diasporas), we also seek to understand contemporary diasporas in the wake of massive geopolitical shifts during the twentieth and twenty-first centuries as wrought by World War I (1914–18), the proposed League of Nations, and post-World War II internationalization, the stock market crash of 1929, and the subsequent onset of the Great Depression (during the 1930s), which had global ramifications, the rise of German Nazism (from 1935 onward), World War II (1939–44), and major shifts since the end of WWII: the Bretton Woods conference of July 1944, which led to postwar economic restructuring and the creation of international financial institutions and regulatory bodies (the International Monetary Fund, the General Agreement on Tariffs and Trade, and the International Bank for Reconstruction and Development, popularly known as the World Bank), the emergence of international law and the founding of the United Nations, the anticolonial struggles of the 1950s and 1960s on the continents of Asia, Africa, and the Americas, the Cold War, which was sometimes "hot" militarily, the proliferation of multinational or late capital (and regional trading zones) since the late 1970s, the precipitous-yet-already-late fall of the Berlin Wall in 1989, and the presumed "demise" of communism and communist economic nation-states since 1990, as well as the post-1990 proliferation of global capitalism and the celeritous multi-state authorization of multinational free trade agreements. In the book's concluding Postface, we will also examine the impact of the terror events of September 11, 2001, the War on Terror, and the wars in Afghanistan and Iraq on international migration patterns, diaspora subjects, and global diasporic communities.

First, to the historical models of diaspora, then an examination of twentieth-century geopolitical shifts, and finally on to the contemporary twenty-first century moment.

"Next Year in Jerusalem"?
The "Model" of the Jewish Diaspora

The Jewish diaspora dates historically to the destruction of Solomon's Temple in Jerusalem by King Nebuchadnezzar in 586 BCE and the subsequent dispersal of Jews from their Holy Land (and homeland) in Judea, beginning a period of Babylonian exile. Contrary to the dominant historical conceptualizations of the Babylonian exile, scholars Robin Cohen and Gabriel Sheffer both demonstrate that the exile was a period of relative prosperity, creativity, and cultural, "religious activity" (Sheffer 2003, 44; Cohen 1997, 4). "Partly because of a shortage of skilled labor that was needed to build the expanding center of the Babylonian empire," Sheffer explains, "and partly because of moderate religious, social, and political views, throughout the sixth century BC the rulers of the Babylonian empire were quite tolerant toward ethnic groups that had either migrated voluntarily or been exiled to Babylon" (2003, 44). Two moments of diasporic return are recounted historiographically and theologically: the great exodus from Egypt, marking the first "return" to Judea; and a "second large-scale return to the Holy Land" in 520 BCE from Persian-controlled territory. Nevertheless, even "beyond Babylon, there were flourishing Jewish communities all over the Hellenic world . . . [and] by the fourth century BC there were already more Jews living outside than inside the land of Israel (Ages 1973: 3–7)" (Cohen 1997, 6). Although the Temple was reconstructed in 515 BCE, it remained periodically violated by imperial powers and imposed religions; following the conquest of the region of Asia Minor, now known as the Middle East, in 330 BCE by Alexander the Great, for example, and following successful efforts to create a Hellenized Judea, perhaps quintessentially symbolized by the Septuagint (the Greek translation of the Torah) from the third to the first century BCE, the Temple was also "Hellenized" (and defiled) as Cohen explains, by the sacrificial slaughter of a pig to Zeus in 167 BCE (1997, 5). As Greece declined and Rome ascended, so too did the fates of Jews in Jerusalem and other parts of Judea also change. In 70 CE, a Jewish revolt against the tyranny of the Roman Empire was squelched by Roman soldiers, and the Second Temple was destroyed by Titus, a Roman general, and a Roman law was passed barring Jews from living in Jerusalem and Judea. Once more, the Jewish people were scattered from Judea and found refuge in the Middle East, Central Asia, North Africa, and Europe. By the advent of Muhammad's preachings in 613 CE, following his first revelation on Mount Hira in 610, and the seventh-century spread of Islam throughout the territory now known as the Middle East, only a small minority of Jews remained in Jerusalem. According to Cohen, Jews were expelled from Medina shortly after Muhammad arrived there in 622 CE, and under the Islamic caliphates, Jews and Christians were denoted as *dhimmi*, inferior nonbelievers, and between 850–4 CE, both were required to "affix wooden images of devils to their houses, wear yellow garb and put yellow spots on the dress of their slaves"; yet, he also notes that until the birth of Zionism in the late nineteenth century, the migration of European Jews to Palestine in the early twentieth century, and the creation of Israel at the mid-century, Jews were "generally," and comparatively, "well treated in Islamic societies" (1997, 12, 11). For example, Jews living in territory ruled by the Ottoman Empire served in "high offices," and as "bankers," "finance ministers and advisers," and as "district governors in Baghdad, Basra, Damascus and Aleppo," yet they were also "kept firmly in their place" (Cohen 1997, 13–14).

Following the 1095 CE call for Crusaders to reclaim the "Holy Land" by Pope Urbanus, anti-Jewish sentiments and practices among Christians erupted in Europe. Brutal anti-Jewish violence spread throughout Germany and other parts of Europe beginning one year later in 1096. Persecuted by Christians in Europe throughout the medieval period, European Jews suffered political persecution, segregation, and expulsions: in 1290, Jews were expelled from England; in 1215, the Pope ordered that all European Jews must wear marks of their "un-faith" on their person, usually a badge or a hat known as a "Jew hat"; in 1306, they were expelled from France; and in the wake of the Black Plague from 1348–50, Jewish Europeans were expelled from Spain, Portugal, Italy, and Poland. Sephardic Jews in Spain and Portugal were forced into exile in the late fifteenth century during the Spanish Inquisition and *Reconquista*: in 1492, under the jurisdiction of inquisitor-general Torquemada, who was ironically a Spaniard of Jewish descent, "between 100,000 and 150,000 Jews fled Spain" (Cohen 1997, 9); while the majority fled to Morocco, Algeria, Tunisia, and other parts of the Mediterranean, some of these Jewish populations ultimately resettled in Poland and in Lithuania during the sixteenth century, eventually migrating further east into Russia. European Jews continued to confront racism, oppression, and violence throughout the late Middle Ages and up until the eighteenth century. Citizenship rights were granted to Jews by the United States of America in 1789, by France in 1791, and by most European countries during the nineteenth century, but not by Russia until the 1917 Bolshevik Revolution.

Jewish European and Russian communities, however, suffered racism and political discrimination throughout the nineteenth century; and in the late nineteenth century, modern anti-Jewish political persecution emerged as European nationalisms with their cataclysmic amalgams of racial purity, folk-citizen, and nation thrived on the continent.[1] Anti-Semitism as a "modern" racist term was first used in Europe in the 1870s and marks the beginning of modern Jewish persecution in the name of European nationalisms, particularly modern and exclusionary incantations of German *Volk* and French *Peuple-Citoyen*. A reaction to late nineteenth and early twentieth-century anti-Semitism, Zionism (the desire to found or reclaim a Jewish homeland) thrived in the 1890s inspired by its visionary leader Theodor Herzl. A Jewish Austro-Hungarian journalist, born in Budapest but working in Vienna for a Viennese newspaper and reporting from Paris while covering the Dreyfus Affair in France in 1894, Herzl authored a book entitled *Der Judenstadt* (*The Jewish State*), subtitled *A Modern Solution to the Jewish Question*, in 1896. Herzl conceptualized a secular state free of religious, racial, and political persecution and founded the Zionist Organization in 1897. According to Cohen, "by 1914 Palestine's Jewish population was 85,000, 12 per cent of the total" (1997, 14). Taking root among uprooted diasporic Jews across

Europe, Russia, Central Asia, and North Africa, the Zionist movement became a political promise in the geopolitical realigning of the Middle East during and after World War I and following the collapse of the Ottoman Empire in the early post-WWI years. On November 2, 1917, Lord Balfour issued the Balfour Declaration to establish a "national home" for the Jewish people. According to Howard Sachar in *A History of Israel From the Rise of Zionism to Our Time* (1976), the Balfour Declaration was tantamount in the eyes of many Arabs and Palestinians to a promise by a European imperial power to create a Jewish state in Jerusalem and the surrounding area, Palestine, without consideration of how this act might displace Palestinians already living there. Riots ensued in Jerusalem and Jaffa in the late 1920s.

Russian anti-Jewish racial discrimination and persecution was also pervasive throughout the nineteenth century, though the 5 million Russian Jews – largely assimilated and secularized – were allowed, on the whole, more political, civic, and education participation in the country than in parts of Europe. This changed abruptly in the late nineteenth century when anti-Jewish sentiment, discrimination, and institutionalized violence toward Russian Jews escalated. Anti-Semitic pogroms brutalized Russian Jews following the assassination of Alexander III in 1881. In May 1882, with the passage of the "Temporary Laws" (also known as the May Laws), a period of extreme racial persecution and religious violence spread throughout Russia lasting until 1917 with the Bolshevik Revolution. During the late nineteenth and early twentieth-century Russian anti-Jewish pogroms, 2 million Russian Jews fled persecution, migrating to the US and European countries during the period from 1881 until the outbreak of World War I in 1914. According to a Russian Census conducted in 1897, the Russian Jewish population numbered over 5 million; during the period of anti-Jewish political persecution, "over half of this number emigrated," with most fulfilling Zionist calls and migrating to Palestine, with others migrating primarily to the United States (Cohen 1997, 17). Between 1903 and 1906, there were 600 anti-Jewish pogroms executed by Russia (Cohen 1997, 17). In 1906, a Marxist-Zionist party, the Poalei Zion ("Workers of Zion") was founded to struggle for the creation of a socialist Jewish state in Palestine. Even after the Bolshevik Revolution in 1917, political persecution continued; and pogroms continued during the Russian Civil War from 1918–21: 100,000 Russian Jews were killed and 500,000 displaced by the violence. Persecution in the 1920s and 1930s, during the height of Stalinist purges, Russian Jews, in order to survive, assimilated culturally and linguistically, if not religiously, to Russia's dominant communist mores, many abandoning Hebrew (which had been banned in the country) and Yiddish, at least publicly, for Russian.[2] Writing for the exhibit "Beyond the Pale: The History of Jews in Russia," the curators note that it is both intellectually reductive and morally exculpatory to singularly blame the Holocaust on the nefarious machinations of one man, Adolf Hitler. Rather, they argue,

it was made possible by a unique combination of factors: the total control over the machinery of a modern state by the totalitarian regime of the National Socialists; the active cooperation or passive consent of a large part of the German population;

the collaboration of like-minded regimes and people in the occupied territories; and a deeply rooted anti-Semitism common to all Christian countries in Europe.

Economic recession in the 1920s and 1930s – following the New York stock market crash in 1929 and the subsequent onset of the Great Depression in the US, which had worldwide ramifications – further exacerbated ethno-national tensions, political quests for racial purity in the national populace, and the racist foundation to nationalist fervor not only in Nazi Germany and Communist Russia, but across Europe and parts of the Americas too. Cohen calls this "the unbreakable link between race, nation and territory" (1997, 14).

Following the rise of Adolph Hitler and the National Socialist German Workers Party, or the Nazi Party, in Germany in the 1930s, Jewish immigrants sought refuge in Palestine. German anti-Semites portrayed Jewish Germans as a double-horned devil with the Christian German nationalist state being threatened, they argued, by both (and quite paradoxically) "Jewish Capital" and "Jewish Bolshevism."[3] Coming to power in 1932, the National Socialists were instrumental in having Hitler become the Reich Chancellor in 1933. Dismantling parliamentary rule and consolidating powers of executive decree, Hitler assumed the role of German dictator, leading the Nazis in power in the 1930s. Nazi anti-Semitism was influenced by eighteenth and nineteenth-century racialized scientific premises that undergirded white supremacist ideals and distinguished "Caucasians" (a term introduced by Johann Blumenbach in 1781) from other presumably "inferior races" – those of African, Asian, Native American, and Jewish descent. Based on these racist pseudo-scientific ideas, most German nationalists claimed and celebrated their presumed "Aryan" descent while vilifying those of "Semitic" and Romanian "Gypsy" origins, persecuting Jews and Gypsies and eventually – in a genocidal program known as *die Endlösung* ("the Final Solution") and, in an expansive effort to forcibly acquire territory, or *Lebensraum* ("living room") – systematically arrested, imprisoned in concentration and death camps (in Auschwitz, Belzec, Chełmno, Lublin-Majdanek, Sobihór, and Treblinka), and then calculatingly exterminated over 6 million European Jews.[4] According to Sachar, as many European Jews (Ashkenazi) arrived in Palestine in the year 1935 as resided there in 1918, one year after the Balfour Declaration. Not surprisingly, ethnic or racial, religious, and political tensions between Jews, Muslims, and Christians in Palestine also erupted in the 1930s. Following the end of World War II and the *Shoah*, or Holocaust, Israel was created in 1948, the same year as the United Nations Declaration of Human Rights (UNDHR).

From the beginning, the Jewish diaspora was (and has remained) fragmented by language, culture, customs, diets, ritual practices, and geographical locations – with Sephardic Jews settling first in Spain and Portugal, or the Iberian peninsula, later in the Maghreb (or Algeria, Tunisia, Morocco, Egypt, and elsewhere in North Africa), the Middle East, and other parts of the Mediterranean; Ashkenazi Jews settling in Northern and Eastern European countries, particularly Germany (or then, the Rhineland), Prussia, the Baltic and Balkan regions, and eventually moving eastward into Russia; and Mizrahi Jews from the Middle East or other parts of the so-called Arab world. The Sephardim traditionally spoke

Ladino, a hybrid Romance language with roots in Hebrew and in Castilian Spanish, while the Ashkenazi spoke Yiddish and the Jewish Middle Eastern population spoke a Judeo-Arabic patois. Jewish diasporas have, however, written and spoken several different languages over the centuries in exile from Jerusalem, including not only extinct or "dead" languages – Knaaic (or Judeo-Slavic spoken in the late medieval Czech Lands) and Zarphatic (once spoken in northern France and parts of Germany, including Frankfurt-am-Main, Mainz, and Aachen) – but also those spoken today by only small communities of scattered peoples: Judeo-Aramaic (with only about 20,000 remaining speakers, most living in Israel, where the language has been eroded by modern Hebrew), Dzhidi (or Judeo-Persian, spoken by Iranian Jews), Juhuri (with approximately 100,000 speakers living in the Caucasus regions of Azerbaijan, but also in Russia and in Israel), Karaim (a Turkik-Hebrew language with Crimean, Trakai, and Lutsk-Halych dialects and spoken by Crimean Karaites and Turkik adherents of the Jewish sect in Crimea, Lithuania, Poland, and the Ukraine), Krymchak (or Judeo-Crimean Tatar, with only 100 or so remaining speakers among the Krymchak people living in Crimea), and Yevanic (also called Romaniote and Judeo-Greek, and spoken into the twentieth century by Jewish Greek communities, but becoming extinct as speakers adopted or assimilated into Hebrew, Ladino, Greek, Turkish, and Bulgarian, as speakers migrated from Greece to Israel and the US, and ultimately as the few remaining Romaniote speakers were massacred during the Holocaust).[5]

Today, Jewish populations reside in many countries across the globe – from Azerbaijan to Uruguay, Argentina to Belarus, Russia to South Africa, France to Romania, Kazakhstan to Iran – with the largest population (according to statistical data compiled in 1991) in the United States (5.75 million), more than the number residing in Israel (4.14 million) at the time. Other large diasporic populations exist in Argentina (213,000), France (530,000), Russia (430,000), the Ukraine (325,000), Brazil (100,000), Great Britain (300,000), and South Africa (114,000).[6]

"Amnesia is the legacy of the New World": Remembering the African Diaspora

"Amnesia is the legacy of the New World," as Nobel laureate Derek Walcott wrote in his 1992 acceptance speech, "The Antilles: Fragments of Epic Memory." Remembrance, or historical memory, is a creative act of diasporic longing, if not the actual recovery of a lost ancestral African homeland, yet it remains a necessary creative act all the same. The transatlantic slave trade began when Portuguese seafaring traders started buying African slaves from the coast of West Africa in the late 1400s; and enslaved Africans, transported in small numbers to Portugal, were imported into the Americas in larger numbers beginning in the early 1500s: slaves were first brought to the "New World" in 1502, only one decade after the arrival of Christopher Columbus in the "West Indies" in 1492, by the Spanish to mine gold in Hispaniola, Isla Espanola (or "Little Spain") after the island was claimed by the Spanish monarchy of King Ferdinand and Queen Isabel, after a governorship was established by the monarch under Ovando, and after Spanish colonialists unsuccessfully sought to enslave the native warrior Arawaks who resisted enslavement and fought to the death. By 1517, large numbers of enslaved Africans were forcibly brought to the Spanish colonial island and, later in the sixteenth century, to other parts of the West Indies and the Americas. Slavery spread rapidly, in fact, throughout the New World, from Hispaniola to other parts of the Caribbean – Jamaica, Barbados, Trinidad, Puerto Rico, Cuba, the Bahamas, and other islands in the archipelago – and throughout the continents of North America and South America (with slaves concentrated in the mid-Atlantic and southeastern colonies, but also later imported into "New Spain," now México, and parts of central America, particularly Belize, and the continent of South America from the northern coastal areas of Guyana, Surinam, and Venezuela, into the Amazonian region of Brazil, and beyond).

African diaspora was crucial to the emergence of American capitalist wealth (as Eric Williams presciently argued in *Capitalism and Slavery*). According to historian Thomas C. Holt (in "Slavery and Freedom in the Atlantic World"), the Americas are unthinkable apart from its Africanist presences, and particularly the contributions to labor, production, and the capitalist accumulations of wealth in European colonies of the Americas:

> By the eve of the American Revolution, the social, political, and economic patterns of intercourse that made up that world order were well-established, and slavery and the slave trade were at their base. By 1770, there were more than 17 million people in the Americas; almost 2.5 million of them were slaves, or about 14 out of every 100 European subjects in the New World were slaves. But it is the distribution of that population that is most significant. The slave proportion of colonial populations ranged from 2 percent of the Spanish mainland to 88 percent for the French, with Dutch, Danes, Portuguese, and British falling in between those extremes – all averaging about 53 percent. But for the largest powers, population-wise, the modal percentage of slaves in their populations was 34 percent; for the most powerful *economically*, it was around 80 percent.
>
> The point here is that the most developed and commercial sectors – the French, the British, and the Dutch – led the way in the exploitation of slave labor. The slave subjects produced commodities that constituted a third of the value of European commerce. They were at the base of a transatlantic commerce that accounted for half a million tons of shipping and employed more than a hundred thousand seamen and dockworkers. (41–42)

From sugar to tobacco to cotton and coffee, enslaved Africans – the sweat of their brows, the blood on their backs, and the toil of their days – were absolutely crucial to the agricultural production, surplus profit for planters, financial success of the American plantation economies, and the massive accumulation of wealth in the colonies. To give only one example, though undeniably the historically salient one: colonial Saint Domingue, known as the "pearl of the Antilles," was the most profitable sugar cane producing island in the Caribbean archipelago, helping to create France's wealth. Slavery was, as Holt forcefully concludes in his essay, "instrumental in fashioning the global architecture of the modern world" (42).

Profit from exploitation, sugar from sweat, wealth from slavery: the equation was soon to be reversed in colonial Saint-Domingue. Haiti is, in fact, singular in the Caribbean, in the Americas, and in the world for its unique history. The Haitian Revolution, which erupted from slave revolts in August 1791 and ended with a formal "Declaration of Independence" in January 1804, culminated in the violent eradication of the French Antillean colony Saint-Domingue, the abolition of slavery in the territory, and the founding of Ayiti, the first free black republic in the world: as historical event, it is arguably one of the most important moments in American hemispheric history, if not in the modern world.[7] Revolutionary heroes – Boukman Dutty, Biassou, Jean-François, Toussaint Louverture, Jean-Jacques Dessalines, Henri Christophe, and Alexandre Pétion – and their nemeses or French military antagonists – Napoleon Bonaparte, General Victor-Emmanuel Leclerc, and General Donatien Rochambeau – have dominated the historiography of the era. The impact of the Haitian Revolution was felt, as historian David Geggus writes, "from the Mississippi Valley to the streets of Rio" politically, economically, and culturally: "The fifteen-year struggle for racial equality, slave emancipation, and colonial independence alarmed and excited public opinion on both sides of the Atlantic. It shaped great power politics, generated migration movements, and opened new economic frontiers. It stimulated slave resistance and new expansions of slavery, while embittering the debates about race and abolition" (247).[8] As Martin Munro underscores in his article "Can't Stand Up for Falling Down: Haiti, Its Revolutions, and Twentieth-Century Negritudes," the Haitian Revolution profoundly affected the larger Atlantic world:

> There could scarcely be a more symbolically important "big bang" in Caribbean history than the Haitian Revolution, an epic act of insubordination whose cataclysmic scale and anticolonial significance remain difficult to fully appreciate even now, two hundred years after Dessalines's final proclamation of independence. This was, let us remind ourselves, an event that sent shockwaves across commodity markets, shudders through the European merchant classes, and ripples of encouragement to other New World slave communities. (3)

Culturally, the heroic gestures of the revolution also inspired European and American artists and writers throughout the nineteenth century, as a small but important wealth of literature reflecting on the Haitian revolutionary heroes attests: William Wordsworth's "To Toussaint Louverture" (1802); Heinrich von Kleist's "Die Verlobung in St. Domingo" (1811); Victor Hugo's *Bug-Jargal* (1826);[9] John Greenleaf Whittier's "Toussaint Louverture" (1833); Alphonse de Lamartine's *Toussaint Louverture* (1840); Wendell Phillips' impassioned abolitionist oratory on "Toussaint Louverture" (1863); and Victor Schoelcher's biography, *Vie de Toussaint Louverture* (1889).

Beyond its intellectual and literary impacts, the Haitian Revolution stilled the hearts of planters and masters throughout the Americas. The Saint Domingue slave revolts – or the Haitian Revolution, as it is known to posterity – began in

1791 when Boukman, a runaway slave, and an anonymous *mambo* (Vodou priestess) sacrificed a wild boar to the *lwas*, or spirits, and then led one of the most violent (and ultimately successful) slave insurrections in the Americas. Following the Vodou ceremony led by Boukman at Bois Cayman, slave revolts broke out into revolutionary struggle that culminated in the 1804 declaration of independence and the establishing of Ayiti, or Haiti, the first black republic and the second republic in the western hemisphere – its revolution following the American Revolution and War of Independence by only fifteen years and the French Revolution by two years. Consequently, African diaspora religions throughout the Americas – Obeah (in the former British Caribbean: Jamaica, Antigua, and elsewhere), Quimbois (in Martinique and Guadeloupe), Shango (in Trinidad), Santería (in Cuba), Gaga rituals (in the Dominican Republic), and Camdomblé in Brazil – were all associated with insubordination, slave revolts, and black insurrection.

Vodou has ever since permeated the American cultural imagination, particularly in the creolized cultures of the South and most notably in the southern coastal cities that received St. Domingue refugees in the 1790s and the first decade of the nineteenth century, such as Savannah, Charleston, and New Orleans, the home of Madam Marie Laveau (born 1794? in either St. Domingue or *le Vieux Carré* of French New Orleans) who earned the title "Voodoo Queen of New Orleans" in the 1830s. Saint Domingue refugees settled in several cities in the US, including New York, Philadelphia, Baltimore, Savannah, Charleston, and New Orleans. New Orleans received the largest numbers of refugees during this period (20,000), some directly from provinces in St. Domingue and others indirectly from Cuba, Jamaica, Martinique, and Guadeloupe. Over 9,000 St. Domingue refugees, en route from Cuba, arrived in 1809 alone (Laguerre 1998, 2, 58, 65). The "slave revolt" in Saint Domingue, of course, stilled the heart of white Americans who feared similar revolts (and the subsequent emancipation of enslaved African Americans) in the US (Laguerre 1998, 58). At the heart of such fear in the American cultural imagination was the African diasporic religion Vodou, regarded as a potent and deleterious black magic. The "horror" of Haiti in the early American imagination (late eighteenth century to early nineteenth century) was, precisely, its success: within nascent national images of the US, the Haitian Republic represented the inverse of the America Republic – slave revolts instead of slavery; Vodou instead of Protestantism; Black Africa instead of European America in the "New World." In the late nineteenth and early twentieth centuries, a period of US expansionism and imperialism in Latin America and the Asian Pacific initiated under the Monroe Doctrine (1823), American vilification of Vodou revealed racist ideas about African diaspora religions, black culture, black sexuality, and above all, black autonomy. This racist ideology, of course, also perpetuated American interests economically and diplomatically.

Nineteenth-century American abolitionists, like Wendell Phillips in his speech "Toussaint Louverture" (1863), highlighted the heroism of the Haitian revolutionaries Louverture, Jean-Jacques Dessalines, and Henri Christophe. If abolitionists lauded Haitian revolt and independence, white southerners feared Haiti, and Vodou was used to demonize the Black Jacobins and the Black Republic. In

"Southern Thought" (1857), George Fitzhugh defended the institution of slavery, writing "Europe and the North can any day abolish slavery by disusing slave products. They should try the experiment, for should they succeed in abolishing it, they will have none of those products thereafter – Jamaica and Hayti prove this." Fitzhugh's statement reveals not only the economic threat posed to the southern (and northern) economies by abolition, but also reveals the implied threat of trade sanctions and imposed economic isolation – using Jamaica and Hayti as examples of the destitution wrought *not* by abolition, but by forced isolation as a punitive measure meant to destroy the economies of freedmen.

Before emancipation, the *Repiblik dAyiti/République d'Haïti* also served as a major point of African American emigration for fugitive slaves and freedmen of color seeking refuge in the only free black republic in the Western hemisphere. Haiti's revolutionary impact was also felt in abolitionist movements across the Americas and across the European continent: the abolition of the international transatlantic slave trade in 1807 and the emancipation of slaves in the British Caribbean colonies from 1833–4 are also direct consequences of the successful slave revolts that began the Haitian Revolution. 1804 thus marked the genealogical beginning of an end to slavery in the New World as the next century witnessed abolition movements across the Americas: following anticolonial revolts, which were financially and politically supported by Ayiti and led by revolutionary Simon Bolivar in South America, slavery was abolished in Chile, Mexico, and Central America in the 1820s; in the French Antillean colonies of Martinique and Guadeloupe in 1848; in other parts of South America in the 1850s – Colombia in 1851, Ecuador in 1852, Argentina and Uruguay in 1853, and Peru and Venezuela in 1854; in the Dutch Caribbean islands in 1863; in the United States in 1865 at the conclusion of the US Civil War; in Cuba from 1880–6; and finally, in Brazil in 1888 (Butler 1999, 122).

One should not forget that "African America" (or Africans within the Americas) – comprised even today of Portuguese-speaking Brazilians from São Paulo, Spanish-speaking Cubanos from Santiago-de-Cuba, English-speaking Americans from Chicago, or from Bridgetown, Barbados and Kingston, Jamaica – has always been linguistically, culturally, historically, religiously, and even ethnically diverse. African Americans, or those of African descent in the Americas, came from manifold ethnic origins, or tribes, speaking myriad languages and holding diverse religious beliefs, practicing unique rituals, customs, and culinary traditions. Enslaved Africans arrived in the "New World" from Benin, Yorubaland, Iboland, the Congo, and other parts of west and central Africa, speaking scores of different languages and practicing religions that were Dahomeyan, Yoruban, Ibo, Congolese, and Islamic in origin. African diasporic cultures all reveal this hybridity: *métissage*, or mixed cultural syncretism, and not unity, defines the scattered peoples of African diasporic origins; and the Caribbean as a region exemplifies this diversity. Multicultural as well as interlinguistic, the Caribbean includes not only African diasporic presences, but also includes people from indigenous, Indian, Chinese, European, and Middle Eastern descents. It is also multireligious, with individuals who are devotees of Christianity, Judaism, Islam,

Hinduism, and African Caribbean religions such as Vodou, Obeah, Quimbois, Shango, and Santería.

The Caribbean, as a region, has also been marked by European colonialism (by the Spanish, Portuguese, Dutch, French, and British), the Atlantic slave trade (in fact, 40 percent of the Africans forced into slavery and brought into the "New World" ended up in the Caribbean); the Middle Passage; plantation forms of chattel slavery; the "Second" Middle Passage (as it has been called by Indo-Caribbean scholars) that brought indentured servants from India, China, and other parts of Asia into the Caribbean following the British abolition of slavery in 1833–4; continued colonial domination in many areas throughout the twentieth century; and US imperialism rationalized by the Monroe Doctrine (1823). As a region, its histories, languages, religions, and peoples have been marked by cultural forms of creolization. It is a region, as cultural critic Stuart Hall defines it, with an African presence, an American (or indigenous) presence, a European presence, and I would add, an Asian presence.

The Caribbean is not only a site of African diasporic translocation, but it is also a region marked by contemporary diasporas and out-migrations, particularly since the late 1940s and early 1950s. Indeed, migration and diaspora have been significant trajectories in twentieth-century Caribbean cultures: following World War II, Caribbean immigrants entered Amsterdam, France, Britain, Canada, and the US in large numbers. The Caribbean, as a region, "has lost more than five million people over the last fifty years." (Kingma 2006, 182). According to Cohen in *Global Diasporas*, 250,000 Caribbean immigrants entered Amsterdam in the post-WWII years; 300,000 entered France; 500,000 entered England; and over 1 million entered the US. Following the 1948 British Nationality Act allowing immigration of individuals from the British colonies and postcolonies, many Caribbean writers settled in and around London, including George Lamming (Barbados), Sam Selvon (Trinidad), Andrew Salkey (Jamaica), Stuart Hall (Jamaica), and Ian MacDonald (Trinidad) arriving between 1950 and 1951 (with George Lamming and Sam Selvon arriving on the same boat) (Procter 2000, 321); and Wilson Harris (Guyana) and Caryl Phillips (St. Kitts) arriving in 1958. (Phillips, seven years old at the time, is one of the Caribbean's most important contemporary writers.) Other Caribbean writers arriving later in Britain include the dub-poet Linton Kwesi Johnson (Jamaica), Kamau Brathwaite (Barbados), Grace Nichols (Guyana), John Agard (Guyana), Fred D'Aguiar (Guyana), and Merle Collins (Grenada), many now living and writing in the US. As Anita Mannur and I wrote in the introduction to *Theorizing Diaspora*,

> This early transatlantic African Diaspora resulted in numerous fractured diasporas in the late nineteenth century and throughout the twentieth century, as Black Africans migrated from south to north in North America and across the western hemisphere – from Port-au-Prince to Montréal, from Kingston to New York – and from west to east across the Atlantic ocean again – from Trinidad to London and elsewhere. (Braziel and Mannur 2002)

Post-Abolition Nineteenth-Century
European Migration to the Americas

Historically, some of the earliest and most persistent patterns of modern international migration, particularly since the mid- to late-nineteenth century, have been economic. In the wakes of the abolition of the international transatlantic slave trade in 1807 and the abolition of slavery in the United States in 1863 (though not fully enforced until the end of the US Civil War in 1865) and in Brazil in 1888, both countries actively sought economic migrants to sustain expansive capitalist development in their post-abolition economies that had been built – quite literally – on the backs of blacks, or from the compulsory labor of enslaved Africans. Consequently, both the United States and Brazil had influxes of economic migrants into their countries and economies in the late nineteenth and early twentieth centuries; and consequently, both are what may be classified as "immigrant countries," having been profoundly impacted by the diverse ethnicities, religions, cultures, languages, and of course, labor of those incoming migrants. Other "settler colonies" established at the height of European colonial expansion and founded on the suppression and displacement of indigenous peoples (Native Americans, Amérindiens, Aborigines, Maori, Zulus) also emerged in the early twentieth century as "immigrant countries" that sought economic migrants (particularly from Europe) to bolster their capitalist economies and to "whiten" their populace or citizenry. It is hardly surprising, then, that national immigration laws in these countries (Brazil, the US, Canada, Australia, New Zealand, and South Africa) were premised on white privilege and racially exclusive categories given the racist legacies of Spanish, Portuguese, and above all British colonialism in these countries during the eighteenth and nineteenth centuries (as we will further discuss in chapter five, "Race and Diasporas"). Crucial, then, to an understanding of historical resonances of the term *diaspora* are post-abolition shifts in migratory patterns, particularly in North and South America: for example, waves of European migration to the US and to Brazil as these countries actively sought out economic migrants after the total abolition of slavery in 1863 and 1888, respectively, radically changed the demographic composition of these countries.

Another important post-abolition diaspora involved the migration of Indian and Chinese individuals, frequently as "indentured laborers" to the Caribbean (Trinidad, Cuba), parts of South America (particularly Guyana, Peru, and Brazil), South Africa (especially in Durban and Natal), the East African coast (Kenya, Uganda, Tanzania, and Zanzibar), and islands in the Indian ocean, such as Mauritius and Réunion, and in the Pacific Ocean, such as Fiji and Hawai'i. "Most indentured labourers (perhaps about 1.5 million in all), were recruited from India," though China and Japan were also sources for these post-abolition economic migrations; and as Cohen further explains, "The movement of Indians to the tropical plantations provides an instructive reminder of how far the planters were prepared to go in keeping their two desiderata – abundant land and cheap labour. . . . Many of the indentured Indians were physically moved into the slave barracks of the former African slaves – a poignant reminder of why they were there" (Cohen, R. 1995, 45). Japanese and Chinese laborers, legal and illegal, also helped to rebuild the post-slavery economies of South American and North American countries, as well as to build infrastructural advances that supported the technological development of American capitalist economies. While Chinese laborers had been in the western United States since the 1830s, in the post-abolition period of the late nineteenth century, they also arrived, for example, in increasing numbers as economic migrants to build the transcontinental railroad.

Nineteenth-century migration to the United States, however, was of largely European origin with Irish immigrants, fleeing hunger and the potato famine of the 1840s, arriving during that decade; and German, Norwegian, and Swedish immigrants arriving in the years 1881–5 and settling predominantly in the upper Midwest. Approximately 1.5 million Catholic Poles arrived in the 1880s, and approximately 2 million Russian and Eastern European Jewish immigrants also arrived during the 1880s, fleeing religious persecution and the racialized violence of Russian anti-Jewish pogroms during the last two decades of the nineteenth century and settling largely in the urban Northeast. Italian immigrants also arrived in the United States in large numbers, entering through Ellis Island from the 1880s to 1890s. Over 100,000 Italians arrived on US shores from 1881 to 1900, but the peak was not until the decade 1910–20, when 2 million Italian immigrants arrived in the country.

While nineteenth-century US immigration policies were under "local jurisdictions" of the port of entry, it was not until the mid-nineteenth century – with the arrival of Chinese economic migrants hired as laborers to construct the transcontinental railroad – that federal regulation of immigrants and immigration was established (Bernard 1992; qtd. in Dow 2004, 6). Ellis Island, opened in 1891, was the port of entry for most immigrants and refugees seeking new lives in the US, and the port remained a major point of entry throughout the opening decades of the twentieth century. Beginning in 1918 under the Wilson administration and continuing throughout the first half of the twentieth century, public alarm and journalistic protests about sanitation, deteriorated facilities, and its "detention-like penitentiary" climate led to the closing of Ellis Island in 1954 after "a US Supreme Court justice called it an 'island prison'" (Dow 2004, 6) – no longer a port of entry for refugees, "poor . . . tired . . . hungry . . . yearning to be free," but rather a site for immigrant detention.

Diaspora Taxonomies, Migratory Patterns

Diaspora as a term historically and typically denotes the scattering of people from their homelands into new communities across the globe. William Safran, in the important essay "Diasporas in Modern Societies: Myths of Homeland and Return," defines the term *diaspora* (in contrast with other related, but distinct categories: *expatriates*; *immigrants*; *refugees*; *aliens*) as characterized by six distinguishing features or characteristics. First, diaspora as a term refers to people who have "been dispersed from a specific original 'center' to two or more 'periph-eral,' or foreign, regions"; second, diaspora applies when those dispersed com-munities "retain a collective memory, vision, or myth about their original homeland – its physical location, history, and achievements"; third, diasporic communities are marked by a firm belief that "they are not – and perhaps cannot be – fully accepted by their host society and therefore feel partly alienated and insulated from it"; fourth, diasporas overwhelmingly, Safran argues, "regard their ancestral homeland as their true, ideal home and as the place to which they or their descendants would (or should) eventually return – when conditions are appropriate"; fifth, diasporic communities firmly "believe that they should, col-lectively, be committed to the maintenance or restoration of their original home-land and to its safety and prosperity"; and sixth, diasporas and diasporic communities typically "relate, personally or vicariously, to that homeland in one way or another, and their ethnocommunal consciousness and solidarity are importantly defined by the existence of such a relationship" (Safran 1991, 83–84).

While Robin Cohen (in *Global Diasporas*) adopts Safran's definition, he also adapts and augments its contours. For Cohen, four additional features may be seen as definitive to diasporas: first, diasporas may include, indeed often do include, "groups that scatter for aggressive or voluntarist purposes," including revolutionary minorities struggling for an imaginary homeland as well as those traveling for commercial trade; second, diasporas and "diasporic consciousness" are predicated on a "strong tie to the past or a block to assimilation in the present and future"; third, diasporas are defined positively, not just negatively, and dia-sporic consciousness involves a "recognition of the positive virtues of retaining a diasporic identity," as well as a "tension between an ethnic, a national and a transnational identity" that is "often a creative, enriching one"; fourth, Cohen also further suggests that "members of a diaspora characteristically sense not only a collective identity in a place of settlement, nor again only a relationship with an imagined, putative or real homeland, but also a common identity with co-ethnic members in other countries" (24–25).

In our own historical and theoretical conceptualizations of the term *diaspora* (in the editors' introduction to *Theorizing Diaspora*), Anita Mannur and I hoped to relocate diasporas within the contemporary critical moments of postcolonial-ism, postmodernity, and late capital precisely in order to articulate the possibility that *diaspora* (as a term) and that diasporas (as migratory formations) are pro-duced and thus circulate with "new currencies" in global discourses, and ones moreover that "confound the once (presumed to be) clearly demarcated param-eters of geography, national identity, and belonging." To theorize the interlocking geopolitical, material, technological, environmental, human, and cultural terrains of the potential "new currencies" for the term diaspora, we suggested that dias-poras work in two directions simultaneously, challenging both the strictures and structures of nationalism and the increasingly imperialist, hegemonic forces of globalization (Braziel and Mannur 2002, 7).

Our theoretical conceptualization of diasporas as a "double-pronged critique of the nation and globalization" (as Gopinath refers to it)[10] merits further critical elaboration, particularly in relation to post-9/11 geopolitical shifts and in relation to the productive, if also restrictive flows of global capitalism, in which financ-escapes, technoscapes, and peoplescapes are often bound up, and at times, find their own flows obstructed by those dominant international strictures of "empire" (Negri and Hardt 2001) and capital. Intermediate to nation and globe, or the structuring forces of nationalism and globalization, diasporas transmit information, finance, remitted capital, and even desire across the international borders of nation-states; diasporas thus typically remain connected to those left behind at home in geographically distant or remote homelands (through cash remittances, long-distance communications through cyber, digital, and telecommunication technologies, expressions of long-distance nationalism, and transnational activism to raise political consciousness and impact foreign policy in their adopted diasporic countries), as well as frequent trips home for those with the financial means to travel. Diasporas are thus transnational "tentacles" of nation-states, both those of the homeland and of the country of adoption; but diasporas are also global capitalist economic formations created by push/pull factors within national economies, regional trading blocs, and even within the production and labor shifts of the global economy, such as the "importation" of multinational corporations (MNCs), or "offshoring" and the "outsourcing" of labor. For many developing countries, the homeland economically depends on extra-territorial "development" strategies: in other words, smaller countries, like Haiti, the Dominican Republic, the Philippines, Albania, and beyond, often depend on outmigration, and thus actively regulate exported human labor and imported MNCs, and then strongly encourage (or in some cases, compel) the remittance of hard currency funds, while too often also working against labor organization, increases in minimum wage, environmental protection laws, etc. in order to keep MNCs from relocating (yet again) in its spiraling rush to the global labor "bottom." And these small-economy development strategies are too frequently assisted by larger economies through the direct (and indirect) influences and legal strictures imposed by international financial institutions (like the World Bank, the International Monetary Fund, the World Trade Organization), regional lending institutions (like the Inter-American Development Bank), and national agencies for international development, notably, the United States Agency for International Development (USAID). That being said, diasporas are not overdetermined migratory formations: diasporas may be produced by the dominant flows of global capitalism, ethnic nationalisms, and corporate transnationalisms, among other forces, but diasporas are not merely receptive, passive structures; diasporas are also productive. Or, to reiterate an earlier point: power may be productive (of diasporas), but it is not always in control of what it produces.

While diasporas may (and undeniably do) contest and disrupt the hegemonic forces of nationalism and globalization, refiguring the dominant discursive framings of nation-state and global capitalism, we must also remain cognizant of the ways that diasporas and diasporic forms of cultural production may also remain complicit or imbricate both with nationalist formations and "with transnational capitalism [and may] shore up the dominance of the latter by making its mechanisms invisible," as Gopinath importantly reminds us (2005, 10).

Diaspora is, though imprecisely and at times inaccurately, often used synonymously with other critical terms such as transnationalism and global capitalism that have had similar moments of historical emergence and intellectual trajectories within post-Cold War discourses that attempt to understand geopolitical and cultural realignments following the fall of the Berlin Wall in 1989. While transnationalism as a term aptly describes the movement of capital, finance, trade, cultural forms of production, and even material forms of production across national boundaries that serve to erode the nation-state as the foundation or ground for capitalist economies, diaspora remains a primarily human form of movement across geographical, historical, linguistic, cultural, and national boundaries: as such, it remains a lived, negotiated, and experienced form of transnational migration; it is in this sense that diasporic subjects may be understood to be transnational migrants, or transmigrants.

Globalization addresses the complex lines of cultural and capitalist exchange that move simultaneously from center to periphery, from periphery to center, and from myriad peripheral points to others. While capitalism may be accurately defined as a system of economic exchange that historically emerged in the Western hemisphere through colonialist expansion, extraction of natural resources, subjugation and even enslavement of labor, the divisions of production, the alienation of labor, the extensification and intensification of capital, and the maximization of surplus capital, global capitalism is defined not merely by financescapes marking the flow of money, resources, labor, and production from the "West" to the "rest," or from the developed countries to the "developing" or "undeveloped" countries (as Benjamin Barber and others may have it), but across multiple, complicated, and many-trafficked peripheries of hybrid exchange (as Appadurai suggests). And while both contemporary forms of diaspora and transnationalism must be contextualized within the period of late capitalism, or global capitalism, and necessarily remain striated by globalization and global forms of exchange, neither term is absolutely reducible to global capitalist cultural flows.

To better understand diaspora (as a theoretical, sociological, anthropological, historical, cultural, and geopolitical term) one must first understand the ways in which migratory patterns and the migrations of various groups of individuals inform what we mean by diaspora. Migration defines the movement of individuals from a native country across national or state boundaries into a new receiving (or "host") country: migrants, however, move for many varied and disparate reasons – some voluntary (such as economic profit, employment, education) and others involuntary (compulsory migration as a consequence of civil warfare, racial or ethnic oppression, religious persecution, dictatorship and state violence, political persecution, and other retaliatory forms of violence). It is thus crucial to differentiate between multifarious types of diasporic subjects, distinguishing between *economic migrants, political asylees, exiles, refugees* (from famine and war), and postcolonial *émigrés* (from places as varied as Algeria, Morocco, Egypt, Jamaica, Trinidad, Barbados, Guyana, Nigeria, Ghana, Kenya, Uganda, Tanzania, and elsewhere), who moved (and continue to move in the twenty-first century) from a formerly colonized home-country to postcolonial metropoles (such as Paris, London, Amsterdam), perhaps initially intent on seeing the "mother country," but also intent on actively seeking education, professional opportunities, or even personal freedom.

Clearly, delineating the taxonomies and typologies of diasporas (or migrants) is complicated by the often indistinct and overlapping boundaries between categories, and yet distinctions are also intellectually important – if for no other reason, though I think that there are other salient reasons – precisely because immigration laws of the receiving countries materially, politically, and legally codify the boundaries between various categories: legal and illegal, documented and undocumented, economic and political, and refugees and illegal aliens, to note the most striking examples. These classifications, though not absolute, enable scholars to make important critical distinctions between – to isolate only a few exemplary patterns here among the many to be addressed in the chapter – Irish immigrants who migrated to North America to escape the potato famine in the 1840s, individuals in solitary exile from their home countries due to political persecution or forcible expatriation and displacement (notably, writers and scholars such as Joseph Conrad, Edward Said, E. M. Cioran, Josef Brodsky, and others), Bangladeshi and South Vietnamese individuals fleeing war and political retaliation in 1971 and 1975, respectively, and Central American and Mexican farm laborers who annually enter into seasonal periods of migration to find agricultural work in the US.

Colonial settlers

At the height of European colonialism, expatriates from Spain, Portugal, Britain, France, and Holland were living outside of their motherlands and dispersed from the continental confines of Europe, scattered to the corners of the "Empire" in sites from South Africa, Zimbabwe, Canada, including Québec and Acadia (or the provinces of "New France"), Australia, New Zealand, México, the Caribbean archipelago, Brazil, and extensively throughout the continents of North and South America. Postcolonial theorists and scholars distinguish settler colonies from exploitation colonies, in which colonial administrations were established in order to expropriate raw or natural resources, goods, labor, and land, but without large colonial settlements (Young 2001). Britain was the colonial empire with the largest number of settler colonies across the globe, from southern Africa to North America to the Pacific islands of Australia and New Zealand.

Transnational corporate expatriates

A significant portion of migrants include transnational corporate expatriates who remain citizens of their country of origin – typically, though not exclusively, one of the "developed" nations of North America, Europe, or East Asia – though they work and reside in extra-territorial sites; unlike traditionally defined *economic migrants*, this class of migrants are typically educated, affluent, upwardly mobile, and above all, they move quite easily and frequently across national borders in the process of "doing business."

Student visas

Individuals admitted to host countries on student visas also comprise an important class of contemporary migrants. Frequently, these students originate from so-called "developing" or "underdeveloped" – or third-world – countries and migrate to so-called "developed" or first-world countries to pursue baccalaureate and post-baccalaureate degrees. Host countries often target students with knowledge, skills, and expertise in specific areas of research, such as engineering, physics, mathematics, and other hard sciences, because these countries believe that the educational experience will reap multiple benefits both for the students and the academic institutions at which they are studying.

Postcolonial émigrés

Important migratory shifts also resulted as a consequence of European colonialist expansion into Africa, Asia, and the Americas, and later from anticolonial independence struggles, decolonization, and migration from postcolony-to-metropolitan centers. For example, twentieth-century migrations and diasporas included the movement of individuals from formerly colonized territories to urban locations in North America (Toronto, Montréal, New York, San Francisco, Chicago), in Australia (Sydney, Melbourne), and in the Asian Pacific region (Hong Kong, Singapore) that thrived in the post-WWII boom in an emergent global capitalist economy. Postcolonial émigrés constitute a major class of contemporary migrants: following anticolonial struggles in the former colonies and the processes of decolonization that occurred after World War II, many postcolonial individuals sought educational, economic, and citizenship rights within the colonial "motherland," and particularly in her metropoles (London, Brussels, Paris, Amsterdam, Berlin, Rome, and elsewhere).

Refugees

Within the fields of diaspora, migration, and immigration studies, refugees are classified as individuals who have been granted political asylum within a host country due to being the target of persecution, state violence, retaliatory civil strife, political repression, or unlawful imprisonment or torture within one's country of origin. According to the most recent global statistics compiled by the UN in 2000, there are 21.5 million refugees worldwide, half of whom are women and children; in fact, there are 8 million children refugees in the world today. UN statistics also document an additional 900,000 *asylum* seekers, or asylees. Forces that lead to refugees seeking refuge in other countries include failed states, despotism or dictatorship, ethnic or religious conflict, civil warfare, and other forms of political violence or minority persecution. While refugees have historically been classed alongside *political asylees* by scholars within these interrelated fields, the tendency to do so has recently abated, a direct consequence of the 1980 Refugee Act in the US and indirectly the statistical decline in the percentage of asylum cases granted since the 1990s. Following the lead of host countries in distinguishing refugees from *asylees* or *asylum seekers* (see definition below), scholars have also begun to distinguish the two categories of migrants: while for the former, the legal distinction casts aspersion on the migratory motivations of asylum seekers until granted asylum and refugee status, for scholars the distinction necessarily points to the material, political, and legal boundaries that demarcate the two groups (see also *detainees* below). Host countries began this classificatory shift "because immigration officials suspected that many more people were 'economic refugees' who were only claiming asylum because they would not qualify for admission as migrant workers" (Stalker 2001, 12). In fact, the percentage of asylees actually granted asylum and given refugee status declined in almost every country in the EU, as well as in the US, throughout the 1990s (in the midst of civil warfare, regimes of "ethnic cleansing," and militarized forms of retaliatory violent local conflicts that marked the Rwandan and Yugoslavian massacres, as well as military coups and violent forms of retaliatory violence in small developing countries like Haiti).[11] In the last decade, the problem of global refugees has resurfaced in strikingly similar ways, as European countries and the EU itself have tightened immigration laws, dramatically reduced the number of refugees admitted into EU states, and denied applications for political asylum, even among applicants fleeing the ongoing Dafour genocide in Sudan.[12]

For all of these reasons, though I acknowledge that both groups have isolable relations, interrelated issues, and overlapping problems or concerns, I too differentiate between *political asylees* (those filing petitions for political asylum and refugee status), *refugees* (those whose petitions for asylum are approved), *detainees* (individuals who are held, or imprisoned, in detentions centers for the duration of time in which their applications for asylum are being processed, and in some cases, for years), and *illegal aliens* (those who have entered the host country through illegal means or measures), some of whom are *undocumented workers* or *economic migrants*, but many of whom may be refugees who feared denial of their asylum applications by the host country.

Following the United Nations' Universal Declaration of Human Rights in December 1948, the organization held the Conference on the Status of Refugees and Stateless Persons on May 28, 1951. In the Covenant adopted on July 28, 1951 under General Assembly Resolution 429 (V) – which also created the UN High Commissioner for Refugees (UNHCR) and which superseded the International Refugee Organization, an earlier refugee organization – the United Nations defined a *refugee* as any stateless individual who

> owing to well-founded fear of being persecuted for reasons of race, religion, nationality, membership of a particular social group or political opinion, is outside the country of his nationality and is unable or, owing to such fear, is unwilling to avail himself of the protection of that country; or who, not having a nationality and being outside the country of his former habitual residence as a result of such events, is unable or, owing to such fear, is unwilling to return to it.

Though the UN Resolution did not enter into force until April 22, 1954, the agreement also guaranteed *refugees* many of the same rights as nationals and aliens within the country of adoption, including nondiscrimination based on race, religion, or national origin (Article 3); the right to freedom of religion and its practice (Article 4); the right to "continuity of residence" (Article 10); the legal claim to "personal status" and the right to marriage within the receiving or host country (Article 12); the right to "movable and immovable property" (Article 13); the right to artistic and intellectual property (Article 14); the "right of association" or freedom of assembly (Article 15); access to the judicial process, courts, legal recourse, and due process (Article 16); the right to "gainful employment" through wage-earning jobs (Article 17), self-employment (Article 18), and professional vocation (Article 19); access to public welfare resources (in countries where available to the public), such as rationing (Article 20), housing (Article 21), public education (Article 22), public relief assistance (Article 23); as well as "labour legislation and social security" (Article 24). The UN Agreement also ensured refugees administrative assistance (Article 25), the right to "freedom of movement" (Article 26), access to identity papers (Article 27) and travel documents (Article 28) such as passports or visas, the right to transfer assets (Article 30), and protection from undue penalties such as "duties, charges, or taxes" (Article 29). Most importantly, Article 32 of the UN Agreement protects refugees from host country expulsion except in the cases of threats to national security or illegal felony offenses, and even in these cases, refugees are to be protected from deportation back to the originating country in which their life and liberty were threatened. Article 33 explicitly prohibits *réfoulement* (or *réfouler*), or return to the native country.

Political asylees (or asylum seekers)

Immigration law within many host countries now distinguishes between *refugees* and *political asylees*, those seeking refuge or asylum within the host country. Once an asylum application has been filed with the host country, the individual filing the application is legally classified as an *asylee* or *asylum seeker*. The individual does not become legally classified as a refugee, with the protection of fundamental rights typically accorded and guaranteed to refugees in accord with the 1951 United Nations Convention on the Status of Refugees and Stateless Persons, until the application for political asylum has been approved. Asylees are held in a liminal state of classlessness: they are not yet refugees, indeed may never become refugees, and yet until their applications for political asylum are either accepted or denied, these individuals effectively have few rights within the host country that they are seeking to enter and within the originating country that they have departed. Although in clear opposition to the 1951 UN Convention and to the 1993 UN Vienna Declaration and Program of Action, intended to update and expand the application of the 1951 Covenant, many host countries now hold asylees in detention (as discussed more extensively below under *detainees*) while their applications for political asylum are being processed.

Detainees

Asylees who are held in detention camps at immigration prisons may be classified as *detainees*. While few citizens of host countries are even cognizant of the fact that immigration prisons exist – both within the domestic borders of those countries and at offshore sites – since the onset of the "War on Terror" and the indefinite detention of individuals at detention camps on US military bases, the public has become increasingly aware of the vexing issues of immigration policies, detention centers, and detainees. Scholars such as Michael Welch, Mark Dow, and Rachel Meeropol, among others, have attempted to bring the plight of detainees to light. Responding to pressure from the United Nations following the 1951 Convention on Refugees and Stateless Persons, the United States also abandoned its "policy of detention" of refugee applicants, but resumed detention under the Immigration and Naturalization Service (INS) in 1980 following the Mariel Boat Lift of over 125,000 Cuban refugees and the massive waves of Haitian refugees – pejoratively referred to as "boat people" (an appellation earlier applied to Vietnamese and other Southeast Asian refugees seeking asylum in Australia, Hong Kong, and elsewhere in the Pacific during the early fallout of the post-Vietnam War years, particularly following the evacuation of US military troops in 1975) – that had already begun in the 1970s, but escalated in 1980. The end of a 26-year period of non-detention immigration policy in the US thus rapidly reverted to a policy of detention under the Carter and Reagan administrations as Cuban and Haitian refugees seeking entry through south Florida ports were detained at Miami's Krome Detention Center (Dow 2004, 7). "Although thousands of Cubans would end up in long-term detention, most Cubans who made it to US shores were welcomed as political refugees since they were fleeing a regime opposed by the federal government" (Dow 2004, 7). Since the Duvaliers were seen as a (necessary) dictatorial wall against the spread of communism in the Caribbean region, the same was not true for Haitian refugees fleeing political violence, but consistently classified and legally determined by US courts and the INS, as well as rhetorically portrayed in the US media, as *economic migrants* fleeing poverty on the island, not state regimes of violence (Farmer 1992, 1994, 1999, 2003; Chomsky, Farmer, and Goodman 2004; Laguerre 1998; Dow 2004; Opitz 2004).

In the mid-1990s, following the military coup d'état overturning the presidency of democratically elected Jean-Bertrand Aristide in 1991 (seven months after his election in 1990), Haitian refugees left the country in the scores of thousands as a "reign of terror" violently deployed against supporters of Aristide and Fanmi Lavalas, the political party he founded, was waged by the de facto regime under Général Henri Namphy and armed rebel groups, like the *Révolutionnaire Front pour l'Avancement et le Progrès d'Haïti* (*Revolutionary Front for Advancement and Progress in Haiti*), more commonly known as FRAPH, which has financial and political ties to both the Central Intelligence Agency and the International Republican Institute. By 1994, the year that saw Aristide restored to power by a US-UN led military intervention (or "intervasion" as critics have dubbed it), almost 45,000 Haitian refugees were imprisoned as detainees in detention camps at the US Naval Base at Guantánamo Bay in Cuba.

Detention of refugees, immigrants, and even permanent residents escalated – as did the active deportation of these groups – after Congress (in direct response to the 1995 bombing of the Murra federal building in Oklahoma City) passed the 1996 Illegal Immigration Reform and Immigrant Responsibility Act (IIRIRA) and the Antiterrorism and Effective Death Penalty Act (AEDPA), generally allowing for more expansive jurisdiction and regulatory latitude for the INS and specifically allowing "the agency to detain and deport any legal (and illegal) immigrant who has been charged with or convicted of a drug offense" (Welch 2002, 2). The "new immigration legislation" both reflected and heightened anti-immigrant sentiments in the US, further serving to criminalize and pathologize refugees who are too frequently regarded as deserving detention (read: locked up) by an unsympathetic US public who also too frequently elide distinctions between refugees, narcotics traffickers, terrorists, and international criminals as the "wars" against immigrants, drugs, and terror collide (as I have elsewhere discussed at greater length). "Under the 1996 immigration act," Welch explains, "numerous crimes were classified as aggravated felonies requiring detention and possibly deportation, including minor misdemeanors such as shoplifting and low-level drug violations" (2002, 3).

In many ways, though, the 1996 immigration legislation only codified as federal law and universally applied to all immigrants what had already become an entrenched institutionalized practice of detention that targeted Haitian refugees, who were dubiously criminalized as "drug traffickers," racially discriminated against in relation to their Cuban contemporaries, and even medically pathologized as HIV-carriers – and indeed, segregated camps were constructed at Guantánamo Bay for HIV+ Haitians who were quarantined on the naval base (Farmer 1992, 1994, 1999, 2003). "The laws also mandated increased detention of asylum seekers and, through a process known as expedited removal, gave low-level immigration inspectors wide authority to return asylum seekers encountered at airports. [And] [t]he number of detainees increased dramatically" (Dow 2004, 9).

Internally displaced persons (IDPs)

Often referred to as "internal refugees," *internally displaced persons* are those who have been uprooted through violence, civil warfare, famine, disease, "ethnic cleansing," political persecution, or religious oppression in their home regions. While not refugees seeking refuge in a foreign country by crossing international borders, internally displaced persons are similar in that they have been displaced from their homes, confront poverty, hunger, persecution, violence, and uncertainty. Displaced from their homes and neighborhoods, they seek shelter not in a foreign country, but in other parts of their own native countries.

Economic migrants

Economic migrants are individuals who move from their home countries to host countries in response to capitalist "push" and "pull" factors within local, regional, national, and global economies. "Push" factors include economic recession or depression, unemployment, scarcity of resources, poverty, and famine in home economies, whether local, regional, or national. "Pull" factors include economic boom in host countries, labor shortages, and increased demand for skilled employees and service-sector workers, whether at the local, regional, national, or even supranational levels (as is often the case for pull factors at the global capital level). Since the 1970s, shifts within global capitalist forms of production have led to a decline in economic migration for manufacturing jobs, as multinational corporations have themselves multiply relocated to so-called "free trade zones" within "developing" countries: some scholars now commonly refer to the immobility of labor and the hyper-motility of production sites, capital, and finance, which predictably migrates toward lowest wages, minimal benefits, and maximal profits. Marxism 101: surplus profit.

Additionally, other factors impact the motility or immobility of economic migrants: overpopulation in urban areas; infrastructural problems in rural areas, particularly in "developing" or "underdeveloped" countries; scarce resources in home countries and economies; environmental degradation; and even neoliberal economic "development" policies as structurally determined, enforced, and regulated by international development agencies (such as USAID, lending agencies such as the World Bank and the Inter-American Development Bank [IADB], and global financial institutions such as the International Monetary Fund [IMF] and the World Trade Organization [WTO]).

For example, during the 1970s and early 1980s, USAID and IABD development strategies for Haiti, Jamaica, and many other Caribbean and American countries included reduced funding for domestic agriculture, increased funding for commodity-specific forms (i.e., Anthurium nurseries) of exportation agriculture, and the establishment of so-called free trade zones for multinational corporations to employ manufacturing workers at substandard living wages (even relative to the countries in question); in fact, USAID dollars were even spent to lobby the Haitian parliament *not* to increase the minimum wage! Too frequently, the impact of these "development" strategies have been deleterious, not beneficial to the "developing" countries: proliferation of foreign-owned agricultural corporations that produce crops for exportation, the erosion of small farming for local consumption, loss of domestic agricultural sustainability, increased dependency on first-world countries for food importation, massive and unprecedented levels of internal rural to urban migration, overpopulation in urban centers of "developing" countries like Port-au-Prince, Kingston, Rio-de-Janeiro, Santo Domingo, San Juan, Panama City, and Managua in response to the *push* of agricultural shifts and the *pull* of multinational corporations, and consequent international migration to other locales.

Undocumented workers ("illegal aliens")

Related to the class of *economic migrants* are *undocumented workers*, those individuals who due to poverty and lack of opportunity seek economic benefits and employment outside of the borders of their home countries, but do so without first obtaining the requisite legal documents to afford them the classification of economic migrants. Undocumented workers are also rhetorically, politically, and often in fact legally defined as *illegal aliens*, a term that effectively strips these individuals not only of legal rights, recourse, and basic protection of human welfare, but also pejoratively casts these individuals as inappropriate criminals who remain outside of the protection of all nation-state borders. Illegal aliens may, then, be said to quintessentially materialize and exemplify what Giorgio Agamben defines as the *homo sacer*, the abject and vilified non-subject without rights or recourse.

In chapter one, we examine the role of diasporic workers in the new global economy, specifically addressing economic migration as diaspora formation. The chapter thus studies how diasporic workers contribute to the capitalist economies of their countries of adoption, but it also importantly elucidates how diasporic remittances also function to develop smaller homeland economies. Because the issue of Mexican migration to the United States has been a historically vexing one (and remains so today) – beginning with the Mexican-American War of 1846 and the territorial fallout over borderlines and indigenous territories – and because economic migration was the definitive form in the post-abolition, capitalist economies of the nineteenth and twentieth centuries in North America, chapter one also foregrounds a case study focusing on transborder migration across the volatile and highly policed zone of the US-Mexican border.

Questions for Reflection and Discussion

- What is your family's personal history of immigration? Do you know when your genealogical ancestors immigrated to the country where you reside? How have race, language, culture, and history shaped your understandings of immigration?
- Louis Mendoza and S. Shankar conclude their introduction to *Crossing into America* by quoting John F. Kennedy's *A Nation of Immigrants* ("Everywhere immigrants have enriched and strengthened the fabric of American life"). How have immigrants been historically foundational to the United States of America, to Brazil, to Canada, as well as to other historically immigrant-receiving countries?
- What roles have immigrants and the historical processes of immigration played in shaping politics and identities (linguistic, ethnic, cultural, even national) in these immigrant-receiving countries?
- Why are immigrants frequently targeted in the media and in popular culture? How are anti-immigrant sentiments (expressed in media or in popular culture) based on limiting stereotypes and prejudices about language, religion, race, culture, or national origin?
- Why is immigration vital to a country? Who is an immigrant? Who may be a citizen? Are the full rights of citizenship always guaranteed?

Additional Research

Thinking through writing

Theorizing anti-Semitism, totalitarianism, and twentieth-century Jewish diasporas

Because it is the *organization*, and not the *ideological content*, that defines totalitarianism, Hannah Arendt (in *The Origins of Totalitarianism*) clears an intellectual path for arguing (*contra* conventional wisdom or even dominant scholarly opinion of the 1950s) for a structural similitude between German Nazism and Soviet Communism. In other words, despite their ideological differences – German Nazism presumably a *national*, rightist movement; Soviet Communism ostensibly an *imperial*, leftist movement – both were *totalitarian movements*. Both were anti-statist or anti-state movements; both were totalitarian, rather than nationalist; and both the structures and the operative mechanisms of the movements were similar. Both Russia (in the late nineteenth century) and Germany (in the late nineteenth and early twentieth centuries) were also sites for virulent anti-Semitism and violent pogroms against Jewish minorities. In this light, read *The Origins of Totalitarianism* and examine how, for Arendt, nineteenth-century European anti-Semitism and colonialism (which was racially inflected and racist in practice) both created fertile ground for totalitarian movements in the twentieth century.

Theorizing African diasporas

Read, compare, and contrast three divergent theoretical approaches to the African diaspora: those offered by Paul Gilroy (in *The Black Atlantic*), Molefi Kete Asante (in *Afrocentrism* and in *The Afrocentric Idea*), and Joseph Roach (in *Cities of the Dead: Circum-Atlantic Performance*). How do these authors deploy the term *diaspora*? How do they complicate or deconstruct this term as an organizing rubric for defining peoples of African descent in the Americas?

1

Diasporic Workers,
New Global Economy

According to the most recent data compiled by the United Nations Population Division, almost 3 percent of the global population, totaling approximately 200 million people worldwide, are immigrants – living and working outside the country of birth. International migration has rapidly escalated over the last quarter century with the number of immigrants today twice that of 1980. And while distinctions must necessarily be made between asylees, refugees, trafficked persons, and economic migrants, or diasporic workers – as demarcated in the Introduction to this book – all international migrants have impacted the global economy, as well as the national economies of home and host countries. The Global Commission on International Migration reports that economic migrants add $240 billion annually to the economies of their home countries, while spending "more than $2 trillion in their host nation[s]" (Leopold 2005). Economic migration, one of the earliest and longest-sustained patterns of international migration, has proliferated over the last few decades, particularly in the years following the oil crises of 1973 (a result of the Arab oil embargo) and 1979 (in part a consequence of the Iranian Revolution), and the subsequent global economic recession of the early 1980s. Diasporic workers in the "New Global Economy," as it has been called, are part of this defining moment of late capitalism: its transnationalization of finance, its international division of production, its "outsourcing" (of labor and services), its "offshoring" (of banking and informational technologies), its commodification of exported (and exploited) labor, its global trade in goods and services, and its capital-monetary flows in remitted salaries, transferred funds, and inflationary-deflationary currency exchanges. While international economic migration has always been part of the extensive and intensive flows of capitalism, diasporic workers in the new global economy are unique in that they contribute not only to their personal livelihood, or even to that of their nuclear and extended families, but more expansively to their hometowns (its infrastructure and public services: roads, bridges, wells, supplies of drinking water, schools, textbooks) and even the modernization or "development" of their native countries, particularly developing countries.

Diasporic workers, or economic migrants, are as diverse as the countries they emigrate from and the countries they migrate to: dominant patterns of international economic migration include Mexican and Central American farm workers or field hands, car-washers, nursing assistants, janitors, cooks, dishwashers, carpenters, and construction workers in the United States; Filipina maids in Hong Kong, Italy, and the US; Filipina and Filipino nurses registered and practicing in Canada, the US, countries in the European Union, Australia, and New Zealand;[1] Chinese working in textile factories outside Los Angeles; Ghanaians driving lorries or working the "Tube," and Mauritian waitresses serving coffee in hotel restaurants off Tavistock Square in London; Pakistani construction workers in the Middle East, especially since the 1980s; Sri Lankan domestic workers in the Gulf States, again since the OPEC oil boom; Cameroonians manning explosives to extract oil in the Ogoni Delta region of Nigeria; Trinidadians drilling for oil offshore in Venezuela; Maghrebis, particularly Algerians, working on car-manufacturing assembly lines or as automobile mechanics in France's Renault; Turks and Kurds waiting tables in Germany; Dominicans *buscando mejor vida*, "seeking a better life," while working retail, answering telephones, or building houses in Puerto Rico;[2] Puerto Ricans working in the "garment district" of New York City, picking apples in western Massachusetts, or cleaning hotel rooms in Miami or the Bahamas; Haitian cane laborers in the DR, *und so weiter*, and so on.

Working to sustain self, family, friends, local villages, and developing nations, diasporas (or diasporic communities) employed overseas also contribute to political campaigns and national candidates back home, as is the case in Haiti and the Philippines,[3] but also civil unrest, funding of revolutionary militant groups, arming of military coups, or supplying weapons, as is the case for some Sri Lankans in Canada, and elsewhere, supporting the "Tamil Tigers" (officially the Liberation Tamil Tigers of Ealam [LTTE]), sometimes through forced remittances (discussed more extensively below).[4] Developing countries – from the Dominican Republic and Haiti in the Caribbean, Pakistan and Sri Lanka in South Asia, and the Philippines in the Asian Pacific – have frequently based their own strategic plans for development on exported labor and imported free trade zones and multinational corporations. In this opening chapter, "Diasporic Workers, New Global Economy," we will probe the interlocking issues of labor, immigration, legal documentation, illegal (or undocumented) workers, and economically driven migration patterns, such as agricultural migrant labor, housing or construction work, and other service-sector forms of employment (particularly in hotels and restaurants). The chapter thus allows readers to understand the push-pull of economic or financial patterns that are directly related to migration influxes-outflows within a country, as well as the relation of economic migration, recession, and the frequently atavistic eruptions of anti-immigrant sentiments that accompany periods of economic decline. It will also address two related issues: the huge impact that diasporic remittances have had and continue to have on small developing economies worldwide; and the global resurgent phenomenon of human trafficking and forced labor.

Taking economic migration and North American worker diasporas as our case study, we will examine the long historical patterns of economic migration across the US-Mexican "border," or *La Frontera* and *La Linea* as it is called in Spanish. Contested territory at least since 1846 when the United States first sent federal troops to the land surrounding the Rio Grande, and acquired "legally" – or as Mexicans might counter-dispute, illegally – by the US at the end of the Mexican-American War two years later in 1848 with the signing of the Treaty of Guadeloupe Hidalgo (which allowed for the official US annexation of Mexican land now comprising the states of Texas, Arizona, New Mexico, Oklahoma, Wyoming, Colorado, Kansas, Utah, Nevada, and California), the border region, or *La Frontera*, between the United States and Mexico remains a violent and liminal zone of economic, material, political, militaristic, judicial, legal, and extra-legal transnational negotiation between the two countries.

This opening chapter thus focuses extensively, in the final case study, on Mexican and Central American economic migration to the United States and examines the often polemical and even violent transnational "border politics" that have accompanied this migration. The case study discusses the multiple series of Immigration and Naturalization Services (INS) "operations" – from the pejoratively named "Operation Wetback" of 1954 to "Operation Secure the Border" proposed in 2006 – implemented in order to control and restrict transborder migration, as well as restrictive state legislative acts like California's Proposition 187, and labor strikes among undocumented workers (for example, the hotel workers' strikes in Chicago, Minneapolis, San Francisco, Las Vegas, and elsewhere in the US). Moving into the contemporary historical moment, the case study also addresses President George W. Bush's deployment of National Guardsmen to work beside border patrol agents in summer 2006, concomitant congressional proposals in the Senate and the House of Representatives to build a fence along the already heavily "patrolled," though still-porous border, and the unsettling and invidious upsurges in transborder violence as vigilante citizen groups such as the Minute Men take up arms and also attempt to "police" the border.

Diasporic Remittances, Small Developing Economies

Throughout the 1990s, diasporic remittances exceeded international developmental aid to many developing countries (Stilwell et al. 2004, 597; cited in Kingma 2006). In 2001, the United Nations Conference on Trade and Development estimated that the annual total for officially transferred diasporic remittances worldwide was $117 billion (cited in Kingma 2006, 194). According to the Report of the Global Commission on International Migration commissioned by the United Nations for 2005, the amount of global economic remittances – US$150 billion annually – exceeded (by three times!) the amount of international developmental aid extended to developing countries for that year.[5] Diasporic dollars remitted to family members and friends in the home country through official channels – money wiring agencies, post offices, banks, or other financial institutions – often comprise a substantial portion of the receiving country's gross domestic product: "for example, 4.5 percent in Benin, 5.8 percent in Burkina Faso, 16.2 percent in Nicaragua, and 26.5 percent in Lesotho" (Kingma 2006, 6). Other countries have benefited even more radically from influxes of diasporic remittances, or what Appadurai refers to as *financescapes*: during 2000 alone, "remittances sent by the diaspora to El Salvador, Eritrea, Jamaica, Nicaragua and Yemen enabled these countries to augment their respective GDP by more than 10 percent" (IOM 2003a, 17, 229; cited in Kingma 2006, 193); and in Tonga, "remittances account for as much as 39 percent of their GDP" (ibid). Moreover, in African countries that are not oil-rich (as are Nigeria and Cameroon), diasporic remittances exceed dollar-for-dollar the amount of foreign capital investment in the country, thus making "an essential contribution to the national economy" (ibid). Other countries with strategic programs designed to export human labor, encouraging massive outflows of economic laborers, like the Philippines and the Dominican Republic, also have incredibly large capital inflows of diasporic remittances, totaling in the billions annually for both countries. Despite the obvious decisive economic boon to developing countries through circulating diasporic remittances and inflows of hard cash, the actual benefit is difficult, if not impossible, to ascertain, since data on global diasporic remittances is based on "official" flows of capital and thus does not, and cannot, account for "remittances channeled through unofficial routes, which in some cases, as for the Arab countries, reach huge proportions," as Glytsos explains (2001, 262). Unofficial diasporic remittances form part of what Choucri (1986) refers to as a "hidden economy" within some national economies (cited in Glytsos 2001, 262).

Not only directly benefiting friends and family, diasporic remittances also stimulate local national economies through increased income and consumer spending, though some scholars believe that this influx of cash-capital may also stimulate inflation, though the evidence is, at this point, "inconclusive" (Glytsos 2001, 263). Diasporic remittances received by family and friends are often used to purchase food, clothing, electronic appliances (refrigerators, stoves, televisions, videocassette recorders), and houses or housing-construction materials; in fact, 73 percent of diasporic remittances to Egypt "went into housing construction" (Glytsos 2001, 263). Diasporic dollars, however, also flow toward infrastructural development projects: helping to build roads, staff local schools, and generously contribute to other "hometown" projects (particularly in countries like Haiti with very few public resources or tax revenues). Diasporic incomes are frequently earned in hard currencies – like dollars, euros, marks, or pounds – and increasingly financial institutions are collaborating with migrant workers to transfer funds internationally without first exchanging the currency into softer ones that are subject to devaluation and erratic deflationary fluxes (Kingma 2006; United Nations Department of Economic and Social Affairs 2005). Other banks and financial institutions have reduced the transfer fees charged for remitting funds internationally, and this reduction in percentage of commission fees has dramatically increased the remittances actually reaching friends and family members in the home countries:

Following a negotiation with the Mexican government and as part of a marketing campaign targeting Latin American workers in the United States, a group of banks agreed to lower the transfer commission rate to 5 percent. As a result a further $1–2 million per year reaches relatives and investment projects in Latin America. Similarly, three banks in Paris offer a special transfer scheme to Côte d'Ivoire, Mali, and Senegal; in 1999 they officially transferred $24 million to Senegal alone.

In countries with high (even staggering) levels of unemployment, diasporic remittances can alleviate national poverty and economic hardship: according to the International Labor Organization, diasporic remittances sent to the country of Senegal "constitute the principal source of household income – almost 90 percent – for those households that receive them." (Kingma 2006, 109, 193)

Developing countries have become, perhaps, so financially dependent upon diasporic remittances sent home by overseas migrant workers annually that national (or global) efforts to reduce international economic migration may have severe and deleterious consequences for the economic sustainability of those countries. Case in point: both Houses of the United States Congress, Senate and the House of Representatives, are amidst ongoing debate in proposed 2006 immigration reform bills currently under legislative consideration; if passed, these bills (S. 2611 and HR 4437) will almost certainly have a negative economic impact on migrants workers ("legal" and "illegal," authorized and undocumented) in the US, their families back home, and sending countries, such as Mexico and Guatemala. In countries sending highly skilled, well-trained, or professionally educated workers (like nurses, physicians, engineers, physicists, professors, and so on), the loss of human capital and potential tax revenues *may* actually exceed the diasporic remittances sent back home, even though migrant professionals with higher salaries tend to remit at higher rates; the data on migrant professionals is inconclusive and a point of scholarly debate among international migration scholars; in countries sending low-skilled, uneducated workers (such as agricultural farmhands, janitors, dishwashers, or maids, though many of these individuals are also admittedly skilled, educated, underemployed at home and abroad, and thus overqualified for their low-paying migrant jobs), however, the diasporic remittances more than amply compensate for or substantially offset the loss in human capital and potential income tax revenues.

Gendered differences are also traceable in patterns of economic diasporic remittances, as María José Alcala demonstrates in a recent study entitled "A Passage to Hope: Women and International Migration." According to Alcala, women migrant workers, who on average earn less than their male counterparts, still send a higher percentage of their earnings home each year to support family, especially children and aging parents, who remain behind. Of the estimated 95 million women immigrants working outside of their home countries, a significant proportion remit "up to three-quarters of their income home" (Barbassa 2006). In the year 2000, "Bangladeshi women working in the Middle East . . . sent home 72 percent of their earnings, on average" (Barbassa 2006). Funds remitted by women economic migrants also typically comprise the majority of total remittances received by their home countries each year. For example, in 1999 Sri Lankan women working abroad (many as domestic workers in the Middle East) remitted approximately 62 percent of "the more than $1 billion the country received in remittances" (Barbassa 2006). According to statistics compiled by the Sri Lankana Bureau of Foreign Employment (SLBFE) for 2003, an estimated 680,000 Sri Lankan women were outside of the country, with "over 80 percent of them [working] as housemaids in the Middle East" (SLBFE 2003; cited in Gamburd 2004). Sri Lankan diasporic workers and their financial contributions to the South Asian island country's economy are discussed at greater length below.

Filipino diasporic remittances have powerfully shaped the Philippine economy over the last few decades. Remittance dollars, in effect, constitute *the* push-pull of the Filipino diaspora: in 1989, annual remittances equaled US$973 million (Hawthorne 2001, 214n2); dollars remitted to the Philippines for 1993 totaled "3.4 percent of the Gross Domestic Product, which is the equivalent of 30 percent of the trade deficit or entire interest payments on the country's foreign debt" (Chang 2000, 130). And according to the Central Bank of the Philippines, the remittances returned to the country by overseas migrant workers from 1974 to 1994 totaled US$18.196 billion (Ceniza Choy 2003, 188). Filipino remittances in dollars and other hard currencies (pounds and euros) have peaked in the early years of the twenty-first century: in 2004, remittances equaled US$8.5 billion (Kingma 2006, 24); and in 2005, US$10.7 billion (Mannes 2006). Rhacel Salazar Parreñas contends it is "impossible to overlook the significance of migrant labor to the Philippine economy. Some 34 to 54 percent of the Filipino population is sustained by remittances from migrant workers" (2005, 39). And the decades-old Philippine historical pattern of migratory outflows and capital inflows is likely to continue unabated, "given the country's massive $46 billion debt to the World Bank, International Monetary Fund, and other lending institutions based in North America," and especially since "overseas workers' remittances have been the country's largest source of foreign exchange" (Ceniza Choy 2003, 188).

Haitian diasporic remittances have similarly impacted the country's developing economy over the last few decades, beginning in the late Duvalier period. Throughout this period, the late 1970s through the mid-1980s, the import-export equation escalated, as Haiti continued to import far more than it exported; and by 1985, Haiti was deep within its economic crisis. According to Hooper, "by that year, the balance of payments deficit reached $25 million, while total debt was estimated at between $519 million and $833 million by August 1987" (1995, 135). Debt coincided with state despotism, the Duvalier dictatorship in the country, and a noose's hold on public political expression, as well as out-migration. Throughout the Duvalier era, in fact, Haitian exiles or diasporic subjects who fled political persecution, brutality, and economic hardship in Haiti for a better life outside of Haiti's borders (whether in Santo Domingo, the Bahamas, Dakar, Paris, New York, Boston, Miami, or Montréal) were regarded as national traitors. Haitians who transferred their citizenship to other countries were considered *apatrid*, or without a country (Glick Schiller and Fouron 1999, 139). In 1990 the relationship between Haiti and its diaspora was radically altered, and it had profound effects on the trans-American reconfigurations of nation-states and diasporas, as well as the country's economic development strategies. (One other consequence is that Haitian diasporic communities more openly expressed concern and engaged in forms of nonviolent political activism to denounce the treatment of Haitian refugees detained both at Guantánamo Bay and at Miami's Krome Detention Center.) As socialist, grassroots candidate in the 1990 Haitian presidential election, Jean-Bertrand Aristide reincorporated the diaspora into the national, if not territorial body of Haiti, referring to the diaspora as the country's administrative "Tenth Department." Aristide directly appealed to the nationalist sentiments of the diaspora, calling for their reinvestment in the homeland in *Pwojè Lavalas* (Project Lavalas), a paper published during his presidential campaign, and promising an important place for all Haitians living in diaspora. The publication proclaimed that "the LAVALAS MOUVMAN, which has adopted a good project of government, supposes the participation of all citizens from all social classes," adding that "a special place will be reserved for peasants, women, all patriotic movements, and all Haitians in diaspora" (quoted in Glick Schiller and Fouron 1999, 135). This appeal to Haitians living in diaspora echoed Aristide's earlier calls for the diaspora to return home in *In the Parish of the Poor* (published in 1987), writing: "My generation is running away from Haiti, with its dark corners and byways. I want to call them back before they begin their fruitless travels. . . . I say to them come back and make a new Haiti" (quoted in Glick Schiller and Fouron 2001, 119). Aristide reconsidered this "politics of return" in 1990, once he realized the positive financial impact of the diaspora (with its constant remittances to family members, its generous campaign contributions, and its fundraising within hometown associations); diasporic dollars were key to rebuilding Haiti, and Aristide even referred to the diaspora, or "Tenth Department," as a "bank" (Glick Schiller and Fouron 2001, 120; cf. Richman 196). In fact, two-thirds of the $300,000 raised for Aristide's 1990 presidential campaign was raised from diasporic contributions (Glick Schiller and Fouron 2001, 120; Jean-Pierre 1995, 202). After his election in April 1991, Aristide raised an additional $600,000 from Haitians living in diaspora to fund development projects under the Lavalas Administration (Jean-Pierre 1995, 202). Remittances (estimated at US$125 million annually) sent by Haitian diasporic communities and family members living in the United States and Canada partially offset the country's trade imbalance (Hooper 1995; Glick Schiller and Fouron 2001). Diasporic remittances also directly impact the foreign policy decisions of host country as well as facilitate (and fund) changes in homeland politics for Haiti.

Sri Lankan diasporic workers have also impacted the country's economy and political structure through financial remittances. Sri Lanka's postcolonial history, vexed by civil warfare and ongoing violence, is crucial to understanding its migratory outflows of both political refugees and economic migrants. Civil unrest erupted in the South Asian island country in the early 1980s: warring factions and nationalist, separatist divisions broke down along ethnic and religious lines with the Sri Lankan Sinhalese Buddhist and Muslim majority first repressing – politically and economically – the Tamil Hindu minority, and then opposing the militant factions and insurrectionist forces within the Tamil minority. Amidst race riots and inter-ethnic strife in the late 1970s and early 1980s, the country's Sinhalese majority (approximately 14.25 million people) persecuted the Tamil minority (approximately 3.2 million people). In July 1983 the Sri Lankan government instituted an "anti-Tamil pogrom," which "left up to 3,000 Tamils dead" (Sriskandarajah 2002, 289, 290). The conflict, though erupting in 1983, was decades in the making:

> Since Sri Lanka's independence from the British in 1948, the Singhalese majority has systematically cut down Tamil rights. The Singhalese-dominated state passed the Sinhala Only Act in 1956, which made Sinhala Sri Lanka's official language. Next, the state attacked Tamil dominance in Sri Lanka's educational system by lowering university acceptance standards for Sinhalese students. Horrific riots in 1977, 1981, and 1983 increasingly polarized the community. (La 2004, 381)

Yet it was undeniably "the events of 1983 [which] mark[ed] the start of the widespread refugee flows from Sri Lanka to India and the rest of the world" (Sriskandarajah 2002, 290). To counter ethnic and religious intimidation by the dominant majority who controlled the Sri Lankan government, the Liberation Tigers Tamil Eelam (LTTE), or the "Tamil Tigers," was founded in 1983. Consequently, the Tamil Tigers entered a revolutionary struggle to secede from Sri Lanka, claiming Jaffna (in northeast Sri Lanka) as a separate, national homeland. According to Sriskandarajah, "the north-east of the island, traditionally home to the island's Sri Lankan Tamil population and base of the largest militant group, the Liberation Tigers of Tamil Eelam (LTTE), has undergone widespread devastation" (2002, 289). From 1983 until the ceasefire negotiated by Denmark and Norway in 2002, almost 65,000 Sri Lankans died during the bloody civil warfare.

During this same period, the country also experienced massive migratory outflows – the Sinhalese economically migrating to the Middle East, and the Tamils seeking political refuge in India, North America (primarily Canada), Europe, and Australia. Thus, out-migratory flows from Sri Lanka may be subdivided into labor and political migrations. While immigration scholar Dhananjayan Sriskanadarajah concedes that "the total migration from Sri Lanka, estimated to be between 1.5–2 million over roughly 20 years, is not particularly large or intense by global standards[,] [w]hat is notable . . . is the scale of this migration relative to population size, its sustained nature, and the notoriety achieved by migration flows from Sri Lanka" (2002, 288). Sriskandarajah distinguishes the "basic characteristics" of the two dominant out-migratory flows in the following ways: the first pattern is defined as a labor migration, predominantly of Sinhalese Muslims, voluntarily, for "economic reasons" and through "formal channels" (or governmentally negotiated international labor contracts) to the Middle East; the second pattern is defined as a "forced" political migration of Tamils due to "conflict-driven" causes and through "informal channels" to India and to the developed countries of the West (2002, 288). Human costs of the armed civil conflict and out-migration have been profound: as Sriskandarajah writes, the conflict has had high direct and indirect costs island-wide in terms of lives, livelihoods, and slower economic growth. Not surprisingly, the largest increases in both migration flows have occurred since 1983. While the majority of political migrants have been Tamils directly affected by the conflict in the north-east, the conflict has also indirectly fueled the increased flows of predominantly Sinhalese labour migration from the south-west. (Sriskandarajah 2002, 289)

To date, approximately 1.5–2 million Sri Lankans live off the island.

Following the national success of the Philippine economic development plan based on exported (yet too often exploited) human labor, the Sri Lankan government followed suit in creating the Sri Lankan Bureau of Foreign Employment (SLBFE) to "promote the country's 'main resource', namely 'its highly industrial and literate people'" (Sriskandarajah 2002, 291). From a national development perspective, the active exportation of labor "eased unemployment problems," resulted in monetary capital inflows to compensate for human capital outflows: the diasporic workers' remittances "contributed to the national income and eased foreign exchange needs at a time when military expenditures and government borrowing were increasing" (Sriskandarajah 2002, 291). Diasporic remittances exceeded US$1 billion by the late twentieth century, representing a significant portion of Sri Lanka's "total annual GDP of less than US$20 billion" (Sriskandarajah 2002, 294). Based on data collected by the International Monetary Fund (IMF), Sri Lankan diasporic workers remitted only US$9 million in 1975, but the amount has increased dramatically since 1980 with a rapid proliferation seen during the 1990s: in 1980, diasporic workers remitted US$152 million; in 1985, US$292 million; in 1990, US$401 million; in 1995, US$790 million; and in 1999, over US$1.05 billion. As Michele Ruth Gamburd affirms, "the Sri Lankan government has grown increasingly dependent on labor migration to relieve local unemployment and bring in much-needed foreign exchange" (2004, 167). While substantial and impressive contributions to Sri Lanka's developing economy, these estimates only include formal remittances sent through official channels (banking institutions, financial centers, post offices, corporate money-wiring agencies) and not those informal remittances sent through unofficial channels (third-party transfers or covert wiring mechanisms).

While Sinhalese diasporic workers have remitted funds to stabilize the Sri Lankan developing economy, Tamil diasporic remittances have often worked to destabilize the country. For example, TamilNet has fostered diasporic remittances intended to further the revolutionary cause of the Tamil Tigers. Diasporic politics have thus continued to influence homeland politics. In posing a tentative answer to his own titular question, "Can Remittances Spur Development?," economist Stuart S. Brown conjectures "yes," affirming that diasporic communities can indeed "influence home country politics as well as host country foreign policy" (2006, 64). In the case of the Tamil Tigers, however, the influence on host countries has diminished as it has resorted to internationally shunned violent tactics (like suicide bombings) in its revolutionary struggle. Or as Sriskandarajah explains, "Tamil diasporic organizations have been actively engaged in shaping Tamil politics, and, generally, in legitimizing Tamil nationalism" (2002, 298), though that effort has been marred in developed countries of the West since the destructive bombing attacks on the World Trade Center Twin Towers, first in 1993 and then again in 2001.

According to UNHCR statistics published in June 2001, an estimated 817,000 Tamil refugees (or asylum seekers) were "internationally displaced" (Sriskandarajah 2002, 293). The majority of diasporic Tamils reside in Canada, Europe, India, the US, and Australia: 400,000 Tamils are in Canada; 200,000 in Europe; 67,000 in India; 40,000 in the US; and 30,000 in Australia. The same UNHCR report ranked Sri Lanka in "the top ten of asylum seeker sending countries" for the year 2000 (Sriskandarajah 2002, 293). According to political scientist and peace and conflict studies scholar John La, "Canada currently hosts the world's largest Sri Lankan diaspora," and most are Tamils living in "ethnic enclaves" in Toronto and Vancouver and who sought and gained political asylum in the North American country following the events of 1983. La documents that Tamil diasporic remittances are not always "voluntary." In fact, La charges that the LTTE – "notorious," he writes, "for using tactics such as political assassination, suicide bombing, and the recruitment of child soldiers" – compels Tamil Sri Lankan Canadians to support its cause by developing "a system to extract remittances from Tamil refugees in Canada by exploiting transnational social ties," and by threatening the refugees, their families, and "the security of relatives or property still in Sri Lanka" (2004, 379). La illustrates how the LTTE exerts control over the Tamil diaspora, detailing how Tamil Tigers "have infiltrated Tamil enclaves in Canada" in order to forcibly "extract" remittances from the diasporic community: these funds "are normally collected by front businesses and charities" such as the Federation of Associations of Canadian Tamils (FACT), an organization alleged to have "raised" and then diverted (or "laundered") an estimated sum "between US$12 million and US$22 million annually for the LTTE" (La 2004, 381). Refusals to remit are often met with veiled threats toward family members back home or worse: "tragic losses of life or destruction of property in the refugee's sending state" (La 2004, 381). Tamil diasporic remittances, thus, often flow through third-party or informal channels, particularly since the designation of the LTTE as a "terrorist organization" by the US State Department in 1997 and FACT as a terrorist organization since September 11, 2001. Consequently, Tamil diasporic remittances are "often funneled through foreign bank accounts or other intermediary institutions that help to cloak these capital flows"; or, at times, the group has actually smuggled money (cash, not virtual) into the country (La 2004, 382).

Economic and infrastructural devastation has also been one impact of the extended armed conflict in Sri Lanka. And "the challenge in [and for] Sri Lanka will be to move from a vicious cycle of conflict, underdevelopment and migration to a more virtuous one" (Sriskandarajah 2002, 283). Writing the case study on Sri Lanka for the International Organization of Migration (published in *International Migration* in 2002), Sriskandarajah remarked in an endnote that "positive signs [were] emerging from Sri Lanka that the main protagonists in the conflict were willing to enter negotiations toward an interim political solution"; and while a ceasefire was agreed to by both groups in 2002, only four years later, violence – allegedly committed by Tamil Tigers armed, supplied, and financially supported by the Tamil diaspora – erupted once more in April 2006. By early autumn 2006, though still ostensibly under ceasefire, almost 700 Sri Lankans had been killed by gunfire, hand grenades, and suicide bombings as the fighting appears to have actively resumed despite the ceasefire. High unemployment in the northeast Tamil populated part of the island, combined with insurrectionist fervor, has made the area "a fertile recruitment ground for Tamil militant groups" and continues to lure Tamil youth into militancy. As La explains, Sri Lanka has been (and continues to be) wounded by a "civil war that has, over the past twenty years, instilled deep-rooted hostilities between Tamils and Singhalese, destroyed Sri Lanka's national infrastructure, and claimed over 65,000 lives" (2004, 382). The point is this: diasporas may have a profound impact on their homelands through remitted funds earned abroad and transferred home; yet at times, those funds may serve destructive ends or aims nationally, politically, and materially. And the forced extraction of remittances, as in the case of Tamil refugees in Canada, further violates the human rights of persecuted individuals who fled their homeland seeking refuge from violence and exploitation. Diasporic remittances, then, are powerful tools to sway homeland politics, but that influence may not always be a beneficial one. As Anita Mannur and I asked several years ago in our editors' introduction to the edited volume *Theorizing Diaspora* (2002):

> In theorizing future trajectories of diaspora and diaspora studies, it will be crucial to schematically analyze the role of cyber-technology and the world wide web within such ideological and capitalistic formations: how, for example, do supporters of specific organizations such as the PLO (Palestine Liberation Organization) and LTTE (Liberation Tigers of Tamil Eelam), who are committed to positing a different version of the homeland, use cyber-space to promote alternative visions of the home and the homeland, while also moving capital across such divides? How does their presence on the Internet allow for faster or easier transnational flows of money?

Having addressed the impact that diasporic workers in the "new global economy" may have on homeland politics and on host country foreign policy through remittances, generally, let's now consider the specific historical, material, cultural, labor, and geopolitical space of the US-Mexico border as a catalytic site for transborder economic migration and even the multinational, third-space of the "borderzone" itself as an important site for global capitalist expansion, production, and diasporic transmigration.

Case Study: "La Frontera": Transborder Migrations, Mexican-American Diasporic Workers

The illegal immigrant is the bravest among us. The most modern among us.

Richard Rodriguez, author of *Brown*

Fences don't work.
Senator Edward M. Kennedy, Massachusetts

It's impossible to deport a population the size of Ohio.
Senator Tim Johnson, South Dakota

There are many Mexicos; there are also many Mexican borders.
Luis Alberto Urrea, author of *Across the Wire*

Given its geographical proximity – indeed land-mass contiguity – with the continental United States (the "border," though porous, only officially delineated in 1853), and given the long and sustained patterns of economic migration south to north, and less frequently north to south, across the border, the US-Mexican capitalist interdependence and patterns of historical economic migration constitute a unique case study. Economic migrants – seasonal farm workers, cattle drivers, ranch hands, and more recently, hotel and restaurant workers and construction workers – have been crossing the border (legally and illegally, documented and undocumented) as long as it has existed; and of course, the indigenous traversing of river, desert, and sparsely settled land in the region that eventually became *La Frontera* predates the actual border itself. According to Haines and Rosen (1999), half of all "illegal aliens" in the United States are from Mexico, and approximately 15 percent are from Central America. Other statistics are equally salient: according to *World Development Indicators*, published by the World Bank in 2003, annual remittances to Mexico totaled an estimated US$4.2 billion in 1996, and US$8.9 billion in 2001; in 2002, "20 million Mexican workers... sent home nearly $10 billion" (Kapur and McHale 2003, 50); most impressively, data published in *Balance of Payments Statistics Yearbook* and compiled by the IMF, as well as estimated figures presented by the World Bank for 2004, estimate that Mexican migrants remitted a whopping US$18.1 billion back home to family and friends in Mexico![6] And as economist Stuart S. Brown reports, the majority of these remittances flow from the US to Mexico, further noting that "the largest single group of remitters has been US-residing Latin Americans, with a disproportionate share of US remittances flowing to Mexico" (2006, 60).

In this case study, then, we will focus on US-Mexico economic migration, placing contemporary transborder movement of workers across *La Frontera*, or the "border," in the historical context of Anglo- and Spanish colonialism in North America from the sixteenth to eighteenth centuries, forcible land acquisitions and westward expansionist movement by the United States throughout the nineteenth century, the Mexican-American War (1846–8), the consequent establishing of the border and demarcation (or cartographic divisions) of North American into US and Mexican territories in 1848 and 1853, the creation of the US Border Patrol, and historical patterns of economic migration across the border in the late nineteenth, twentieth, and early twenty-first centuries.

North America, throughout the eighteenth and nineteenth centuries, was defined by British, French, and Spanish colonial territorial acquisition, expropriation of native or indigenous lands, and boundary disputes. By 1800, the British colonies had both declared (in 1776) and won (in 1783) independence from King George's Britain; and Charles IV of Spain had ceded "Louisiana" to France under coercion by Napoleon Bonaparte. Three years later in 1803, fighting a losing battle against the "Black Jacobins" revolting against slavery and French colonial rule in the Antillean island of Saint-Domingue, Napoleon sold the Louisiana territory to the United States of America during the administration of President Thomas Jefferson, who orchestrated the "Purchase," for a monumental $15 million, money sorely needed to subdue slave revolutionaries declaring their own independence under the political and military leadership of Toussaint Louverture (in 1791, two years after the storming of the Bastille that started the French Revolution in 1789). Despite the dispossession of France from its second largest North American colony (after Québec in the northeastern continental territories) and the massive monetary acquisition, the French colonial empire still lost its most wealth-producing and profitable colony, Saint-Domingue, as the revolutionary soldiers declared the independence of the République d'Haïti (Republic of Haiti) one year later in 1804. Annexationist and expansionist in nationalist fervor, President Jefferson claimed that the Louisiana territory "included all lands north and east of the Rio Grande, thus laying claim to Spanish settlements such as San Antonio and Santa Fe" (Nevins 2002, 16). The young United States of America thus entered early nineteenth-century negotiations with imperial Spain and the Spanish colonial empire in North America to establish the "exact location of the boundary between Spanish Texas and the Louisiana territory" (Nevins 2002, 17). Battles and border disputes raged in the early nineteenth century – Napoleon invading Spain in 1808, and the USA invading western Florida in 1810 and eastern Florida, both regions under Spanish colonial rule, in 1818. In 1819, the US and Spain signed the Adams-Onis Treaty authorizing the US to acquire all of Spanish Florida in exchange for the country's "recognition of an international boundary between Texas and Louisiana," which extended US territory to the 42nd parallel but allowed Spain to retain control over Texas. According to Joseph Nevins, the treaty not only established the precursive historical ground for the Mexican-American War, but also established "a US pattern of seizing territory by force" (2002, 17). The United States of America thus pressed southward and westward, pursuing what many believed to be its "Manifest Destiny" – a term coined and popularized by *Democratic Review* editor John Sullivan – and that "combined the ideas of Anglo-Saxon superiority with capitalist territorial expansionism" (Nevis 2002, 17). Winning independence from Spain in 1821, Mexico also "acquired the challenge of protecting its northern border" from US "barnstorming" incursions and from "transboundary Indian raids," native battles to hold onto indigenous lands desired by both countries – Mexico to the south, the USA to the north (Nevins 2002, 17, 23).

1823: another historically momentous year: in January, the USA officially recognized Mexico's independence and sovereignty, although reluctantly and only under pressure form anti-colonialist sympathizers in the country; in March, the newly-born Mexico faltered as "both Central America and Chiapas," still a rebellious region, seceded from the republic; in October, a newly-consolidated "United States of Mexico" was created; and in December, designed to foil and prevent Spanish colonial efforts to re-establish control of Mexico, but also to establish the dominance militaristically, politically, economically in the western hemisphere, the United States Congress passed the Monroe Doctrine under the presidential administration of James Monroe, "pronouncing that the Americas were off limits to European intervention and colonization and that the United States would not tolerate such activity. (Nevins 2002, 18)

By the 1820s, Anglo-American settlers (many "proslavery southerners" and cotton planters) were a well-established presence in Mexico's Texas (Nevins 2002, 18). In 1830, the Republic of Mexico illegalized and abolished slavery in the country, which led to tensions between the Mexican government, Anglo-American slaveholding settlers in the territory, and wealthy Tejanos who were sympathetic to both slavery and US capital inflows. Tensions arose during the decade of the 1830s, and in 1837, secessionists supported by US capital, or "dollar diplomacy," Anglo slaveowners and separatist Tejanos were able to win independence from Mexico. Although the Republic of Texas asked the US to annex the territory, President Andrew Jackson, swayed by northern abolitionists, refused; however, Texas was later annexed by the US in 1845 under the proslavery administration of President John Tyler (Nevins 2002, 18–19).

Geopolitical shifts in North America during the 1830s and 1840s exacerbated boundary disputes and territorial tensions between the United States of Mexico and the United States of America, leading up to the onset of the Mexican-American War in 1846. Aggravating the situation, President James Polk deployed federal troops to the Rio Grande in early 1846: tempers flared; "skirmishes . . . ensued"; "full-scale war" was waged (Nevins 2002, 19). Following two years of military battles between the countries, US troops seized Mexico City, forcing the Mexican government to concede defeat. With the bi-national signing of the Treaty of Guadeloupe-Hidalgo in February 1848, Mexico "ceded half of its territory to the United States" – a vast expanse of land covering "one million square miles" and stretching across the current boundaries of ten states – from Texas, Arizona, and New Mexico in the south, to California in the west, and as far north as Utah, Colorado, and Wyoming (Nevins 2002, 19). Additionally, the United States "absorbed 100,000 Mexican citizens and 200,000 Native Americans living in the annexed territory" (Nevins 2002, 19). After the end of the war and the discovery of gold in California in 1848, boundary tensions, particularly between the ore-rich areas of New Mexico, Sonora, and Chihuahua, continued to mar US-Mexican relations. Political and geographical expansionists in the US sought Mesilla (in contemporary southern New Mexico) as US territory. In 1853, the US government sent representative James Gadsden to Mexico to diplomatically (or if necessary, under threat of force) resolve tensions and normalize "trade relations" between the two countries. At the threat of a second US military invasion, Mexico ultimately agreed to sell Mesilla to the US for $10 million (Nevins 2002, 21).

In 1864, the US government passed the Act to Encourage Immigration, establishing the first US Immigration Bureau to increase immigration so that US industries would have a sufficient labor supply during the Civil War (Nevins 2002, 193); rendering "official" and legislatively codified what had already been historically actual (that is: US-Mexico transborder economic migration), the act operated according to the economic principles that international migration scholars refer to as *push-pull* – in periods of economic hardship, decline, or recession, citizens and immigrants are "pushed" out; and, conversely, in periods of economic upturn or boom, resulting in higher employment levels and an increased demand for laborers, migrants are "pulled" toward vacant jobs and supply that needed national labor. Thus began what some migration and diaspora scholars refer to as the "revolving door" located at the border or *La Frontera*, one constantly moving or revolving, yet one which opens or shuts at political will "depending on the needs of domestic economic interests" (Nevins 2002, 35).

Although battles had been fought and lives lost to acquire land and to firmly demarcate the US-Mexico border (as far south as possible in the North American continent), the border remained a porous, well-traversed, high "traffic" zone – by citizens (of both the USA and Mexico); Native Americans, Chinese laborers (pejoratively referred to as "coolies"), and European economic migrants; black-market bootleggers; and even cattle (one of the sorest points of contention between the two countries and the first *raison d'être*, in fact, for "border patrol") – throughout the remainder of the nineteenth century and into the early twentieth century. The late nineteenth century was not, despite frequent and largely unregulated border traversals, a peaceful or free century; rather, it remained a cultural "contact zone" (Pratt 1992) that was often brutally, if unofficially, a site marked by violence, southern Texas being the "site of the bloodiest fights" between Anglo-Americans, Tejanos, Mexican border-crossers, and Native Americans. David Chapman, in fact, historically documents the brutal lynching by vigilantes of 24 Mexicans in Texas between 1889 and the 1920s (cited in Rosales 1999, 119); and Francisco Rosales documents white and black civilian violence against Mexicans in the southwestern United States from 1900 to 1935 (1999, Appendix A, 203–211). Violence escalated during the early years of the twentieth century as the border, or *La Frontera*, became the site for transborder crime (smuggling, rustling, raids, gang violence, and vigilantes).[7] Volatility further increased during the Mexican Revolution from 1910 to 1920, as well as in the failed revolutionary attempt, which was fomented in the "Plan de San Diego" uprising of 1915 to "liberate" the oppressed African, Mexican, and Native populations of southern Texas and which called for the vengeful killing of all white adult males over the age of 16; given the failures of the "Plan," however, what actually transpired was a "reign of terror" waged against Mexican Americans in southern Texas; and while 21 white men were killed during raids, over 300 Mexicans were killed in retaliation (see Acuña 2000, 177).[8] Smuggling posed a particularly troubling transborder activity, with everything from "diamonds, watches, textiles, opium, booze, Chinese 'coolies,' garlic and just about anything that could be transported" being moved across the US-Mexican border (Nevins 2002). In fact, initial efforts by the US to control and restrict human movement across the border was a response to immigrant smuggling of Chinese and Europeans across *La Frontera*: the former being racially and strategically excluded from immigrating to the US following a series of Anti-Asian Exclusion Laws (or Chinese Exclusive Acts) beginning in 1882, which "barred all Chinese laborers from entering the country for ten years and prohibited Chinese immigrants from becoming naturalized citizens" (Lee 2003, 2); and the latter arrested for entering the country illegally. It was not until the early twentieth century that US "controls over the transboundary flow of immigrants coming from Mexico began to emerge," and even then, laws restricting immigration were not legislated in response to Mexican transborder migration, but in response to Chinese and European transborder migration (Nevins 2002, 25). "With the exception of the Alien Acts of 1798," Nevins explains, "there was no federal legislation restricting immigration into the country until 1875" (2002, 25). Post-1875 (and especially following the 1882 "exclusion" acts that were racially, ethnically, and nationally discriminatory), the concept of "illegal alien" – one to be excluded through controlled, regulated, enforced legal means and methods – was born in the United States. But "as legislative prohibitions against certain types of immigrants increased, so did the efforts of would-be immigrants to enter the United States without authorization, thus the origins of the 'illegal' immigrant" (Nevins 2002, 26). Ken Ellingwood, writing in *Hard Line: Life and Death on the US-Mexico Border*, affirms: "It was Chinese immigrants, not Mexicans, who were the main targets of US efforts to mind the borders, following passage of the Chinese Exclusion Act of 1882" (2004, 19–20). A failed act of anti-immigrant legislation, the Exclusion Act "failed to end Chinese immigration" into the US, and from "1882 to 1943, an estimated 300,955 Chinese successfully gained admission into the United States" (Lee 2003, 12).

Contradictions abound, of course: even as Chinese laborers were being smuggled across the US-Mexican border in the 1880s and 1890s, having first arrived in the West in the 1830s, or when they were landing ashore in Florida or the Gulf Coast from Cuba, where "more than 30,000 unemployed Chinese immigrants on the island" awaited their chance at illegally entering the US in the 1920s, Chinese Americans were contributing and had already contributed their blood, sweat, tears, and labor to building the gold-mining economies of the West Coast in the 1840s-1850s and working for Union Pacific to construct the transcontinental railroad, completed in 1869 (Nevins 2002, 28; see the entire section, pages 25–28). Similar contradictions held true for the US industrial capitalist economy and Mexican migrant laborers: although in direct violation of the Alien Contract Labor Law, passed in 1885, US railroad companies actively recruited and hired Mexican migrants. As Balderrama and Rodríguez explain, "Agricultural expansion stimulated extensive railroad construction in the Southwest[; and b]y 1909 there were six railroad companies servicing the region," which "employed more than six thousand Mexicans to lay track and to maintain the right-of-way" (1995, 16).

The Mexican Revolution (1910–20) was a period of chaos, violence, and anarchy; and consequently, many Mexicans fled violence by crossing the border north into the United States. It was also a period of anti-Mexican backlash and retaliatory, anti-immigrationist violence by Anglo-Americans against their migrant neighbors, popularly known as the "Brown Scare":

> Because the part of the upheaval that took place on the northern border had anti-American overtones, often manifested by threats against American property, border raids, and angry anti-"Gringo" rhetoric, many Americans took out their frustrations on immigrant workers who were not involved in any of this activity in a hysteria that historian Ricardo Romo has dubbed the "Brown Scare" (fear of Mexicans during the Mexican Revolution). (Rosales 1999, 3)

From 1911 to 1915, "tens of thousands of Mexicans" were legally admitted to the United States to work and contribute to the US economy (Nevins 2002, 32). With the onset of World War I, border patrolling guardsmen were deployed not only to prevent illegal entry and transborder migration, but also, and more pressingly, to ensure wartime border security. But, as Rosales explains, "World War I-induced xenophobia increased the fear of Mexicans and caused more doubt about the loyalty of those living in the United States" (1999, 20). At the time, as previously mentioned, most illegal immigrants – Chinese and European – entered from Mexico, Canada, or Cuba. US immigration legislation passed in 1917 mandated literacy tests and a head tax (to the amount of $8 per person); as a result, entry was "denied to 5,745 Mexican immigrants" in the first year. Yet, transborder migrants simply found other (covert and illegal) modes of entry: "After the 1917 Immigration Act," Rosales writes, "ferrying [immigrants] . . . across the Rio Grande illegally became a lucrative trade" (1999, 69). Postwar economic recession from 1920–1 led to fierce anti-immigration hostility and bureaucratic efforts to "repatriate" Mexican economic migrants who had arrived during the war (Balderrama and Rodríguez 1995, 98). Still, Mexican economic migrants continued to pour across the porous border, and "by the 1920s, Mexicans could be found harvesting sugar beets in Minnesota, laying railroad tracks in Kansas, packing meat in Chicago, mining coal in Oklahoma, assembling cars in Detroit, canning fish in Alaska, and sharecropping in Louisiana" (Nevins 2002, 32). In fact, during the "roaring" 1920s that witnessed an economic bounce, Mexican economic migration to the US was at a record high level; and according to Balderrama and Rodríguez, "at least half a million Mexicans entered the United States legally between 1899 and 1928" (1995, 7). The Quota Act of 1921, however, curtailed international migration to the US, restricting entry of new immigrants based on national-origin groups already present in the country and limiting the number to 3 percent of that immigrant's population based on the 1910 US Census. The Johnson-Reed Immigration Act, passed in 1924, allocated $1 million for "additional land-border patrol," and administratively created the US Border Patrol "out of the previous boundary policing unit" (Nevins 2002, 29). The Johnson-Reed Immigration Act of 1924 placed the US Border Patrol under the jurisdiction of the Department of Labor Appropriations Act (Nevins 2002, Appendix, 194). It also made the 1921 quota system a permanent part of immigration law, utilizing the 1890 US Census as the basis for restrictive and restricting national quotas. "In theory," according to law professor and legal immigration scholar Leti Volpp, "the 1924 act left immigrants from the Western Hemisphere free to immigrate. But, while not subject to numerical quotas or restriction on naturalization, Mexicans were profoundly affected by other restrictive measures enacted in the 1920s, including deportation policy, the creation of the border patrol, and the criminalization of unlawful entry" (2003, 259). Yet economic considerations often swayed political opinion and local enforcement, and during periods of agricultural labor demands (growing and harvesting season), border patrol agents, sympathetic to local farmers, simply did not apprehend transmigrant Mexican field hands or farm workers (see Balderrama and Rodríguez 1995, 9).

Other legislative measures passed during World War I and the interim postwar years also attempted to restrict legal points of entry. Having designated official ports of entry in 1917, requiring passports for entry in 1918, and illegalizing (as a misdemeanor) all other ports or points of border crossings into the country in 1929, making reentry after deportation a felony, the US government thus criminalized "illegal aliens" and controlled entry of legal migrants. Initially legislated as wartime efforts to secure the territorial borders of the United States during World War I, the measures ultimately impacted the rural cattle hands, tenant farmers, and migrant field workers who seasonally crisscrossed, recrossed, and then cyclically crossed again the border each year from early spring to autumn harvest.

Migrating legally and illegally to the United States during the entire decade of the 1920s, despite a rise in anti-immigrant sentiments during the post-WWI years of economic recession, which "deepened hostility toward Mexicans" (Rosales 1999, 120), and despite periods of deportation and coercive or forcible "repatriation" during the decade, Mexican economic migrants continued to arrive, to seek and find employment, and, when and as long as possible, to stay; and "by 1930, more than 10 percent of Mexico's population was living in the United States" (Nevins 2002, 32). Census records for 1930, as Balderrama and Rodríguez write, "calculated that approximately 1,422,533 Mexican Nationals and Mexican Americans lived in the United States" (1995, 7). With the 1929 stock market crash and the onset of the Great Depression (or *La Crisis*),[9] however, the fates of Mexican diasporic workers took a radical turn for the worse: following the October 1929 "crash" and the rapid descent of the US economy, which had worldwide ramifications, in the 1930s, both Mexican immigrants and Chicanos, or Mexican Americans who were US citizens, suffered mass deportation, racially charged anti-immigration hatred, discrimination, and even brutal violence during the six-year period from 1929 to 1935. During the "mass deportations" of the 1930s, "an estimated 415,000 Mexicans" were forced to leave and an additional 85,000 voluntarily departed under fear of coercion and violence (Nevins 2002, 33). According to Nevins, "some estimates of the deportations run as high as one million including tens of thousands of US citizens of Mexican descent" (2002, 33). Deportation "sweeps," referred to as *levas* or *razzias* in Spanish, often resulted in the arrest, detention, interrogation, and ultimately, deportation of all people of Mexican background, whether undocumented workers, or "illegal aliens," documented legal migrants, or US citizens, as Balderrama and Rodríguez (1995, 55) clarify. During the 1930s, in fact, Mexicans "constituted 46.3 percent of all the people deported" by the US (1995, 53). Half of all expelled Mexicans and Mexican Americans were those residing and working in Texas, where cotton farmers and the planter economies of the state were devastated by *La Crisis*, or the Depression (Acuña 2000, 221). Mexican migrant farmers were also targeted because of the growing popularity of the Communist Party and immigrant labor organizations among this group of migrant workers (see Acuña 2000, 228–248). In 1933, President Hoover formed the Immigration and Naturalization Service (INS) by merging the Bureau of Immigration and the Bureau of Naturalization; still under the jurisdiction of the Department of Labor, anti-immigrationist efforts were fueled by nationalist fervor, patriotism, economic depression, competition for jobs, and supported by war veterans, including members of the American Legion and the Veterans of Foreign Wars, as well as by "native" labor activists, including members of the American Federation of Labor (Balderrama and Rodríguez 1995, 53). In 1940, the INS was moved from the Department of Labor and placed under the jurisdiction of the Department of Justice (Nevins 2002, Appendix, 195).

Efforts to regularize and control the movement of transborder economic migrants, or diasporic workers, came in 1942 with the Bracero Program, a "guestworker program" or "contract labor program" legislated and inaugurated during World War II. From an immigration control perspective, the Bracero Program had merit; from a labor perspective, however, it was flawed legislation: "given the great shortage of farm labor during World War II, the Bracero Program was [essentially] created to import hundreds of thousands of Mexicans without labor protections" (Volpp 2003, 259). Overall, the Bracero Program, most vibrant from 1942 until 1947, "provided more than 219,000 workers to agricultural employers," with California farms employing "63 percent of the braceros during the regular growing season and 90 percent of the braceros in the offseason (January–April)" (Nevins 2002, 205n90; citing Calavita 1992, 20–21). Due to several factors (higher labor cost, fees, filing of papers for legal guestworkers with authorized contracts), however, the program dramatically failed to prevent illegal transborder entry and to prohibit undocumented "aliens" from working in the US. The 1940s thus saw massive deportations of illegal Mexican immigrants – 57,000 in the first half of the decade, but "almost 856,000 in the second half" (Nevins 2002, 33).

In 1952, the McCarran-Walter Immigration and Nationality Act was passed by US Congress: the law was overdetermined by Cold War ideology and anti-immigration *ressentiment* that regarded immigrants as "'indigestible blocks' which could not assimilate," "featured a provision that barred from entry those who had ever written or published or circulated writings advocating certain political views, including communism, anarchy, or overthrowing the US government, or all government" (Volpp 2003, 260), and as "an expression of the Cold War era, legislated strict quotas, created an area called the 'Asia-Pacific triangle' based on a strategically territorial mapping, and contained language delineating the exclusion of and right to deport any alien who has engaged or has had purpose to engage in activities 'prejudicial to the public interest' or 'subversive to national security'" (Lowe 1996, 9). Two years later, in 1954, under President Dwight D. Eisenhower, the US Congress also authorized "Operation Wetback," an Immigration and Naturalization Services program not only bearing a racist name, but also implementing racially charged policies of massive detention and deportation of "illegal" Mexican migrant workers in the US, particularly in the border states, the very ones once comprising part of the territories claimed by both the United States of America and Mexico. Although the government tried to compensate agricultural losses of illegal farm workers with an increase in braceros admitted post-1954, the late 1950s saw a decline in "bracero contracts" from 1959 until the program was administratively discontinued in 1964 (Nevins 2002, 35). "The recession of the early 1950s," as Volpp explains, thus resulted in the massive "deportation of more than one million Mexicans, many without hearings," through the racist and discriminatory policies of Operation Wetback (2003, 259).

Throughout the United States, the 1960s was a period of violent cultural clashes, civil rights movements, student activism, anti-war protests, immigration legislation, and changing demographics in the country. Governmentally, the 1960s was a period of political concession, expressed in a willingness to tackle social inequities (through civil rights legislation, for example) and other big problems (the "war on poverty"), and even of optimism expressed in LBJ's envisioning of the "Great Society." Not since FDR's New Deal to rejuvenate the US economy and end the hardships of the Great Depression had (big) government acted on behalf of so many common citizens; and yet it was also a period of tragedy and persistent discrimination – rising casualties and mounting losses in the Vietnam War, as well as human rights atrocities committed against Vietnamese civilians during the war (notably, the March 1968 massacres at Mai Lai, thảm sát Mỹ Lai, in which 504 Vietnamese were brutally beaten and murdered by US soldiers); continued segregationist politics and racial violence in the South; institutional discrimination and race riots in the Northeast and Midwest; the political assassinations of JFK (1963), Malcolm X (1965), MLK (1968), and presidential candidate Bobby Kennedy (1968); and the exploitation of Mexican migrant farm workers in the San Joaquin Valley and elsewhere in agricultural fields across the rural heartland of the country.

The Hart-Cellar Immigration Act, passed in 1965, has had a profound impact on the changing demographics of the United States over the last few decades, as well as on the newer diasporic communities (Asian, Latin American, Caribbean) arriving, settling, and working in the US. The Hart-Cellar Act eliminated immigration quotas based on "national origins" and legislated by the 1952 McCarran-Walter Immigration and Nationality Act, establishing new criteria for admitting immigrants to the US. It established "an overall ceiling of approximately 300,000 immigrant visas, which were divided between the Eastern Hemisphere, set at 180,000, with a maximum of 20,000 per country, and 120,000 for the Western Hemisphere" (Volpp 2003, 261). Specifically, the 1965 Immigration Act established seven preferential categories for admitting immigrants to the US:

(1) unmarried adult sons and daughters of citizens; (2) spouses and unmarried sons and daughters of permanent residents; (3) professionals, scientists, and artists of "exceptional ability"; (4) married adult sons and daughters of US citizens; (5) siblings of adult citizens; (6) workers, skilled and unskilled, in occupations for which labor was in short supply in the United States; and (7) refugees from Communist-dominated countries or those uprooted by natural catastrophe. (Lowe 1996, 181–182n16)

The seventh and last category was inflected by Cold War politics and remained a powerful ideological commitment by the US government to anti-communist rhetoric and political foreign policy up until 1989. As proved to be the case, the seventh category was often used to ideologically determine which asylees of those applying for political refuge in the US would be admitted as a refugee and which would be denied asylum. As Volpp explains, "In 1965 Congress created a new immigrant category, for aliens fleeing persecution in a 'Communist-dominated' country, or a country 'within the general area of the Middle East,' or for those 'uprooted by catastrophic natural calamity.' Those fleeing repressive non-Communist governments outside the Middle East received no protection" (2003, 264).

1965 was also a momentous year for migrant labor activism in the United States. In September 1965, César Chávez called for and organized a strike among grape workers in Delano, California. After years of striking against grape growers in the San Joaquin Valley, the United Farm Workers (UFW) called for a total "boycott of table grapes" in 1968 (Vargas 2005, 377). By 1970, five years after the strike was initiated by Chávez, "grape growers recognized and negotiated contacts with the union" (2005, 377). A period of labor agitation and worker rights organization, the 1960s was also a period of social unrest and activist mobilization for Mexican American students and anti-war protesters.

Influenced by the African American civil rights movement, the Chicano Liberation Movement emerged, demanding equality, equal access to education, housing, and employment, and espousing an identity politics grounded in the pursuit of social justice. Disproportionately impacted by the Vietnam War – in fact, Chicanos were heavily drafted into the war effort, and from 1961 to 1967, "over 19 percent of US Army casualties and 23 percent of Marine Corps casualties had Spanish surnames" (Vargas 2005, 377) – Chicano student and anti-war protests also embraced a collective political identity defined by *Chicanismo*. In 1969, Corky González organized the Chicano Youth Liberation Conference held in Denver, Colorado. At the conference, González introduced the political ideal of "Atzlán" as a Chicano "homeland" (one in which Chicanos both dwelled and yet had been removed from geopolitically): the concept of Atzlán was thus a Chicano reterritorialization of what had been "occupied territory" – taken by the US from Mexico and dispossessed from indigenous peoples in the Southwest. By the early 1970s, the impact of the Chicano movements and the concept of Atzlán had "spread throughout the barrios" (Vargas 2005, 377). Inspired by the Black Power Movement, the 1970s also witnessed the emergence of the Brown Power Movement that denounced the war and demanded social, ethnic, political, and labor justice for Mexican Americans. The Brown Berets, modeled on the Black Panthers, organized in East Los Angeles to protest police violence and discrimination against Chicano youth and Chicano communities in the city. In August 1970, the Chicano Anti-War Moratorium brought together "more than 30,000 Chicanos gathered in Los Angeles" (Vargas 2005, 377); riots ensued; and three protesters were killed, including "prize-winning Chicano journalist Rubén Salazar" (Vargas 2005, 378). Mobilizing politically, not only as alternative social justice grassroots organizations, but also as political parties, Chicanos rallied behind *La Raza Unida* Party, a Chicano political party, created in Texas in 1970 by José Angel Gutiérrez. *¡Ya basta!*, or "Enough," became the resounding cry of the movement. Influenced by these movements, the period of the mid-to-late-1970s was one of growing political enfranchisement, civil rights, and increasing political power as a minority in the United States.

By the 1980s, Chicanos were "the country's fastest growing minority, compris[ing] two-thirds of the more than 27 million Latinos in the United States" (Vargas 2005, 440). Following a period of increased political clout, minority representation, and economic gains in the US, the Reagan years saw Chicano setbacks in the US. The 1980s may be alternately defined as "Reaganism," which politically witnessed a period of social conservatism marked by "white backlash" against civil rights gains by American ethnic minorities during the 1960s and 1970s and a "suspension of affirmative action efforts" (Vargas 2005, 440); or as "Reagonomics," a period of conservative fiscal policies marked by reductions in corporate and personal income taxes, increases in military deficit spending, and infrastructural cuts to human welfare programs). The period thus saw the political-economic hegemony of the "New Right," its growing cultural conservatism, a reversal of hard-won civil rights, and the coining of reactionary concepts like "reverse racism" and "political correctness" – or "PC," as it became known in common parlance. In 1986, the US Congress brokered major immigration reform legislation passing the Simpson-Mazzoli bill into law as the Immigration Reform and Control Act (IRCA). Although the IRCA "cracked-down" on employers who hired "illegal aliens" or undocumented workers and required the completion and submission of I-9 forms verifying legal status through a passport, social security card, or driver's license for all employees, the act also permitted all illegal immigrants who had resided in the country since 1982 to apply for and obtain "legal" status. In effect, and at end, the IRCA became a sort of "amnesty" legislative act – lauded by proponents of amnesty, excoriated by opponents – and ultimately granting legal status to approximately 2.5 million immigrants previously considered illegal.

During the 1980s, the US government also diminished both the man-size and economic allocation of the Border Patrol, and the number of illegal Mexican and Central American immigrants, or undocumented workers, also, unsurprisingly, increased during this period. By 1989, the estimated number of "illegal aliens" or undocumented workers totaled 2.5 million, approximately 50 percent from Mexico alone. Border populations also increased in these decades, as did the number of *maquiladoras* (Mexican-located, but US-financially centered multinational textile corporations) located in border towns like Tijuana and Ciudad

Juárez. In 1992, Canada, Mexico, and the United States signed the North American Free Trade Agreement. Intended to open economic (trade, production, and financial) borders, while closing geopolitical boundaries for illegal transborder migration, NAFTA was an intracontinental pact designed to facilitate the transnational buying and selling of goods and services, the multinational scattering of production sites (reversing the historical flows of economic migration in which workers relocate for jobs), and the international fiduciary and financial exchanges between the three countries. NAFTA, because of its emphasis on the free movement of capital, not people, set a chilly tone for immigrants in the "get tough" years of the Clinton administration that fueled global capitalism, while eroding the progressive (if expansive) social policies of the Post-New Deal/ Post-Great Society Democratic Party of FDR and LBJ. The Clinton rallying cry: open the borders to "free trade," reform (or end) the welfare state, usher in neoliberal economics. Truly, it was almost as calculatingly pro-capital and pro-business, if administratively less brutal, than its Republican counterpart and successor: George W. Bush's so-called "compassionate conservatism."

NAFTA was implemented in 1994, the same year that California voters passed ballot initiative Proposition 187 to end all public assistance and welfare benefits (including food stamps, medicare, Medicaid, and public education) to "illegal aliens" residing in the state; Californians also subsequently voted to "abolish bilingual education" (Vargas 2005, 440). Under the Clinton administration, the INS and the US Border Patrol also massively expanded border security efforts along the US-Mexico boundary. The INS unleashed a series of "operations" to prevent illegal entry and human smuggling across the border. Anti-immigrant state "propositions" and INS "operations," in fact, defined the early 1990s or post-NAFTA period; and by 1996, the US Congress was once again passing major immigration reform legislation, answering the call of growing anti-immigration sentiments among the US citizenry and in the "crackdown" wake of the 1995 bombing of the Mura federal building in Oklahoma City by Timothy McVeigh, falsely but widely and preemptively assumed by media and public alike to be the act of foreign terrorists. Three major bills were passed by Congress: the Antiterrorism and Effective Death Penalty Act of 1996; the Personal Responsibility and Work Opportunity Reconciliation Act (PWORA) of 1996; and the Illegal Immigration Reform and Immigration Responsibility Act (IIRIRA) of 1996. The first act expanded the legal ground for the "deportation" of immigrants who broke the law and were convicted in court (Volpp 2003, 265). PWORA, following California's Proposition 187, "made even permanent resident aliens ineligible for most federal means-tested benefits, like food stamps and Supplemental Security Income" (Volpp 2003, 265–266). It also required that "prospective immigrants" document that they had the financial resources to be self-sustaining if admitted to the country (Volpp 2003, 265–266). IIRIRA focused on tackling the issue of "undocumented" or "illegal" immigrants: it further expanded the legal ground for deporting immigrants and permanent residents, including those guilty of misdemeanor offenses; it "instituted mandatory detention for many classes of immigrants seeking admission – including potential asylum seekers – through 'expedited removal' if they had no papers or had papers that seemed fraudulent"

(Volpp 2003, 266). It also "immunized many administrative decisions from review by a federal judge, since immigrants were thought to be clogging the courts with meritless appeals with the collaboration of attorneys and progressive judges" (Volpp 2003, 266). And finally, the IIRIRA authorized the INS and the US Border Patrol to construct a fence along the Tijuana-San Diego part of the border, a high-traffic point for illegal entries. Consequently, traffic and smuggling simply moved farther eastward into the arid Arizona desert. Transborder economic migration thus continued unabated throughout the 1990s, and into the twenty-first century, despite a series of other failed INS programs – both "Operation Blockade" and "Operation Hold-the-Line" (El Paso) implemented in 1993; "Operation Gatekeeper" (San Diego) in 1994; "Operation Safeguard" (Arizona) in 1995; and "Operation Rio Grande" (Brownsville) in 1997 – to prevent the "illegal entry" of Mexican migrant workers; however, points of entry moved further eastward away from the metropolitan borderzone of Tijuana-San Diego and into small, rural towns and arid, perilous, and literally deserted parts of the desert.

US President George W. Bush and former Mexican President Vincente Fox, considered by many to be strong hemispheric allies and political collaborators, first began negotiations for a guestworker program to allow Mexican immigrants to cross the southwestern US border and legally work in *el Norte* on temporary contracts in 2000, and though many in Senate supported Bush's call for the program, it remains unclear whether an immigrant work program will be authorized by both houses of Congress. Following a decade-long cycle for immigration reform, US Congress yet again took up the issue in 2006, as it did in both 1986 and ten years later in 1996. The US House of Representatives passed an immigration reform bill H.R. 4437 in December 2005: the bill included punitive anti-immigration measures, including detention and deportation for all illegal entries, making illegal entry itself a felony criminal offense and a bar against ever being admitted to the US as a legal or documented immigrant, and calling for the construction of a 1,200-mile fence along the 1,900+-mile US-Mexican border. A few months later, on March 28, 2006, at midnight (considered by many a surreptitious move), an immigration reform bill passed through the Senate Judiciary Committee. Over the next three days – from the morning of March 28 until the last day of the month – debate of the bill on the floor of the US Senate ensued while nationwide protests by immigrants, concerned citizens, and student activists erupted in major cities – Los Angeles, New York, DC, Chicago, Boston – as well as in smaller cities – Des Moines, Atlanta, Birmingham, Cincinnati, Cleveland, and Minneapolis – and even in more remote, rural locales across the country, taking to the streets to demand legal status, fair treatment, minimum wages and benefits, and equitable immigration policies in the country. Protests and Senate debate filled the media-waves of the US alongside news from the North American Summit, held in Cancun, Mexico on March 30–31, 2006, and bringing together US President George W. Bush, then Mexican President Vincente Fox, and newly elected (and conservative) Canadian Prime Minister Stephen Harper. Rallies, marches, and other organized acts of nonviolent protest continued throughout spring 2006; and on May 25, 2006, the Senate passed S. 2611, a comprehensive immigration reform bill that included measures to regulate immigration flows across the US-Mexico border, create a guestworker program (which both Presidents Bush and Fox supported and promoted binationally), and to establish a path toward "legal" status for undocumented workers – an estimated 11–12 million – who had already been residing, working, and mostly law-abiding in the US for an extended period of time.

As US Congress recessed at the end of spring 2006, the House of Representatives deferred a final vote and delivery to Senate on H.R. 4437 until the next congressional term began in autumn and planned a series of summer "town-hall meetings" and citizen "talk-back-live" sessions in border towns in the southwest from Brownsville through Nogales all the way westward to San Diego. Believing that Congress would fail to achieve consensus on a "comprehensive" immigration bill and that the more punitive measures within the H.R. bill would fail to win support and thus be approved by the Senate before the November midterm elections, the House decided to break up H.R. 4437 and deliver it piecemeal to the US Senate for legislative approval. According to Joel Havemann, staff writer for the *LA Times*, the "fence bill" (as it has been dubbed by the press) is a strategic effort by the House of Representatives to get their legislative act (H.R. 4437) approved by Senate: "The House, unable to win Senate support for its relatively punitive legislation, plans to break its bill into pieces and to send them to the Senate either as free-standing bills or as riders to spending bills."[10] On September 13, 2006, Representative Peter T. King of New York introduced the first of these piecemeal bills to the House: H.R. 6061, or the "Secure Fence Act of 2006," intended to establish operational control over the international land and maritime borders of the United States, was passed the next day on September 14, 2006 by a 283–138 vote.

H.R. 6061 calls for the construction of a 730-mile, two-layer reinforced fence along the southern land border of the United States, the "systematic surveillance" of the border through "personnel and technology," including "unmanned aerial vehicles, ground-based sensors, radar coverage, and cameras" in order to prevent "all unlawful entries into the United States, including entries by terrorists, other unlawful aliens, instruments of terrorism, and other contraband."[11] The Secure Fence Act of 2006 also amends IIRIRA of 1996 (Public Law 104–208, 8 USC. 1103 note), which authorized the construction of a fence along the US-Mexico border near Tijuana-San Diego, expanding the geographical points of construction from Tecate and Calexico, California to Douglas, Arizona and from Columbus, New Mexico to El Paso, Del Rio, and Eagle Pass, Texas and further east from Laredo to Brownsville. It calls for a "virtual fence," or "interlocking surveillance camera system," to be fully installed by May 30, 2007 and for the physical barrier or actual "fence construction" to be completed 12 months later on May 30, 2008. Additionally, the bill allows border patrol agents the authority not only to "stop vehicles" attempting to cross the line, but also to "review the equipment and technology available to United States Customs and Border Protection personnel to stop vehicles" through technology designed to arrest vehicular movement. H.R. 6061 also grants the Department of Homeland Security (DHS) the authority to "achieve and maintain operational control over the entire border" and "requiring DHS to provide all necessary authority to border personnel to disable fleeing vehicles, similar to the authority held by the United States Coast Guard for maritime vessels."[12] Finally, the bill also authorizes "a study on the feasibility of a state-of-the-art infrastructure security system along the northern international land and maritime border of the United States" with Canada, including surveillance of the Great Lakes. While the fence will be constructed at "high traffic" points along the border, other measures – lights, cameras, motion sensors, road blocks – will also be built or installed in other less traversed points along the border.

On the same day that the House of Representatives passed H.R. 6061, it delivered the bill to Senate where it was "received and read the first time"; on the following day, September 15, 2006, the Senate "read the second time and placed on the calendar"; two weeks later on September 29, 2006, the Senate, following a file for cloture by Senator Bill Frist of Tennessee to limit debate and prevent a filibuster (particularly by Senators who opposed the bill outright or who strongly favored more comprehensive legislation on immigration issues), passed the bill "without amendment by Yea-Nay Vote" of 80–19 (Library of Congress: Record Vote number 262). In effect, despite widespread Senate support for comprehensive immigration reform (passed as Senate bill S. 2611 in May 2006), the Congress ultimately capitulated to anti-immigrationist sentiments in passing a "fence"-only bill instead of a broader act (including plans for a guest-worker program and a potential path toward obtaining legal status, permanent residence, or citizenship) designed to address the economic, political, and social problems created by having high levels of undocumented workers in the US. As Rachel L. Swarns writes in the *New York Times*, even "the Republican architects of the Senate bill – including Senators John McCain of Arizona, Lindsay Graham of South Carolina, Mel Martinez of Florida, and Chuck Hagel of Nebraska – supported the decision to bring the fencing measure to a final vote," despite many Senators favoring "the legalization of illegal immigrants" and a guestworker program to support sectors of the US economy (agriculture, construction, cattle ranching, chicken processing, and hotel and restaurant management).[13]

Dissenters such as Ted Kennedy of Massachusetts denounced the bill as "'a good-feel, bumper-sticker vote' designed to energize conservative voters before the midterm elections."[14] Further criticizing the fence bill as wasteful spending, Kennedy "noted that nearly half of the illegal immigrants in the country entered the country legally, without sneaking across the Mexican border, and overstayed their visas."[15] While H.R. 6061 authorized construction of the fence, it does not include the requisite funding (an estimated $7+ billion)[16] to actually build it: however, funds were authorized in a separate homeland security spending bill (totaling $35 billion) that allocates $1.2 billion to begin fence construction along the border. The Secure Fence Act and the homeland security spending bill, both passed before the fall 2006 recess, also authorized and allocated "money to hire 1,500 new Border Patrol agents, increasing the force to 14,800, and to add 6,700 detention beds" along the border (Swarns, "Senate Moves"). In an article written by Carl Hulse and Rachel L. Swarns for the *Times* on September 30, the journalists further explain that "the fence legislation was one of the chief elements to survive the broader comprehensive bill that President Bush and a Senate coalition had hoped would tighten border security, grant legal status to most illegal immigrants and create a vast guestworker program to supply the nation's industries."[17] Despite passing H.R. 6061, which authorizes the construction of a 730-mile fence, Congress appropriated "only enough money to complete about 370 miles of it."[18] Critics of the bill maintain that "the failure to agree on a guestworker program" would lead to a "severe shortage of agricultural workers."[19] Harry Reid, Minority Leader of the Senate, decried the bill as a "clear repudiation of President Bush's call for comprehensive legislation."[20] Other Senators derided even the very idea of a "fence" as yet another international "wall" – to add to China's and Berlin's historically isolationist and lockdown attempts against citizens and foreigners to wall in the former and keep out the latter – and this one planned as a high-tech, highly surveyed "virtual" boundary with a highly militarized and physically wired border. Mexican officials were also angered by the so-called fence bill; advocates of the bill, however, believed that a fence was necessary to secure "the porous border," which "could be used," they aver, "by terrorists who want to sneak into the US undetected."[21] Although promoted as a "security" bill, specifically to promote "homeland security," the rhetoric usually revolves around and returns to immigration and "widespread panic" about "illegals": describing the line as "inexcusably porous," Senator Frist wrote on his political blog that "one of the most effective ways that we can stop illegal immigration is through the construction and proper maintenance of physical fences along the highest trafficked, most commonly violated sections of our border with Mexico." Speaking with prophetic zeal, and patriotic, isolationist fervor, Frist proclaimed: "A nation that can't 'secure' its borders can't secure its destiny or administer its laws."

Thus, in 2006, the Bureau of Citizenship and Immigration Services, under the aegis of the Department of Homeland Security, was also working hard to pass and implement "Operation Secure the Border," or "Operation Jump-Start" as border patrol agents have dubbed it. While Senate bill S. 2611 initially called for the construction of a 370-mile fence along the US-Mexico border, and while the House of Representatives bill H.R. 4437 hoped for the eventual construction of a 1,200-mile fence along the 1,950 mile *linea*, or line, both houses of Congress have compromised in authorizing a 730-mile fence. Already in late spring 2006, President George W. Bush had called for funds to construct a "virtual fence" utilizing surveillance technologies, motion detectors, and unmanned aerial vehicles to patrol the border, as well as to hire an additional 6,000 border patrol agents – supported and supplemented by 6,000 National Guardsmen to be deployed along the border (2,500 to have been deployed by June 2006, though the numbers fall short of that figure) in what is tantamount and will be (materially, politically, technologically, and legally) a massively militarized borderzone. Not surprisingly, the very same US-based energy, aerial technology, and weapons-manufacturing corporations – Boeing, Lockheed Martin, Raytheon, and Northrop Grumman – that have received bids for postwar "nation-building" and post-bombing-strikes reconstruction efforts, as in Iraq and Afghanistan, have also submitted bids for the "multibillion dollar federal contract to build what the administration calls a 'virtual fence'."[22] By October 2006, Boeing had already received "a three-year, $67 million contract to implement the first part of a plan to reduce illegal entry along thousands of miles of border with Canada and Mexico using better technology, including cameras, sensors and even unmanned airplanes."[23]

For future generations along the border, in both neighboring North American countries, and for diasporic workers in the new global economy, the most pressing question that remains may well be this one: where and how to locate doors and windows that mitigate against and allow movement across the erected boundaries of fences, the apparent closures of walls?

Questions for Reflection and Discussion

- What do diasporic workers contribute (materially, financially, politically) to a country?
- What are the costs of guestworkers or economic migrants for a host country?
- How do diasporic workers support families, hometowns, and national development projects through financial remittances?
- What are the economic structural relations of global capitalism, international migrations, and contemporary diasporic formations?
- Should host countries allow economic migrants who support national economies to fully participate in the country's political process? Why or why not?

Additional Research

Thinking through debating

Working in small groups, students will debate the "affirmative" and "negative" sides of one of the following topics related to recent US immigration reform (still underway in 2006–7): begin by outlining ideas "for" and "against" a stance on the issue. Compile "evidence" (data, statistics, testimony) to support your argumentative points. For each argumentative point, outline potential critiques. Additionally, student collaborative groups should anticipate "alternative perspectives" or "counter-arguments" to their own stance and formulate potential rebuttals for those arguments.

If useful to do so, imagine that your group is (a) writing a letter to the editorial board of the *New York Times*, the *Washington Post*, the *Wall Street Journal*, the *LA Times*, the *Cincinnati Enquirer*, the *Chicago Tribune*, or an international newspaper such as the *Guardian*, *Le Monde*, or *Der Spiegel*; or (b) giving a speech at a local organization (the Rotary Club, the College Republicans, the Young Democrats, or some other group); or (c) participating in a televised political debate for a local office (mayor, city council, school board).

1 Guestworker program

President Bush supports "guestworker programs" (an H2A visa already exists for migrant farm workers) to allow immigrants to temporarily enter the country as "guestworkers" in order to fill employment positions that are either in shortage, in high demand, or that other US citizens and legal immigrants do not typically fill. Do you support such a program? Why or why not? What impact would the program have on the US economy?

2 "Border"

US Congress has legislatively supported President Bush's call for US Reservists to guard the US-Mexico border and for the construction of a "wall" along the border to prevent individuals from Mexico, Central America, and other countries from entering the country illegally. Do you agree that the United States should build a wall along the border? Why or why not?

3 Amnesty

As of 2006–7, approximately 11.5 million "illegal aliens" – or undocumented workers – work and reside in the US. In 1986, President Reagan supported and the US Congress passed legislation that granted "amnesty" to those law-abiding workers in order to alter their status from "illegal" to "legal" and that allowed them to remain in the country, work, and contribute to the US economy. Should "illegal aliens" be granted "amnesty" in 2006–7 as they were in 1986 under the Reagan administration? Why or why not?

2

Gender and Diasporas

Despite what some scholars have referred to as the "feminization of migration" (Castles and Miller 2003; Momsen 1999; Ehrenreich and Hochschild 2002), and despite a marked "feminization of the contemporary Filipino overseas workforce" (Ceniza Choy 2003, 188) since the 1970s, as discussed more extensively in the case study at the end of this chapter, gender as a category of scholarly analysis only entered into international migration studies during the 1980s. According to Stephen Castles and Mark Miller's landmark study *The Age of Migration* (1998), gendered patterns of economic migration emerged almost four decades ago: "Since the 1960s, women have played a major role in labor migration," and since the 1990s, "women workers [have] form[ed] the majority in movements as diverse as those of Cape Verdians to Italy, Filipinos to the Middle East and Thais to Japan" (1998, 9). Gendered patterns of economic migration have also coincided with and escalated during the period known as the "globalization of migration" (Castles and Miller 1998, 18), roughly from the international standardization of monetary currency in the early 1970s until the current moment, but rapidly proliferating post-1989 with the so-called death of communism, and revealing both a "globalization of women's work" and "global redivision of women's traditional work" (Ehrenreich and Hochschild 2002, 12, 11). Feminist scholars working in the areas of gender, globalization, development, and migration have referred to this material migratory "exchange" not only as a source-country "brain drain," but also a "care drain" – siphoning off skills and providers – and a "mommy drain," since many economic migrants working in the service sector are mothers (single and married) who leave their own children behind in the care of other women (other mothers, grandmothers, aunts, sisters, or more distant relatives) when they migrate. Castles and Miller demonstrate how "immigrant servants – from the Philippines, Indonesia, Thailand, Korea and Sri Lanka – allow women in the richer economies to take up new employment opportunities" (1998, xi). Dominant theme, globally recurrent pattern: as Ehrenreich and Hochschild explain: "The 'care deficit' that has emerged in the wealthier countries as women entered the workforce *pulls* migrants from the Third World and postcommunist nations; poverty *pushes* them" (2002, 8).

Patterns of economic migration, then, are mapped along myriad gendered lines of power and disempowerment in relation to capital, mobility, nation-state, and even family.[1] Gender – what it is, what it means, how it is defined, how it is performed, when and where it becomes legible or illegible, visible and invisible, operative and inoperative, privileged or subaltern – and thus transnational gender relations must be understood relationally: in other words, and often in other worlds, gender in one context must be contextualized relationally and intersectionally with multiple interrelated and yet often contradictory categories such as race, class, sexuality, nationality, education, literacy, religion, and, though less frequently noted or specifically isolated, historical forms of economic ideology (capitalism, communism, socialism) and political state formation (autocracy, democracy, monarchy, plutocracy).

In this chapter, we will survey major migratory patterns that have gendered parameters, examining the economic migration of service laborers and focusing primarily on nurses, maids, and other domestic workers. The chapter overviews, for example, economic migrants from Mexico, Central America, Southeast Asia, and the Asian Pacific region, who have largely worked as domestics, and discusses the global services trade in nursing (Africa, Australia, Canada, the Caribbean, East Asia, the Philippines, the UK, the US, and New Zealand). Female economic migrants overwhelmingly make up those holding domestic service positions as cooks, nannies, maids, or personal attendants worldwide. Historically gendered as women's work, domestic service remains so today. Nursing – also historically coded as feminine and as part of the contemporary global trade in services – has dramatically reconfigured the international division of sexual labor and the global capitalist market for care. Indeed, nursing has become a global trade service with trained and highly skilled nurses heavily sought after and commonly migrating from one country to another in pursuit of better employment opportunities. Consequently, nurses typically (and understandably) migrate from economically deprived countries to wealthier ones, creating a paucity of nurses in less developed countries. Textile manufacturing constituted another dominant, if not globally pervasive form of gendered economic migration in the 1970s and 1980s before the post-Cold War era of multilateral and regional free trade agreements: for example, before the signing of the North American Free Trade Agreement in 1992 between Canada, Mexico, and the United States, most female economic migrants working in the US were employed by the textile and garment manufacturing industries either within the continental borders of the country or actually along the border in upstart *maquiladoras*; since the implementation of NAFTA in 1994, multinational corporations have not "imported" migrant labor, but rather relocated in offshore locales – "exporting" the manufacturing plant and "outsourcing" the labor. Since this production-based pattern of economic migration has virtually disappeared, or has at least become vastly diminished, beginning in the mid-1990s, having been replaced by services-based patterns of economic migration, it is omitted from the discussion of gender and diaspora here; it is, however, clearly related to (and must be kept in mind) when

considering the economic migratory patterns related to the global trade in services
– healthcare, domestic service, and the sex industry – that are outlined and foregrounded in this chapter. While some forms of gendered labor (such as textiles)
shifted post-NAFTA, service jobs continue to attract economic migrants from
poorer countries to wealthier ones.

While the chapter focuses heavily on gendered work and patterns of economic
migration, it also examines diasporic formations that foster these gendered patterns of economic migration, with extended family and ethnic community networks often supporting (physically, emotionally, and – crucially – monetarily)
migratory patterns. Diaspora as a term may refer to ethnic enclaves in the host
countries, or as is increasingly the case, may refer administratively within origin
countries to "overseas" departments of scattered expatriate citizens who remit
dollars, support local economies, and facilitate both further out-migrations of
under- or unemployed natives and inflows of information and capital. Diasporic
linkages thus facilitate gendered patterns of economic migration as "whole networks and neighborhoods leave to work abroad, bringing back stories, money,
know-how, and contacts," and as "one domestic worker in New York, Dubai,
or Paris passes on information to female relatives or friends about how to arrange
papers, travel, find a job, and settle" (Hochschild 2002, 19).

Overviewing international migration patterns of nurses, domestic workers,
and (in chapter three) sex workers, we further examine what scholars have
described as both the contemporary "feminization" and "globalization" of
migration. At the end of this chapter, we will thread together the two streams –
nursing and domestic service – with a final case study on Filipinas, especially
since the "diasporic" aspect is most pronounced in the out-migratory flows of
women from the Philippines – i.e., outflow routes and information inflows are
charted along certain dominant paths in relation to ethnic and working enclaves
of Filipinas in the US, Hong Kong, and Italy, respectively, for nurses, domestics/
nannies, and prostitutes (although there are diasporic Filipinas working in these
vocations across the globe). One cannot help but wonder, in fact, if only the most
destitute, illiterate, elderly, disabled, ill, and underprivileged Filipinas stay home,
since most migrating women from the archipelago are graduates, those who have
earned high school diplomas or college degrees, not only those who migrate
abroad to work in ER wards of hospitals or attend to the elderly in nursing
homes, but also those who migrate abroad to clean bathrooms, or to blow tod-
dler's noses, sing nursery rhymes, and clean stubbed toes.

Nurses and Migration

Across the globe, nurses migrate seeking better educational opportunities, salaries, benefits, and professional work conditions: pushed out by myriad and
diverse factors – famine, war, exploitation, violence, poverty, unemployment,
poor work conditions, harassment, and limited national mobility;[2] pulled toward
advanced medical technology, capital, resources, pharmaceutical supplies, and
intellectual and clinical challenges, nurses are on the international move – from

Russia to Israel, South Africa to Ireland, Ghana to England, Jamaica to Canada, India to Australia, Bangladesh to Saudi Arabia, China to the United States, and from the Philippines to scattered corners – metropolitan, suburban, and rural – across Europe, the Americas, the Middle East, and Asia. While historical and colonial linkages often determined initial postcolonial migratory patterns of international nursing migration in the post-World War II and decolonization periods up until the 1970s – for example, nurses moving from North and West African countries like Senegal, Ivory Coast, Tunisia, and Morocco to France; from the Philippines to the United States; or from Commonwealth countries in Africa, Asia, and the Caribbean, as geographically dispersed as Ghana, Bangladesh, and Antigua, to the United Kingdom – increasingly, the migratory trajectories are less frequently determined and not so easily mapped onto histori-cal (cultural, educational, and of course, linguistic) colonial relations. Today, one might find Chinese and Korean registered nurses (RNs) practicing in hospitals or nursing homes in global cities of overdeveloped countries in Europe, North America, East Asia, and the Asian Pacific as one would earlier have found nurses from South Africa, Trinidad, Pakistan, and other English-speaking countries.

Typically, though, nurses – like other highly skilled economic professionals arriving with intellectual capital and passport nursing "caps" – migrate from rural, remote areas to larger metropolitan sites, from developing countries to developed (or overdeveloped) countries, and from low-wage positions to higher-income employment, although some migration currently exists among developing countries – for example, nurse migration occurs within and among sub-Saharan African countries (primarily, but not exclusively, from Lesotho, Zimbabwe, Botswana, and Malawi to South Africa), and within and among the Caribbean countries who are political members of the Caribbean Community (CARICOM), and even from the Philippines to the more affluent and technologically developed countries of South Africa, Saudi Arabia, the United Arab Emirates, and elsewhere worldwide. Statistically, the numbers are stark, even overwhelming: a few exam-ples suffice to make this point: according to Buchan and Sochalski (2004), "in 2000 more than 500 nurses left Ghana to work in other industrialized countries"; similarly, "in Malawi, between 1999 and 2001 over 60 percent of the entire staff of registered nurses in a single tertiary hospital (114 nurses) left for jobs in other countries"; and "between 2000 and 2001 alone, 10 percent of nurses in Barbados left the nursing sector, the majority of whom left the country for employ-ment elsewhere" (588).[3] Statistically, Kingma also documents similar third- to first-world migratory patterns for registered nurses: "Today, there are more Bangladeshi nurses in the Middle East than in Bangladesh," paralleling the recurrent problem in the Philippines, where since the 1970s there have been periods in which "there were more Filipino nurses registered in the United States and Canada than in the Philippines" (2006, 173). In Ghana, the "loss of 382 nurses" in 1999 "represented 100 percent of the annual output of its nursing schools"; and in Jamaica, approximately two-thirds of the country's nursing graduates have emigrated to other countries since the mid-1970s (Kingma 2006, 173). More starkly, particularly given the AIDS crisis in South Africa, according to DENOSA, the country's professional nursing organization and labor union, "three hundred nurses leave the country every *month* to practice abroad" (cited in Kingma 2006, 173). Healthcare industries in receiving (or "importing") countries may be as profoundly impacted as those in source (or "exporting") countries: according to Kingma, foreign nurses represented "nearly 98 percent of the 4,417 nurses employed in hospitals and other health facilities in 1999" in the United Arab Emirates (UAE), and similar patterns hold for other Gulf States such as Saudi Arabia, where 84 percent of all registered nurses were foreign immigrants (2006, 173).

International recruitment for nurses has indeed entered the global market with highly skilled, trained, educated, licensed, and registered nurses migrating cross-nationally and even transcontinentally toward countries offering the highest salaried positions with great benefits packages, continued education, housing accommodations, fewer caseloads, and shorter shifts, and away from countries that are not competitive within this global employment market: typically, the migratory trajectory from nurses has been from third-world countries in Africa, the Asian Pacific, and the Caribbean toward wealthier first-world countries in Europe, North America, and the Asian Pacific. "Exporter" countries for nursing include Ghana, the Philippines, Trinidad, and Jamaica; "importer" countries for nursing include the US, Britain, Ireland,[4] Canada, New Zealand, and Australia, including some migration within and without the UK with nurses moving from Scotland to Britain and from Britain to the US and Australia. Most nursing scholars and healthcare professionals, including the International Council for Nurses, agree that the issues surrounding nursing migration are complicated – nurses' labor and migrant rights in tension with a country's need to sustain its healthcare system, and the global migration pattern the result of myriad, inter-related "push" and "pull" factors, such as problems with nursing education, retention, and administrative support for healthcare as well as salary and benefits. Critics, however, rightly aver that global migratory patterns for nurses, though propelled by national nursing shortages, ultimately result in severe or critical nursing shortages in the exporting countries, even those like the Philippines that have historically fostered out-migration of nurses to encourage and sustain the remittance of US dollars and euros back into the Filipino economy, and a consequent "brain drain" in those countries with educated and skilled professionals literally "siphoned" off by richer countries like the US, Canada, Australia, and Britain.

Overall, increased demand for nurses in the developed (or overdeveloped) countries, like the UK, US, Canada, Australia, and New Zealand may be linked with myriad factors: increased aging of post-WWII "boomer" populations; Reagan-era economic vitality starting in the late Cold War period of the late 1970s and 1980s; national nursing shortages due to lack of internal recruitment and lack of investment in nursing education; a lack of retention of nurses who maintained registration but practiced or worked in other corporate-sector jobs, sometimes, but not always, in related healthcare or pharmaceutical fields; as well as external factors, including the over-production of nurses in Asian and African countries relative to the GDP of those countries during the same time period. Smaller, developing countries, consequently, were unable to absorb the highly skilled, highly educated natives into their national economies, leading to under- and unemployment in the healthcare professions, including nursing (a "push" factor) and the subsequent "pull" toward the wealthier countries mentioned above.

Three key works address international nurse migration and the global market in healthcare services, authored by major scholars in the fields of nursing and migration history: James Buchan's *Nurses Work: An Analysis of the UK Nursing Labour Market* (1998), which addresses the multinational nursing labor force on the UK registry; Catherine Ceniza Choy's *Empire of Care: Nursing and Migration in Filipino American History* (2003), which places post-1965 nurse migratory patterns to the United States within the context of US imperialism in the Philippine archipelago in the late nineteenth and early twentieth centuries; and Mireille Kingma's *Nurses on the Move: Migration and the Global Health Care Economy* (2006), a comprehensive study examining the political, economic, and material factors related to international nurse migration and shortages in the global healthcare market. In this section, I first detail international nurse migration, then offer a special case study of Filipina nurses abroad and the diasporic networks that support and facilitate nurse migration.

Migration toward capital and resources may falsely suggest what Mireille Kingma has called the "global treasure hunt"[5] in nursing – the belief that transnational relocation ineluctably improves the lot of migrant nurses; yet, international nurse migration has its own unique (and not so unique) set of problems – fraudulent recruitment contracts that are not honored by institutions once the nurse arrives, exploitation and exploitative labor tactics (including in media-publicized cases, the employer confiscation of the nurses' travel documents), racism and anti-immigrant sentiments in the work place and in the diasporic location.[6] As James Buchan writes, "In the summer of 2001 the media in the UK highlighted the poor treatment of Indian and Filipino nurses who had been recruited to UK private sector nursing homes" (2001a, 204). International nurse migration, while a "big business" multinationally for some enterprises, especially recruitment agencies, also poses real material costs to source countries: brain drain (which Kingma defines as "a transfer of human capital from one country to another"),[7] the attrition of skilled practitioners, the lost investment in nurse education for the individual who has left the national registry to practice abroad, and loss of income tax on nursing salaries as a source of future revenue (Kingma 2006, 177). Problems for source countries "will continue to be severe," since "they are losing scarce, and relatively expensive to train resources" (Buchan 2001a, 204). Source countries not only lose skilled professionals in the field, but also "future leaders in the profession" (Buchan 2001a, 204). Whether or not these material and intellectual losses for source countries are offset by fiscal gains in the form of diasporic remittances by exported laborers remains a key question, as addressed below.

A decade-long post-Cold War period of global economic restructuring and austere financial policies imposed on developing countries by World Bank and IMF "structural adjustment plans" (SAPs), which massively reduced developmental loan funding for and investment in the public sector, including healthcare, in the sweep toward "privatization" as part of the "Washington consensus," the 1990s also brought a concomitant period of privatization and corporate "down-sizing" in hospitals of the developed countries. These late capitalist fiscal policies quite literally wrecked havoc on fragile healthcare systems across the world, resulting in chronic nurse and physician shortages as well as diminished access to healthcare in both the poorer and wealthier countries. Consequently, and subsequently, chronic medical shortages spiked demands: within years, competi-tion for healthcare providers on the global market and the international "trade in services" commanded incredible profits.

Partially regulated by the General Agreement on Trade in Services (GATS),[8] passed in 1995, the World Trade Organization (WTO), regional and multilateral free trade agreements, professional regulatory organizations like the International Council of Nurses (ICN) and the World Health Organization (WHO), and national immigration laws, international nurse migration now constitutes a major economic gain to hospitals, international recruitment agencies, private or corporate-based nurse training programs or schools, financial institutions and banks, and for the gross domestic product (GDP) of the source countries. While GATS and regional trade agreements do not directly impact national immigration laws or nurse licensure requirements, these agreements do indirectly influence the multilateral and international motility of nurses and other medical providers as part of the global labor market in healthcare services. For example, the North American Free Trade Agreement (NAFTA), passed in 1992 and implemented in 1994, created a special Trade NAFTA (TN) visa allowing for nurse migration from Canada and Mexico into the United States with no cap on nurses migrating from Canada yet limiting the number of nurses migrating from Mexico to 5,500. Another example is Trans-Tasman Travel Arrangement enacted in concordance with the Australia-New Zealand Closer Economic Relations Agreement: under this regional trade agreement, both countries recognize degrees, certification, and licensure of the other country, and registered nurses may seek employment – without work restriction or further authorization – reciprocally within the two countries. Similarly, the European Economic Community, inaugurated with the European Community Treaty, negotiated by all members of the European Union (EU), recognizes credentials, licensure, and the right to move at will throughout the territory to seek professional employment or advancement. Like nurses, domestics – predominantly employed as maids or nannies – also migrate across national borders seeking better lives and livelihoods.

Migrant Domestic Laborers: Maid Trade and Nanny Politics

Dirt, from an anthropological perspective, was defined as matter "out of its place" by Mary Douglass in *Purity and Danger* (1969). Regrettably, for the 2.9 percent of the world's population, a staggering 175 million immigrants – 85 million women, 90 million men – they too are often seen or regarded as misplaced bodies, nameless statistics, faceless laborers. Almost one half of all legal and illegal economic migrants are women, the vast majority from developing countries yet working in developed countries across the globe as "domestics" – in other words, doing the "dirty work" historically gendered as feminine, "woman's work," for the privileged who can afford to contract their services (Heyzer and Wee 1994, 31–32). And this "dirty work" – like dirt – embodies often exploitative and discriminatory patterns of dislocation. As cultural and materialist critic Barbara Ehrenreich writes, "Dirt . . . tends to attach to the people who remove it" and "to be cleaned up after is to achieve a certain magical weightlessness and immateriality," a kind of affluent virtual existence beyond dirt.

Mary Romero's *Maid in the USA* (1992), Nicole Constable's *Maid to Order in Hong Kong* (1997), and their echoed titles in Doreen Mattingly's journalistic essay "Maid in the USA" (1998) and Barbara Ehrenreich's "Maid to Order" in *Global Woman* (2002), as well as Grace Chang's *Disposable Domestics* (2000) and Bridget Anderson's *Doing the Dirty Work?* (2000), all address the material disparities of wealth and power between immigrant domestics and their affluent employers. In 1998, the US Census Bureau documented "549,000 domestic workers," legally residing and working in the United States; and according to Ehrenreich, in 1999, 14–18 percent of US households employed maids (2002, 91, 90). Overwhelmingly, though, immigrants working as domestics – maids, cooks, personal care attendants, nannies – are unaccounted for statistically: undocumented, they are officially invisible. Nevertheless, statistics for those working legally in these positions are still quite revealing: according to the Bureau of Labor Statistics, the median income for a domestic laborer was a mere $223 per week, "$23 below poverty level for a family of three" (Ehrenreich 2002, 92–93). As Mattingly affirms, "the annual incomes of even the busiest domestic workers are below $10,000 (the US poverty level for a family of four is about $15,000)." And these are recorded median salaries for legally documented workers!

Invisibility for immigrant women working as domestics is compounded by their unique work environment: "isolated in private households [often] without papers or legal protection," these women "are strikingly vulnerable to abuse"; and the work (ranging from hands-on-knees scrubbing; cooking all day and sometimes into the night; caring for the invalid, the elderly, or preschool children; washing cars; unclogging toilets; and emptying litter boxes) can be "singularly degrading" (Anderson 2002, 107). According to statistics maintained by Kalayaan, a British nonprofit organization (NGO) that supports immigrant women working as domestics in the UK, 84 percent "reported psychological abuse"; 34 percent "physical abuse"; and 10 percent "sexual abuse" (Anderson 2002, 108).

Maids, or immigrant domestic laborers, are overwhelmingly women within established ethnic enclaves settled and working (both legally and illegally) in North America, Europe, Asia, the Middle East, and elsewhere. In the United States, the majority of immigrant maids – or "disposable domestics" (as Chang notes in identifying the way that they are all too often regarded by their immensely more privileged employers) – are from Mexico and Central America; in the European Union, immigrant maids arrive from multiple locations – "the Philippines, Sri Lanka, Thailand, Argentina, Colombia, Brazil, El Salvador, and

Peru" (Ehrenreich and Hochschild 2002, 7), but with Asian immigrant women primarily residing and working in the United Kingdom, Maghrebi or North African women in France, and Turkish or formerly East German women in Germany. Regionally in the US, the ethnic origins of domestic laborers also vary, with Chicanas and Latinas providing the majority of the legal and illegal labor pool in the Southwest and West Coast, Caribbean immigrants in New York and other parts of the Northeast, rural underclass Anglo-Americans in more remote parts of New England, and indigenous peoples doing the "dirty work" for wealthier settlers in their own native Hawai'i (Ehrenreich 2002, 92).

"Maid trade," in fact, now constitutes a major form of gendered economic out-migration globally in Asia, Africa, Eastern Europe, the Caribbean, Mexico, and Central America. A five-year study from 1987 to 1992 undertaken by the Kuala-Lumpur based Asian and Pacific Development Centre (APDC) Research Project, and published as *The Trade in Domestic Workers* in 1994, documented how the regional and transcontinental maid trade resulted in massive out-migration waves for poor countries in South Asia, Southeast Asia, and the Asian Pacific to wealthier countries in East Asia, the Asian Pacific, and the Middle East. According to the APDC Research Project, major geographic patterns of female migration include the following international routes, both legal and illegal:

Legal routes
- from Indonesia to Saudi Arabia;
- from Manila, Philippines to Hong Kong, Malaysia, and Bahrain;
- from Sri Lanka to Bahrain, Hong Kong, and Singapore.

Illegal routes
- from Bangladesh to Pakistan;
- from Burma [Myanmar] to Pakistan;
- from Mindanao, Philippines to Malaysia.

Statistics compiled by the APDC group reveal an out-migration exodus of women seeking work as domestics cross-regionally, particularly from the Philippines, but also from Indonesia and Sri Lanka:

Estimated out-migration by source country

	Low estimate	High estimate
Philippines	275,000	275,000
Indonesia	100,000	240,000
Sri Lanka	100,000	175,000
Bangladesh	2,000	15,000

Gendered patterns of economic migration from these source countries, particularly those migrating to the Gulf States before and after the 1991 Gulf War, are still salient migratory patterns: for example, Filipina women constitute 50–70 percent of the overseas workforce (Ehrenreich and Hochschild 2002, 6; Ceniza Choy 2003, 188–189); and Sri Lankan women comprise 84 percent of all economic migrants arriving for work, or reporting for duty, in the Middle East. (Other gendered patterns of economic migration from South Asia to the Middle East during the same period, but which are beyond the scope of this chapter, include Bangladeshi and Burmese [Myanmar] women working in domestic service in Pakistan, and Pakistani men migrating and working in construction in the Gulf States.)

Similarly, statistics for estimated totals of immigrants entering receiving countries in East Asia and the Middle East are high, particularly for Saudi Arabia, the country that "imported" the overwhelming majority of South Asian, Southeast Asian, and Asian Pacific migrant women employed as domestic workers:

Estimated in-migration by receiving country

Saudi Arabia	750,000
Bahrain	40,000
Hong Kong	65,000
Singapore	65,000
Kuwait	28,000
Malaysia	27,000

According to Heyzer and Wee (1994), in the late 1980s and early 1990s, "an estimated 1 million to 1.7 million women . . . [were] working as domestic workers in Asia and the Middle East" (40). As with international nursing migration, economic domestic labor migration patterns reveal the Philippines to be a special case, as discussed further below.

In their edited collection *Global Woman: Nannies, Maids and Sex Workers in the New Economy* (2002), Barbara Ehrenreich and Arlie Russell Hochschild outline four dominant "cross-regional flows" for gendered economic migration of women: from Southeast Asia to East Asia and the Middle East; from Eastern Europe, countries formerly part of the Soviet Union, to Western Europe; from South and Central America and from Mexico to other parts of North America; and finally, from Africa to Europe. Concurring with the findings of the APDC in 1994, Ehrenreich and Hochschild first map a dominant migratory flow of women "from Bangladesh, Indonesia, the Philippines, and Sri Lanka to Bahrain, Oman, Saudi Arabia, Hong Kong, Malaysia, and Singapore" (2002, 6). The second pattern of female migration moves east to west, "from Russia, Romania, Bulgaria, and Albania to Scandinavia, Germany, France, Spain, Portugal, and England" (2002, 6). The third migratory route flows south to north in the Americas, primarily, but not exclusively, "from Mexico to the United States, which scholars say is the longest-running labor migration in the world (2002, 6), already extensively discussed in chapter one of this book. The fourth major migratory movement for immigrant women also flows from south to north, but transcontinentally from Africa to Europe, with France receiving "female immigrants from Morocco, Tunisia, and Algeria" and Italy receiving "female workers from Ethiopia, Eritrea, and Cape Verde" (2002, 6). All of these transmigratory routes are significant in examining gendered patterns of economic diasporas, but our case study focuses on the Filipina diaspora worldwide.

Case Study: Filipina Working Diasporas in the US, Hong Kong, and Italy

The Philippines offers a unique geopolitical standpoint from which to comparatively examine the three forms of gendered economic migration and global trade in services – nursing, domestic labor, and sex work, discussed more extensively in the next chapter. The Philippine government's strategic institutionalization of exported human labor as national economic policy in the mid-1970s, combined with its highly educated population, has resulted in one of the world's largest diasporas, predominantly the result of sustained, managed economic out-migration over several decades. Exported labor was Ferdinand Marcos' presidential answer to a twofold national problem: high rates of unemployment in the country and a massive external debt owed to international financial institutions (IFIs). The Labour Code, legislated in 1974, envisioned the exportation of human labor as a short-term, or stop-gap, measure to address the unemployment crisis and the national "shortage of foreign currency for development" (Raj-Hashim 1994, 122). Once legislated, however, exported labor proved highly profitable and became permanent national policy. The Philippines Development Plan (PDP) and the Philippines Development Plan for Women (PDPW) helped to facilitate emigration and labor exportation. Hard currency cash flows into the Philippines, usually in dollars, fueled the outflow of Filipinos leaving the country. And, in 1974, once "foreign exchange remittances" totaled US$1 billion, Marcos issued Presidential Decree 442 (P.D. 442) and the Philippine government implemented the Overseas Employment Development Board (OEDB), under the jurisdiction of the Labour Ministry, "to design and implement policies" (Raj-Hashim 1994, 123). According to Rita Raj-Hashim, the Philippine government "provided incentives to lower the cost of emigrating, reduced travel tax, established one-stop centres for processing, and removed customs duties for returnees"; and most significantly, in terms of reaping the financial benefits of its investment in human capital, "it also forced the overseas migrants to send remittances through official channels" (1994, 123).

Philippine policy not only actively encouraged economic out-migration as an administrative answer to widespread national unemployment, but also created an entire bureaucratic state apparatus to sustain and bolster the Filipino diaspora as an extra-territorial and fiscal "department" – if only unofficially – of the homeland. Consequently, Filipinos departed from the archipelago in droves seeking employment abroad as seamen, domestics, nurses, and workers in the entertainment and sex industries. Executive Order No. 857, issued in 1983, "made it mandatory for overseas workers to remit 50 to 70 per cent of their earnings," and granted oversight authorization to both the Bangko Sentral ng Pilipinas (Central Bank of the Philippines) and the Foreign Ministry, which collaborated in establishing "mechanisms for . . . enforcement with penalties, such as non-renewal/extension of passports for non-complicance with the ruling" (Raj-Hashim 1994, 127). According to Lesleyanne Hawthorne, in 1990, "700,000 Filipinos left to work overseas as documented workers, 'to join the stock of an estimated 5.7 million Filipinos in some 160 countries'" (2001, 215; internal quotation from Asis 1995, 328). Initially, the out-migratory flows were predominated by men, but by 1987, "83 percent of Asia-bound Filipino workers were female, contributing to the US$800+ million returned in remittance per year" (Hawthorne 2001, 214).

Remittance dollars, in effect, constitute *the* push-pull of the Filipino diaspora: in 1989, annual remittances equaled US$973 million (Hawthorne 2001, 214n2); and according to the Central Bank, the remittances returned to the country by overseas migrant workers from 1974 to 1994 totaled US$18.196 billion (Ceniza Choy 2003, 188). Remittances in dollars and other hard currencies (pounds and euros) peaked in the early years of the twenty-first century: in 2004, remittances equaled US$8.5 billion (Kingma 2006, 24); and in 2005, US$10.7 billion (Mannes 2006). Financial necessity and monetary return compel the outflux of Filipinos from their homeland. Every day, an average 2,531 Filipinos leave the archipelago to work abroad as overseas contracted labor:

> They include engineers toiling in the oil rigs of Gulf region countries; nurses caring for the elderly and sick in Saudi Arabia, the United Kingdom, and the United States; domestic workers cleaning the homes of the affluent in Asia, the Gulf region, North America, and Europe; seafarers manning cargo ships the world over; and teachers safeguarding the classrooms of public schools in Texas and California. (Parreñas 2005, 12)

It is, Rhacel Salazar Parreñas contends, "impossible to overlook the significance of migrant labor to the Philippine economy. Some 34 to 54 percent of the Filipino population is sustained by remittances from migrant workers" (2002, 39). And the decades-old Philippine historical pattern of migratory outflows and capital inflows is likely to continued unabated, "given the country's massive $46 billion debt to the World Bank, International Monetary Fund, and other lending institutions based in North America," especially since "overseas workers' remittances have been the country's largest source of foreign exchange" (Ceniza Choy 2003, 188).

One of the largest source countries for international nurse migration, the Philippines also provides an interesting case study on the historical, cultural, educational, and material parameters influencing global healthcare. Catherine Ceniza Choy's *Empire of Care* documents the exporting of Filipino nurses in the global market for healthcare in the context of US imperialism in the Philippines and the continued postcolonial ramifications of transnational political and economic relations between the two countries: rather than linking the historical patterns (more recently and exclusively) within the post-1965 shifts in immigration in the US and the strategic economic policy shift of the Philippine government toward the exporting of human labor as economic migrants in the 1970s, as do most scholars, she places the contemporary phenomenon of high-skilled, high-education economic migration of Filipino nurses within the longer historical context of US imperialism in the archipelago beginning in 1898 and continuing throughout the period of US occupation until 1946. Specifically, Ceniza Choy documents the "importation" of nursing into the Philippines during the Spanish-American War, the Philippine-American War, and the early occupation period at the beginning of the twentieth century: she then traces the American promulgation of nursing as a gendered profession in the Philippines through the end of the occupation and into the 1950s, demonstrating that Filipina nurses were instrumental both in the post-WWII US economy, after the congressional passage of the Asian Exclusion Repeal Acts in 1946, and in the post-1965 period of massive Filipino migration to the US following the legislation of the Hart-Cellar Immigration Act. To do so, Ceniza Choy's *Empire of Care* documents the impact of the three mid-to-late twentieth-century transnational shifts on the over-production of Filipino nurses during the decades from the 1950s to the 1970s: the inauguration of the US Exchange Visitor Program (EVP) during the Cold War, the 1965 Hart-Cellar Act (specifically, the third category of preference for highly skilled immigrants), and the "institutionalization of exported labor" and "dollar repatriation" by the Marcos administration in the 1970s.

During the post-1965 period, over 70,000 foreign nurses migrated to the United States: of this number an estimated 25,000 Filipino nurses entered the US healthcare labor force (Ong and Azores; cited in Ceniza Choy 2003, 1). In 1989, Filipino immigrant nurses working and residing in the US constituted 73 percent of all foreign nurse graduates in the country, Canadian nurses comprising the "second largest group," yet only 12 percent of all US employed nurses (Ceniza Choy 2003, 2). Under former President Marcos, the Philippine government institutionalized the export of human labor as economic policy encouraging out-migration of under- and unemployed laborers and implementing the "dollar repatriation program" that secured the inflow or return of hard currencies through foreign-earned salaries remitted back to family members, Filipino banks, and homeland business, education, and public infrastructural investment opportunities (Ceniza Choy 2003, 116–117). "According to the Central Bank of the Philippines, between 1975 and 1994 Filipino overseas contract workers sent remittances totaling $18.196 billion" (Ceniza Choy 2003, 188). And Ceniza Choy predicts that the "massive $46 billion debt to the World Bank, International Monetary Fund, and other lending institutions based in North America" make it "unlikely that the export of Filipino laborers abroad will end or even decrease in the near future, when overseas workers' remittances have been the country's largest source of foreign exchange" (2003, 188). Filipino nurses are overwhelmingly Filipina nurses, with female migrant women constituting 41 percent of the overseas workforce compared to 36 percent of the "domestic workforce": in fact, these highly skilled migrant workers form, as Ceniza Choy aptly concludes, a "worldwide diaspora of Filipino women working in Japan, Canada, the Middle East, several European countries," and the United States (2003, 188).

That "worldwide diaspora" of Filipinas also includes domestic laborers, those who tend to the elderly and the young, do the shopping, prepare meals, wash dishes, clean houses, and otherwise remain on call to the small demands and menial tasks of the wealthy. Parreñas, in the opening paragraph of her book *Servants of Globalization: Women, Migration, and Domestic Work* (2001), informs her readers that "the majority of Filipina migrants scattered all over the globe are domestic workers" (2001, 1). Of the 7 million Filipinos living in diaspora, over 3.5 million (some estimates are as high as 4.9 million) are women; among these diasporic Filipinas, two-thirds are employed as domestic workers (Parreñas 2001, 1). Despite their varied diasporic locations, Filipina domestics have a similar and common "shared role as low-wage laborers in global capitalism" located primarily in its urban "economic centers" (2001, 3). For this reason, Parreñas aptly refers to these migrant women as "global servants of global capitalism" (2001, 3). In this way, Filipina diasporic domestics form a global community of workers dislocated into low-wage labor by the economic turmoil caused by global restructuring in the Philippines.

While Parreñas' study compares Filipina domestics working in Rome (since the 1970s) with those working in Los Angeles (where Filipinos have a longer historical presence dating to the early decades of the twentieth century following the Spanish-American and Philippine-American wars), we should keep in mind that Filipina domestics are also working and residing in other scattered locations across the globe – Hong Kong, Singapore, Bahrain, London, New York, and scores of other metropolitan sites, both big and small. Some statistics from her study, however, saliently demonstrate that the lives of Filipina domestics and the diasporic communities they dwell in are not in all ways and in every place similar: for example, in Italy 70 percent of all Filipino economic migrants are women, and 98.5 percent are employed as domestics; by contrast, in the US, about 50 percent of Filipino economic migrants are women (Parreñas 2001, 4). From the first waves of economic migration in Italy in the 1970s until 1995, approximately 200,000 Filipinas have arrived, with an estimated 100,000 centered in the capital city of Rome; in contradistinction, an estimated 200,000 Filipino economic migrants – both men and women, but overwhelmingly "never-married single men" –were already in Los Angeles as early as 1965, three decades before they reached this number in Rome (2001, 6). As a direct consequence of the 1965 Hart-Cellar Immigration Act, the Filipino migration to the US is "second in size only to the Mexican migration flow" into the country (2001, 6). According to the 1993 US Census, there were more than 1.4 million Filipinos in the country (2001, 6).

Too often separated from a larger ethnic community in their living and working environments, isolated in individual houses, cleaning or caring for the very old and the very young, solitarily for long hours, Filipina domestics nevertheless do come together, speak Tagalog, exchange information, buy goods, or transfer money. Ethnic grocery stores and "bank-sponsored remittance centers" are two common meeting points (Parreñas 2001, 13). Remittances not only connect Filipina diasporas to family and home in direct material exchanges, they also bring migrant women together, even if only briefly: "remittance agencies represent collective locations among geographically distanced migrant workers," simultaneously connecting those in diaspora to those remaining at home and those dwelling in separate diasporic residences in the same city (2001, 13). Filipina domestics – in Hong Kong, Italy, the US, and elsewhere – thus maintain transnational families by telephoning, emailing, recording cassettes, and sending packages (as well as money) back home to aging parents, sisters and brothers, teenage children all remaining in the Philippines; however, they also sustain long-distance communication and familial contact (or "transnational family ties") with other diasporic siblings, cousins, aunts, or uncles living elsewhere. Finally, magazines circulating in diasporic cities, like *Tinig Filipino* or *Diwaliwan*, connect migrant women to a sense of long-distance Philippine identity despite their geographical dislocation from the country (2001, 14–15).

Performing menial tasks and numerous, thankless chores, Filipina domestics are still, like their nurse compatriots, often college-educated and extremely literate individuals: they have chosen overseas unskilled (or low-skilled and low-waged) work that is frequently under-appreciated, routinely under-compensated, and often disgusting too: this choice is one of economic necessity. As Parreñas explains: "Even with a high level of education attainment, Filipino women migrate and enter domestic work because they still earn higher wages as domestic workers in postindustrial nations than as professional workers in the Philippines" (2001, 19–20). In Rome, for example, Parreñas found the domestic workers average between 1,083,000 and 1,844,000 lira – or between US$722 and $1,229 – monthly salary. More likely to be paid weekly in the United States, domestic workers in Los Angeles averaged between US$350 to $425 per week. By contrast, the women Parreñas interviewed earned only an average US$179 monthly while working in the Philippines in the 1990s. Not only are wage differentials between the homeland and diasporic countries of adoption stark, compelling Filipinas to leave professions in the Philippines to work as domestics abroad; differences in living standards are also stark. For example, while living at home, "Filipina rural women have reported going without power for four to eight hours of every day and coping with little or no water. Urban women from the Philippines reported working an average 18-hour day doing domestic work, [or] laundry work outside their homes" (Chang 2000, 127). Endemic unemployment and poverty compound the daily problems confronted by Filipinos who stay at home. Disparities are even more stark for uneducated women working as domestic workers in the Philippines before migrating to work as domestics abroad. Poverty, unemployment, lack of investment in the public sector (and a strategic deinvestment in healthcare, education, and welfare programs through structural adjustment plans imposed on developing countries by international financial institutions) all make life in the Philippines precarious at worst and uncertain at best for those who remain behind (see Chang 2000, 123–154).

According to Grace Chang's *Disposable Domestics* (2000), citing the familiar statistics on Filipina overseas migrant workers (70 percent work as domestics; proportionally, more are employed abroad than at home), the massive waves of out-migration of women from the Philippines, as "exported labor" (or as those more critical of governmental policy might rebut, as commodities), "have led to public outcries that the Philippine government is selling or trafficking women" (2000, 129). Cheap labor abroad: sources of "huge sums" of remittance dollars at home: big business and high profit returns for recruitment agencies: Filipina domestics sustain economies and profit-flows – or what Appadurai calls *financescapes* – for the Philippines, for scores of host countries, for recruitment agencies (Chang 2000, 129). Remittance dollars for 1993 totaled "3.4 percent of the Gross

Domestic Product, which is the equivalent of 30 percent of the trade deficit or entire interest payments on the country's foreign debt" (2000, 130).

For the Philippines, as for some other developing countries, exporting labor has replaced exporting goods as a source of national revenue. Unsurprisingly, Filipina domestics have been lauded as diasporic "heroes" of the Philippine homeland, both by President Corazón Aquino in a state visit to Hong Kong in 1988 and by the Freedom from Debt Coalition (FDC) (Chang 2000, 136). Despite promises of upward mobility abroad, too often Filipina domestics are often regrettably deceived about expected salaries, compensated poorly for their near round-the-clock toil, subjected to racist discrimination, confronted with haranguing or humiliating verbal or mental abuse, and have even, at times, suffered violence at the hands of the employers whose houses they share (2000, 134–136). Profits for national economies; servants for affluent families from Hong Kong to Toronto, Rome to LA – Filipinas are too often indeed regarded as "disposable domestics." As Chang writes: "The trade in women from the Philippines and elsewhere has proven immensely profitable to sending countries' governments and entrepreneurs, and highly 'economical' to the governments that recruit them and the elite who employ them" (2000, 151). More forcefully, she concludes: "When debtor nations export their women as migrant workers in the futile effort to keep up with debt payments, these women live and work in conditions of debt bondage, mirroring the relationship between their home and 'host' countries" (2000, 151).

Catholic Institute for International Relations (CIIR) statistics, published in 1987, document "over a million and a half Filipinos employed as contract workers in over 120 countries worldwide" (1987, 18; cited in Constable 1997, 20). Nicole Constable records the diasporic experiences of Filipina domestics working in Hong Kong, where in-migratory flows of domestic workers began in the 1980s as the Philippine economy declined, with soaring unemployment and rapid devaluation of the peso even as the Hong Kong economy, alongside those of the East Asian "tigers" or "dragons," thrived and the HK dollar swiftly increased in value. As Constable notes, "Hong Kong's phenomenal capitalist growth, high standard of living, and low rate of unemployment, is often contrasted to the economic instability, growing international debt, high rate of unemployment, and poverty in the Philippines" (1997, 30): although written in 1997, just before the British political "return" of Hong Kong to the Republic of China, Constable's words still remain apropos today. Taking over the domestic labor of two-income professional families, Filipina domestics allowed Hong Kong women upward social mobility carefree of "domestic chores" (1997, 21). Filipina domestics, thus, work at the sometimes vexing intersections of ethnicity, nationality, gender, and class. Private is not only public, as second-wave Anglo-American feminists asserted: it is also political and economic. As Constable writes, "shifts in the global economy, the development or underdevelopment of industrial capitalism, and political and economic changes in mainland China, the Philippines, and other regions of Asia, all have a bearing on the pattern of household work in Hong Kong" (1997, 21). Constable also sees myriad historical, political, and economic factors as operative in structuring the Philippine phenomenon of

exported labor: "Colonialism, neocolonialism, political corruption, and underdevelopment explain why the Philippines is the largest exporter of workers in the
Asia-Pacific region" (1997, 21). And these two fields – household work in Hong
Kong and Philippine labor exportation – are structurally interrelated, explaining
"why Filipino workers have come to be viewed as 'commodities' that can be
'sold' or 'traded' to solve economic problems in the Philippines and as 'resources'
that can be tapped as part of a 'natural' scenario of capitalist development in
Hong Kong" (1997, 21).

Three notable political-economic shifts are salient here: (1) the change in the
gender composition of the Hong Kong workforce; (2) the move from a production-based economy to a service economy in the country; and (3) an increase
(though marginal relative to US, European, or especially Philippine standards) in
the unemployment rate in 1995 following a low level of unemployment throughout the 1980s. First: women first entered the Hong Kong workforce in noticeable
numbers beginning in the 1960s to 1970s, increasing in the 1980s and 1990s
(Constable 1997, 24n3). "As educated women increasingly found jobs, provisions had to be made for childcare and housework" (1997, 26). Second: from
the 1970s to the 1990s, Hong Kong moved from a production-based economy
to a service economy, and reflecting similar geoeconomic patterns also discernible
in the US, manufacturing and other production-based jobs "moved across the
border" into mainland China following economic liberalization in that country,
which escalated during the ten-year period from 1980 to 1990 (1997, 25). Third:
economic boom in Hong Kong's service sector pulled migrant laborers into the
country in order to fill service jobs, especially since unemployment at the time
"remained low by US standards," never rising "above 2 percent" throughout the
1980s and into the early 1990s, although it did reach "3.5 percent in 1995"
(1997, 25). Consequently, anti-immigration sentiment and public outcry against
foreign workers, including Filipina domestics, also increased in the mid-1990s.
"Despite the increase in the unemployment rate in 1995, the demand for full-
time, live-in foreign domestics remained steady" (1997, 26). Local uneducated
Chinese women worked primarily in textiles and manufacturing in the 1970s and
in low-end service jobs (hotels, restaurants, cleaning services for corporations) in
the 1980s, preferring these jobs to in-home domestic work, which was regarded,
and indeed probably was, demeaning or debasing.

Worldwide shifts and national ones impacted the Philippines during the 1970s:
in 1972 Ferdinand Marcos, opposing labor organization and union activism
among workers in foreign-owned multinational corporations that "repatriated ... 90 percent of their profits," declared "martial law" in the country
(Constable 1997, 31); the global "oil crisis" in 1973–4 led to high crude profits
among the Gulf states but economic recession in consumer countries, including
the Philippines, which were negatively impacted by short supplies and exorbi-
tantly high oil prices. In 1973, the Hong Kong government instituted a policy of
allowing foreign nationals to work as domestic servants, which led to the migratory in-flow of Filipinos.[9] According to the International Labor Organization
(ILO), the Philippine unemployment rate hit 25 percent in 1974, the year that
Marcos initiated the Philippine policy of exported labor; and by 1975, "over 40

percent of families ... could not afford 'basic nutritional requirements'"
(Constable 1997, 32). Internationally, an increase in interest rates in 1979–80,
preceding a global economic recession from 1980 to 1982, led to a concomitant
increase in interest payments on international debts (Leahy; quoted in Constable
1997, 33); and by the 1980s, "about two-thirds of the Philippine population
lived below the poverty line" (Constable 1997, 32; according to CIIR 1987, 1).
In response, Marcos mandated remittances from overseas workers in E.O. 857,
denounced by the ILO and diasporic working Filipinos; the mandate was lifted
on May 1, 1985 after international criticism and diasporic activism by United
Filipinos against Forced Remittances, which formed in Hong Kong in 1984.
Unemployment: exported labor: human consequences. Monetary success of the
Philippine policy of exported labor is, as the Asian Migrant Centre explains,
"achieved at the cost of national dignity and unquantifiable human costs – broken
families, uncared for children at home, [and] rootless lifestyles" (1992c, 20;
quoted in Constable 1997, 33–34).

In the mid-to-late 1980s, Filipina domestics became targets of Hong Kong
ressentiment and discrimination: decried as demanding, spoiled, ungrateful, lazy,
and too uncooperative or intractable, Filipina domestics were also described by
employers, the media, and the public alike as incompatible "with the hardwork-
ing ethics and serious attitude of the Chinese" (Constable 1997, 36). Racist
charges and discrimination against Filipina domestics in Hong Kong led to the
Philippine government under the Aquino administration to ban "new contracts
for Filipino domestic workers in 1988," although it was only a "short-lived
moratorium" (1997, 35, 36).[10] Despite the influx of Indonesian and Thai women
immigrants into Hong Kong in the late 1980s to mid-1990s to work as domestics,
Filipinas – never replaced – have become so culturally and linguistically associated with domestic service "that the term *banmui* 'Philippine girl' is used inter-
changeably with 'maid' or 'servant'" (1997, 38). Most Filipinas working as
domestics entered the country through fee-based recruitment agents who profit
in the global trade in domestic services: advertisements circulated by the agencies
often pejoratively depict Filipinas as "commodities" to be bought, sold, circulated, replaced: "The domestic worker is marketed as though she were an inani-
mate household appliance: she comes in various models, goes on sale, includes
a warranty, and can easily be replaced if the customer is not satisfied" (1997,
62). Migrant domestic workers, from the Philippines and elsewhere, are often
regarded as commodified bodies and purchased labor circulating in the new
global economy.

In the next chapter, "Global Traffic," we will thus further address the notions
of commodified bodies and bought labor, as well as examine how these are gendered phenomena. We will also open the discussion of diaspora and diasporic
studies to the more nefarious realities of international human trafficking – both
sexual trafficking and labor trafficking – and coerced work under global capitalist
economies worldwide. While not the solitary focus, the chapter will foreground
the issues of prostitution, trafficking in women, the multinational sex industry, sex
work, and the distinctions between voluntary and involuntary sex workers with
comparisons to other forms of human trafficking and contemporary slave labor.

Questions for Reflection and Discussion

- What are historically gendered patterns of economic migration?
- How has there been a "feminization of migration" since the 1970s? If so, what led to this shift?
- How and why have some forms of manufacturing and service-sector jobs led to gendered patterns of economic migration?
- Why, in your opinion, do manufacturing and service-sector industries target women, specifically, as economic migrants?
- Is there an international "trade in care" (healthcare, childcare, elderly care, cleaning care)? If so, what are the material benefits to the host countries receiving these service care workers? And what are the costs (material, national, medical, psychological, emotional, or other) to the exporting countries who lose these service care workers to out-migration?
- How do gendered forms of economic out-migration not only lead to a "brain drain," but also a "care drain," or even "mommy drain" (considering that many women migrate to support children who remain behind at home with siblings, parents, or other relatives)?

Additional Research

Thinking through writing

Conduct independent research through surveys, telephone interviews, or written correspondence with a local hospital administrator or nurse recruitment officer in your town; and then write a research paper that overviews your findings. (If possible, and feasible, compare statistics in your municipality with those in a town nearby.)

Questions to consider about research
- What percentage of the nursing staff (RNs, LPNs, and NAs) are foreign-born immigrants?
- Where were the nurses recruited? By whom? How?
- What recruitment packages does the local hospital offer as incentives for nurses who migrate to work in this institution?

3

Global Traffic

Sexual economic migrations present a vexing set of intractable issues. Even the terms of the argument are not immediately clear or transparent: contested, continually debated and revised, fractiously and ideologically divided, the arguments seemingly devolve into dichotomized perspectives: sex work or coerced prostitution? Voluntary trade in sex services or involuntary violence against women? Sexual migrations or human trafficking? Both: it depends. Yet the distinctions are too often obscured, too often reduced to *indistinction*; and what is ultimately lost is our ability to discern and thus document those differences. Trying to survey the vast, vexing, and seemingly landmine-pocked landscape of migrants working in the sex industry is indeed a difficult task. There are many unresolved distinctions, ideologically debated terms, and other intractable problems within the existing scholarship. For example, are these migrations voluntary or involuntary? Are these patterns of movement forms of sex migrations or examples of illegal global human trafficking? Is the contracted service an example of sex work or prostitution, which some feminist organizations define as inherent "violence against women"? Are these migratory patterns a global feminist issue, a human rights issue, or an international labor issue? Should these illegal migrations result in a universal effort to abolish all sex work and all sex industry services, or local, national, and regional efforts to legalize and regulate those industries while also cracking down on human trafficking? Who should spearhead these efforts – the United Nations, the International Organization for Migration, or the International Labor Organization? Well, it all depends on who you ask. Compounding the moral, political conundrum of these unresolved questions is another vexing ineluctable reality: almost all forms of "human traffic" (or "migrant smuggling") are illegal, covert, and nearly impossible to document statistically; and the international routes and modes of smuggling are often identical for the woman forced (or duped) into prostitution and another woman, perhaps sitting right beside her, who voluntarily chose to travel illegally and pay (or incur the debt of) the fees for falsified documents, contracted employment, and perilous transportation crossing the Adriatic sea from Albania to Italy in a high-speed boat or riding across the Nepal-India border at night!

Actually, the answer to some of these seemingly contradictory questions is an un-paradoxical "yes": yes, some women (and children) are trafficked illegally and internationally for sexual exploitation in both black market and legally authorized brothels, pornography rings, telephone sex servicing companies, and street prostitution; yes, some women voluntarily choose to sell (or rent out) the only property owned outright in their names – their bodies – and choose to pay often exorbitant fees or incur debts to be repaid in order to be illegally smuggled across national borders. "However distasteful the idea may be to certain groups," Melissa Ditmore writes, "sex work is a form of labor," and the International Labor Organization (ILO) "estimates that the sex sector accounts for between 2 and 14 percent of the GDP of Asian countries; namely Indonesia, Malaysia, the Philippines, and Thailand (Lim 1998, 7)" (2005, 120).

Poles along the spectrum of this debate are manifest in the approaches, objectives, and points of contention between two of the major organizations involved: the Coalition Against Trafficking in Women (CATW) and the Global Alliance Against Trafficking in Women (GAATW). Founded in 1988, CATW is an international feminist nongovernmental organization that attained Category II Consultative Status with the United Nations Economic and Social Council in 1989; co-directed by Janice G. Raymond and Dorchen A. Leidholdt, the NGO has a powerful voice and profound political sway in international debates over and national policies on human trafficking and prostitution. Adopting a feminist approach to human trafficking, the major objectives of CATW include defining all prostitution as "violence against women"; abolishing all forms of "human trafficking"; eradicating all forms of prostitution and "buying and selling" in sex services related to trafficking in women and children, including pornography, phone sex, and cybersex. CATW has been in the lead in efforts to establish a United Nations Convention Against Sexual Exploitation, which it hopes to see adopted by the UN as an article of international law. Founded in 1994 in Thailand as a dissenting voice to the abolitionist feminist principles of CATW, GAATW adopts an intersectional approach to the issue of human trafficking that tackles the issue from feminist, human rights, and labor perspectives. Major objectives of GAATW include distinguishing between involuntary sexual slavery/debt servitude and voluntary sex work; advocating for the legalization and regulation of the sex industry; pressing for labor rights (minimum wage, standardized practices, and worker protections/benefits); and abolishing all forms of involuntary "human trafficking" (abduction, deception, coercion).

Scholars and activists associated with CATW include, in addition to Raymond and Leidholdt, Melissa Harley, Esohe Aghatise, and Gunilla Ekberg. Scholars and activists associated with GAATW include Kamala Kempadoo, Jyoti Sanghera, Bandana Pattanaik, Lin Chew, and Elaine Pearson, and this research-policy group has worked on legalizing and legitimating sex work and sex workers' rights as well as anti-trafficking efforts. Independent scholars working on issues related to the international trafficking of human beings include Marjan Wijers, Melissa Ditmore, Jo Doezema, Lisa Law, Kevin Bales (founder of Free the Slaves), David

Feingold (a consultant for UNESCO), Lin Lean Lim, Ronald Skeldon, John Frederick, and Anand Tamang. Francine Pickup (1998) has eschewed the international "politics" in sex trafficking research, suggesting that an anthropological lens may be more useful and less ideological in research on the issue. Ronald Skeldon (2000) argues that the cultural, historical context of the sex industry in Southeast Asia is unique and cannot be simply explained or definitively categorized as "trafficking" *tout simple*. Julie Cwickel and Elizabeth Hoban (2005) similarly argue for intellectual and theoretical approaches that navigate (or mediate) the ideologically overdetermined presuppositions that too often drive, fuel, and fund research on sex traffic and prostitution. Another dissenting voice, Laura Agustín (2006) has been critical of the monolithic approach to prostitution as human traffic and as inherently violent, by definition, and has pressed for opening the terrain of sex-work migration to alternative theoretical approaches, including those offered by the theoretical lenses of migration, diasporic, and transnational studies.

Common routes are discernible in sex migration, smuggling, or trafficking. Points of arrival often include Australia, New Zealand, the United States, the United Kingdom, Greece, Germany, Italy, Spain, and other countries in the European Union, the Middle East, particularly the Gulf states, Japan, Taiwan, and other developed East Asian countries, as well as Thailand, India, and Pakistan. Migratory points of departure are frequently countries in the Caribbean, particularly the Dominican Republic, Russia, Albania and other countries in Eastern Europe, including "newly independent states" (NIS) that formed when the Soviet Union collapsed, as well as Thailand, Myanmar, Nepal, Bangladesh, the Philippines, and other developing Asian and Pacific countries. In South Asia and Southeast Asia, especially the Mekong region (Cambodia, China, Laos, Myanmar, Thailand, and Vietnam), there is also a great deal of inter-regional migration of prostitutes. Roberta Espinoza, in *Global Woman*, lists geographical migratory routes for sex-trade smuggle or traffic. Two well-traveled roads include the journey from the Philippines to Italy and from Nigeria to Italy (Espinoza 2002, 277–278). Although Italy is a common point of arrival for those working in the sex industry, many of the women arriving on Italian shores or through Roman airports are almost certainly dispersing to other European cities that have a thriving sex industry, such as Berlin and Amsterdam. Less dominant but still traceable routes include movement from Guatemala to Spain; Colombia and Brazil to Western Europe; the Philippines to Japan, Taiwan, Hong Kong, and Malaysia; Cambodia to Thailand and Malaysia; Vietnam to Thailand and Cambodia; Myanmar (formerly Burma) to Thailand; Bangladesh to Pakistan and India; Nepal to India; India to Pakistan and Sri Lanka; Sri Lanka to Pakistan; Albania to Greece; Romania to Turkey; and Russia and the Ukraine to Western Europe (Espinoza 2002, 280).

That involuntary and voluntary forms of illegal smuggling related to the international sex trade coexist and often travel the same paths is a testament to the scholarly need for critical distinctions among the terms of the argument: trafficking; smuggling; sex work; sex slavery; debt bondage; recruitment loans. "Trafficking" is the illegal and coercive buying, selling, trading, circulating, and transporting of humans against their will. "Smuggling," though also illegal, is not synonymous with trafficking: smuggling is the illegal but voluntary transportation and border-crossing (nationally, regionally, internationally) of undocumented migrants, those traveling without passports, visas, or other official documents explicitly authorizing that person to enter a country; likewise, smuggling includes individuals crossing borders with falsified or fraudulent documents. "Sex work" includes the voluntary trade for monetary profit in sexual services that includes an array of sex acts – oral, anal, genital, receptive, penetrative – as well as other erotic practices: dancing, stripping, whipping, verbal fantasizing, mutual masturbation, and scores of countless other paid services from the sanitized to the hardcore graphic for sexual arousal and pleasure; it may also include, but may not be limited to, all sorts of pornography, from photography to film to live performance. (One can imagine the rest of what it may include, if one so desires.) Key to defining "sex work," however, are two words: consenting adults. "Sex slavery," in contrast, includes a similar range of sex acts and erotic practices with one crucial distinction: it is not voluntary. Sex slaves are those (men, women, children, heterosexual, homosexual, bisexual, or transsexual) who are coerced into prostitution or any other sector of the sex industry against their will through deception, debt bondage, or coercion that need not be physical, but may also be psychological or financial. Sex slaves are victims not only of coerced labor, sexual exploitation, and human rights, but also of intimidation, mental abuse, violence, and more. "Debt bondage," a common form of financial coercion into sexual slavery, is the practice of forcing individuals to "work off" the costs of transportation, housing, clothing, and food incurred during their movement across national borders and their residence once there: this is common when individuals knowingly migrate for economic reasons, sign "contracts" agreeing to repay transportation costs, but are deceived either about the sexual nature of the work contracted or the exploitative work conditions; it is less common, of course, when trafficked individuals are actually abducted and sold into slavery, whether sexual or domestic or other forms of compulsory labor. And finally, "recruitment loans" – a common form of contractual obligations of economic migrants to recruiting agents and agencies – are the work-repayment of all the same aforementioned costs (transportation, housing, clothing, and food) incurred during and after movement. In the former case, the "debt" is used to manipulate, coerce, and control the indebted individual; in the latter, while the same could also be arguably true, it is typically regarded as an opportunity for economic migrants, sex workers or maids, to migrate even if they initially lack the financial resources to do so alone.

Sex workers voluntarily working in the industry do not change the reality that women and children are illegally and involuntarily trafficked daily into sexually exploitative forms of labor. My point, then, is not that sex trafficking does not exist: it does. Rather, my point is this: critical distinctions are absolutely necessary in order to obtain and document accurate information about migratory flows, legal and illegal, and about economic migrants in the sex industry, voluntary and involuntary. We must also remain cognizant of the fact that the new posterchild (or woman) – of "slavery's new face" – of human trafficking does not render all sex work slavery. As Skeldon explains,

The image of the young girl sold out of poverty to unscrupulous brokers, or kidnapped from a village and transported to the city where she is kept in sordid conditions to serve an endless procession of men until she is eventually released to return home to die of AIDS, is a powerful driving force for many to seek the elimination of the worst forms of trafficking and child labor. (2000, 17)

Rhetorically persuasive, emotionally compelling, this image has become the icon of anti-trafficking campaigns internationally, leading to calls for the universal and unconditional abolition of not only human trafficking, but also of prostitution and the entire sex industry worldwide. This image – compelling though it is – does not tell the whole story, though it undeniably tells part of the story; yet to deny that the image is a partial or fractional one is intellectually dishonest, politically myopic, and profoundly unjust to the ones who do suffer such indignity and debasing sexual enslavement. "That such events occur," Skeldon continues, "seems indisputable. How common they are is much more difficult to access" (2000, 17). More pointedly, Agustín writes, "numerous feminist and activist authors insist that hundreds and thousands of women have been forcibly 'trafficked' to Europe, that 'prostitution' can never be a job in the conventional sense of the word and that those disputing these ideas are actually enemies of migrant women themselves" (2006, 40).[1] At end, though, we agree that sexual enslavement of the poor and vulnerable by powerful, wealthy, organized crime rings, or even by small-time, petty local criminals, occurring "at all appears an indictment of modern patterns of development," and more precisely, of uneven development (Skeldon 2000, 17). But, as Skeldon importantly clarifies, "perhaps the most critical contribution of the debate has been," and will continue to be, the "move away from the woman as victim interpretation . . . to an acceptance of the complexity of the sex sector" (2000, 18).

Collapsing distinctions between voluntary and involuntary forms of sexual migrations not only clouds the international issue and "murkies" already umbrous waters, but could exacerbate the perils, risks, and abuses for those involved. For example, sex workers entering the profession voluntarily confront a host of issues that might be easily eradicated if prostitution and other sex services were legalized, regulated, and governmentally sanctioned: violation of labor laws; minimum wage requirements; violence in the work place; employer abuse; unsafe sex practices; illegal trafficking of drugs by clients; and so on, and so on. And making the sex industry legal might destigmatize (and obviously, decriminalize) sex work, exculpate those working from criminal punishment, and make it more likely that legal sex workers would help authorities identify and protect those involuntarily there. Other problems exist within the current scholarly writing on the issue: the feminist focus in the wealth of scholarly studies on the issue over-emphasizes the institutional "victimhood" of sex-trafficked women and children sold into sex slavery or debt bondage, obscuring the fact that many involved in the migratory selling of sex (and their bodies) are adult men and transsexuals.

Add to this problematic the irrefutable fact that human trafficking and forced labor are not just operative within the sex industry, but also within a wide array of other forms of labor. Unsurprisingly, less "sensational" forms of coerced labor and human traffic get scant attention by comparison. Human trafficking is undeniably an international phenomenon in the new global economy: trafficked individuals are persons – adults and children, men and women, boys and girls – who are bought, sold, traded, bound by debt, and then transported involuntarily across borders (local, national, regional, or trans-continental) for the purpose of forced labor, whether that compulsory labor be in offshore fishing, quarry mining, domestic service, or the sex industry. While the international trafficking in women and children who are sexually exploited victims of the sex industries in prostitution, pornography, and other areas have drawn the most media (typically sensationalized) and government attention, other forms of human trafficking are just as pervasive, if not more so. Many factors have exacerbated the illegal trafficking in human subjects: the closing or tightening of legal routes of entry into countries through restrictive immigration laws; the anti-immigrant sentiments that have led to the international closing of national borders, including to those seeking political asylum, which has led to a "refugee crisis" since the 1990s; the international traffic in drugs and narcotics trans-shipment that facilitates illegal routes of entry and "outlaw" modes of cross-border movement; organized multinational corporate crime rings; disorganized, small, petty, but no less pervasive business in the traffic of persons; and the lack of international regulation over multinational corporations, not to mention black markets and disorganized microbusinesses. All of these facts suggest that human trafficking is an international labor, human rights, and migration issue, not simply a feminist one. To reduce human trafficking to the "traffic in women" not only erroneously equates voluntary sex work with coerced forms of sex slavery, which is clearly misguided, but also turns an indifferent, blind eye to the anonymous millions who are forced into other physically excruciating, mentally debilitating, debasing, humiliating, mundane, or menial – not to mention compulsory! – forms of coerced labor that exist across the world today. Having established that critical and conceptual distinctions are necessary, let's review some of what we do know and can account for (from interviews and other research) on sex work, sex trafficking, and the larger global phenomenon of human trafficking (all forms of labor, not merely sexual).

Sex Work

For every statistic documenting, or estimating, the percentage of involuntary migrant sex workers in a country or region, there is an ineluctable inverse reality: the statistics for those who are voluntary migrant sex workers. By inverting (or reframing) some of the international estimates above for sex trafficking and sex traffic victims, we see a different picture of the sex industry and the voluntary presence of not only women, but also men and FTM and MTF transsexuals in it. To take a hypothetical example, if 45 percent of the sex workers in a massage parlor in Berlin, or 32 percent of migrant street prostitutes in Milan, can be documented as sex trafficking victims through detention and deportation records, or through prosecutory state testimony, asylum applications, and NGO interviews, then an inverse picture of sex industries in these two European cities may also come into view: that is, as many as 55 percent of sex workers in the Berlin parlor and 68 percent of migrant prostitutes working the streets of Milan may be there voluntarily. Just as it is incredibly difficult to ascertain the number of sex traffic victims, it is equally difficult to discern the precise number of individuals who enter sex work by choice. The sex trade is often covert, criminalized, and unregulated; yet it is big business and multinational, if not global, trade. For precisely these reasons, and because so many individuals worldwide – women, men, and transsexuals – do choose to voluntarily enter sex work for both migratory and monetary reasons, international nongovernmental organizations like the Network of Sex Workers Projects (NSW), founded in 1991, and GAATW, formed in 1994, have led efforts both to abolish human trafficking – not simply of sex workers, but of all coerced workers – and to advocate on behalf of voluntary sex workers for the protection of human and labor rights.[2] For these international NGOs and for many sex workers' rights advocates, anti-trafficking campaigns are too frequently anti-migrant, anti-prostitution, anti-labor; or as Josephine Ho writes, their efforts have formed an international, hegemonic "anti-sex industry" (2005, 98).

In the edited collection *Global Sex Workers*, Kamala Kempadoo and Jo Doezema document a global sex workers' rights movement, which began in the United States and Western Europe in the late 1970s and early 1980s but spread throughout the "developing" world – South America, the Caribbean, West and South Africa, Australia, New Zealand, and Asia and Pacific countries – during the 1990s, giving an account of the struggle of prostitutes to gain recognition as sex workers in an industry that should be legalized, regulated, and sanctioned if in violation of their labor rights. "If sexual labor," Kempadoo and Doezema explain, "is seen to be subject to exploitation, as with any other labor, it can also be considered as a basis for mobilization in struggles for working conditions, rights and benefits and for broader resistances against the oppression of working peoples, paralleling situations in other informal and unregulated sectors" (1998, 8). These prostitutes, as Kempadoo and Doezema saliently note, were not organizing for the abolition of prostitution, but rather for its legalization and governmental labor regulation. Because the women and men and transsexuals coming together to demand their rights, benefits, and protection did not identify as "victims," the editors also do not identify them as such; they demanded the right to be taken seriously and protected from exploitation, violence, and abuse as sex *workers*. It is also important to note that the women, men, and transsexuals also did not identify as prostitutes (or more pejoratively, as whores), but insisted on prostitution as a form of work, not as a psychic or emotional ground for their identities as working people. And the scope of the sex workers' rights movement, like sex work itself, is transnational in its industry practices (sex migrations, sex trade online, sex tourism),[3] and global in its scope. Following the founding of prostitute rights organizations in France, Britain, Germany, Australia, Canada, and the United States in the 1970s and 1980s, the International Committee for Prostitutes' Rights (ICPR) formed in 1985, and the first World Whores Congress was held in the Netherlands during the same year, which culminated in the World Charter of Prostitutes' Rights.[4] In 1982, the Ecuadorian Association of

Autonomous Women Workers was founded and the organization sponsored a prostitute strike in 1988 to demand better work conditions and rights. Prostitutes in Brazil held a conference in 1987 that led to the forming of the National Network of Prostitutes and the formation of the Network of Sex Work Projects (NSWP) in 1991 (Kempadoo and Doezema 1998, 20). Similar prostitute organizations – fighting not only for labor rights but for safe-sex requirements in the industry and government enforcement to combat the spread of HIV/AIDS – emerged across South American countries in the early 1990s, including in Chile, Peru, Venezuela, and Suriname, and then rapidly into Central America (Nicaragua, Guatemala), Mexico, and parts of the Caribbean. Similar efforts and activist battles were taking place across the globe from Kenya and South Africa to India and Indonesia, Tasmania and Taiwan, Thailand and Japan (Kempadoo and Doezema 1998, 21–22).

Kempadoo has been a leading voice in efforts to represent the daily struggles and labor rights activism of sex workers globally, paying key attention to the activist efforts of prostitutes and sex workers in the Caribbean. *Sun, Sex, and Gold: Tourism and Sex Work in the Caribbean* (1999), edited by Kempadoo, examines the intersections of global capitalism, tourism, and the impact of sex tourism on the small developing countries of the Caribbean (with essays focusing specifically on sex tourism in Cuba, the Dominican Republic, Jamaica, Barbados, St. Maarten, Curaçao, Belize, Suriname, and Guyana) in the historical context of European colonial domination and slavery in the region. It also explores the intersections of sex tourism and the desire to buy and sell the sexual "exotic" with the political economy of race, gender, and sexuality in the archipelago.

Kempadoo explores the Caribbean sex industry further in the book *Sexing the Caribbean* (2004), as does Denise Brennan in *What's Love Got to Do With It?* (2004). Both note the phenomenon of cross-regional sex migrations, particularly sex worker or prostitute out-migrations from the Dominican Republic to other parts of the Caribbean, including Haiti, Curaçao, Antigua, Panama, St. Maarten, and Suriname (Kempadoo 2004, 142). According to Kempadoo, by 1996, "50,000 Dominican women were estimated to be engaged in sex work outside the country" (2004, 142). Kempadoo also documents cross-regional sex migrations by women sex workers from Guyana to Suriname, Trinidad and Tobago, and Barbados, from Trinidad to Barbados and Colombia, and from Haiti to the Dominican Republic (DR), Curaçao, and Barbados, as well as from countries in South and Central America (Brazil, Colombia, Honduras, Guatemala, and El Salvador) into the Caribbean region. And finally, she notes patterns of male sex worker migration from Jamaica to the DR and Cuba (2004, 142). Importantly, Kempadoo discovered through brothel interviews with sex workers in Curaçao that about 50 percent of the workers who migrated to the Antillean island after signing employment contracts admitted that they knew that the contracted work was sex work, and further notes that "there was little evidence that the women were enslaved or physically held against their wills, yet [also notes that] some freedoms and rights were curtailed and impinged upon and [that] the women faced specific types of economic coercion" (2004, 150–151). Loans to cover incurred costs and resultant accumulated debts were, as expected, common in sex work migrations to Curaçao, Cuba, Colombia, and the DR (2004, 151). Other violations were common: smuggling, indebtedness, or worker financial entrapment, and deception during the "recruitment" process. It is not only recruiters and pimps who are exploitative, but also clients (or "johns") and even police: according to Amalia Lucía Cabezas, "sex workers in Belize, Colombia, the Dominican Republic, Guyana, Jamaica, and Suriname have reported many instances of harassment, robbery, extortion, coercion, and violence" (2005, 203).

Focusing exclusively on the Dominican Republic, Denise Brennan examines the contemporary phenomenon of transnational out-migration strategies by both Dominican male sex workers (pejoratively called "sankies" or "sanky-pankies")[5] and female Dominican sex workers who try to turn paid trysts with sex tourists in the country into romantic liaisons and potential marriage proposals as a way out of Dominican poverty and the country, and of securing a visa into a wealthier country where they can migrate-by-marriage, which the anthropologist describes as a postmodern, global capitalist *sexscape* (drawing on the algebraic vocabulary of Arjun Appadurai to name discordant movements or diasporic flows within the traffic of the global economy). For these migrant sex workers, the ultimate sex act, or sexscape, is, as Brennan writes, "performing love" transnationally: "sex workers and resort workers are hard at work selling romance along with the other goods and services they deliver" (2004, 91, 98). While sex tourists visiting the DR from Canada, the UK, the US, Germany, or other countries may be seeking "sun, sex, and gold" – to quote the title of Kempadoo's edited collection – and above all fun and pleasure, the sex workers that they hire may be deliberately planning post-erotic strategies for asking their clients to visit again, plan trips together, wire money, apply for visas, and more (2004, 98, 110). Like other prostitutes from Latin America and the Caribbean who have formed part of the global sex workers' rights movement, the men and women of Sosúa, Dominican Republic have organized to address the issues of violent clients and police harassment (Brennan 2004, 155–161). Dominican women – both those who are sex workers and those who are not – but who frequent tourist resorts and night clubs are also subjected to police harassment: "Nightly, police arrest women *en masse* as they exit discos or congregate in the streets and restaurants of tourist resorts in the Dominican Republic" (Cabezas 2005, 202). Cabezas also notes that

> the state stigmatizes and criminalizes, as potential sex workers, local women who visit tourist areas. Particularly vulnerable are young women without male companions, but ultimately all women are subject to these disciplining tactics and face restrictions on their freedom of movement. Charged with "bothering tourists," they are subject to arbitrary arrest and detention and to bodily harm, sexual violence, and verbal abuse from police officers. (2005, 202)

As in many geographic locations across the globe, Dominican sex work is opportunity and exploitation, money and abuse, choice and violation of rights. Still, Dominican sex workers, at a UN-sponsored conference on sex work in Latin America and the Caribbean, actively opposed efforts to abolish prostitution in the country and also rejected the language of abolitionist discourses, including "trafficking in women," as "elitist and male-dominated," and inapplicable "to the Latin American context" (Cabezas 2005, 219). And like Kempadoo and Cabezas, Brennan documents exploitation as well as agency and choice in the Dominican sex industries, providing "a nuanced picture of women [and men] who confront the inequities of globalization" (2004, 182).

On the sexual economics of voluntary sex work and the *choice* to do it, both in the United States and in less affluent geographical locations, Amber L. Hollibaugh (in *My Dangerous Desires*) makes a point that may seem obvious to some, but disputable to others who see agency and choice in different terms: "The bottom line," Hollibaugh maintains,

> for any woman in the sex trades is economics. However a woman feels when she finally gets full tilt into the life, it always begins as survival – to pay the rent, buy medicine for the kids, buy drugs for yourself, run away from an abusive home, live despite lack of documentation, live out a "bad" reputation, flee from incest. Yes; it always starts with just trying to get by. (2000, 181–182)

Regardless of what other factors may enter into the decision to do sex work, economics is definitely part (if not the sum total) of the equation. Geetanjali Gangoli, documenting voluntary sex work in East India, agrees: "There are close connections between migration, poverty and women who enter into sex work" (2006, 214). In Kolkata, West Bengal and in Orissa, the two states in Eastern India that she researched, Gangoli asserts that "acute poverty is the single most important reason for women joining sex work" (2006, 215). Like others working under the "sex work" theoretical paradigm, rather than the "sex traffic" model, Gangoli notes that "while many women started off by narrating stories of coercion and violence, once a relationship had been established, their stories often changed," suggesting that women in sex work defensively learn a "script" dictated by shame, social stigma, criminal activity, and potential punishment that fosters accounts of "innocent victimhood," when the reality may be complicity and choice (2006, 216). "Truth" in this context may be almost impossible to uncover, but certainly "voluntary" sex work seems to be a constrained choice or option, one impacted by poverty, lack of opportunity, illiteracy, and other factors.

Although not focusing explicitly on sex worker smuggling, or the international migratory patterns of Southeast Asian sex workers, Lisa Law's anthropological research (published as *Sex Work in Southeast Asia*) on sex work and the sex industry in Southeast Asia, generally (and Cebu, Philippines, more specifically), also offers trenchant insights for rethinking the dominant ideological discourses that position all prostitution as violence against women, and all sex work migration as trafficking. Drawing on feminist theorizations of the body (influenced by the writings of Michel Foucault, particularly *Discipline and Punish* and *The History of Sexuality*) that posit bodies as material formations that are constructed through power, play of forces, and ideological discourses, Lisa Law suggests that prostitute bodies are the objects of a disciplinary power that polices morals and public health, and become marked by the practices they engage in (e.g. when and where they engage in business, who their customers are, whether or not they use condoms, etc.). These practices are surveyed, regulated and controlled – usually but not exclusively through the machinery and technologies of the "state" – and this exertion of power creates much knowledge about a pathologized subject ("prostitution"). (2000, 24)

Linking these more deterministic ideas about corporeality as a "construct" with geographical writings on space and how bodies move though space, alter spatial configurations, and yet are also altered by space and spatial relations, Law also insists that prostitutes are not passive or docile receptacles of power, but rather are active, moving agents that are constructed through power relations: "The bodies of Southeast Asian sex workers make movements through space: through red light districts, health clinics, through local communities and the spaces their customers also inhabit (e.g. clubs, hotels and beach resorts" (2000, 24). Provocatively, Law also suggests that the writings of postcolonial scholars influenced by Foucault, such as Edward Said (in *Orientalism*) and Ann Laura Stoler (in *Race and the Education of Desire*), reinforce notions of the "Orient," of "orientalism," and thus also of Asian people in ways that implicitly reinscribe geographical and corporeal terrains as both passive and feminine, reinforcing, perhaps unconsciously, pejorative and pervasive stereotypes about Asian women (2000, 128n3).

Significantly, following Doezema and others, Law also intellectually and politically disrupts the *prostitute victim/sex worker agent* binary so foundational to feminist and labor activist discourses on the sex industry, illustrating how feminist discourses too often position prostitutes as "victims" in need of rescuing or saving from enslavement in sex trafficking enterprises and how labor rights activists, with whom Law is clearly more sympathetic, define the same individuals as sex "workers." International HIV/AIDS prevention campaigns led to both a renegotiation of the terms of the debate and direct collaborative efforts to work with sex workers, rather than simply on behalf of them. As Law explains, "Because 'empowering' women to protect themselves from HIV/AIDS is considered an urgent priority, perspectives that characterize women as victims have been challenged by an agency-centred, participatory approach to education[, which] . . . introduces a new prostitute subject: a 'sex worker' agent capable of managing her own destiny" (2000, 97). Perhaps unsurprisingly, "activism around sex work as a form of work as well as an issue of rights has occurred more frequently at international HIV/AIDS conferences than at conferences about women" (2000, 98).

Members of GAATW and individual scholars have also collaborated on transnational activist, policy-based, and scholarly research projects, including the edited volume *Trafficking and Prostitution Reconsidered: New Perspectives on Migration, Sex Work, and Human Rights* (Kempadoo, Sanghera, and Pattanaik 2005), which was the culmination of "feminist participatory action research" workshops held by the international NGO in 2000 and 2001. Co-edited by Kamala Kempadoo, a social science researcher and transnational feminist activist, the collection of essays approaches the issue of trafficking "not as the enslavement of women, but as *the trade and exploitation of labor under conditions of coercion and force*, [as] analyzed from the lives, agency, and rights of women and men who are involved in a variety of activities in a transnationalized world" and attempts to disrupt "the contemporary hegemonic discourse on trafficking, and [also] advance an approach that supports the humanity, agency, and rights of the poor" (2005, viii, ix). In her chapter to the book, Jyoti Sanghera critiques the hegemony of global (and universalizing) discourses of human trafficking and the political-policy sway that these feminist discourses have had in the United Nations and other national organizations, such as the United States Agency for International Development (USAID) and the US State Department. Ratna Kapur, in her chapter to *Trafficking and Prostitution Reconsidered*, argues that trafficking has become an international migration and border control (or border patrol) issue that reinforces global inequality among rich and poor states, affluent citizens of developed countries and displaced, impoverished migrants of the developing (or underdeveloped) countries. Phil Marshall and Susu Thatun address the misguided efforts of abolitionist organizations and the negative impact that their anti-trafficking agendas have actually had in the Mekong region.[6] In her essay, Lin Chew traces her own personal shift from a feminist anti-trafficking perspective (through work in the Dutch nongovernmental organization STV) to a labor- and human rights-based one. Josephine Ho details how anti-trafficking discourses are both anti-prostitution and anti-sex, revealing a white, middle-class, protestant, and affluent "panic" about sex, sexuality, and sex acts. Melissa Ditmore, also critical of the anti-sex focus of anti-trafficking advocates (particularly those who equate all sex work, even voluntary, with violence against women), deconstructs the ideological underpinnings of an internationally dominant anti-trafficking coalition that unites abolitionist feminists, Christian conservatives, and neoconservative politicians in the United States. John Frederick similarly unpacks the "myth" of sex trafficking of Nepali women in India. Kampadoo, in an edited chapter in the book, collects the first-person accounts of individuals affiliated with sex workers' rights organizations in Hong Kong, India, China, and Thailand. Kalpana Viswanath, in collaboration with the research organization Jagori, compiles a forceful and compelling documentary on human trafficking and coerced labor in non-sex sectors of the global economy, revealing that the overemphasis on sex trafficking worldwide obscures the larger reality of slave labor in less scandalous, less sensationalizing, less moralizing, and perhaps even less "sexy" forms of work. Jan Boontinand, recounting anti-trafficking efforts led by GAATW in the Mekong region, describes how the international NGO actively collaborated with sex workers and women's organizations in the region, particularly in Vietnam and Cambodia. Aftah Ahmed provides both an alternative definition of trafficking and a new model for anti-trafficking efforts. For Ahmed, a "second-generation" definition of trafficking is one that deemphasizes illegal crossing of national borders and contrarily underscores exploitative conditions post-migration, including violation of labor and human rights of victims, as well as one that does not myopically focus on sex traffic while eclipsing other forms of human traffic. Natasha Ahmad, in the final chapter of the book, tackles the "tenuous line between 'trafficking' and 'migration'" – or between trafficked humans and economic migrants moving from Bangladesh to India – and directly and indiscriminately advocates for the human and labor rights of all migrants, regardless of their legal, political, or economic classification (Kempadoo 2005, xxviii).

Sex Trafficking

Still, global sex trafficking paints a grim and brutish portrait of the world, its malefaction, its greed, its rottenness: according to a report published in 2001 in the *Trafficking in Migrants Quarterly Bulletin*, a venue affiliated with the International Organization of Migration (IOM), approximately 700,000 to 2 million women and children (mostly, though not always, girls) are trafficked "across international borders every year," including the following breakdowns by geographical region: 250,000 from Asia; 100,000 from the former Soviet Union; 100,000 from Latin America and the Caribbean; and 50,000 from African countries (quoted in Watts and Zimmerman 2002). No doubt, sex trafficking in women and children yields massive profits globally to those involved in it, whether large-scale multinational crime rings or local, low-capital smugglers, creating the "third largest source of profits for organized crime, after guns and narcotics, at some US$6 billion" (Skeldon 2000, 13). While profits in sex-trade traffic are typically estimated at approximately US$7–10 billion annually, some estimate as high as $12 billion (Cwikel and Hoban 2005, 306). Admittedly, estimates of sex traffic profits are merely "guestimates" predicated upon other estimates – the number of women and children trafficked each year, the known revenues of the global sex industry by country or region, and adjusted rates to account for unknown elements and transactions in the buying and selling of sex (Cwikel and Hoban 2005, 306). According to Interpol, sex trafficking is "the fastest-growing crime category today" (Sulavik 2003; quoted in Cwikel and Hoban 2005, 306). Precise profits are unknown, perhaps even unknowable, though it is certain that the amount "is vast compared with the $54 million" allocated by the US State Department to combat trafficking internationally (Cwikel and Hoban 2005, 206). Although the United Nations estimates that between 700,000 and 2 million women and children are sex traffic victims, as already noted, other estimates are as high as 4 million (Estes and Weiner 2001; Raymond 2001; US State Department 2002; all cited in Cwikel and Hoban 2005, 306). Estimates of sex traffic victims, like profits, are also guestimates, since these victims are most often "an invisible labor force," smuggled across international borders under perilous conditions without official travel documents (Cwikel and Hoban 2005, 306). "There will never be an accurate census of trafficked persons," Cwikel and Hoban lament, "because of the ramifications of their illegal status: they are mobile, may have illegal papers or lack documents such as national identity cards or social security numbers, and will not answer phones or mail" (2005, 313).

Jan Raymond, a leading scholar and activist in the global anti-trafficking campaign and co-director of CATW, outlines nine factors that have led to the proliferation of sex trafficking since 1989: the global spread of capitalist economic policies since the dissolution of the former Soviet Union and the "death" of communism; the consequent globalization of the sex service industry, which, like other multinational corporations, both "imports" labor and "outsources" services; the increased demand for sexual services in a globalized market in which prostitution is increasingly legal and some countries (notably, Cambodia, Thailand, Costa Rica, Mexico, and the Philippines, to which one may soon be able to add Australia, New Zealand, the Netherlands, Germany, and Italy) have strategically based their national economies on sex tourism; the persistence of sexism and the political inequality of women (and children) in many countries worldwide; the commodification of sex and thus also of women's and children's bodies as erotic objects to be bought, sold, traded, used, discarded (as Bales astutely comments: "Trafficking, enslavement, forced prostitution, and kidnapping share the distinction that they are crimes in which the victim is also the money-making 'product' of the criminal enterprise");[7] the rampant reality of the sexual abuse of children internationally; the racializing and colonialist belief that "the exotic is erotic" (Cwikel and Hoban 2005, 308); armed military conflict and warfare worldwide in a post-communist period of ethnic fighting, state dissolution, and new state formation that too often conflates sex and violence (witness rape as a tactic of war); and finally, but not inconsequentially, the closing of international and national borders as many states have legislated and implemented "restrictive immigration policies" (Cwikel and Hoban 2005, 308).

The United Nations has provided definitions – which scholars and activists, depending where their convictions may be plotted along the ideological and political spectrum, have either been formative in establishing or have contested – for both "trafficking" and "smuggling." Article 3 of the United Nations Protocol to Prevent, Suppress and Punish Trafficking in Persons, Especially Women and Children, introduced in 1993 and passed by the UN General Assembly in 2000 but still unratified by some member states, legally defines the "trafficking in persons" as constituted by all of the following:

(a) "Trafficking in persons" shall mean the recruitment, transportation, transfer, harbouring or receipt of persons, by means of the threat or use of force or other forms of coercion, of abduction, of fraud, of deception, of the abuse of power or of a position of vulnerability or of the giving or receiving of payments or benefits to achieve the consent of a person having control over another person, for the purpose of exploitation. "Exploitation" shall include, at a minimum, the exploitation of the prostitution of others or other forms of sexual exploitation, forced labour or services, slavery or practices similar to slavery, servitude or the removal of organs.

(b) The consent of a victim of trafficking in persons to the intended exploitation set forth in subparagraph (a) of this article shall be irrelevant where any of the means set forth in subparagraph (a) have been used.

(c) The recruitment, transportation, transfer, harbouring or receipt of a child for the purpose of exploitation shall be considered "trafficking in persons" even if this does not involve any of the means set forth in subparagraph (a) of this article.

(d) "Child" shall mean any person under eighteen years of age.

For comparative purposes, it may be useful to juxtapose the legal definition of "smuggling" offered in Article 3 of the United Nations Protocol against the Smuggling of Migrants by Land, Sea and Air, also unratified by some member states:

(a) "Smuggling of migrants" shall mean the procurement, in order to obtain, directly or indirectly, a financial or other material benefit, of the illegal entry of a person into a State Party of which the person is not a national or a permanent resident;

(b) "Illegal entry" shall mean crossing borders without complying with the necessary requirements for legal entry into the receiving State;

(c) "Fraudulent travel or identity document" shall mean any travel or identity document:
That has been falsely made or altered in some material way by anyone other than a person or agency lawfully authorized to make or issue the travel or identity document on behalf of a State; or
That has been improperly issued or obtained through misrepresentation, corruption or duress or in any other unlawful manner; or
That is being used by a person other than the rightful holder.

(d) "Vessel" shall mean any type of water craft, including non-displacement craft and seaplanes, used or capable of being used as a means of transportation on water, except a warship, naval auxiliary or other vessel owned or operated by a government and used, for the time being, only on government non-commercial service.

Critics of these UN definitions, as further discussed below, insist that the legal definitions of "trafficking" and "smuggling" focus more on the illegal means and methods of human transportation and overemphasize state control of national borders and the need to combat illegal immigration to the detriment of those trafficked or smuggled: in other words, these critics argue, the UN should pay more attention to the plight of those suffering through these illegal means of transport and national border-crossing than to the state's control of these crimes.

While exact global numbers of sex trafficked victims are impossible to know, for all of the aforementioned reasons, sample statistics for various region-specific and country-based studies are still revealing: from roughly 1989 until 1998, according to reports issued by the Ukraine Ministry of Interior in 1998, an "estimated 400,000 Ukrainian women [had been] . . . trafficked during the previous decade," and from 1991 until 1998, according to the IOM, an estimated 500,000 Ukrainian women became victims of sex trafficking to the Netherlands, Germany, Turkey, Greece, Cyprus, Italy, Spain, the former Yugoslavia, Bosnia and Herzegovina, Hungary, the former Czech Republic, Croatia, the United Arab Emirates, Syria, China, Japan, and Canada (Hughes 2000, 627); following the dissolution of the USSR, over 800,000 Russian and Soviet Jews immigrated to Israel, and sex traffickers stealthily "used this cover" (the massive wave of post-Soviet migration) to import 10,000 Russian and Ukrainian women as sex-trafficked victims, creating a burgeoning illegal sex industry worth US$450 million annually in the Middle Eastern country (Hughes 2000, 629); of the 80,000 to 100,000 Thai migrant prostitutes "working in Japan's sex industry in 1993," at least some are believed to have been trafficked into the country (Skeldon 2000, 19); according to researchers Liz Kelly and Linda Regan in a study on sex traffic in the United Kingdom, "500,000 women were trafficked into the EU in 1995" alone; since the mid-1990s, the ILO reports, approximately 5,000 Moldovan children and teenagers, almost exclusively girls, are trafficked from the newly independent state into Russia to forcibly work in the Russian sex industry every year (2000, 1); in 1998, the Bangkok Centre for the Protection of Children's Rights released a report claiming that over 10,000 Cambodian and Burmese [Myanmar] children were trafficked into the Thai sex industry annually; in 1999, 40 Thai sex workers were detained – at least half and possibly all were believed by authorities to be sex traffic victims – and the profits for the prostitution of these women was "at least $1.2 million" (Cwikel and Hoban 2005, 315; citing Ford 2001); in 2002, an "estimated 20,000 children prostitutes [were] working in Cambodia, many . . . from neighboring Vietnam" (*Contemporary Sexuality* 36.9: 2093).

Since the 1980s, Italy has been a common point of entry and transit for both sex trafficking and migrant smuggling of voluntary sex workers; however, according to a report in *The Lancet*, Germany is now "the main destination for trafficking of women in Europe," since the Bundesrepublik Deutschland legalized prostitution in brothels in 2003. (In May 2003, New Zealand also legalized prostitution in brothels; the Netherlands, Australia, and Italy have all since followed suit.) According to the UK-based medical journal, approximately 10,000 women from Central and Eastern European countries are trafficked into Germany each year (1954). According to the 2005 "Report of the Eastern and Horn of Africa Conference on Human Trafficking and Forced Labor," Kenya is a major transit country for sex trafficking to Germany, other parts of Europe, the Middle East, and South Africa; it is also a major destination country for regional sex traffic: women and children from Burundi, Ethiopia, Rwanda, and Tanzania frequently end up in Nairobi's sex industry (2005, 23). The same report estimates that there are 12,000 children and adolescent teenagers in Kampala, Uganda who have been trafficked into the country for "commercial sex" (2005, 25). According to Europol, citing the most recent data compiled by the IOM, estimates that 500,000 women across the globe "have been trafficked into prostitution in Europe" alone (Europol 2005, 5).

One consistent pattern persists: a few profit; others suffer profoundly. Worldwide, theirs is an all too common narrative of exploitation and misery: abducted, lured, or deceived, then transported, bought and sold, forced into prostitution or other sectors of the global sex industry, these women and children are coerced into believing that they are not only contractually bound to work, but also indebted to their traffickers for the "costs" of transporting, housing, feeding, and clothing them; isolated, vulnerable, often beaten or physically tortured and threatened, these victims are often raped by their captors and mentally "broken down" until they, fearfully, become submissive and compliant. Young girls are often the unsuspecting victims of "boyfriends" (strategic suitors who deliberately prey on the weak and seek out lonely, displaced adolescents to "befriend" and then entrap) who persuade them to run away from home or move to another country, nurtured by the false hope or ill-guided fantasy of starting a new life together abroad: they are promised love, happiness, greater opportunities for making money (in short: a way out); once trafficked out of their home countries, they are delivered into a world of illicit (and involuntary) sex trade, indebtedness, and loneliness. Difficult as it may be to believe, in some countries, girls are occasionally sold into prostitution or pornography by their own impoverished, desperate parents. Women who become victims of sex trafficking are frequently deceived into signing phony employment contracts for jobs in restaurants, bars, hotels (and making them, at least in their own susceptible minds, "responsible" for all costs incurred) – in essence, promised a chance to earn money and get out of crushing poverty – when in reality, the work will be in prostitution, sex clubs, or pornography. Trafficked into a foreign country, these women and children are frequently arrested and then deported in police crackdowns on prostitution, in countries where it is illegal, or crackdowns on illegal smuggling of migrants. And so the cycle continues. Back home, traffickers still hold them to "debts" and a life of sexual bondage, and they are traffic victims once more. Or, if they manage to escape, they are often shunned by unsympathetic families or socially ostracized. Still, the Global Fund for Women acknowledges that "while many women and girls are trafficked for the purposes of sexual exploitation, the majority of trafficked persons are exploited for their labor in the industrial and agricultural sectors, or forced into domestic servitude" (1). For this reason, it is thus crucial to place sex trafficking and sexploitation within the larger phenomenon of human trafficking and labor exploitation under global capitalism in the world today.

Human Trafficking

The Global Fund for Women defines human trafficking as "a form of modern-day slavery in which persons, predominantly women and children, are recruited by threat, deception, abduction or coercion into situations of forced labor. Human trafficking encompasses all processes of buying, selling, and moving people from one location to another against their will or by means of trickery, and it constitutes a grave violation of human rights" (1). Most scholars and activists concur with this definition and the urgency of abolishing human trafficking; given that "trafficking is a hugely complicated and multimillion dollar business," abolition may prove difficult, if not nearly impossible (Skeldon 2000, 12). United together multilaterally, nations must strive to do precisely that, however arduous. To hope to abolish human trafficking it is crucially important to understand and to tackle the global problem head-on – in other words, as a "hugely complicated and multimillion dollar business." Contrary to popular belief or media focus, human trafficking – of men, women, and children – is largely for forced economic labor, not sex work. In 2005, the ILO estimated that there were 9.5 million trafficking victims in the continent of Asia alone, but of this number only about 10 percent were victims of sex trafficking (Feingold 2005, 26). And the most recent information released by the United Nations estimates that the victims of human trafficking total 12.3 million (Kristof 2006). However, "worldwide, less than half of all trafficking victims are part of the sex trade" (ILO; cited in Feingold 2005, 26). According to the "Trafficking in Persons Report," issued by the US State Department, "the annual number of women and children trafficked for sexual exploitation" prior to 2000 was "more than 1 million, including 250,000 from Southeast Asia" (Skeldon 2000, 13). The US State Department Report for 2003 estimated that 800,000 to 900,000 people had fallen victim to human trafficking for that year. In 2006, the State Department Report estimated that 600,000 to 800,000 people were trafficked, reflecting a decline in approximately 200,000 cases in the last three years. Of this number, the State Department estimates that 70 percent were female, and 50 percent children. Europol, citing findings by the Organisation for Security and Co-Operation in Europe, estimates that 1.2 million children are trafficked annually "for exploitation and farm work, in mines and the commercial sex industry and [are] being used for begging or petty crime" (Europol 2005, 5).

Usually attributed exclusively to global organized crime, human trafficking is actually more frequently the result of numerous small-scale, disorganized crime gangs. "Trafficking *is* big business," Feingold clarifies, "but in many regions of the world . . . trafficking is mostly 'disorganized': individuals or small groups linked on an ad hoc basis" (2005, 28). Similarly, Skeldon describes trafficking as a "fissiparous operation requiring little start-up capital and little in the way of organizational capital," frequently the work of "individual entrepreneurs and petty criminal groups," or "the product of diverse groups constantly shifting in composition and alliance as the need arises" (2000, 12). The ILO estimates that "the total illicit profits produced by trafficked forced laborers in one year to be just short of $32 billion"; this amount, though very high, is only one-tenth of drug trafficking profits – a "$320 billion international trade" (Feingold 2005, 28). Two points are worth underscoring: "trafficking is fundamentally about people who need to move" (Pearson 2005); and "trafficking is often migration gone terribly wrong" (Feingold 2005, 32).

Human trafficking and coerced migrant labor is a global phenomenon with worldwide ramifications: each year approximately "50,000 Chinese may be smuggled to the US," largely from the Fujian province, "on purpose-bought ships, containers on regular shipping routes, and most commonly, on commercial airlines using both genuine and forged documentation" (Skeldon 2000, 13). According to a report published by the University of California, Berkeley Human Rights Center in 2005 documenting human trafficking in California, 57 cases of human trafficking and forced labor occurred involving "500 individuals from 18 countries" in the state during a five-year period from 1998 to 2003: the traffic victims included 36 Thai workers, 104 Mexican workers, 53 Russian workers, and 3 US workers (UC-Berkeley HRC, "Freedom Denied" 1, 9). Of these state-wide cases, 47.4 percent involved prostitution (or sex work), 33.3 percent domestic labor, 5.3 percent mail-order brides, 5.3 percent sweatshop labor for manufacturing, and 1.8 percent agricultural labor or farm work. Although only 5.3 percent of the cases related to sweatshop manufacturing, those cases involved 143 total forced laborers ("Freedom Denied" 9). A collaborative study between the NGO Free the Slaves and the UC-Berkeley Human Rights Center from 1998 to 2003 across 90 different US cities documented 11,821 cases of human trafficking: of the total, 10,000 traffic victims were Chinese; 1,500 Mexican; 250 Vietnamese; and 71 US citizens (*Hidden Slaves*; cited in "Freedom Denied"). Most cases of human trafficking in the US were found in four states – California, Florida, New York, and Texas – with both large immigrant populations and either large agrobusiness corporations or textiles manufacturing corporations. In his research on human trafficking, Skeldon documented "60 different routes from China to the US" (2000, 14). "The journey . . . can be dangerous, with dozens of people crammed into tightly confined spaces, alongside cargo shipments, often with little air, terrible sanitation, and insufficient food and water. Death through suffocation, drowning, freezing, or starvation is not uncommon" ("Freedom Denied" 11). While the Fujian province is the source of many trafficked and coerced laborers, the sources are lamentably manifold: Cambodian boys forced into deep-sea fishing (Feingold 2005, 26); Cameroonian adolescent girls working as live-in (or as is too often the case: locked-in) nannies in Washington, DC (France et al. 2000); Tamil Sri Lankans working in Western Europe; Pakistani men forced to work on construction sites in the Gulf region of the Middle East; Bangladeshi boys abducted and forced to work as camel jockeys in Dubai; or Albanian women forced to work as prostitutes in Athens, Rome, or Berlin; and Moroccan male prostitutes in Madrid. And while the "trafficking of women and children (and, more rarely, young men) for prostitution is a vile and heinous violation of human rights, . . . labor trafficking is probably more widespread" (Feingold 2005, 26). The United Nations Office on Drugs and Crime (UNODC) estimates profits in human trafficking at US$7 billion; the UN Children's Fund estimates the annual profits at US$10 billion (Feingold 2005, 28). Interpol estimates profits as high as US$19 billion (CATW 2005 Annual Report). Exactitude may be a lost cause, but clearly, people are profiting exorbitantly by buying and selling the involuntary labor of others!

Moving now from involuntary global (labor) traffic and voluntary patterns of sex workers' migrations – though the two often travel along the same international routes and through similar means of illegal migrant smuggling across borders – addressed in this chapter, to the migratory patterns of marginalized, oppressed sexual minorities in the next chapter on "Queer Diasporas," we will next trace the diasporic (border-crossing) movements and the global movements (i.e., through activist organizations) of queer politics as individuals who are sexual minorities both traverse national borders and consequently create multiple forms of transnational politics around issues of sex, sexuality, sexual freedom, sexual nonconformity, and queer community within larger diasporic communities worldwide.

Questions for Reflection and Discussion

* What is the relationship between "smuggling" and "trafficking"? How are these two terms defined? How are these two terms contradistinguished legally, politically, and materially?

- How are the phenomena of human trafficking (for coerced labor) and sex trafficking (for coerced prostitution) interrelated? How are the migratory routes, transport mechanisms, and patterns of forged documentation often similar in both cases? How are the two phenomena different?
- Why is it extremely difficult to obtain reliable statistics that distinguish voluntary and involuntary sex work?
- Why is it necessary to distinguish the terms "prostitution" and "sex work"?
- How and why is voluntary sex work a labor issue and an international migration issue, as well as a transnational gender issue?
- What are the limitations of using a gendered framework that underscores "women and children" (as in the internationally deployed and globally circulated term "trafficking in women and children") for understanding the global phenomena of sex work and sex trafficking? (Consider, for example, the roles of men, transgendered individuals, and transsexuals in the sex industry, voluntarily or involuntarily.)

Additional Research

Thinking through debating

Research the two international non-governmental organizations – Coalition Against Trafficking in Women (CATW) and the Global Alliance Against Trafficking in Women (GAATW) – which are both involved in the worldwide campaign to abolish human trafficking, but take different political stances on prostitution/sex work. In a structured debate with affirmative and negative arguments against prostitution or for sex workers' rights, outline and articulate the positions of these two international NGOs.

Thinking through writing

Using the same prompt, write a research paper that overviews the international campaign to abolish human trafficking and the roles that CATW and GAATW have played within this worldwide campaign. Also consider the roles of the United Nations and other international NGOs.

4

Queer Diasporas

Over the past decade, theorizations of "queer diaspora,"[1] which complicate the interrelated terrains of non-heteronormative practices and international migrations, have emerged as important critiques of both the heterosexual framings of diasporic studies and the nationalist (i.e., US) framings of queer studies. Moving simultaneously in two directions or along two interrelated discursive paths – *queering* diasporic studies and *diasporizing* queer studies – scholars, artists, and writers such as Kobena Mercer, Dionne Brand, the late Assotto Saint, Arnaldo Cruz-Malavé, Achy Obejas, the late Reinaldo Arenas, Juana Maria Rodriguez, Martin F. Manalansan IV, Gayatri Gopinath, David Eng, Jasbir Puar, José Esteban Muñoz, David Román, Benigno Sánchez-Eppler, Cynthia Patton, and others have offered new ways of thinking the terms *queer* and *diaspora*. Recent theorizations of queer diaspora have also sought to understand the gendered and sexuated foundations of nations, nationality, and migration, challenging both the heteronormativity of diasporic discourses – or what Gayatri Gopinath refers to as the "hegemonic nationalist and diasporic logic"[2] – and the nationalist framing of queer discourses.

Shifting from gender as the organizing category of analysis (as it was in chapters two and three), to sex, sexuality, sexual identity, sex migration, and diasporic sexual minorities, this fourth chapter discusses the globalization of sexual politics, which has moved simultaneously in two directions: the *queering* of diasporic communities; and the *diasporization* of queer communities. Queer communities have been rightly challenged for racial, national, class-based, and gender normative assumptions by working-class or poor queer folks, transgender queers, intersexed queers, FTM and MTF transsexuals, queers of color, and diasporic queers: consequently, queer studies has striven – at times, painfully – to become increasingly sensitive to racial, national, class, and gender-normative forms of privilege that negatively impact its communities; in contrast, David Eng argues that "mainstream gay and lesbian scholarship fails to embrace queerness as a critical methodology for the understanding of sexual identity as it is dynamically formed in and through racial epistemologies," also lamenting the paucity of "sustained class-based analyses of racial-formation" in gay and lesbian studies, queer studies, and ethnic studies (2001, 218). Similarly, diasporic communities have been challenged by queer individuals for their heteronormativity and patriarchal notions of gender and sexuality. As Eng contends, "the patriarchal complicities" of "cultural nationalist project[s]," including minoritarian counter-nationalist movements and their "disciplining of the domestic, the[ir] forced repression of feminine and homosexual to masculine, of the home to the nation-state, is a formation in need of queering" (2001, 210–211). Eng also importantly asks, "How might we invoke a queer and diasporic assumption of the domestic to denaturalize claims on the nation-state and home as inevitable functions of the heterosexual?" (2001, 211). This chapter further explores that question.

The chapter thus addresses queer diasporic activism – both in the country of adoption and in the country of origin – and transnational alliances among queer communities across the globe. Magazines, newsletters, GLBT organizations, and other forms of coalitional media have sought to safely "out" queer communities across the globe; however, as vocal diasporic and postcolonial queer critics have importantly noted, even homosexuality may have its class- and nationality-based normative codes, and "out" may not be the only gay way globally. It thus also examines critiques of global gay activism as being grounded within (and thus perpetuating) colonialist impulses to universalize experience and prioritize first-world over so-called third-world sexual sensibilities. In this chapter we will also detail legal political asylum cases in which sexual minorities have claimed right to asylum as individuals who have been persecuted because of their sexual orientation. The chapter also probes the legal discourses surrounding sexuality, migration, and legal protection for queer diasporic subjects, outlining the contours of sexual migration by queer individuals. (It also connects, in salient ways, to the discussions of sex tourism, sex trade, sex worker migrations, and the illegal forms of sex trafficking discussed in chapter three, since some forms of sex tourism and sex trade diasporas are queer.)

Queer Migrancy/Queer Migrations

Metaphors of migrancy abound in queer sexual discourses: "coming out" stories, for example, are structured like migration narratives with a pivotal or transitional movement from a sexually repressive space of secrecy, shame, and invisibility into one of openness, pride, and visibility (Binnie 2004, 86). The closet, being in or out, also evokes migration and metaphorical migrancy for queer subjects, yet it remains an admittedly "nebulous" zone (Eng 2001, 260n6). "The closet," David Eng suggests, "becomes an impossibly blurred space of private concern and public regulation," and the "continual blurring of in and out – and of public and private space – divests queer subjects of access to traditional notions of citizenship (e.g., the right to privacy) in a bourgeois ordering of the nation-state and public sphere" (2001, 261n6). (Issues of rights, citizenship, asylum law, anti-sodomy laws, and demarcations of the public/private are taken up again at the end of this chapter.) Noting that "anxieties about loss of home remain psychically central to queer (as well as racialized) cultural projects," Eng explains that "the often literal ejection of queers from their homes – coupled with their marginalization by pervasive structures of normative heterosexuality" and the "traumatic displacement from a lost heterosexual 'origin'" that never properly exists "dog the queer subject in a mainstream society impelled by the presumptions of compulsory heterosexuality" (2001, 205).

Alan Sinfield also argues that all queers are in diaspora – too often exiled from heterosexual homes into gay urbanscapes, longing for return but fearing rejection; and yet, for Simon Watney, diasporic queers may find new homes in metro gay bars across the globe, or in the transient pleasures of gay cosmopolitics. For Watney, then, all queers are in diasporic dislocation from heterosexual homes and public cultures, until they pull up a stool at the local "gay bar," a private or communal space of queer "relief" and "identification" (1995, 61). Disrupting Watney's metaphoric imagining of queer diasporic longings and metro gay bars worldwide as multiple sites of endless queer homecomings and cocktail rounds, Manalansan asks what "contradictions, discomfort, and disparities" might mar the possibilities of universal queer community – in Watney's queer imagining: "relief . . . in a gay bar or a dyke bar in a strange city in a foreign country[, e]ven if one cannot speak the local language" (1995, 61). What difference, Manalasan might ask, does it make whether or not one speaks "the local language" – French or German, Tagalog or Kreyòl? And what difference does it ineluctably make as to who is ordering martinis and who serving them in such imagined queer homes?

Rejecting the notion of queers in diaspora, Michael Warner suggests that we are without a homeland – no home to leave, no home to which we can return. For Warner, queerness cannot "be in diaspora, having no locale from which to wander" (1993, xvii). Similarly, Bob Cant also asserts that "lesbians and gay men differ from other groups of migrants in that there is no homeland that can validate our group identity" (1997, 1; quoted in Binnie 2004, 85). Yet as long as the "fear of a queer planet" persists, there will be perverse longings for queer imaginary homelands.

Queer Nation, capitalizing on notions of queer homelessness, sought to carve out queer nations within the larger fabric of heteronormative nation-states, much in the way that black nationalism modeled itself on and yet defined discourses of nationalism predicated on racial exclusion and racist segregation. For Eng, "the political monikers of activist groups such as Queer Nation, which tenaciously locate questions of membership within a larger national collectivity, propose that home as a regulating principle might, on reflection, constitute one of queer activism's organizing conditions of possibility" (2001, 205). "In its alignment with the nation-state," he continues, "home becomes the site of validation, the privileged location for the benefits of citizenship, the central place of belonging," and thus, "Queer Nation might offer potential ways to disturb traditional understandings of membership in the US nation-state" (2001, 205–206). David Bell, however, challenges utopic umbrella models of queer family, home, or nation, exposing and critiquing how bisexuals are often regarded as "outsiders," or sexual tourists in queer nations, interlopers situated at a remote "place on the margins" – "just here on a day trip" and then safely back to a (presumably straight) home (Bell 1995; Binnie 2004, 90).

And of course, as Gayle Rubin documented in her groundbreaking essay "Thinking Sex" (1984), queers do migrate – not only within nation-states like the United States or Canada from rural, isolated hetero-hometowns to urban centers with openly gay neighborhoods (such as from "Anywheresville, USA" to San Francisco's Castro district; from Farmington, Maine to Northampton, Massachusetts; or from Québec City to Montréal), but also, and as importantly, from countries with laws criminalizing and harshly punishing homosexuality to countries with more liberal attitudes (and laws) toward sexual minorities (for example, from Guayguayare, Trinidad or from Colombo, Sri Lanka to Toronto; or from Harare, Zimbabwe to London).

While Jon Binnie believes that "to speak of a queer diaspora is both necessary and highly problematic," he also insists that queer communities remain cognizant that "there are very real obstacles and barriers to movement, in the form of heteronormative and homophobic migration policies, . . . as well as the very real economic and emotional costs of migration" (2004, 81, 85). Suffice it to say, *some* queer communities do not need to be reminded that metaphorical migrancy differs materially and politically from the actual lived experiences of queer migrations and the formation of queer diasporas. They have lived it. They have experienced it. Still, Binnie's points are important and valid ones in this queer "migratory" debate. Despite the growing emphasis on "motility" in social theory (and overly abstract theorizations of migrancy, migration, travel, diaspora, tourism and so on), the concrete and material reality is that some individuals are prohibited from moving, from crossing borders; and "there are limits on the movement of sexual dissidents" in particular (Binnie 2004, 88). For persecuted sexual minorities, queer flight (or a perverse version of the American Dream) may be fueled less by diasporic dreams or desires for illusory metropolitan gaytopias in (mythically, or at least only fractionally) affluent "global cities" – San Francisco, London, Paris, Berlin, Miami, New York, Toronto, or elsewhere – and more by a necessity to escape the "very real fear and threat of persecution in the country of origin" (Binnie 2004, 88). Political asylum for persecuted sexual minorities was first granted in the United States in 1994, two years after the Canadian Immigration and Refugee Board (CIRB) granted asylum to a gay applicant in 1992. Like the US and Canada, the United Kingdom also now grants political asylum for sexually persecuted minorities – motivated by homophobia and hate violence against gays – grounded in the UNHCR legal definition of "'persecution' based on 'membership of a particular social group'" (Binnie 2004, 95). Political asylum in the US for persecuted sexual minorities is discussed at greater length in the second half of this chapter. And while Binnie rejects the idea that sexual persecution alone leads to queer migration, or compels queers to migrate, it is certainly (in and of itself) a *compelling* reason for cross-border movement, however difficult that may actually prove to be, though other reasons (desire for queer community, pursuit of sexual passion, desire for romantic companionship, allure of imagined metropolitan chic, and so on) clearly also entice queers toward seductive travel, or toward the at times alluring, though never easy or simple, and always fraught decision to leave one's country and migrate to another.

So when we speak of queer diaspora, we need also to speak of queer diasporas; and when we speak of queer diasporas, we are necessarily talking about (or should be) the queer migrations of individuals across international borders – i.e., those who have actually migrated. Migrancy may be metaphorical, but always in figurative relation to a concrete or literal experience of movement or migration. Our discussion of queer diasporas, then, will be grounded within specific legal, material, cultural, national, and historical moments and movements – from Mumbai or Manila to New York, from Colombo to Toronto, from Santiago de Cuba to Miami, from Rio de Janeiro to San Francisco, from Beijing to Los Angeles, or from Milan to Montréal – as scholars working on the issue all brilliantly illustrate.

Queer diasporic studies have been largely historical, cultural, or qualitative rather than quantitative analyses in methodological approach, written by scholars working in anthropology, geography, ethnic studies, gender studies, cultural studies, and literary, filmic, or visual studies. Key works in the still-emergent field include Juana María Rodríguez's *Queer Latinidad* (2003), José Quiroga's *Tropics of Desire* (2000) and *Cuban Palimpsests* (2005), José Esteban Muñoz's *Disidentifications* (1999), David Eng's *Racial Castration: Managing Masculinity in Asian America* (2001) and *Q&A: Queer in Asian America* (1998), edited with Alice Y. Hom, Martin F. Manalansan IV's *Global Divas: Filipino Gay Men in the Diaspora* (2003) and *Queer Globalization* (2002), edited with Arnaldo Cruz-Malavé, Gayatri Gopinath's *Impossible Desires: Queer Diasporas and South Asian Public Cultures* (2005), Anne-Marie Fortier's *Migrant Belongings* (2000), and earlier essays collected in *¿Entiendes? Queer Readings, Hispanic Writings* (1995). Most, though not all, of these scholars are US-based – living in university towns or metropolitan cities and "professing" in American universities – and their studies focus almost exclusively on queer diasporic communities in the context of the United States, with the notable exception of Anne-Marie Fortier who lives and works in the UK and whose work examines Italian queer diasporic communities, or Italian diasporic communities from a queer perspective, in Canada, the UK, and the US. For example, Gayatri Gopinath's research, deploying literary and cultural studies methods, explores the contours of South Asian queer diasporas in the US, the UK, and Canada, while David Eng's book probes the racialized, sexualized constructions of queer diasporic masculinity and Asian Americanness from a psychoanalytic perspective among Chinese American gay men. Manalansan, a pioneer in the field, relies on cultural studies, ethnography, and other qualitative anthropological research methods (case studies based on field work, interviews, and analysis) to document the fractured lives of Filipino gay men and *bakla* (a Tagalog term difficult to translate, but that loosely describes the culturally specific phenomenon of transgender and transvestite gay men from the Philippines) in the US.[3] Rodríguez traces the material and political implications of race, sex, gender, class, and nationality among discourses (legal, cyber, activist, corporeal, and literary) that construct identity among Latin American queer diasporic subjects in the US, what she refers to as a collective *Queer Latinidad*.

Influenced by the fields of literary, cultural, filmic, and performance studies, Eng also deploys a queer diasporic framework to understand the complex and imbricate constructions of race and masculinity among Asian American men, generally, and among Chinese American (and Japanese American) gay men, specifically, in his book *Racial Castration* (2001). In the book, Eng offers queer diasporic readings of various Asian American literary, filmic, and staged texts – *China Men*, *Donald Duk*, "The Shoyu Kid," *M. Butterfly*, *Eat a Bowl of Tea*, *Pangs of Love*, *Paris is Burning*, *The Wedding Banquet*, and *Rolling the R's* – as well as of Asian American queer diasporic masculinities through analyses grounded in psychoanalysis, critical race theory, ethnic studies, and literary criticism. The opening chapter, "Racial Castration," theoretically probes the vexing intersections of race and masculinity for Asian American men, which Eng describes as "feminized and emasculated Asian American masculinity within the domestic borders of the United States" (2001, 33). In the conclusion, "Out Here and Over There: Queerness and Diaspora in Asian American Studies," Eng offers a theoretical intervention in ethnic studies and areas studies from a queer diasporic perspective, arguing that queer methodologies illustrate the ways in which the racialized marking of excluded others operated (*par example*, those excluded from US immigration and citizenship by the Chinese Exclusion Acts of the 1880s) and continues to operate through constructions of gender and sexuality, specifically as feminine and homosexual. Resisting the extremes of "yellow peril" and "model minority" that prevent full political and cultural (or unhyphenated) belonging in the US, Eng ultimately asks in the conclusion whether diaspora and exile might not be better theoretical rubrics for understanding Asian America and Asian American identities than the more dominant ones of "immigration" and "settlement."

"Where is Asian America?" Eng queries in "Impossible Arrivals" (2001, 204). Moving between nation-states (the one departed from and the one where one "impossibly" arrives) and the *intermezzo* movements of diaspora – both departures and arrivals, but also the liminal movements back and forth from home to host country – Asian Americans, Eng conjectures, are "suspended between departure and arrival, . . . permanently disenfranchised from home, relegated to a nostalgic sense of its loss or to an optative sense of its unattainability" (2001, 204). And yet the very term and concept of "Asian America" represents a diasporic yearning for home, but also a desire for countercultural minoritarian nation building (like black nationalism or Queer Nation) within and without the larger United States of America. Asian America is, as Eng writes, "a siteless locale with no territorial sovereignty"; or as Sau-ling Wong writes, "a yearning for the kind of containing boundaries and contained site enjoyed by the dominant society, a nation-state" (1995, 4; quoted in Eng 2001, 204). Yet one must ask: what becomes walled out, or forcibly contained within, the "containing boundaries" of the nation-state? How porous and malleable, at moments, despite carefully guarded gates, erected walls, and 24–7 military surveillance might the presumably all "contained" borders and boundaries of the larger nation-state

actua   ? And how metastable
migh   :tually guarded, might
they   disintegration,   near
disag

O   mmigration-settlement-
assii   melting pot" paradigm
in th   ora became *the* question
grip   versary in the academy"
(20   vas to press "how queer-
nes   erica (2001, 260n2). Eng
thu   arameters, particularly in
the   eployments in the period
of i

ng critical emphasis from
n-states; the transnational
pital; the global commodi-
of flexible labor; and the
:tronic media, communica-

Eng   orical parameters (grounded
in   it, in many ways, remained
het   tering of seeds" and patriar-
cha   connecting diaspora to new
glob   :he wake of "the apotheosis
of global capital under the Reagan and ___ administrations, the collapse of
communism in the Soviet Union and Eastern Europe, and the dismantling
of prolabor movements and unions" (2001, 218). While Eng maintains that
diasporas *can* be scattered transnational sites of resistance to the hegemonic
structures of nationalism and global capitalism, or to nation-states and global
regulatory bodies and international financial institutions, he also concedes that
diasporas "*can [also] function* as unusually conservative sites of nationalism as
well" (2001, 207; emphasis added). Eng thus reminds us of the ways in which
global capital, following Saskia Sassen and others, "exerts its demands within
the localized space of the nation-state" and within diasporas, which may function
as transnational or extra-territorial extensions of the nation – in effect, as national
outposts (2001, 214).

In *Global Divas* (2003), his ethnographic study of Filipino gay men in New
York, Manalansan theoretically frames the lived experiences of queer diasporic
transmigrants through linguistic play, sexual play, performance, and ritual. For
example, Manalansan explores the complex interplay between *bakla* and gay
sexual identity among diasporic Filipino men, suggesting that while the two are
in sexual creative translation, some elements are untranslatable: they do not
"travel," as Manalansan says. He also analyzes the importance of *swardspeak* –
or Filipino gay slang – in constructing a sense of diasporic and sexual identities,

as well as how everyday lives require cross-cultural and cross-linguistic performance. Two other key moments are foregrounded in *Global Divas* – first, the
Stonewall rebellion, the role that working-class Filipino and Latino gay men
played in it, obscured in most commemorations of the event, and how these diasporic gay men differently identify – or *disidentify* – with the event as a US "queer
national moment"; and second, "the Santacruzan, a traditional Filipino religious
ritual . . . performed by a group of Filipino queers" that allows Manalansan to
examine "Filipino gay men's negotiations in the public arena" (2003, 20). Finally,
Manalansan reports on the impact of AIDS among Filipino gay men in diaspora,
an analysis that again underscores cultural-linguistic translation and performance, since the men have coined the disease *Tita Aida*.

Noting that "ideas about diaspora and globalization have invaded even the
most mundane aspects of queer lives," and further suggesting that "words [such]
as globalization . . . index or mark sophistication and cosmopolitanism in queer
culture," Manalansan also warns that gay scholarly skeptics "have used the
words as ominous signs of more insidious processes such as Western capitalist
expansion and queer cultural imperialism and exploitation" (2003, 5). In contrast
to impersonal transnational flows of capital, technology, and information, and
also counter-juxtaposed to what vociferous critics decry as the nefarious ills of
global homogenizing forces (the McDonaldization of Queer, or McQueer),
Manalansan's vibrant ethnography details with verve, panache, relevance, and
irreverence how Filipino gay men in New York actively live the transnational
and navigate the global, or how they negotiate the transmigratory and queer
diasporic lived experiences of global exchanges and transnationalist flows: their
lives are mapped in and through those hybrid exchanges. Yet Manalansan also
remains vigilant about how "scholarly works focusing on the global and transnational . . . as symptomatic of the proliferation of gay and lesbian social
movements" may also position diasporas as "insignificant after-effects . . . of
queer globalization," rather than as integral and vital components of global
capitalist restructuring and transnational refigurations of national economies,
notions of citizenship or political belonging, long-distance nationalism, diasporic
participation, and public cultures; these scholarly works, thus, "unwittingly posit
a *white* gay male gaze" (2003, 5–6).

Conversely, Manalansan defines the emergent field of "new queer studies" – or
what he describes as a "transnational turn in queer studies" – as one that inter-
rogates "the political stakes" risked in migration or diasporic movements that
must be contextualized within the larger moment of transnational or global
capital. "New queer studies," which may also be named queer diasporic studies,
"expand" or "trouble" the "seemingly stable borders" of both queer studies and
diasporic studies "by illuminating the different ways in which various queer
subjects located in and moving in between specific national locations establish
and negotiate complex relationships to each and to the state" (2003, 8). Queer
diasporic studies also pays attention to and critically examines "the vicissitudes
of the intensified movement of people, capital, ideas, and technology across
borders" (2003, 8). And finally, queer diaspora scholars, like "immigrant queers
of color," also cannot ignore "how mobility is not only about the actual physical

traversing of national boundaries but also about the traffic of status and hierarchies *within* and across such boundaries" (2003, 9).

Gopinath's *Impossible Desires* organizes its analyses of female erotic desire around three structural rubrics: queer diasporas, "impossibility," and South Asian public cultures. For Gopinath, theorizing the cultural, historical terrains of "a queer South Asian diaspora" makes significant contributions to the fields of diasporic studies, globalization studies, queer studies, and popular or public cultural studies. As Gopinath explains in the introduction to *Impossible Desires*, conceptualizing South Asian diasporas from a queer theoretical perspective serves to accomplish all of the following critical tasks:

> First, it situates the formation of sexual subjectivity within transnational flows of culture, capital, bodies, desire, and labor. Second, queer diaspora contests the logic that situates the terms "queer" and "diaspora" as dependent on the originality of "heterosexuality" and "nation." Finally, it disorganizes the dominant categories within the United States for sexual variance, namely "gay and lesbian," and it marks a different economy of desire that escapes legibility within both normative South Asian contexts and homonormative Euro-American contexts. (2005, 13)

All of these critical interventions are significant ones. As Gopinath explains, neither the contours of queerness (same-sex desires, affections, practices, sex acts, "gender trouble," or gender-bending, trannie "outlaws"), nor those of diaspora and diasporas may be understood outside the transnational machinations of global capitalism and the circulating market of bodies, ethnicities, and identities; however, queer diasporas may create discordant counter-flows within the dominant or hegemonic motions of capital, heterosexuality, nationality, and even those of globalized gay cultures that too frequently remain premised on uninterrogated notions of race, class, gender, and nationality.

"Impossibility," the theoretical *intermezzo*, thus opens new spaces for rethinking the frameworks of nation, diaspora, globalization, and even queer diasporas; and it is here that Gopinath makes her most important intellectual and political contributions. In articulating queer diasporic female desires and identities (or thinking the unthinkable, imagining the unimaginable, and demanding the impossible), Gopinath suggests that it is queer female diasporic subjects who embody this "impossibility" within hegemonic constructions of nation and diaspora – not only patriarchal, heteromasculine constructs, but also postcolonial feminist ones founded within a presumed heterosexism or compulsory heterosexuality and gay white homonormative paradigms grounded in racially, ethnically, and nationally exclusive ways.

Queer Nation/Queer Diaspora

Theorizations of queer diaspora, above all, have offered a powerful rejoinder to the model of "Queer Nation" that was dominant in GLBT discourses of the 1990s. Drawing on earlier precursors such as black nationalism, Queer Nation was founded at an ACT UP meeting in New York in April 1990 and more visibly emerged – as a concept and as a political organization – during the 1990 New York Pride March, when a group of activists distributed the Queer Nation manifesto "Queers Read This" as a public refusal to remain invisible, quiet, or passive in the face of overt and violent forms of homophobia or institutionalized forms of heterosexism – or even in the face of gay and lesbian attempts to enter into the domestic, if not erotic, economy of heterosexuality through emphasis on monogamy, marriage, and other more normative behaviors, instead of on open and explicit forms of sexual diversity.[4] Described by Alan Sikes as "a loose federation of local organizations whose defiant denaturalizations of normative heterosexuality frequently hinge upon parodic rearticulations of 'straight' society and subjectivity," Queer Nation refused heteronormative social, cultural, and political strictures, staging "kiss ins" and planning "mall takeovers."[5] Although Queer Nation marked an important moment in queer activism in the United States, it risked erecting and normalizing another unacknowledged boundary among GLBT or queer communities: that of nationalism or nationality. According to Terry Goldie,

> the "nation" of Queer Nation has two rather opposed interpretations. One is a belief in a community which supersedes the traditional view of the nation-state. In this the nation is a greater tie between the two homosexuals than between a heterosexual and a homosexual of the same state. The other interpretation is what might be called "a life of irony." This is the one explored by Berlant and Freeman, who consider the camp way that gay and lesbian activists in the United States use symbols of patriotism such as the flag. The traditional American patriot stands in front of the Stars and Stripes, his hair cut to marine length, holding a gun. The queer nationalist is in the same pose, with the same hair cut, but has traded the gun for a dildo, and is quite likely a she. This is not so much a greater nation as the old one turned upside down. (2)[6]

Not surprisingly, that unacknowledged nationalist framing was invisibly, but undeniably, inflected as US[7] Diasporic queer activists press the questions: What are the limits of applicability of the terms "Queer Nation" (or even "queer" for that matter) for speaking to diasporic or global homosexual practices and identities? And how is the concept of "queer nation" grounded in US-based ideas about "gay liberation" and even national identity? As a term and as a coalition, then, Queer Nation may have had its geopolitical limits within the US, and Queer Nation risked becoming gay globalization, a commodified and exported discourse of sexual identity, or, as cynics note, just another form of capitalist imperialism.

As the myriad cultural-geographical terrains of queer diasporas challenge the singularity of queer nation, so too do they explicitly critique the notion of "global gays." A review of some of the literature touting gay globalization suffices to reveal how problematic such formulations can be. For example, in the article "Speaking Its Name: Inventing a Gay and Lesbian Studies," Ken Plummer pronounces, "Homosexualities have become globalized." Plummer envisions the global terrains of queer sexualities, writing,

Certainly the late modern world cannot be understood without seeing the interpenetrations of countries: of their economies; their cultures; their technologies. There is a worldwide process in which modern technologies have quite simply made the global world a local one: one in which news can be simultaneously consumed in many countries across the world at the same time . . . And homosexuality is part of this.

He continues, "Indeed, the gay and lesbian movements house identities, politics, cultures, markets, intellectual programmes which nowadays quite simply know no national boundaries."[8] Plummer's transnational queerness, however, fails to address sites at which national borders are closed – both to insiders seeking to leave or to outsiders seeking entry – and it ignores the asymmetry of transnational or global relations (often mapped through global capital and the international divisions of labor).

Resisting transnational (or global) "queering" as a form of universal sexual imperialism in the essay "Something Queer about the Nation-State" (1995), Warner writes, "both the word 'queer' and the concept of queerness turn out to be thoroughly embedded in modern Anglo-American culture," adding that "we should be more than usually cautious about global utopianisms that require American slang" (361; quoted in Hayes 2000, 6). Dennis Altman's critiques of global "queering" have been harsher and more sustained, arguing that ideas (or fantasies) about "global gay" identities are merely old forms of Western imperialism in queer clothing.[9] In resisting "queer" as the commodified forms of imported "Western" gay identities, Jarrod Hayes uses "queer" as a transitive verb, not as an adjective, in his pioneering study *Queer Nations: Marginal Sexualities in the Maghreb*. "In spite of the potential applicability of the term 'queer' to the Maghreb," Hayes writes, "I shall use it here less as an adjective to describe sexual acts than as a verb to signify a critical practice in which nonnormative sexualities infiltrate dominant discourses to loosen their political stronghold" (7). These critiques of a "queer" universal are important; it is also important to remember, however, that the "West" has no monopoly on queer sexualities, desires, and identities; queer circulates globally and diasporically, often altering and resisting Western forms of sexual identities, if at times, mimicking them. Queer diasporic critics like Gopinath, Manalansan, and Eng, among others, are resolute on this point. Aijaz Ahmad's critique of Fredric Jameson's theorization of "third-world texts," thus, is also relevant to theorizations of global gays/gay identities globally. Ahmad argues that Jameson's theory assumes that capital belongs to the "first world" and that socialism emerges from the "third world"; however, Ahmad aptly notes that both capitalism and socialism are global phenomena. Likewise, queer (or non-heteronormative sexualities) are global, even if the language of articulating "perverse" sexualities and acts varies across national boundaries and transnational iterations.

Unlike Altman, Warner, and others, who place queer identity in relation to global shifts, many emergent scholars examine the theoretical conjunctures of queer identities and diasporic relations. (Whereas "global" maintains, at least provisionally, a hegemonic relation to the ideas of the "first world" through the dominance of the US in global capitalism, diasporic studies examines the

realignments globally enacted through postcolonial migrations, transnational
subjects, and myriad diasporas worldwide.) Sexually marked migrants also press
others to consider how the rubrics of "home" and "homeland" may be vexing
sites or terrains for queer individuals in diaspora. According to Patton and
Sánchez-Eppler, when "a body that carries any of many queering marks moves
between officially designated spaces – nation, region, metropole, neighborhood,
or even culture, gender, religion, disease – intricate realignments of identity,
politics, and desire take place," carefully noting, though, that "the effects of
movement, of tectonic shifts between differently produced and carried identities
and differentially textured places are far from uniform."[10] In these movements,
neither bodies and identities, nor places of travel are "static"; rather, bodies,
desires, identities, and places are all forms of a "mobile imaginary."[11] For Patton
and Sánchez-Eppler, "what must be interrogated" is "the intersection, the collision, the slippage between body-places; the partial transformation of those places;
the face installed by dissimulation in place."[12] Suggesting that identities so con-
figured need to be theorized as "tactical" instead of "strategic" (*à la* de Certeau),
Patton and Sánchez-Eppler add that "if frantic realignment is all we do, we
risk . . . underutilizing the power of tactical maneuvers, of queer timings, to alter
territory, to leave burn marks as our trace, to get a face from defacement."[13] In
theorizing queer diaspora and historicizing queer diasporas (or queer migrations),
however, we also need to consider how these frameworks are not separate or
separatist ones. In other words, while distinctions between queer diaspora and
queer nation, or queer diaspora and global gay, are necessary and even critical
ones, we need to understand how these all too easily offset binaries may also be
mutually constitutive sites or material-political formations.

How might queer diaspora be not only a creative perversion and desired
profanation of the presumed purity of patriarchal, heterosexual nation, but
perhaps, also, an extension of queer nation, a diasporic formation that is both
resistant to yet complicit or imbricate with queer imaginary homelands (however
inaccurately framed as white, middle class, first world, affluent, or even *homo-
masculine*!), yet complicit with its discordant notions of national belonging and
dissident (or diva)[14] citizenship, or its *disidentifications* with nationality as a
framework for politics and participatory notions of group membership? How
also might queer diasporas reveal an imbrication, even but not only through vocal
critiques, with the concept of "global gays," or the global gay rights movement,
which often operates and circulates through international nongovernmental
organizations and disseminated pamphlets, publications, and "on the ground"
homosexual work with its utopic aspirant desires for scattered transnational
queer utopias of trans-global safe sex zones for sexualized minorities? And its
admittedly noble goals (even when grounded in exclusionary presuppositions
around issues of development, even when ill-executed) not only for queer political
"acceptance," but also queer political mobility and gay activism (or, a global
"acting up"), as well as important international efforts in the areas of HIV/AIDS
prevention and treatment, the eradication of homophobia and anti-gay violence,
and a desired end to the multiple, disparate, but no less perilous, transnationalized forms of institutionalized heterosexuality?

"Queer Nation" and "Global Gay," after all, are driven by transnational desires for queer social justice worldwide, even if all too often deployed and positioned in undeniably exclusionary and privileged ways that implicitly (or even explicitly) reinforce colonialist, imperialist notions of historical progress, linear evolution, and teleological models of capitalist "development" that hold the "developed West" up as the *telos* for all the aspirant, yet still "developing Rest" (read: backward or less civilized). Yet, queer nation and global gay thrive on subaltern spaces and queer diasporas as sites of radical resistance to the too often deployed mechanisms of power and privilege. We would do well to remember and heed Gramsci's warning about hegemony: it consolidates itself through assimilated dissent and difference; counterhegemonic forces may always be incorporated to shore up hegemony.

It is, however, within this last terrain – how theorizations of queer diaspora unsettle the ground of both the conceptual fields of queer nation and global gays – that I would like to similarly unsettle ground, at least provisionally. It may have become too easy, after all, to establish certain dichotomies in our discussions of queer diaspora. *Par example*:

Queer Diaspora v. Queer Nation
Queer Diaspora v. Global Gays

For Gopinath, queer diasporas may contest the heteropatriarchal assumptions of nation and diaspora and challenge the homogenizing and hegemonic forces of global capitalism; however, queer diasporas may also operate in tandem and complicity with the structuring forces of nation and globalization. Queer diasporas, thus, are always *in relation* and *in tension* with nation and globe. Despite this triangulation of nation-diaspora-globe in Gopinath's conceptualizations, she clearly demarcates the terrain of queer diasporas from that of global gays, and one might assume that she would also demarcate queer diasporas from queer nation. Yet how might queer diasporas also stand in relation and in tension with both queer nation and global gays, just as diaspora stands in tense relation to nationalism and global capitalism? In other words, it may now be time to deconstruct and unsettle the too easily offset binaries of *Queer Diasporas v. Queer Nation*; or, *Queer Diasporas v. Global Gays*.

For example, while not unproblematic in its at-times imperialist presuppositions about sexual minorities from other countries, legal work in the US (and in other countries) to establish sexual persecution as grounds for political asylum necessarily relies on national state apparatuses, such as the US judicial branch of government, as well as nationally located nongovernmental organizations striving for legal equality for sexual minorities, as well as on the efforts of international nongovernmental organizations committed to queer work and the conventions and protocols of international law and global regulatory bodies, such as the United Nations, in working to protect sexual minorities who are seeking refuge. And while we must also necessarily interrogate and mitigate against legal and critical arguments that ineluctably position "developed" nations as sexually liberatory spaces – clearly not the case! – and counter-position "developing" countries as sexually repressive ones, we must also collaborate transnationally for sexual-social justice for queer subjects across the globe in both their home-dwellings and in their queer migrations.

Sexual Asylum and Immigration Law: Queer Diasporic Refuge?

Sexual asylum, and its global impact on national immigration laws, is a new and still largely unnavigated legal terrain. Important contributions to the emergent and transnational field of marginalized sexual minorities and the question of political asylum have been made by Juana Maria Rodriguez (in *Queer Latinidad*), by Eithne Luibhéid, Lionel Cantu, Jr., Timothy J. Randazzo, and Siobhan Sommerville (in *Queer Migrations*), by Alice M. Miller, Brad Epps, Bill Fairbairn, and Matthew E. Price (in *Passing Lines: Sexuality and Immigration*), by Jessica Chapin in a cultural studies article published in *GLQ*, and, significantly, by legal scholars Sonia Katyal, Tracy J. Davis, Jin S. Park, Lucy H. Halatyn, and Suzanne Goldberg in law review journals. Within the national context of the United States, scholars and legal activists have focused their efforts in three areas: immigration law, political asylum cases, and judicial court rulings. Two immigration laws have been heavily scrutinized for their exclusionary measures targeting homosexual migrant subjects: the 1952 Immigration and Nationality Act, or the McCarran-Walter bill; and the 1996 Illegal Immigration Reform and Immigrant Responsibility Act (IIRIRA). Other scholarly and activist efforts have been committed to reviewing political asylum applications filed with the former Immigration and Naturalization Service (INS), or with the Bureau of Citizenship and Immigration Services (BCIS), appeals filed by asylees with the Board of Immigration Appeal (BIA) to dispute application denial by the INS, and finally immigration judge court rulings in the federal circuit court of appeals if the denial is also upheld by the BIA. Three appeals filed with the BIA claiming the right to political asylum in the US on the grounds of sexual persecution have been historically significant: *Matter of Acosta* (1985); *Matter of Tobosa-Alfonso* (1986); and *Matter of Tenorio* (1993). Two 9th Circuit Court of Appeals cases also represented clear victories for activists, lawyers, and asylees working for the right to political asylum for persecuted sexual minorities: the rulings of immigration judges in both *Pitcherskai v. INS* (1997) and *Hernandez-Montiel v. INS* (2000) against the Immigration and Naturalization Service – in denying political asylum and the BIA upholding of that decision to deny asylum – opened the door for new applicants.

   Matter of Acosta (1985), though not specifically addressing the issue of sexual orientation as ground for political asylum, did establish that "membership in a particular social group" – as outlined in the United Nations 1951 Convention on refugees and the 1967 Protocol – does constitute ground if that group is a persecuted one and group membership is determined either by an "immutable characteristic" or characteristics that one "should not be required to change." The "immutable characteristic" precept differentiated the ruling in *Matter of*

Acosta from an earlier court ruling in *Sanchez-Trujillo v. INS*, 801 F. 2d. 1571 (9th Cir. 1986) that emphasized "a voluntary associational relationship." The BIA ruling in *Matter of Acosta*, by contrast, established the following criteria for claiming right to asylum by virtue of group membership: "Whatever the common characteristic that defines the group, it must be one that the members of the group either cannot change, or should not be required to change because it is fundamental to their individual identities or consciences" (*Matter of Acosta*, 19 I&N Dec. 211 [BIA 1985]; quoted in Musalo et el. 2002 and in Randazzo 2005, 32).

Matter of Acosta became key for the issue of sexual asylum in the US, however, when an immigration judge ruling on another appeal, *Matter of Toboso-Alfonso* (1986), cited it as precedence. The second appeal was filed by a Cuban asylee named Armando Toboso-Alfonso, whose 1985 petition for political asylum had been denied by the INS, despite the fact that as a gay Cuban man – i.e., his "membership in a particular social group" – he was registered as a "homosexual" by the Cuban government and periodically required "to submit to detention and interrogation," which included physical abuse and police harassment. In 1980, during the Mariel boatlift, "Cuban authorities ordered Toboso-Alfonso to leave the country or spend four years in prison for being gay" (Randazzo 2005, 32). While determined ineligible for political asylum in the US due to minor brushes with the law, the immigration judge did "withhold deportation," allowing Toboso-Alfonso to stay in the country. Withheld deportation – though not a full grant of political asylum, has a similar end result: i.e., allowing the asylee to remain in the country – but legally requires a higher degree ("clear probability") than the lesser proof ("well-founded fear of persecution") required for political asylum (quoted in Randazzo 2005, 33). Basing its dissent of the immigration judge's ruling squarely on US immigration law that barred homosexuals from immigrating to the United States under a provision of the 1952 Immigration and Nationality Act, or the McCarran-Walter bill (as it is more popularly known) that barred entry of those with a "psychopathic personality or sexual deviation, or a moral defect," a law upheld by the Supreme Court to include homosexuals, the INS appealed the ruling of the judge to the Board of Immigration Appeals. In the appeal, the INS argued that considering homosexuals to be members "in a particular social group" "would be tantamount to awarding discretionary relief to those involved in behavior that is not only socially deviant in nature, but in violation of the laws or regulations of the country as well" (quoted in *Matter of Toboso-Alfonso*, 20 I&N Dec. 819 [BIA, March 12, 1990], 822; quoted in Randazzo 2005, 33). "In 1990," the same year that immigration law reform overturned or repealed the 1952 provision barring gays and lesbians from immigrating to the United States, "the BIA dismissed the INS's appeal and granted Toboso-Alfonso's petition for withholding deportation" (Randazzo 2005, 330).

Timothy J. Randazzo, while acknowledging the precedent established by *Matter of Toboso-Alfonso*, also remains critical of the rhetorical language of the BIA ruling in the case; according to Randazzo, the BIA established protection by virtue of the claim of *being* homosexual (i.e., having presumed and presumably *biological* "membership in a particular social group"), but not for *behaving* gay.

As Randazzo writes of the ruling: "Though unprecedented, the case was not a total victory for gay and lesbian asylum seekers. Addressing the INS's concern that 'socially deviant behavior' should not be made the basis for refugee protection, the board distinguished between homosexual *behavior* and *being* a homosexual" (2005, 33). Within the legal terms of the INS appeal and the current immigration laws at the time of the ruling, however, it could be reasoned that the board made a legally strategic argument, yet one that clearly relied on juridical presuppositions that both reasserted queer sex acts (or gay behavior) as criminal and codified being gay as biological or essentialist. In its ruling the BIA thus left unchallenged the presumed right of governments (both the Cuban and the US governments) to enforce anti-sodomy laws (keep in mind: at the time, *Bowers v. Hardwick* was the "law of the land") and to punish so-called offenders; it also explicitly disavowed that the ruling established any legal precedence for claim to "gay rights" (Randazzo 2005, 33). The BIA ruling reads: "This is not simply a case of assertion of 'gay rights'" (*Matter of Toboso-Alfonso*, 822; quoted in Randazzo 2005, 33 and 56n12). That representatives of the Cuban government ordered Toboso-Alfonso to leave the country or face imprisonment – interpreted by the board as "the government's desire that all homosexuals be forced to leave their homeland" (ibid) – seems to have played a crucial role in the BIA ruling. Despite the explicit problems with the language of the ruling and its legal implications about *being* v. *behaving* gay, however, "the ruling is significant in that the board permitted sexual orientation to form the basis for membership in a particular social group" (Randazzo 2005, 34). However, since the board did not publish its ruling it was not permissible as "legal precedent" in other political asylum cases regarding sexual orientation and persecution for that orientation (Randazzo 2005, 34).

Four years later, with numerous political asylum cases based on sexual persecution awaiting decision, then Attorney General Janet Reno issued a June 16, 1994 Memorandum establishing *Matter of Toboso-Alfonso* as legal precedence on the issue. Internationally, the legal decision was a strategic and crucial one for international human rights law since Canada had granted political asylum on the grounds of sexual persecution in 1992 and eight other countries in Europe (Austria, Germany, Denmark, Finland, the Netherlands, Sweden) and the Asian Pacific (Australia and New Zealand) had also done so by 1994. Ironically, three months earlier, on March 8, 1994, the INS – even as they were in the midst of a legal appeal in *Matter of Tenorio* – had granted political asylum to Ariel da Silva, a Mexican gay man who had filed his application based on sexual persecution by the Mexican police who raped and beat him; however, the INS made the grant explicitly an individual one and not one extendable to a special group or "class of people" (quoted in Randazzo 2005, 34).

Matter of Acosta also served as legal precedence in a third asylum case, *Matter of Tenorio* (1993). Following a brutal experience of anti-gay violence, Marcelo Tenório, a Brazilian gay man who was the victim of "gaybashing" and violence in his home country, filed for political asylum in the United States on the basis of sexual persecution after "illegally" migrating to the US and relocating in San Francisco, where his court of appeals trial was held. Again citing *Matter of Acosta* as precedence, in 1993, Immigration Judge Philip Leadbetter ruled that Tenório's homosexuality made him part of a "particular social group" that subjected him to violence and discrimination in his homeland. In the ruling, the judge determined that because Tenório "is openly homosexual, a characteristic the court considers immutable, and one in which an asylum applicant should not be compelled to change," he should be granted political asylum and refuge in the US. Following the affirmative decision by the immigration judge, the INS appealed the ruling with the Board of Immigration Appeals, which "dismissed the appeal" in 1999, upholding the judge's initial decision to grant Tenório political asylum based on sexual persecution and thereby allowing him to remain in the country (Randazzo 2005, 34).

In "The Subject on Trial: Reading *In re Tenorio* as Transnational Narrative," chapter three of *Queer Latinidad*, Rodríguez offers a rhetorical analysis of the court of appeals trial based on the transcript, including an incisive analysis of the "interstitial dark, queer refugee" (as Marcelo Tenório was constructed in the trial, in mainstream media coverage, and in the gay and lesbian press). Rodríguez does so by examining how the singular depiction of Tenório as "gay-bashed" Brazilian asylee obscured the other material realities of his life (particularly "poor Black Brazilian") as intersectionally mapped through race, class, nationality, and the particular reality of his having been orphaned at the age of eight following an accident that killed both of his parents. According to Rodríguez, "The dictates of the law require an erasure of the way Tenório's life is impacted by the enmeshed particularities of nationality, color, class, age, voice, and positionality, or what the legal critic Kimberlé Crenshaw terms 'multiple intersectionality'" (2003, 95). Rodríguez thus intersectionally reads the transcript of the trial *In re Tenorio*, no. A72 093 558 (as well as the often mixed or hybrid codes of Tenório's body and Rio de Janeiro's and San Francisco's queer-metrosexual geography) for its/their contradictory rhetorical constructions of race, class, nationality, homosexuality, heterosexuality, brutality, barbarity, and civility through the actual *testimonios* of Marcelo Tenório himself, the expert witness Dr. Luiz Mott called to testify about homophobia and anti-gay violence in Brazil, Tania Alvarez, the immigration attorney representing Tenório, Allen Lee, the attorney representing the INS, and Philip Leadbetter, the immigration judge presiding over the appeals trial.

"In the nine years since the first cases were granted in 1994," Randazzo wrote (in 2003), "approximately six hundred people have received asylum based on sexual orientation" (2005, 30). While "official figures are not available[,] the Asylum Program of the International Gay and Lesbian Human Rights Commission (IGLHRC) has been able to track many of the cases it has come into contact with through its outreach and advocacy efforts on behalf of asylum seekers" (Randazzo 2005, 43). Although progress has clearly been made in the legal rights of persecuted sexual minorities to claim asylum in the United States, other disparities still persist: "The Asylum Program has recorded 686 asylum grants to men and just 87 to women, illustrating a severe gender disparity in the asylum process" (Randazzo 2005, 43). Though not yet documented, similar disparities demarcated along the lines of race or ethnicity, nationality or geographical region of origin, religion, education, and class (or what Pierre Bourdieu calls "cultural capital") almost certainly exist too. And since 9/11, asylum cases have been imperiled and sexual minorities (along with other racial-religious minorities, heterosexual or homosexual) increasingly subjected to detention and deportation (as further discussed in the closing chapter of this book).

There are, of course, other contradictions within US (and UK) efforts to protect sexual minorities: for example, many countries that grant political asylum based on sexual persecution also require HIV/AIDS testing of all individuals attempting to legally migrate into the country and, moreover, explicitly bar entry of seropositive migrants, thus restricting access to individuals who, if both gay and HIV+, may actually suffer additional persecution in the country they are trying to leave. Such are, regrettably, one of the manifold contradictions of sexual asylum and queer international migrations. And asylees held in US detention are too frequently not only not protected from abuse and violence, but actually subjected to it by immigration prison guards, as lamentably was the case of Christina Madrazo, a Mexican transsexual woman who was raped twice by a security guard while being detained at Krome Detention Center in Miami, Florida in April 2002.[15] That political asylum in the US is being awarded to protect gays, lesbians, bisexuals, transsexuals, transgender outlaws, and other queer deviants or marginalized sexual minorities is, in many ways, an ironic gesture and sadly so given the multiple acts of gay-bashing, anti-gay hostility, homophobic violence, and overt hate crimes in this country – not only the most notorious cases of rape, mutilation, and murder (including the brutal killing of Matthew Shepherd whose massacre galvanized queer activists and public outrage too), but also the countless acts of discrimination, abuse, and harassment that occur throughout the US, not only in rural counties and on backroads of southern and midwestern states, but also, strikingly, even in supposedly queer-friendly metropolitan areas of the Northeast and West Coast – Boston, New York, DC, Seattle, San Francisco, and Los Angeles. According to the New York City Gay and Lesbian Anti-Violence Project, there were 151 murders of queer individuals reported from 1992 to 1994, the two-year period in which *Matter of Tenorio* was being appealed by the INS in the circuit court of appeals, and "close to 60 percent of these murders were marked by an extraordinary degree of violence or 'overkill'," which usually is defined as "dismemberment, genital mutilation, bodily mutilation, and an extraordinarily high level of gratuitous violence" (Rodríguez 2003, 101). Rodríguez notes two distressing, though perhaps not unsurprising trends (particularly given the violent admixtures of homophobia and racism in US cultures) within the acts of anti-gay violence documented by the New York City Gay and Lesbian Anti-Violence Project: first, "'African American and Latino/a victims were more likely to be 'overkilled' than white victims'; [and] second, 'if the victim was a person of color, it was less likely that the case was solved'" (2003, 101). Even presumably safe queer zones, like San Francisco's Castro district, are not only not free of anti-gay violence, but are often the very site of it: Castro has "become the focus for many gay-bashings" because of its queer "visibility" and "the largest number of reported gay bashing incidents [in the city] take place" in this neighborhood (Rodríguez 2003, 106, 91). As Rodríguez concludes, "What happened to Marcelo Tenório in Rio de Janeiro could have just as easily taken place in San Francisco or in any other city or town in the United States" (2003, 106).

Two 9th Circuit Court of Appeals cases have also been instrumental in fostering the protection of queer transmigrant refugees in the US – *Pitcherskaia v. INS* (1997) and *Hernandez-Montiel v. INS* (2000). The first case involved Alla Pitcherskaia, a Russian lesbian who applied for political asylum in the United States: in her petition, Pitcherskaia maintained that, if deported to Russia, she would be forced into psychiatric hospitalization and be subjected to electric shock therapy administered to "treat" and "cure" her homosexuality; Pitcherskaia, unsurprisingly, regarded this form of "medical treatment" for sexually "deviant behavior" as a form of torture or punishment. The immigration judge presiding in the case disagreed, and to the surprise of many, the judge, ruling on behalf of the INS, denied political asylum to Pitcherskaia. Appealing the decision to the Board of Immigrant Appeals, Pitcherskaia was again denied: the BIA ruling stated that the "psychiatric treatment . . . did not constitute persecution because it represented an attempt to 'cure' rather than 'punish' her for her sexual orientation" (Randazzo 2005, 36). In the 9th Circuit Court of Appeals, the judge determined that "a supported benevolent intent . . . [did] not preclude an act from falling under the statutory definition of 'persecution' under US refugee law," reversing the BIA ruling, granting the petition for review, and remanded the case back to the board for additional review (Randazzo 2005, 36). As of September 2006, the BIA had "ordered an immigration lawyer to review her claim" and to determine whether or not her "fear of persecution is 'well founded,'" but no decision has yet been made. Although clearly not a victory (yet) for Pitcherskaia, queer activists and legal scholars do see the 9th Circuit Court of Appeals finding that maleficent intent is not necessary in defining persecution "as an important victory for [potential] asylum seekers fleeing similar forms of abuse" (Randazzo 2005, 37).

The second political asylum case with queer political import that was heard before the 9th Circuit Court of Appeals was *Hernandez-Montiel v. INS* (2000). Key to the case was the issue of "sexual identity," and whether or not queer identities such as transgender, transsexuality, and transvestism, which are not so easily mapped along a heterosexual-homosexual binary of sexual orientation, also "constitute a protected 'particular social group' under US asylum law" (Randazzo 2005, 37). Geovanni Hernandez-Montiel, a Mexican transgendered sex worker, filed a petition for political asylum and for withholding deportation in the United States after being beaten and raped by police officers in Mexico. Denied by the immigration judge initially ruling in the petition and by the BIA, both claiming that Hernandez-Montiel's persecution was not the result of any "immutable characteristic" that made him ineluctably part of a "particular social group" persecuted in Mexico, but rather that it was the result of "changeable" characteristics – i.e., as simple, in fact, as a change of clothes: boots instead of stilettos, silk dress changed for jeans, lipstick for a pocket knife. While the rulings clearly avoided essentialist definitions of sexual identity, seeming rather to embrace the performative, obviously it is (and was not) as simple as a change of clothes, or desires, or identities at will. It is important to note too that neither the immigration judge, "nor the BIA had questioned the credibility of his testimony regarding harassment from his family and authorities, including at least two incidences of rape by Mexican police. Accordingly, the elements of persecution were clear under even a conservative test: serious harm at the hands of state agents in Mexico" (Miller 2005, 150). Ultimately, the negative ruling by both the immigration judge and BIA rested on the determination that Hernandez-Montiel was not persecuted because he was a gay man, but because he was a transgender cross-dressing sex worker – in other words, pathologizing, criminalizing, and denying asylum of a queer individual deemed nationally "undesirable" (or too sexually deviant) to be granted asylum and admitted into the country to turn his trannie tricks in the US. "One of the adjudicators," in fact, specifically associated Hernandez-Montiel's "transvestism" with his sex work as a "male prostitute" (Miller 2005, 150). As Alice M. Miller explains, the denials "demonstrate the extent to which claimants need to simplify [and sanitize] their self-representations to portray immutable [and desirable] identity, as well as to adjust them to fit pre-existing norms and standards of acceptability (cross-dressing is not only not essential to a person's selfhood, doing it to sell sex is also unacceptable" (2005, 150; quotation slightly modified for emphasis). Rejecting the INS and BIA rulings that classified Hernandez-Montiel as a gay male cross-dresser, the judge presiding over the 9th Circuit Court of Appeals ruled that he was a gay man "with a female sexual identity" (Miller 2005, 151). Relying on expert scholarly testimony that distinguished the active, penetrating man from the passive, penetrated man in same-sex anal or oral intercourse, typifying the former as heteromasculine and the latter as homo-feminine in Mexican culture, the judge found that Hernandez-Montiel, as a persecuted female-identified homosexual man, should be awarded political asylum (*Hernandez-Montiel v. Immigration and Naturalization Service*, US Court of Appeals, 9th Circuit [225 F.3d 1084]; Miller 2005, 151; Randazzo 2005, 37). Citing *Matter of Acosta*, which defines membership in a "particular social group" as an "immutable characteristic," and quoting *Matter of Tenorio*, which defines "sexual orientation" as an "immutable characteristic," the court found that Hernandez-Montiel's sexual orientation was expressed "by adopting gendered traits characteristically associated with women" and was part of a "particular social group" of "gay men with female sexual identities" (*Hernandez-Montiel v. Immigration and Naturalization Service*, US Court of Appeals, 9th Circuit [225 F.3d 1084]; partially quoted in Randazzo 2005, 37).

If the denial of asylum rulings by both the INS and the BIA rejected the idea that Hernandez-Montiel's sexual identity rested on an "immutable characteristic" that defined him as a member in a "particular social group," then the judge's ruling, which granted asylum (a positive outcome for the asylee, of course), rested its decision on an argument that seems to define female-identified gay men as an "immutable" identity – i.e., as an essential or essentialist one. As Miller reasons: "In the *Hernandez-Montiel* case, the 9th Circuit re-shapes a loosely gendered form of conduct (dressing as a woman) into a naturalized identity-related conduct (female sexual behavior), which the court then erects into an immutable (sexual) identity" (2005, 152). We should ask, following Miller, "have we won the claim by reifying a category that will now freeze out other identities?" (Miller 2005, 152). Unfortunately, legal arguments – often grounded in essentialist notions of identity – *do* reify and codify those frameworks with respect to the law; and of course, legal categories – *par example*: race in US law prior to the 1954 Supreme Court ruling in *Brown v. Board of Education* – can and do have long-term material and political effects, and ones that can be deleterious to social justice in the US. Yet, given that the UNHCR defines a refugee as one belonging to a "particular social group" that is subject to persecution and US asylum and refugee law has interpreted membership to be premised upon an "immutable characteristic" that one either cannot change or should not be required to change, it is difficult indeed to imagine how Geovanni Hernandez-Montiel would have won his petition for asylum without deploying such a legal argument within the constraints of the law as now defined. And as Randazzo importantly notes, the ruling will almost certainly "make it easier for other transgender asylum seekers to win their claims along the same lines of reasoning" (2005, 37). Yet these battles do represent future legal and juridical terrains for securing political asylum for all persecuted sexual minorities and for queer legal activists in the US. "Still," Miller writes, "it is worth considering how legally successful strategies (ones culminating in a grant of asylum) might be informed by the more complex, culturally specific knowledge about sexuality that is emerging today" (2005, 153). She asks: "Can successful arguments recognize that the meaning of sexual conduct changes over time, that conduct will not *always* be congruent with identity or, more accurately, that conduct will not always be congruent with the identities that asylum judges recognize? How, in short, will advocates with a more nuanced appreciation of sexuality make their arguments and win?" (2005, 153).

Supreme Court cases have also shaped gay civil rights struggles, and these rulings are as relevant to queer immigrants or queer diasporic subjects in the US as to queer citizens, however *disidentified*.[16] Two Supreme Court cases have been central: *Bowers v. Hardwick* (1986) and *Lawrence v. Texas* (2003). The Supreme Court ruling in *Lawrence v. Texas* (2003), which hinged on a violation of due process, and overturning the notorious ruling in *Bowers v. Hardwick* (1986), was also a landmark legal moment in the battles for sexual minorities' rights, both those of US citizens and those of queer immigrants in the country. Writing the majority opinion (held by Justices Stevens, Souter, Ginsburg, Breyer, O'Connor, and Kennedy), Justice Anthony M. Kennedy asserted that "the State is not omnipresent in the home" (1; quoted in Epps et al. 2005, 189), thereby determining that the court had violated the right to privacy in its 1986 ruling that criminalized sodomy between consenting adults of the same sex (*Bowers v. Hardwick*). Although lauded by legal scholars and gay civil rights activists in the US as an important reversal of an ill-guided and discriminatory court decision to criminalize homoerotic sex acts (even those done in the privacy of one's own home!), other scholars, notably Katyal (2006), contend that the 2003 ruling operates according to a legal desire to "contain"' homoeroticism to private spaces, implicitly making public spaces "out of bounds" or "off limits" legally; therefore, the ruling reinscribes the notions of gay sexual identities as private affairs (another governmental incarnation of the *don't ask, don't tell* policy) to be hidden within the home and reasserts the heteronormativity of public spaces. Katyal speculates "whether *Lawrence* is yet another symbol of a global wave of change, or whether it represents an ultimately unfulfillable goal worldwide, particularly in places where gay civil rights movements have been met with considerable backlash" (2006, 1433). Quoting Manalansan and Cruz-Malavé (in *Queer Globalizations*), who argue that "in a world where what used to be considered 'private' is ever more commodified and marketed, queerness has become both an object of consumption . . . and an object through which queers constitute their identities in our contemporary consumer-oriented globalized world" (2002, 1), Katyal reasons that the *Lawrence* decision and "case law that . . . flourished in its wake" too often operate according to "an implicit logic of containment that has relegated the exercise of sexual autonomy to private, rather than public, spaces" (2006, 1434). Ultimately, "a politics of privacy," Katyal concludes, "must be melded to a broad notion of equality in citizenship if the concept of *true* sexual autonomy is to be effective"; and for that to be accomplished, a more dynamic understanding of the interrelation between the private and public spaces of queer citizenship must be imagined (2006, 1492). Queer critics would do well to heed Katyal's calls to trouble the private/public distinction on which the decision rested: a relegation of queerness to private spaces ineluctably reinscribes public space as heteronormative. As Calhoun explains, "the rhetoric of privacy arguments can do as much to sustain sexuality injustice as to intervene in it" (253; quoted in Rodríguez 2003, 107). For Kendall Thomas, the necessary legal battle "must begin to take rigorous and relentless critical aim at the ideology and institution of normative heterosexuality" (1806; quoted in Rodríguez 2003, 107). And Juana María Rodríguez agrees that "the ideology and institution of normative heterosexuality is what extends property rights, health benefits, life insurance, power of attorney, inheritance, child custody, adoption rights, tax incentives, and a host of other benefits to those who publicly declare heterosexuality through state-sanctioned marriage, including the right to extend US citizenship to one's spouse" (2003, 108).

Queer legal scholars and activists have also challenged and questioned the "rights-based" framework for gaining political ground on issues of migration, asylum, and immigration. In an earlier law review article, Katyal (2002) probes the legal implications that rights-based laws protecting sexual minorities in the US might have transnationally or in a global gay rights movement if those national laws and their ideological underpinnings or presuppositions about identity, identity politics, and civil rights were "exported" to other countries across the globe. US-based civil rights models of legal struggle for sexual minorities' rights too often exclude alternative models of sexualities found in non-Western countries (Katyal focuses on Thailand, India, and Mexico), with US gay rights organizations viewing "same-sex sexual activity that does not fit [the dominant] mold as 'underdeveloped'" (2002, 175). Instead, Katyal underscores the need "to focus on sexual autonomy, and its expressive and deliberative aspects" (2002, 176). In discussions of global gay rights movements, and perhaps especially in discussions of international migration for queer subjects and sexual dissidents,

Jon Binnie also suggests that "a narrow focus on rights can lead us down a theo-retical cul-de-sac" (2004, 87). Nevertheless, sexually marked minorities do suffer acts of homophobic hate violence, which often compel queer migrations and lead to queer diasporas, attest to the need – legally, strategically, materially, politi-cally, and intellectually – to think "sexuality transnationally" (Muñoz and Barrett 1996).

Questions for Reflection and Discussion

- What are the rhetorical, political, material, and epistemological interrelations of the terms "queer" and "diaspora"?
- How are the terms different? How and why may it be useful to distinguish the two terms as well as to conjugate the terms?
- What does it mean to use these terms as verbs, not adjectives: that is, how might we understand efforts to "queer" diasporas and efforts to "diasporize" queer communities? What are the benefits and risks of these efforts?
- How do queer migrations alter diasporas and diasporic formations?
- How do diasporas and diasporic subjects alter queer communities?
- How do queer diasporic subjects further complicate the notions of home, homeland, and nation-state, as well as a sense of political belonging within these spaces?
- What are the structural interrelations of exile from a homeland and a sense of ejection from a home (one's nuclear or extended family)?
- How has queer studies deployed migrancy metaphors in ways that obscure real material migrations?
- How are international laws on political asylum and refugees being used by queer diasporic legal activists to protect sexual minorities who have suffered discrimination, abuse, even violence?

Additional Research

Analyzing film and visual cultures

Pratibha Parmar (Indo-Kenyan) is a queer diasporic film director who now lives and works in the UK. In 1991, Parmar directed and produced a short documen-tary film about queer sexualities in India and in India's diasporas for Channel 4 in Britain. View the film *Khush* (1991) and write a short essay about how Parmar explores queerness and migrations through her filmic lens.

5

Race and Diasporas

Echoing W. E. B. DuBois more than a century after he first wrote the words in 1903, we may be tempted (indeed, we are) to pronounce that one of the most intractable problems of the twenty-first century remains "the problem of the color line,"[1] even in the midst of interreligious conflicts, the illegal trafficking in weapons of mass destruction (WMDs), global terrorism and counter-terrorist wars too often driven by nebulous if also dangerous notions of the "clash of civilizations," or more ironically, the "clash of fundamentalisms," as well as secret military prisons, and international concerns about detention, torture, and the flouting of long-established and honored precepts of international law (codified in the Geneva Conventions), all addressed in this book's "Postface," not to mention environmental degradation, global warming, and the trafficking in human subjects for profit; but if we do, it is not naively so: in other words, it would not be to do so without being fully cognizant of the globally inflected and manifold forms of racism, its historical variations, its deleterious potential for metamorphosis and material alteration, as well as its radical information by gender, class, sexuality, nationality, and transnational inflections with religion, geopolitical shifts, international realignments, transborder migrations, and diasporic formations. Yet, in many ways (both resurgent and residual), it seems impossible to think the contemporary moment without doing so – at least in part – through the parameters of race, racialization, and regionally, nationally, and globally deployed racisms. And diasporic communities, like other international transborder migrants, like detained "asylees" or even detained "enemy combatants," are too often racialized by hegemonic power structures in their countries of residence or of detention, as the case may alternately be. In fall and winter 2005, this fact was all too materially apparent, if not transparent, on national and international fronts with the near-simultaneous eruption of media-labeled "race riots" in France (from October 27 until November 12, 2005) and in Australia (December 11–12, 2005).[2]

This chapter tackles the vexing and often volatile social problematics of race, immigration, and debates about citizenship, both in home countries of origin and those of diasporic adoption. The chapter has three primary objectives. First, it offers a historical overview of race and diaspora and various diasporic communities that have been negatively racialized in their diasporic countries of adoption or that have been expelled from their home countries as racialized minorities. Second, it examines the theoretical conjunctures of race, racism, and diaspora. Third, it also schematically distinguishes specific types or models of "raced" or "racialized diasporas" and provides historical examples in two case studies. After outlining the theoretical intersections of race, racism, and racialized forms of diasporic movement, or the racialized forms of diasporic immobility, or lack of movement, we will examine historical examples of racialized diasporas around two thematically organized case studies: (1) *outsiders within* – the post-migratory racialization of economic migrants; and (2) *barred entry* – the racialization of refugees by intended countries of destination that bar entry to these communities seeking political asylum. A third pattern, though not foregrounded in a separate case study in the chapter, includes racialized diasporic communities who are ultimately *forced out* – i.e., those diasporic communities (like South Asians in East Africa, generally, but Indian-Ugandans, specifically, who were violently expelled by General-cum-President Idi Amin in 1972) who are forced into new diasporas because they are targeted as ethnically "impure" bodies within the nation-state.

The first case study examines economic migrants who, following pull migratory flows, resettle in a diasporic country and who, following the reemergence of push factors (economic recession, high levels of unemployment, competition with citizens for jobs), find themselves negatively racialized and pejoratively characterized as unwanted foreigners – *étranger*, or *Ausländer* – even if they are in fact second-generation citizens in the country: such has been the case for Franco-Maghrebi migrants and second-generation children of immigrant parents, who are in fact French citizens, and for Turkish *Gästarbeiter*, or guestworkers, in Germany. Although the case is true for both Franco-Maghrebis and Turkish Germans, the case study focuses on the example of Algerians in France. The second case study examines racialized refugees who suffer the discriminatory immigration practices and repressive asylum policies of the countries in which they are actively seeking refuge. Within this paradigm, the refugees are actually barred entry into the country, frequently being intercepted at sea or at the intended port of entry, detained in offshore immigration prisons, and then ultimately deported back to their home countries despite the real, not merely perceived, threats of political retaliation, violent repression, imprisonment, torture, and even death. Although race is rarely deployed as the state rationale for the barring of these refugees into the intended countries of adoption, race and racialization are inflected within the administrative language, as well as within the public debates surrounding these refugees. This has been the case for both Vietnamese and Haitian refugees, who were seeking political asylum in Australia and the United States, respectively, and who were pejoratively referred to as "boat people" by the national and international media.

Race and Diaspora: Historical Overview

The Nazi-designed and SS-orchestrated Holocaust of the late 1930s and early 1940s led to the annihilation of 6 million European Jews, a genocide fueled by anti-Semitic racism, fascist class warfare, and fatal, systemic, and institutionalized violence. European Jews who survived the labor and death camps, or who were able to escape arrest, detention, and death were permanently displaced from their homes and homelands. In the years immediately following the end of World War II in 1945, the world continued to witness massive displacements, racialized bloodshed, and violent ethnic strife among warring factions and along volatile borders, many cartographically created following the war: during the Partition of India from Pakistan in 1947 as both countries won their independence from Britain, 15 million Muslims, Hindus, Sikhs, Punjabs, and Bengalis were forced into a religious-ethnic diasporic division, many being slaughtered while trying to cross the borders dividing these two newly independent countries. Nation-state division along religious and ethnic lines set a dangerous postcolonial and post-World War II precedent that has continued to plague the globe throughout the twentieth and into the twenty-first century through racial civil warfare, genocide, and other forms of "ethnic cleansing," although nationalistic divisions along religious and ethnic lines must be contextualized within earlier post-World War I cartographic restructuring of nation-states that have ethnic-religious dimensions, including the dissolution of the Ottoman Empire, the geographic separation of Albania from Yugoslavia, and the border tensions between Greece and Turkey, among other salient examples. Racial and religious demarcations also reveal colonial legacies and may be seen as consequences of British colonial censuses that ruled by divide-and-conquer tactics that literally separated the South Asian or Indian subcontinent into regions defined by religious and ethnic classification. As in South Asia, so in the Middle East. In 1917, the Balfour Declaration was signed, granting Jewish Zionists British-occupied land for the creation of a "homeland." In 1948, Israel was created out of Palestine territory, and consequently, communities of Arab Palestinians, Christians, and Muslims were displaced from their homes and homelands.

The *Shoah*, as the Holocaust is known in the Hebrew language, and these other "postcolonial" and post-WWII violences ultimately led to international efforts to eradicate racial violence, religious persecution, and political discrimination, as well as to protect the rights of refugees and to guarantee asylum to those in need. In 1948, the United Nations issued and passed the Universal Declaration of Human Rights, and in 1951, the international political organization held the conference on the Status of Refugees and Stateless Persons which led to General Assembly Resolution 429 (v) protecting the rights of refugees. Despite the post-World War II initiatives, the world has remained plagued by multifarious forms of racism and racialized or ethnic violences at the local, regional, national, and even global levels. A few examples will suffice to illustrate this point: although economic migration from North Africa and the Middle East into Europe dates to the nineteenth century, the period from the early post-WWII years and postcolonial period from the 1950s and 1960s saw a rapid proliferation of these economic migrants seeking work in Europe. Maghrebi economic migrants in France and Turkish *Gästarbeiter* in Germany came to those countries seeking better incomes and educational opportunities. During the early postwar decades of economic boom, these economic migrants were actively sought out to contribute production power for the French and German post-WWII economies; in the periods of economic recession beginning in the 1970s and continuing into the 1980s, however, these same economic migrants were regarded by French and German citizens as interlopers, unwanted immigrants who were vying for the best jobs, pressing wages downward, and competing with nationals for economic and educational advancement: during those down cycles in the French and German economies, Franco-Maghrebi and Turkish German migrant workers, and even second-generation children of economic migrants, have become the targets of virulent forms of European racisms that crystallize around ethnicity, nationality, religion, class, and economic push-pull factors.

Racialization of diasporic communities in Europe have coincided with other examples of racialized diasporas, including forced diasporas or race-based expulsions: in 1971, during the Pakistani Civil War, which led to the division of the postcolonial country into two states – Pakistan and Bangladesh – 10 million refugees crossed the border between India and the former territory of East Pakistan (now Bangladesh), fleeing ethnic violence and religious warfare; in 1972, as emergent postcolonial African nation-states sought political autonomy and economic development, Idi Amin's regime expelled an estimated 40,000 to 80,000 South Asian Ugandans of Indian and Pakistani descent from the country, despite the fact that many had been born in Uganda. Amin came to power following a military coup against the first postcolonial Ugandan president. In the immediate wake of the fall of Saigon in 1975 and the end of the Vietnam-American War, scores of thousands of Vietnamese refugees, fleeing violence, persecution, and economic destitution, fled the Southeast Asian country of Vietnam for Europe, the United States, and countries within the Asian Pacific, particularly its more affluent metropolitan centers such as Sydney and Hong Kong. In the Asian Pacific, most of these Vietnamese "boat people" were not only denied political asylum, but also routinely intercepted at sea and detained in immigrant prisons by the Australian government. Similarly, Haitian refugees – also pejoratively referred to as "boat people" by the US media – fleeing political violence, state despotism, military coup d'états, and poverty in their home country were intercepted, detained, and eventually deported back to Haiti during the period of late Duvalierism, *Déchoukaj* ("Uprooting"), and the post-Duvalier period known as "Duvalierism without Duvalier" from the late 1980s until the mid-1990s.

In the "refugee crisis" of the mid-1990s, the world witnessed a proliferation of racialized violences, systemic forms of "ethnic cleansing," and racial genocides, with the breakup of the former nation-state of Yugoslavia following the death of Josip Broz Tito in 1980, and the outbreak of genocidal violence in 1994 between the Tutsis and the Hutus in Rwanda, which culminated in the shocking deaths of 800,000 Rwandans (mostly Tutsis) in a mere 100 days.[3] Both civil wars led to genocidal regimes of violence, internally displaced persons (IDPs), and a flood of international refugees seeking asylum (miserably concomitant with a notable and significant decline in the number of asylum applications being approved by European, North American, and wealthier Asian Pacific countries, such as Canada, the US, Britain, France, Germany, Australia, and New Zealand). The 1990s were thus a period of shocking racist violence, "ethnic cleansing" pogroms, and genocidal warfare. In the wake of 9/11, Arab and Muslim immigrants across the globe have also suffered racial and religious persecution as backlash against these immigrant communities has escalated during the War on Terror and since the onset of the Afghan and Iraqi wars in 2002 and 2003, respectively, despite administrative efforts – real and rhetorical – by the US government to quell discrimination against these groups. For example, autumn 2005 witnessed what has been called "race riots" among Arab immigrants both in France and in Australia. In the mid-years of the first decade of the twenty-first century, and continuing as this book was finished, the question of racial violence and ethnic genocide has recurred in the Dafur region of Sudan.

Race and Diasporas: Theoretical Conjunctures, Transnational Disjunctures

Race is a vexing term with myriad connotations and historical, cultural resonances. Race may be defined in biological, cultural, historical, material, political, and legal or juridical parameters. For example, while biological definitions of race that distinguished human beings geographically and ethnically in terms of phenotypical difference first emerged in the eighteenth-century anthropological writings of Linnaeus, Blumenbach, and Buffon, as well as the philosophical writings of Enlightenment thinkers such as Locke, Hobbes, Hume, Kant, and Hegel, and then proliferated in the nineteenth century with the "pseudo-scientific" theories of race and racial difference (such as in Comte de Gobineau's *On the Inequality of the Races*), biological definitions of race progressively lost sway, if they did not totally vanish, in the twentieth century under the critiques of anthropologists like Franz Boas and other social scientists who argued that so-called racial differences were not biological, but rather cultural, inculturated, and thus changeable (not fixed, essential, or immutable), as "scientific" definitions of race and racial difference had long held. For Boas, as for most scholars of the twentieth century, race is a cultural construct, a product of language, culture, history, and power relations among individual communities. Some scholars (notably Stephen Castle, Paul Gilroy, and others) assert that "race" is no more than a secondary byproduct of racism: in other words, racism creates and sustains hierarchical relations of power among various groups of people based on artificial distinctions (such as phenotype or skin color) among human groups.

Definitions of race are manifold, contingent, and changeable. Thus it is crucial that we remember that definitions of race are culturally variable, historically specific, nationally determined, and internationally inflected or deployed as well. In other words, when we speak of racism, it is urgent that we understand first and foremost that race is a cultural construct that is historically malleable and differently deployed at different moments in time and in varying national contexts. There are, however, recurrent patterns to how race is defined and deployed as a discriminatory rubric across multiple geographical settings and historical periods. For example, during the emergence of European colonial conquest in the sixteenth through the eighteenth centuries, and at the height of the British and French colonial empires in the late nineteenth century, race and racism were largely defined by imperial beliefs in white supremacy – through often cloaked under the veil of European "civilization," African barbarism, and Asian orientalism that was exotically represented as racial alterity. Within European colonial contexts, then, particularly where white settler colonies defined their own sense of racial superiority in contrast with indigenous groups, race operated as a mark of social divide, cultural difference, and power differentials (those of possession – of land, natural resources, education, capital, and power – and dispossession, among those dispossessed, often through piracy, theft, and conquest, of those very material and intellectual objects). This was equally and consistently true of Anglo-American and Dutch settlers in South Africa who created violent systems of racial apartheid and dispossessed the native Africans of land, resources, and political representation; of Anglo-American settlers in Australia and New Zealand who committed genocidal acts against the aborigines and Maori in those British settler colonies; of Anglo-American settlers in North America (in the territories that are now the US and Canada), who expropriated land and resources, restricted movement, waged war, and committed acts of genocide against myriad Native American tribes; and no less true of Dutch settlers in Indonesia, or of Spanish colonial settlers in North America (now the southwestern United States and Mexico), central America, and the Caribbean who dominated the Aztec, Mayan, Arawak, Taino, and Caribs in these regions. Even in European colonial holdings that were not primarily settler colonies, such as the British colonial rule in the Indian subcontinent and British and French colonial territories in north, west, east, and southern Africa, white racial privilege and hierarchical deprivileging of yellow, brown, or black natives held sway for several centuries defined by European appropriation of capital, wealth, land, resources, and the powers of manufacturing and production. And, of course, the European slave trade, the transatlantic Middle Passage, and the enslavement of millions of individuals of west African descent in the Americas and in parts of Europe from the sixteenth through the nineteenth centuries formed one of the most egregious examples of institutionalized racism, forced diaspora, racial domination, and "race" as a category of dehumanization, subjugation, and violent exploitation.

Throughout the twentieth century, these centuries-old beliefs in white racial supremacy and African, Asian, and American inferiority have, regrettably, continued to inflect and negatively determine postcolonial configurations of race, racial difference, national racisms, and international racisms, both in former settler colonies that are now independent nation-states, such as Canada, the US, Australia, New Zealand, and South Africa, as well as in postcolonial countries that won independence from European colonial rule, such as India, Pakistan, Bangladesh in South Asia, myriad African countries from Algeria and Morocco in the north, Nigeria, Ghana, Cameroon, and Senegal in the west, Kenya, Somalia, and Sudan in the east, and Zimbabwe, Botswana, and Malawi in the south, as well as throughout the Caribbean and Central and South America.

In the postcolonial and post-abolition world, the racialized forms of colonialism and slavery persisted into the late nineteenth and throughout the twentieth centuries across the globe in disparate continental and national locales: for example, racial segregation – particularly of "white" and "black" individuals – persisted in South Africa under the sharply divisive and disenfranchising system of apartheid; in the United States under post-Reconstruction Jim Crow laws and extra-legal forms of racial discrimination and in racially inflected criminal laws and penalties; in Canada where African Caribbean immigrants have been targets of police and public discrimination grounded in race; and in Britain where "black British" postcolonial immigrant communities have remained culturally, politically, materially, and socially marginalized from civic rights, citizenship, and employment and academic opportunities.

To understand race, we also need to understand and define racism as a critical term that also has multivariate forms and problematic, if nuanced, contours. Pedagogically and intellectually, we may distinguish variant forms of racism: "everyday" racism; biological racism; cultural racism; violent racism; historical or political racism; and institutional racism. Although it is important for political and intellectual reasons to distinguish and differentiate these various forms of racism, it is also important to note that the levels may be multiply-present, overlapping, and even difficult to disentangle in real-world contexts. Let's consider the following definitions for operational forms and levels of racism:

"Everyday" racism: individual acts of prejudice, antipathy, discrimination, or hatred.
"Biological" racism: the prejudicial beliefs that characteristics or traits are in-born or intrinsic to given races.
"Cultural" racism: the prejudicial belief that races possess distinct characteristics (typically regarded as negative) due to learned, cultural differences.
"Violent" racism: brutal acts of violence, even murder, due to profound levels of prejudicial hatred (lynching, police brutality, or other hate crimes).
"Historical/political" racism: broad historical moments defined by widespread injustice, prejudice, and disenfranchisement against a targeted race or ethnic group (segregation, Jim Crowism).
"Institutional" racism: the resilient forms of race prejudice and ethnic bias that were historically formative in the structuring of legal documents (such as the US Constitution), laws (property laws, criminal laws, civil laws), municipal policies, academic disciplines, or other forms of knowledges. This level of racism almost becomes invisible decades or centuries after it becomes inscribed into law or policy, but intractably remains as residual, yet very real, forms of material racism that is very damaging to disadvantaged communities.

Unlike segregation laws in the US, which were overtly racist, property laws for example were predicated on a legal definition of citizenship as "white male property owner" and others excluded from this terrain (African slaves, Chinese economic migrants); even after legal definitions of citizenship were altered by constitutional amendments, levels of racialized presupposition and privilege still have trace remainders in old statutes and laws that are not overtly racist, but remain racially marked nonetheless.

Racisms, like cultural-historical constructs of race, are neither monolithic, nor universal and transhistorical; they vary according to circumstance, opportunity, advantage, disadvantage, strategic or perceived necessity, or material profit. Racisms, though, do have a recurrent feature: they are inherently about social, political, material relations of power; they are about social hierarchy, control, possession, and dispossession.

So how does race inflect diaspora, diasporic movements, or trans-relocations, and diasporic communities across the world? It may be argued that all migratory patterns and human migrations are inflected by race and have decisively racialized parameters – whether overt and openly discriminatory, or more subtly interwoven with issues of class, ancestry, ethnicity, and religion. So what may be defined as the distinctly racialized parameters of diasporas? Race may also undeniably operate as an identity category for diasporic individuals, forming a sense of shared cultural heritage and common experience forged historically in response to racism in the host country of adoption. Race may also operate as an exclusionary category or an actual barrier to movement, to transborder migration, and cross-border motility: historically, the racial classification or categorization of a group determined one's mobility, one's right to move or relocate, or conversely, restricted one's right to resettle, based on the prejudicial or racist exclusions of the "receiving" (or rather, unreceptive) country. In conceptualizing the racialized parameters of diasporas, three salient patterns emerge: the racialization (post-immigration) of economic migrants during periods of recession and competition for jobs; the barring of entry to immigrants, even imperiled refugees, based on racialized (and racist) criteria in the country denying admission; and finally, the expulsion of immigrants, permanent residents, and even naturalized citizens based on racist pogroms of national exclusion from the citizen-body. The first two patterns are examined more extensively in separate case studies below.

Case Study: Outsiders Within: Les Beurs and France's "Crise des banlieues"

During the months of October and November 2005, diasporic youth (children of immigrants from the Maghreb, also called *les Beurs*, sub-Saharan Africa, and the Antilles) the majority of whom are French citizens, took to the streets – marching, protesting, rioting, torching, and vandalizing public property – following the gruesome deaths by electrocution of two teenagers. According to Elaine Sciolini and Ariane Bernard writing for the *New York Times* on the first year anniversary of the riots, which were marked by the irruption of street violence, the *banlieues* (suburbs) of Paris were "aflame with the rage of unemployed, undereducated youth, mostly the offspring of Arab and African immigrants."[4] Sciolino and

Bernard's description is not only pejorative, but also only partially true: the French youth are *French* youth, and while most are of Franco-Maghrebi descent (whose parents were indeed immigrants from Algeria, Tunisia, and Morocco), joined by a minority whose parents are from other parts of Africa or the Caribbean (Senegal, Cameroon, Martinique, Guadeloupe, and elsewhere), they are almost all without exception citizen youth born in France; yet they remain, in many ways, an unassimilated, disenfranchised, and racially targeted minority who are ubiquitously referenced as *les immigrés*, "immigrants." Expatriate African American writer James Baldwin, who sought refuge from US racism and racial discrimination, like so many before him, in Paris, once bitingly noted that the Maghrebi were France's "niggers" (*les nègres*). Understanding how race and racism have inflected the Franco-Maghrebi diaspora (from the end of the Algerian Revolution in 1962 up until the 2005 riots in Parisian banlieues) is, thus, of crucial importance. First, let's overview the crisis of 2005, and its anniversary in fall 2006, then examine the post-WWII immigration from the Maghreb to France, as well as cultural marginalization, political disenfranchisement, overt and covert forms of racism suffered by this diasporic community, and religious discrimination against Franco-Maghrebis throughout the country, even in her "city of lights."

In Clichy-sous-Bois, a banlieue outside Paris, 15-year old Bouna Traoré and 17-year old Zyed Benna died by electrocution after running into an electric transformer while seeking refuge and evading police arrest on October 27, 2005.[5] Heated debate and volatile exchanges have centered around whether or not the police chased the teenagers into the transformer. According to *Le Monde*, "Les autorités affirment que les policiers n'ont pas poursuivi les victimes" (The authorities affirm that the police did not pursue the victims). That affirmation, however, has been challenged by French youth and immigrant communities who daily confront police harassment and discrimination, if not more open acts of violence (beating, stun-gunning, shooting) that have also plagued minority youth in US cities like Cincinnati, New York, and Los Angeles. Despite these administrative disavowals of police complicity in the deaths, the official rhetoric was skeptically received, if not outright rejected, and during the night of the 27th, "Une quinzaine de véhicules sont incendiés" (About fifteen vehicles were torched). Some estimates total 23 cars. Incensed youth also set fire to public buildings (*bâtiments publics*).[6] On October 28, a Friday evening, approximately 400 youth affronted and confronted an estimated 250–300 police officers and armed guards (*gendarmes*), and car torchings broke out in Chêne-Pointu. In total, 30 cars and 10 garbage dumpsters were set afire by angry youth. Thirteen youth were placed under police surveillance for the night. On Saturday, October 29, a "Marche silencieuse en hommage aux victimes" (Silent March in honor of the victims) drew about 500 people from Clichy-sous-Bois and surrounding *villes* and *banlieues*. Marchers wore white t-shirts with the names of the victims on the back side and the words "Mort pour rien" (death for nothing, *or* death in vain) on the front. Although fire bombings, car torchings, and arrests continued on the third night following the deaths of Traoré and Benna, no direct physical violence erupted.

In a televised interview on Sunday, October 30, then Minister of the Interior Nicolas Sarkozy (now conservative French President) reaffirmed that "*'les pol-*

iciers ne poursuivaient pas les jeunes' électrocutés" (the police did not pursue the electrocuted youth), pledged "*'la tolérance zéro*' en matière de violences urbaines" (zero tolerance on the issue of urban violence), and ordered additional police and mobilized soldiers (*gendarmes mobiles*) to reinforce the officers already present in Clichy-sous-Bois. Azouz Begag, Minister Delegated to the Promotion of Equal Opportunity and well-known "Beur" writer and activist, openly criticized his colleague Minister Sarkozy on France 2 television, averring that the incident was no longer merely about the two electrocuted youth, but more generally about the treatment of minority youth by French police. Minister Begag also objected to Minster Sarkozy's negative depiction of youth protesters as a *racaille*, a gang or mob. On the night of October 30, in Forestière Quarter, tear gas bombs – a type commonly utilized by the Compagnies Républicaines de Sécurité (CRS) – were thrown into the interior of a mosque. Muslim worshippers accused the police of having launched the *grenade lacrymogène* (tear gas grenade). Angry protests, heated arguments, and hostile confrontations between angry Franco-Maghrebi citizens and the French police erupted later that night.

Minister Sarkozy offered to meet with the victims' families, who refused, demanding instead to meet with Prime Minister Dominique de Villepin: according to Siyakah Traoré, one of the victim's brothers, the families refused to see Sarkozy because they believed he had proven himself incapable of addressing the violence: "'En aucun cas, nous n'irons voir Sarkozy qui, pour nous, est incompétent. Nous demandons à être reçus par Dominique de Villepin" (In any event, we do not want to see Sarkozy who, for us, is incompetent. We demand to be received by Dominique de Villepin). Acknowledging that *la bombe lacrymogène* was likely "*en dotation des compagnies d'intervention* (CRS)" (a technical device associated with the CRS), Minister Sarkozy nevertheless denied that that fact irrefragably tied the action itself ("la bombe lacrymogène lancée à la mosque," hurling the tear gas bomb into the mosque) to the police. That same day, October 31, Minister Begag denounced what he perceived to be a rhetorical battle by a "semantic warrior" ("une sémantique guerrière"):

> quand on nomme un préfet musulman, quand on dit vouloir donner le droit de vote aux étrangers et qu'on envoie des CRS contre les jeunes des banlieues, il y a un déc alage. . . . C'est en luttant contre les discriminations dont sont victimes les jeunes qu'on rétablira l'ordre, l'ordre de l'égalité. Pas en amenant plus de CRS.

> when one names a Muslim prefect, when one claims to desire to extend the vote to immigrants, yet deploys the CRS against youth in the banlieues, there is a contradiction. . . . It is in the struggle against discrimination that victimized youth hope to reestablish "order," the order of equality. Not in more discrimination by the CRS.

Tensions, popular and political, continued to increase. Politically, tensions increased within the ministerial cabinet as Minister Sarkozy called for Minister Begag's resignation from office; and popularly, tensions increased as police officials charged that insurgents in Clichy-sous-Bois fomented acts of youth copycat violence in other neighborhoods: "les émeutiers de Clichy avaient fait des émules à Sevran, Neuilly-sur-Marne et Bondy" (agitators in Clichy have inspired imitators in Sevran, Neuilly-sur-Marne and Bondy). On Halloween night, amid fears of street unrest by youth, French national police were deployed to Clichy-sous-Bois; the night, however, remained relatively calm. But it proved to be only a fleeting moment of calm preceding tornadic storms of youth unrest, arson, vandalism, and waves of police repression.

On Tuesday, November 1, Prime Minister de Villepin met with the victims' families, reassuring them that a full investigation into the circumstances surrounding the boys' deaths would be undertaken. To the public, the Prime Minister insisted on "la nécessité d'un retour au calme" (the necessity of a return to calm). Seconding this official plea, Minister Sarkozy asked for the concerted "efforts de toutes les parties intéressées pour faire revenir le calme dans les banlieues concernées" (efforts of all involved parties to restore calm in the impacted banlieues). Despite these public statements, violence not only continued, but also spilled "dans trois autres départements: la Seine-et-Marne, les Yvelines et le Val-d'Oise" (into three other departments: Seine-et-Marne, Yvelines, and Val-d'Oise). On the following day (November 2), President Jacques Chirac convened a meeting of the ministerial cabinet, calling not only for a "retour au calme," but also for a "respect de la loi" (respect for the law) and a restoration of order. Tensions within the ministerial cabinet continued as Minister Begag openly condemned Minister Sarkozy for neglecting to confer with him about the youth unrest and the police crackdown, adding that "Nicolas Sarkozy n'est qu'un ministre sur 31" (Nicolas Sarkozy was not the only minister on the 31st). Despite government efforts to restore order, youth agitation and police confrontations continued in Seine-Saint-Denis. In the mid-afternoon of November 2, part of the business district in Bobigny 2 was vandalized; and throughout that night, car torchings and arson of public buildings in Aulnay-sous-Bois, Seine-et-Marne, and Hauts-de-Seine ensued. Amid nocturnal street violence in the area, Minister Sarkozy returned to Bobigny in order to meet with police leaders, the Prefect Jean-François Cordet, Department Direct Jacques Méric, and Christian Lambert, Central Director of the CRS. Violence erupted during the night: approximately 400 cars were torched in Ile-de-France with *brûlées* (burnings) in Dijon (centre-east), in Seine-Maritime (west), and in Bouches-du-Rhône (southeast).

By the evening of November 4, arson and violence had erupted across the capital city of Paris and Parisian banlieues with 897 cars torched during the night, 253 youth arrested, and widespread burning of public and commercial buildings, marking a ninth night of "violences urbaines" (urban violence) in "la region parisienne," including the surrounding French *villes* of Toulouse, Rennes, Nantes, Lille, Le Havre, Soissons, Dijon, Pau, and Strasbourg. After fiery conflagrations in Aulnay-sous-Bois through the night of November 4, between 2,000 and 3,000 people marched in streets filled with "les carcasses de voitures calcinées" (the shells of burnt-out cars) on Saturday, November 5. Convening the Interior Security Council on November 6, President Chirac declared " 'la priorité est le rétablissement de la sécurité et de l'ordre public' dans les banlieues" ("the priority is the reestablishment of security and public order" in the banlieues), following a twelfth night of violence, arson, vandalization, fighting, militarized police presence on the streets, and youth arrests. Explosive hostilities and increasing street volatility led the Council of Ministers to declare a *état d'urgence* (state of emergency). In a televised statement on TF1, Prime Minister de Villepin authorized prefects to impose a *couvre-feu* (curfew) to combat the looting and arson, which nevertheless continued with "1,173 véhicules . . . brûlés . . . et 330 personnes . . . interpellées" (1,173 vehicles burned . . . and 330 individuals arrested) during November 7, the first night following the declaration of a state of emergency, and "617 véhicules sont brûlés pendant la nuit" (617 vehicles being set afire during the night) on November 8. Prefects in Rouen, Le Havre, Amiens, Orléans, and other areas imposed curfews on November 9; however, prefects in Seine-Saint-Denis, Paris, and Val-d'Oise decided not to impose curfews. Despite the widespread curfews, and despite Minister Sarkozy's comment (or perhaps because of it?) that prefects should "expulser '*sans délai*' tous les étrangers qui seraient condamnés dans le cadre des violences urbaines" (expel without delay all foreigners sentenced for committing crimes of urban violence), violence continued with 482 cars torched and 203 arrests. Minister Sarkozy's statement blatantly ignores a social-political truth while rhetorically promulgating an openly public lie: that the youth agitators are militant foreign immigrants, not angry, disenfranchised French citizens. Minister Sarkozy still urged "la paix" (peace) on November 10, yet the violence did not subside: 463 cars were burned, 201 people arrested, and eight police officers from Seine-Saint-Denis suspended for unnecessary violence and brutality against a 19-year-old youth. On November 11, the capital was placed under a state of "haute surveillance" (high surveillance), "sécurité est renforcée à Paris pour le week-end" (security was reinforced in Paris for the weekend), and authorities prohibited protest, marches, and all other political gatherings on streets and in public places on Saturday and Sunday. In spite of these "emergency" restrictions against free speech in Paris, violence remained undiminished: "502 véhicules sont incendiés et 206 personnes interpellées dans la nuit" (502 vehicles were burned and 206 persons arrested during the night) of November 11. But by the evening of Saturday, November 12, for the first time since the deaths of Traoré and Benna on October 27, violence began to abate, with only 374 car torchings over the entire weekend, down (though not substantially) from those of the preceding days.

The state of emergency and the curfew both remained in effect until November 15, and two days later, on November 17, the police signaled a "retour à la normale" (a return to normalcy), but the "Crises" had already brought massive devastation in France: 10,000 cars burned, the destruction or vandalization of 300 buildings, and 6,000 arrests.[7] Financially, the impact was also profound: the cost of torched cars totaled 23 million euros, and the cost of public buildings destroyed by arson reached an estimated 80–150 million euros, bringing the total estimated cost to 200 million euros.[8] Less than one month after the crisis drew to a close, Jean-François Copé, Minister Delegated to the Budget, indicated that "l'État n'interviendra pas financièrement dans ce dossier" (the State would not financially intervene in this case).

Socially and culturally, the impact of the October 2005 crisis and the November 2005 riots has been equally profound. According to Luc Bronner writing for *Le Monde* on January 5, 2006, "Les violences urbaines d'octobre et novembre

2005 ont remis les banlieues au centre du paysage politique, intellectuel et média-
tique" (the urban violence of October and November 2005 placed the banlieues
back at the center of the political, intellectual, and media landscape).[9] In an article
entitled "Colère noire" (Black Anger), published in *Le Monde* on December 10,
2005, Benôit Hopquin describes the problem of the banlieues as an intersecting
one of race-class nexus, which geographically displaced "noirs à l'extérieur"
(blacks to the exterior) and placed "blancs à interieur" (whites at the interior).
Fearful of violent resurgences during the holidays, the French government
deployed "la police national" (the national police), a total of "16,000 policiers
et gendarmes supplémentaires" (16,000 police and supplementary armed guards),
in order to prevent "flambées de violence dans les zones urbaines de France la
nuit du 31 décembre" (inflammatory violence in France's urban zones on New
Year's Eve).[10]

Political fallout of the 2005 "Crise des banlieues" has also continued to be
part of the post-2005 landscape in France. Regarded by many as a xenophobic,
rightist, nationalist hardliner, Nicolas Sarkozy, though the front-runner and
eventual winner in France's presidential elections held in spring 2007, was nevertheless radically challenged by Ségolène Royal, the Socialist Party candidate.
Unsurprisingly, on January 3, 2006, French activist political groups and grassroots organizations in France (including ACT UP and Cimade) denounced
Sarkozy's proposal to reform immigration law, calling the proposal "une néga-
tion radicale des droits fondamentaux de la personne" (a radical negation of
fundamental human rights). Following brazen popular criticism by rapper Joey
Starr, tennis player Yannick Noah, and soccer players Lilian Thuram and Vikash
Dhorasso, Sarkozy struck back: "L'anti-sarkozysme est une mode" (Anti-
Sarkozyism is fashionable).[11] Other activist organizations include "Tour de
France de la diversité" and AC le feu (loosely translated as *AC the fire* but also
an acronym for the Association collectif liberté, égalité, fraternité ensemble et
unis), which was "fondé en novembre 2005 à Clichy-sous-Bois en réaction aux
violences urbaines" (founded in November 2005 in Clichy-sous-Bois in reaction
to urban violence). On the eve of the anniversary of the events of October and
November 2005, Mehdi Bigaderne, a founding member of AC le feu, commented
on the fear among immigrant youth in France: "Les immigrés font peur aux
Français, . . . les jeunes aimeraient pouvoir marcher dans leur cité sans se faire
contrôler par la police" (Immigrants are fearful of the French . . . the youth would
like to be able to march in their cities without being controlled or examined by
the police). According to activist Samir Mihi, the core issues that must be
addressed include "logement, l'emploi, les inégalités et les discriminations"
(housing, employment, inequality, and discrimination).[12]

In October 2006, as the first anniversary of the deaths of Bouna Traoré and
Zyed Benna approached, violence re-erupted in Parisian banlieues, including
Marseille, which did not experience unrest in 2005. On October 26, one day
before the anniversary of the deaths of Traoré and Benna, hundreds of Franco-
Maghrebi youth and citizen protesters marched through the streets of Paris in
order "to present a collection of 20,000 complaints to lawmakers and urge the
disenfranchised to make themselves heard with a vote, not violence."[13] Despite

this political appeal for nonviolent protest, a new spate of violence – including clashes between youth and police, arson, car torchings, and a new tactic: bus burnings – re-erupted during the anniversary week of the youth deaths in Clichy-sous-Bous. In a bus burning in Marseille, a *ville* not marked by violence in 2005, a Senegalese French woman named Mama Galledou was critically wounded.[14]

Since the "Crise des banlieues" in autumn 2005, the French government has been criticized for refusing to reimburse citizens and public municipalities for lost property, as well as for failure to invest in the banlieues and for failure to propose strategic development plans to combat unemployment, housing problems, police discrimination, administrative harassment, and public racism. Many politicians and activists fault the French government for failing to improve living conditions in the banlieues in the interim period, many arguing that conditions (unemployment, poverty, housing problems, discrimination, and despair) had actually worsened in the last twelve months. Consequently, and unsurprisingly, violence has proliferated in these already hard-hit areas. According to French law enforcement officials, Seine-Saint-Denis, "the infamous district north of Paris that includes suburbs like Epinay-sur-Seine," has in the last year become defined by a "climate of impunity" (Sciolino and Bernard 2006). As Sciolino and Bernard explain, "last year's unrest did not trigger a coherent plan to create new jobs, better housing and education and more social services – or even to raise the consciousness of the citizenry" (A8). Clichy-sous-Bois (the "town of 23,000" where the deaths of Traoré and Benna occurred) is "far worse than many other suburbs," having "no local police station, no movie theater, no swimming pool, no unemployment office, no child welfare agency, no subway or interurban train into the city" (A8). Although the French parliament passed "legislation promoting the 'equality of chances'" in March 2006, the act has been "largely ineffectual" in alleviating the devastating effects of poverty, unemployment, housing, discrimination, and lack of extensive political representation (A8). And other legislative acts or proposed bills have had deleterious ramifications on Franco-Maghrebi diasporic communities, who remain targeted as inassimilable "others," immigrants (*immigrés*), or foreigners (*étrangers*), even though most are French citizens. "Another law," Sciolino and Bernard explain, "aimed at curbing illegal immigration – and deporting youthful offenders – ignored the fact that most suburban youths are French" (A8). Most Franco-Maghrebis are Maghrebi French – that is, they are French citizens – but are nevertheless still treated as second-class citizens or foreigners; additionally, those who identify as Beur are primarily the children of Maghrebian migrants, although most of the so-called "second generation" Franco-Maghrebis have not themselves emigrated. According to MacMaster (1997), the percentage of Algerians who had acquired French nationality by 1990 was only 12.7 percent, although some Beurs (granted citizenship by birth in France) refuse to file the official papers for citizenship (219).

Writing presciently on September 13, 2005, Patrice de Beer examined the interlocking problems of racism, unemployment, inadequate housing, and social services in France's Parisian banlieues, and the community struggle for "social justice" and "global security."[15] As de Beer wrote just weeks before the unrest that began in October and continued into November 2005:

The integration of immigrants, whether first-generation or those who have become French citizens, has been reduced to a myth. Africans (including those from the Maghreb countries) especially find it more difficult than other immigrants to get a good education and find a job; and they are segregated by public housing in suburban ghettos where lack of decent public services and increased vandalism reinforce their isolation and dismal living conditions. This creates fertile ground for petty crime, drug-peddling, and Islamic extremism.

In France as elsewhere, the "war on terror" starts at home and can't be limited to a law-and-order policy. It also has to be conducted in the stairwells and hallways of public-housing units and in the job market. It is a matter of social justice as well as public security.[16]

Problems enumerated by both Patrice de Beer in 2005 and Samir Mihi in 2006 have, however, existed for decades among immigrant populations or diasporic communities living in France's banlieues. That racialized diasporic history is key to understanding the 2005 crisis and the re-eruption of violence on the anniversary in October 2006. Let's turn, then, to a historical overview of migratory patterns from the Maghreb to France, first in the years immediately following the end of World War II and then following the Algerian Revolution.

Economic migration into France began in the nineteenth century, including migrants from Italy, Belgium, Portugal, Spain, and North African countries such as Tunisia, Morocco, and Algeria. Periodically, economic recession resulted in a cessation of economic migration and even deportation of migratory laborers out of France. Algerians, as citizens of a French protectorate, frequently were not subject to deportation, as were most other migrant laborers. The number of Algerian economic migrants in France steadily increased in the period from 1914 to 1930, with the number increasing from a mere 13,000 at the beginning of World War I and escalating to 130,000 by 1930.[17] Two years later, in 1932, France passed the first law establishing quotas for immigrants, limiting immigration to economic laborers with identification cards.[18] Subsequent to this legislative act, France increased the number of economic migrants in 1930–9 due to internal labor shortages (MacMaster 1997, 3). Algerian emigration to France rapidly increased before, during, and after the Algerian Revolution (1954–62): in 1954, the number of Algerian immigrants in France totaled 211,000; by the end of the war, in 1962, the number had increased to 350,000 (MacMaster 1997, 189). One paradox of the Algerian Revolution, according to Neil MacMaster, "was that it almost doubled the number of immigrants in the metropolitan heartland of the colonial power with whom Algerians were at war" (189).

In a bloody and shockingly violent event known as the "October Massacre" (1961), the French government brutally suppressed Algerian migrants peacefully demonstrating against France's colonial presence in their home country. Protesting French colonial occupation in Algeria, many Algerian immigrants organized to march in support of the FLN and their efforts to liberate Algeria. The nonviolent protesters, 40,000 in number, who angered the French by chanting "Algérie pour les Algériennes!," were attacked by a police assault that resulted in the death of many demonstrators. According to Neil MacMaster, 200 Algerian immigrants were killed (some were bound and thrown into the Seine), while another 11,500 demonstrators were arrested; and "for a period of about six weeks, from 1 September to 18 October, police squads were given carte blanche to engage in killings with relative impunity, as long as they covered their tracks" (200).

Even Algerian independence did not slow Maghrebi economic emigration to France. Following the end of the Algerian War in 1962, the number of Algerian immigrants in France continued to increase – from 350,000 in 1962 to 530,000 in 1968. This massive migration was largely the result of economic hardship in Algeria due to the devastations of colonialism, war, and postcolonial isolation economically. The rapid increase in Algerian immigrant populations in France from the end of WWII through the end of the Algerian War led to hostile racism in the French press and police force, especially as many of the former colons occupied positions of administrative power in France, particularly in the southern Provence region. The bitterness of the former colons, the *pieds noirs*, about the loss of Algeria and the humiliating defeat in the war became manifest in anti-immigrant (specifically, anti-Algerian) sentiments politically among the French right, although this overt form of racism, in the press and by the police, was tolerated by the silence of the French citizenry. In the late 1960s, perceived loss of governmental control over immigration among the French public also impacted the treatment of migrants and immigrants. Racial violence and racist slurs toward legal immigrants and illegal aliens – particularly Algerian and other Maghrebian migrants, referred to pejoratively (and reductively) as *les Arabes* – increased during this period. "In France," according to Begag, "the word 'immigré' progressively became synonymous with Algerian, the North African and finally Arab. In most cases, the 'problem' of immigration is thought of as the problem of the Arab-Moslem-Maghrébin families."[19] Such anti-immigrant sentiments were exacerbated by the economic recession of 1973, and in 1974 (with the number of Algerian migrants in France totaling 845,000), the French provisionally halted migration into France, permitting only the entry of political refugees and war exiles (such as the Vietnamese after the fall of Saigon). Despite French anti-immigration policies during the seven-year period from 1974 to 1981, the number of foreigners (including illegal aliens) did not decrease.

Neil MacMaster, writing about Franco-Algerian migrants in *Colonial Migrants and Racism: Algerians in France, 1900–62* (1997), notes the link between post-1973 waves of anti-Arab racism in France (especially in southern France where large populations of repatriated *pieds noirs* live) and violent eruptions in 1973, the year before the French halt to economic migration. As MacMaster explains, "The first large-scale manifestation of anti-Arab racism after Algerian independence came with a wave of violence and killings which swept through the south of France between June and December 1973" (212). Maghrebis demanded rights and an end to racist discrimination in France: "this racism was in part inspired by French perception of Algerians displaying arrogance, an assertiveness that took the symbolic form of the immigrants 'invading' the public spaces of the central city which had been the preserve of the French. The Algerians, it was felt,

were now refusing to remain 'hidden' in the segregated slums and HLM estates"
(212). Moreover, anti-Maghrebi violence in southern France was the direct result
of the increasing political influence of le *Front National* (National Front) – formed
under the leadership of former Algerian colons, such as Jean-Marie Le Pen, "the
populist-racist and former Algerian paratrooper" who virulently attacked (both
rhetorically and politically) the French "immigré," by which Le Pen meant Arabs,
generally, and "the Algerian minority," specifically (213).

The mid-to late 1980s thus saw an increase of anti-immigrant feeling among
the French right, especially among the followers of Le Pen, the leading political
voice of le *Front National*, an extremist right-wing political party. Le Pen consistently foregrounded immigration and anti-immigration policies as core issues
within the political platform of le *Front National*. Gaining momentum in France
throughout the 1980s, despite overt racism, Le Pen and his political party
expressed racist and anti-immigrant views, regrettably, "with which many French
[were] in silent agreement."[20] Le Pen's anti-immigrant rhetoric, in fact, specifically
targeted (and continues to target) the Arab or North African immigrant populations in France. Arguing that cultural differences (racial, religious, cultural,
historical) between French citizens and Arab immigrants make assimilation into
French culture impossible, all the while demanding cultural and linguistic assimilation, and further claiming that economic migrants increased unemployment
among the French, Le Pen advocated (and continues to advocate) the deportation
of all temporary migrants. Le Pen and the National Front remain popular, if still
relatively minor conservative voices in French anti-immigrationist politics and
sentiments.

According to Alec G. Hargreaves and Mark McKinney, editors of *Post-
Colonial Cultures in France* (1997), "almost 80 percent of violent acts officially
classified as racist and more than 90 percent of racist murders in France are
committed against Maghrebis, though they account for less than 40 percent of
the foreign population."[21] Begag, a Beur writer and activist throughout the 1970s
and 1980s, similarly wrote that "almost two hundred youth and adults of North
African origin have been victims of racist attacks."[22] Clearly, issues of citizenship,
immigration, migration, and "foreignness" are often imbued with the sociocultural constructions of "good" and "evil" by a particular society. Societies often
scapegoat immigrants for a number of societal ills, issues such as unemployment
and economic recession, that are unrelated to the migrant populations. Also,
differences (of language, race, religion) between migrant populations and citizens
of the dominant or hegemonic population further exacerbate cultural misunderstanding. As Begag notes, "immigrants may be treated as the scapegoats for
worries about the future. Hence, the emergence and strengthening of far-right
parties defending the purity of the national cultures in Western Europe."[23]

Thomas Holt argues that racism is created and circulated through "everyday"
social activities and that through these micropolitical (or quotidian) interactions,
"racist ideas and practices are naturalized, made self-evident, and thus seemingly
beyond audible challenge. It is at this level that race is reproduced long after its
original historical stimulus . . . has faded."[24] Too often "this 'common sense'
racism attributes specific negative qualities to different racialized categories

('Arabs', 'Blacks', 'Chinese')" (MacMaster 1997, 210). And *le Arabe*, within stereotypical French perceptions, is often pejoratively coded as dangerous, sexually promiscuous, or dirty. Following an alleged sexual assault on a child by Maghrebi migrants in November 1966 (unsurprisingly a mere two years after Algeria won its independence from France), *Le Parisien Libéré* denounced the sexual attack and warned of the ostensibly perilous environment created by Maghrebi migrants in France's urban areas, writing "it's like a jungle for women alone . . . At Bagneux, Luce (14 years) was sexually assaulted by four Algerians within 50 meters of a council block." Later, the charges were dismissed after the girl admitted that she had lied; however, *Le Parisien Libéré* failed to correct its histrionic report, printing only that the girl had lied.[25]

Racialized conflicts around issues of immigration, citizenship, and integration have continued to haunt French politics since the early post-WWII period and revolutionary anticolonial struggles of the 1950s and 1960s, particularly as economic migrant communities have increasingly stabilized into permanent immigrant populations. According to a October 1984 article published in *Le Monde*, almost 11 million French citizens are descendants of recent immigrants. "During the last fifteen years immigration, the integration of ethnic minorities, and racism have become central issues in French politics," according to MacMaster, who further writes: "A 1990 opinion poll found that immigration was the second most important domestic concern after social and economic equality."[26]

The late 1970s and early 1980s was also a period of artistic creation, political organization, and community formation among Franco-Maghrebi migrant populations. Concomitant with the rise of anti-Arab sentiment and anti-immigrant legislation in France, the second-generation children of Maghrebian migrants – referred to as Franco-Maghrebis or Beurs – entered a period of artistic and political awakening known as "Le Mouvement beur", "The Beur Movement." In the fall of 1983, Franco-Maghrebis organized a political march, protesting "Pour égalité et contre le racisme" (For equality and against racism). The march, popularly known in the media and by the public as the *Marches des Beurs*, began in Maghrebian banlieues of Lyons and ended ten weeks later with 100,000 protestors gathered at President François Mitterrand's office in Paris. Hargreaves, a prominent scholar on Franco-Maghrebian communities, explains that "one of the factors which prompted the political mobilization of the Beurs was a spate of racist killings during the summer of 1983 directed particularly against younger members of the immigrant community."[27] Hargreaves elsewhere writes that "the immigrant community found itself faced with an upsurge of racist attacks in what became known as 'l'été meurtier' of 1983," the "murderous summer of 1983."[28] These racist attacks galvanized the young Franco-Maghrebi communities across France.

Such political and social organization was possible only after 1981, when the newly elected Socialist Party (under Mitterand's leadership) lifted restrictions on "freedom of association for foreigners" (Begag 1990, 3–4). Hargreaves notes that despite the fact that the Socialist platform had promised immigrants the right to vote in local elections, the promise was abandoned once Mitterand took office on the rationalization that such a proposition ran counter to public opinion

(1987, 109). The mid-1980s saw a further distancing of the Socialist Party and Mitterand's presidency from migrant issues, largely due to the increasing popularity and influence of Jean-Marie Le Pen and *le Front National*. Following a brief period of ethnic pluralism in the late 1970s and early 1980s – heralded under the slogan *le droit à la différence* – the republican model and its emphasis on integration has dominated political dialogue over nationality, citizenship, and immigrants (Blatt 1997, 48–50). "Confronted with the revival of popular and political xenophobia," David Blatt explains, "mainstream political elites responded by reviving and reconstructing traditional models of citizenship, which claimed to offer ethnic minorities full membership in the nation as long as ethnic origin was kept out of the public sphere and expressed only individually rather than collectively" (52).

Subsequent Beur marches were held in 1984 (*Convergence 84*) and in 1985, but with diminished success (Hargreaves 1987, 109). In 1985, extreme-right political organizations proposed reforms in the Nationality Code that would no longer make citizenship automatic for children of migrants born in France (Hargreaves 1987, 110), but these efforts failed. Post-nationality reformation debates created new tensions among citizens and migrants. This period was one of continued immigrant political organization, although the fracturing of immigrants (*Maghrébin* vs. non-*Maghrébin*) and among Franco-Maghrebi communities along national-origin, ethnic, and generational lines weakened the force of such activism. One prominent group organized "contre racisme" was SOS-Racisme, founded by Harlem Désir (a member of the Franco-Caribbean community) (Hargreaves 1987, 109). France-Plus, headed by Areski Dahmani (a young French Algerian professor at Paris-Villetaneuse University), sought to create political representation for Franco-Maghrebi communities. According to David Blatt, France-Plus was influential in mobilizing the electoral registration of Beurs and other Franco-Maghrebis and in placing Franco-Maghrebis on the ballots of major political parties (with the exception of *le Front National*, of course) in local elections (1997, 50). In the national French elections for the European Parliament in June 1989, two young Franco-Maghrebis were elected, and these leaders led efforts to facilitate community organization and to resist cultural integration (or homogenization) within French culture. SOS-Racisme, however, took a more republican stance; even Harlem Désir and SOS-Racisme advocated cultural integration of minorities in a 1987 television interview (Blatt 1997, 49). Whereas SOS-Racisme was a broad-reaching coalition of minorities and French youth organized primarily "contre racisme" and against the politics of the extreme right, France-Plus was more concerned with the political interests and community needs specific to the Maghrebian migrant community.[29] The 1986 death of Malik Oussekine, who was killed by police during student demonstrations in Paris, fueled further protests, political organization, and activism among young Franco-Maghrebis; however, this rise in political consciousness occurred simultaneously with the increasing influence of *le Front National* in local and regional elections in 1987. The same year also brought greater prominence to Beur artists and writers: the popular literary show *Apostrophes* aired interviews with two Beur writers – Azouz Begag and Mehdi Charef – and the French Prix Goncourt was awarded to the Franco-Moroccan writer Tahar Ben Jelloun (Begag 1990, 7–8).

Case Study: Barred Entry: Haitian and Southeast Asian Asylees in the US and Australia

Though the question of immigration detentions pervades the evening news in many countries across the world today in the wake of the internationally controversial decision by the United States to detain immigrants, asylees, "enemy combatants," and terrorist suspects in the global War on Terror since September 11, 2001, both the United States and Australia institutionalized the policy and practice of detaining asylees seeking political refuge in their respective countries during the 1990s. In both cases, "boat people" – refugees arriving on the coastal shores of the United States and Australia by boat – were negatively and racially targeted as "undesirables"; and in both cases, accusations of racism as informing (and deforming) political asylum decisions were lodged against the countries. During the late 1980s to early 1990s, Australia detained Southeast Asians, seeking political asylum, in immigrant prisons; and in the mid-1990s, the United States instituted a similar policy of interception, detention, and deportation of Haitian refugees seeking asylum.

"Detained in the Pacific": Southeast Asian Refugees in Australia

Like the United States, Australia has enforced detention of asylum seekers since the late 1990s, particularly those arriving by boat from Southeast Asia. Since the fall of Saigon in 1975 and the end of the Vietnam-American war, Australia has experienced three waves of "boat people" arrivals from Southeast Asian countries: the first wave, from 1976 to 1982, brought Vietnamese refugees to the country, most of whom were admitted by the Determination of Refugee Status (DORS) Committee, which was created in 1978 to facilitate the asylum process by the Fraser Coalition Government; the second wave, from 1989 to 1994, brought both Chinese nationals fleeing China after the Tiananmen Square massacre in 1989, who were granted group refugee status, and Cambodian nationals – asylum seekers who were not only routinely denied refugee status, but were also held in detention while their applications for asylum were being processed; and the third wave, beginning around 1994 and continuing into the final years of that decade, brought Chinese arrivals to the country, many of whom were Vietnamese refugees from Hong Kong and Indonesia who had been resettled in southern China by the United Nations High Commissioner for Refugees (UNHCR) provision allowing for resettlement of refugees in a "third country" and who were thus denied refugee status by Australia. Again, policies of detention, denial, and deportation prevailed. While exceptions to this policy were made in response to the fall of Saigon and the end of the Vietnam-American war in the years immediately following 1975, and again in response to the Tiananmen Square massacre in 1989, Australia has largely held to a policy of detention of Southeast Asian asylum seekers, particularly of "boat people," denial of asylum application, and deportation to the country of origin; and this policy has had decisively racialized parameters, with the Australian public and media alike denouncing the "invading hordes" from the north and anti-immigrant rhetoric grounded in historically discriminatory fears of a "yellow peril."

The first wave of Southeast Asian arrivals in Australia occurred between 1976 and 1979, in the years immediately following the end of the Vietnam-American war. In April 1976, five Indochinese arrived onshore; by June 1979, 51 boats had arrived on the northern and western Australian coasts, transporting 2,011 Vietnamese asylum seekers, most of whom were being relocated from temporary refugee camps in Thailand (Tazreiter 2004, 140). These arrivals, though relatively small in number, propelled the Fraser Coalition Government to legislate a Refugee Policy in 1977 to revise the Migration Act 1958 to include refugees seeking asylum from war-torn countries, and particularly those trying to escape communist regimes. Following the arrival of 1,043 refugees in 1977 through early 1978, the Fraser government also created the Determination of Refugee Status (DORS) Committee in March 1978 to facilitate and expedite the processing of asylum applications for Vietnamese war refugees. While 11,872 Indochinese refugees were ultimately admitted to Australia in June 1979, "only 2,011 were boat people" (McMaster 2001, 72). Under UNHCR guidelines, the Australian government legally changed the definition of "refugee" to concur with that proposed by the UN on March 16, 1982 (McMaster 2001, 72). During the first wave of arrivals, "just over 2,000 boat people entered Australia, . . . while over a million migrants entered in the regular migration program" (McMaster 2001, 73), revealing that the mode of arrival decisively impacts whether or not refugees are admitted into the country. That being said, however, "even though many of these 'first wave' of asylum seekers arrived on boats, they were not classified as 'unauthorized arrivals' and became the first significant group of Asians to arrive in Australia since the end of the White Australia Policy" (Tazreiter 2004, 140), an immigration policy (not abolished until 1973) that was unapologetically premised on race: i.e., that stipulated "whiteness" as a racial prerequisite to immigration. Overall, the total number of Indochinese refugees granted political asylum by Australia and admitted into the country totaled 96,262, making the country the fifth largest receiver of postwar refugees – after the United States (which granted asylum to 583,049 refugees), China (which granted asylum to 262,853 refugees), Canada (which admitted 98,827 refugees), and France (which admitted 97,827 refugees) following the end of the Vietnam-American war (Tazreiter 2004, 140).

The second wave of Southeast Asian boat arrivals along the northern Australian coastline occurred from 1989 until 1994, following a period of "no boat arrivals from 1982" until 1989, with the arrivals departing almost without exception from Cambodia. On November 28, 1989, 36 Cambodian nationals arrived in Australia. On March 31, 1990, an additional 119 Cambodians arrived seeking political asylum and refuge. All were denied refuge by Australia; and all were detained by the Australian government while their political asylum cases were being decided; 47 Cambodians remained in detention until January 17, 1994, four to five years after their arrivals and the dates of filing their petitions for asylum (McMaster 2001, 73–74). According to McMaster, "Between November 1989 and January 1994, eighteen boats arrived in northern Australia. Most of the arrivals were from the Kompong Som region of Cambodia, mainly Cambodian, Vietnamese and Chinese nationals. One-third of them remained in detention to the end of that period" (74). By legal loopholes (residual elements still enforceable under the Migration Act 1958), the Cambodian asylees could be legally detained, even indefinitely, since the law stipulated that they were to be returned upon the ship or boat on which they had arrived: in most cases, the individuals had been either smuggled on board or been stowaways on merchant vessels, ships not ready, required, or willing to return these "illegal" immigrants; in some cases, the boats had been quarantined and then destroyed because they had been in violation of health codes. As McMaster explains, "Legislation decreed that the boat people, as illegal entrants without authorized visas or entry permits, could be detained until their boat could be turned around. With their boats destroyed, boat people could be detained indefinitely" (74). While legal technicalities determined the plights of Southeast Asian refugees in Australia, so too did foreign policy in the midst of the late years of the Cold War.

True of Australian policy, it was also equally true for many developed countries post-1989 following the fall of the Berlin Wall. 1989 thus marks the beginning of a notable shift in international asylum and refugee policies: the year witnessed not only a significant increase in "illegal trafficking and smuggling of people," but also a sharp rise in the number of "global refugees" (Tazreiter 2004, 142). Exceptions were made, however: following the events at Tiananmen Square in 1989, when the repressive government of the People's Republic of China crushed a student uprising and democracy movement by violently squelching the rights to political dissent and struggles for the freedom of political expression, the Hawke government in Australia "granted permanent residence status to 27,359 Chinese students who had arrived before 21 June 1989, as a 'special group'" (Tazreiter 2004, 142). As in the case of Cambodia and Cambodian asylees, the Australian immigration decision was motivated by international foreign policy and geopolitical realignments in the late Cold War period. Following the second wave of arrivals, Australia established the Refugee Review Tribunal, which "grants protection visa applicants the right to appeal a primary decision with an oral hearing of their claim in a non-adversarial setting" (Tazreiter 2004, 144–145).

While legal technicalities and foreign policy considerations may explain the mechanisms that authorized detentions, they do not explain the political will to detain. Fueled by fear of "inundating" floods of Cambodian refugees arriving in rickety boats all along the northern coastline of Australia, a hyperbolic and excessive fear given the meager numbers of actual boat arrivals from Cambodia, drove the Immigration Department and Gareth Evans, Minister for Foreign Affairs, to openly announce "that the Cambodians were unlikely to be accepted as refugees"

(McMaster 2001, 74), a rhetorical effort to dissuade others from setting sail toward Australia. Prime Minster Hawke also weighed in on the issue, asserting that "We're not going to allow people to just jump that queue by saying we'll jump into a boat, here we are, bugger the people who've been around the world" (quoted in McMaster 2001, 75). Claudia Tazreiter and Don McMaster both contend that anti-Asian racism, particularly targeting poor and presumably low-skilled Southeast Asians arriving by boat, has fueled the policies of detention, deportation, and denial by the Australian government. "Racism in refugee policy in the Australian system," Tazreiter further notes, "has been under renewed scrutiny" given "the issue of mandatory detention of illegal arrivals" (2004, 50n9). In addition to racialization and racist political rhetoric (to be discussed further below), foreign policy also played a role in Australia's denial of Cambodian refugees. Gareth Evans assumed a "major role in the Paris Peace Agreements" between Cambodia's warring factions, and the government believed that "the agreements would be undermined if Australia accepted refugees from Cambodia" (McMaster 2001, 75). To admit Cambodian refugees, the government believed, was tantamount to sending the international political message that "the negotiations" were "untenable" (McMaster 2001, 76). As Don McMaster forcefully concludes, "Cambodian boat people detained in Australia at this time were at the mercy of Australian foreign policy and a minister's desire for a grand triumph" (76). Contradictions between ministerial advocacy of human rights for Cambodian nationals at home and the inhumane treatment of those very individuals fleeing human rights violations and seeking political refuge in Australia, however, were all too apparent. And according to McMaster, those subjected to immigrant detention "were detained solely on the basis of their method of arrival" (76). The second wave also "marks a departure in the Australian approach to boat arrivals and illegal arrivals more generally" (Tazreiter 2004, 141). As McMaster persuasively argues, "Cambodian asylum seekers . . . produced a sustained political response of unprecedented hostility" in Australia, and "boat people," specifically, "became the scapegoats of refugee policy in this period" (89), leading to sensationalized media headlines proclaiming the "invasion" of Southeast Asian refugees: "Boat people flood feared"; "Refugees at peak since Vietnam"; "Boat people slip past security" (90). By the mid-1990s, racist anti-Asian rhetoric flourished not only in the media, the public, and parliament, but also in political campaigns. In September 1996, Pauline Hanson declared before the Australian parliament that "we are in danger of being swamped by Asians" (quoted in McMaster 2001, 127).

The restrictive Australian policy of detention, denial, and deportation persisted during the third wave of Southeast Asian refugees seeking asylum and arriving on the northern and western coasts by boat (with the majority of arrivals during the three-year period from 1994 to 1997, although arrivals continued up until 1999). Third-wave arrivals were largely, though not exclusively, of Sino-Vietnamese and Chinese ethnic origins, but also included smaller numbers of Iranian, Afghan, and Iraqi boat arrivals in 1999. Although most of the boats arrived from China, with the exception of a "few boats of Vietnamese coming from Galang detention camp in Indonesia," the third-wave boat arrivals "caused concern" since they "were predominantly Vietnamese asylum seekers resettled in southern China in the 1980s," but now hoping to relocate in Australia (McMaster 2001, 90). The refugees were seen by many – officials and citizens alike – as "forum shopping" (McMaster 2001, 91). Following periods of detention in immigration prisons such as Port Hedland's detention centre, many of those denied asylum were ultimately deported.

"Detained in the Atlantic": Haitian Refugees in Guantánamo, 1991–1994

One of the largest and longest periods of out-migration from Haiti occurred during the despotic Duvalier dictatorship (from 1957 to 1971 under the rule of François "Papa Doc" Duvalier; and from 1971 to 1986 under his son and successor Jean-Claude "Baby Doc" Duvalier). Some internal or return migration occurred following the overthrow of Baby Doc Duvalier in 1986; however, from 1991 to 1994, years of political turmoil in Haiti, refugees once again fled, *en masse*, political persecution, militarism, and extreme poverty. During the early 1990s alone, especially following the exile of Jean-Bertrand Aristide in 1991 until his return to Haiti in 1994, thousands of Haitians fled anti-Lavalas and military junta violence, taking to the seas in small, ill-constructed *kanntès* or *batos*: the specters of "boat people" stunned concerned communities throughout the Americas, perhaps especially Haitian diasporic communities in the US and Canada, as well as in the Dominican Republic; however, this response was not the only, nor even the dominant, narrative. Stirred by anti-immigration sentiment, often racist and racially charged, the US public, the mainstream media, and governmental institutions (Immigration and Naturalization Service, US Coast Guard, Krome Detention Center, Guantánamo Bay Naval Base) – seemingly less concerned with the welfare of Haitian refugees and more so with public state resources and the financial costs of granting refugees asylum in the US (and in the Bahamas) – prompted the US government to adopt the detain-and-deport policy first implemented by agreement between former President Ronald Reagan and Jean-Claude Duvalier in 1981, later affirmed in George H. W. Bush's Kennebunkport Order issued in 1992, and reaffirmed in William Jefferson Clinton's willingness to uphold the elder Bush's policy, despite having campaigned against it. The Atlantic, like the Pacific, is thus a highly striated and regulated zone: the ocean is not a borderless, malleable terrain; it is, like landbound areas, a territorialized sphere. The plight of Haitian refugees adrift on highly regulated transatlantic waters forms a powerful rejoinder to Paul Gilroy's metaphoric ship as chronotope for transatlantic cultural production and exchange as theorized in *The Black Atlantic: Modernity and Double Consciousness*, for as Joan Dayan asserts, "what is missing [in Gilroy's study] is the continuity of the Middle Passage in today's world of less obvious, but no less pernicious enslavement" (1996, 7). While Gilroy himself suggests examinations of the Atlantic as "one single, complex unit of analysis" (1993, 15), the sociologist's own analysis, regrettably, fails to incorporate Haiti's contemporary transatlantic traumas into his theorization of the "black Atlantic": that is a profound oversight, especially given the historical context of the early 1990s in which the book was written and published.

Haitian out-migration profoundly impacted (nationally and diasporically) the small island country and the countries of destination in North America, primarily the US and Canada: out-migratory flows began during the Duvalier period and continued into the post-Duvalierist years. François Duvalier, who became the Haitian president in 1957, declared himself "President for Life" in 1964, the same year that the US Congress passed the Civil Rights Act of 1964 (Laguerre 1998, 76). In 1965, the first boatload of Haitians arrived in Pompano Beach, near Miami, Florida (Dunn 1997, 322). 1971 saw the genealogical "transfer" of Haitian political power to Jean-Claude Duvalier and the death of his father François Duvalier (Laguerre 1998, 75); the following year, 1972, is usually noted as the year of massive waves of Haitians fleeing the homeland by boat and heading toward Miami (Jean-Pierre 1995; Laguerre 1998; Dash 2001).[30] Whereas earlier external migrants from Haiti in the late 1950s have been characterized as wealthy, educated, and mulatto,[31] the external migrants of the 1970s have been stereotypically (and in some cases, negatively) described as poor, illiterate, and black (Jean-Pierre 1995; Dash 2001);[32] these very characterizations reveal the fractures of race and class within Haitian society, divisive fractures that are often recreated in diaspora.[33] External migrants in the 1970s through the 1990s have also been pejoratively referred to as "boat people" ("bòt pipol"; "boat peuple") by the international media. Racism against these migrants, particularly in the United States, shaped US policies toward Haitian refugees under the Carter, Reagan, Bush, and Clinton administrations.

In 1978, under the Carter administration, the "Haitian Program" was established by the US State Department and INS in response to the so-called flood of Haitian migrants toward Florida's shores; according to Laguerre, the program "evolved into the wholesale deportation of Haitian refugees" (1998, 81). The US policy shifted slightly in 1980, first when the Refugees Act (passed in March 1980) expanded the legal definition of "refugee" and again, in July of the same year, when the State Department's Haitian Program, which had been "under attack by human rights lawyers," was ruled unconstitutional by Judge James L. King (Laguerre 1998, 81). However, in 1981, under the Reagan administration, the US policy toward Haitian refugees became more officially repressive. Reagan signed an agreement with Duvalier allowing for the interception and forcible repatriation of Haitian migrants, and on September 29, 1981, Reagan "issued an executive order directing the US Coast Guard to patrol the water between Haiti and Florida and prevent boatlifts of refugees from entering the US"; according to Laguerre, "this interdiction program carried out on the high seas, precluded applicants from any access to legal advice" (1998, 82).

The 1980s also saw dramatic political shifts in Haiti. On February 7, 1986, political unrest and popular uprisings of Haitian citizens supported by grassroots movements throughout the country successfully overthrew the rule of Jean-Claude Duvalier, who was forced into exile in Paris, effectively ending 29 years of despotic Duvalier rule in Haiti. Initially, Haitians living in diaspora returned to their homeland in a desire to "rebuild" Haiti:

For a brief period, thousands of Haitians poured back into the country. Some completed construction of the homes they had starting building years ago; others established new businesses. But when the military – taking advantage of the democratic movement's divisions – stepped in to fill the political vacuum, these new returnees turned around and left. Once again, Haitians in the diaspora entered a state of limbo. (Jean-Pierre 1995, 198)

The post-Duvalier years remained plagued by oppressive police tactics under the tonton macoutes, the military police institutionalized under Duvalier; by violent and repressive militarism; and by economic depression. Referring to this period as "Duvalierism without Duvalier," Laguerre writes: "It was characterized by the emergence of new political actors, an army that found itself in a new environment and without a script to follow as before, clashes between various sectors of society, and endemic street violence" (1998, 26). The period from 1986 to 1990, though plagued by Duvalierists, prepared the country for democratic elections and "democracy";[34] it also witnessed the emergence of the diaspora as an important "extra-territorial" political organism, to use Laguerre's term, that operated transnationally; the diaspora affected both Haitian and US politics. During Henry Namphy's administration in the late 1980s, the Haitian government created the Office of Diaspora Affairs as a branch of the Ministry of Foreign Affairs, acknowledging the diaspora as an important political unit but effectively defining and designating it as "foreign" or external to the nation (Laguerre 1998, 163).

Massive waves of Haitian refugees fled the country yet again following the military coup d'état that overturned the presidency of democratically elected Jean-Bertrand Aristide in 1991, seven months after the Salesian priest was elected *Président d'Haïti*, President of Haiti. During the mid-1990s, in fact, Haitian refugees were detained at the US naval base in Guantánamo, where, not coincidentally, 660+ "enemy combatants" detained during the Afghan war beginning in 2001 are now held. Late twentieth and early twenty-first century detentions strikingly parallel the detention of war prisoners at this site in the late nineteenth century during the Spanish-American War. Following the military coup d'état in 1991, which overturned Aristide, thousands of desperate and vulnerable refugees – fleeing political persecution, violence, and retaliation – left the island in *kanntès*, small, rickety boats designed for transporting agricultural cargo, not humans. Approximately 34,000 Haitian refugees were intercepted at sea and detained at Guantánamo Bay. At the highest point, more than 45,000 Haitians were held in detention camps at the base. Many Haitian refugees remained in the Guantánamo camps for years without legal representation of their asylum cases before INS. Openly discriminatory in its policies, the INS also sanctioned the isolation of HIV+ Haitian refugees in special cells at Guantánamo: throughout the 1980s, and even into the 1990s, Haitians had been openly targeted by the Centers for Disease Control as one of the *4Hs* (*homosexuals, hemophiliacs, heroin-users*, and *Haitians*),[35] those negatively labeled as HIV-carriers. Haitian refugees remained at Guantánamo until autumn 1995; many, intercepted later, are still being detained at Miami's Krome Detention Center.[36]

Laguerre's theorization of "liminal citizenship" is a useful model for rethinking the "black Atlantic." Border control and vigilance about national boundaries –

here, those of Haiti and the US – place Haitian refugees (the "boat people") between national borders and states of citizens. "Refugees are *liminal citizens*," Laguerre writes, "betwixt and between two states, and struggling to be incorporated in a new country" (1998, 76). Laguerre defines this Haitian diasporic condition as a particular one that leaves the refugee in a position of liminality. Refugees, Laguerre theorizes, "are experiencing a liminal phase in their life, a passage, a transition after separation from the homeland but before incorporation in another territory" (76). According to Laguerre, "Boat people at sea, those who congregate or are placed in refugee camps, and those who are waiting for a formal hearing on deportation, exclusion or political asylum hold the status of *liminal citizenship*, a particular form of the diasporic condition" (76). As refugees are liminal citizens, they occupy a perilous and metastable site that is neither within the homeland nor the country of hoped-for destination, and yet refugees are paradoxically under the jurisdiction and control of both countries. The destination country regulates entry of immigrants and refugees through systematic forms of control, surveillance, detention, and sometimes even deportation that further destabilizes the citizen-rights of refugees, and "this system of surveillance is regimented in such a way as to produce *flexible bodies*, ready to be disciplined for incorporation once they are admitted to the country" (76). In the case of Haitian "boat people" seeking refuge in the United States, the period from 1970 to the present has witnessed an increasingly restrictive and even repressive policy of detainment and deportation with very few individuals actually being granted asylum, despite pervasive forms of political retaliation and torture among those applying. The US-INS system – or *regime of control*, as Laguerre accurately coins it – relies directly upon five mechanisms of control: *departure* or *embarkation control*; *disembarkation* or *border control*; *maritime control*; *internal control*; and as the ultimate mechanism of surveillance, *carceral control*. These "control procedures" of the US-INS, Laguerre explains, operate as mechanisms of "exclusion and admission" (77).

Though Dash speculates in *Culture and Customs of Haiti* (2001) that "the specter of a massive exodus of impoverished black Haitians to the shores of Florida may ultimately have been the single most important factor in the deployment of US troops to Haiti to dislodge the de facto military regime and reinstate constitutional rule, thereby making the case for political asylum untenable" (46), both Laguerre and Glick Schiller and Fouron attribute the US-led UN intervention to political pressure from the diaspora who protested, ran political advertisements in widely circulated newspapers such as the *New York Times*, and lobbied the US Congress, the Congressional Black Caucus, and the TransAfrica Group led by Randall Robinson (who held a hunger strike to protest what he regarded as a lack of US responsiveness to the plight of Haiti and Haitians).[37] "After three years of officially condemning the Haitian military but actually providing it with various kinds of economic and military assistance," Glick Schiller and Fouron write, "the United States changed its stance leading a United Nations military intervention and occupation in October 1994 that restored Aristide to power" (2001, 122). Jean-Pierre agrees with their assessment, noting that "while the international community led by the United States, waffled, the Tenth

Department kept the issue of President Aristide's return alive for three years" (1995, 204).

Measurable differences and historical disparities between how the INS processes Haitian and Cuban refugees also significantly complicate "against race" models of the "black Atlantic." From 1970 to 1980, although almost 50,000 Haitians applied for political asylum in the United States, only 25 were granted asylum. From 1981, the beginning of Regan's "interdiction program," until 1991, the year that Aristide was ousted by a violent military coup, only 28 Haitians were granted political asylum in the US, although 24,000 had applied (Laguerre 1998, 82). Additional statistics by Laguerre also demonstrate the unequal treatment and the striking diasparity between the INS processing of Haitian and Cuban refugees:

> In 1993, 7,421 and in 1994, 10,4000 Haitians filed *refugee applications* with INS. Only 17.8 percent of those were approved. Also in 1993, 10,908 and in 1994, 9,499 filed *asylum applications* with INS. The asylees fared better: 42.7 percent of the applications were approved. For the same period, the Cuban refugees had a rate of approval of 71.7 percent. However, after these applications were processed, a handful of Haitian immigrants were granted asylum. (87, 89)

How the US government and the INS determined these individuals to be economic migrants, rather than political refugees, given the "abysmal human rights record of the Duvalier regime" (Dash 2001, 46), and the post-Duvalierist military dictatorships in Haiti, is intractably difficult for some to comprehend. Many Haitian Americans have even openly denounced the policy as utterly incomprehensible; but on this basis, Haitian refugees were denied asylum in the United States. Many activists reason thus: to grant asylum would have been tantamount to admitting the complicity of the United States in Duvalier's human rights abuses, since the CIA and the US government had upheld the Duvalier dictatorship, while denouncing Cuba's Castro, and had also supported the military coup d'état in 1991. Unsurprisingly, Duvalier allowed US capitalist influence in the country and condemned both Marxism and Cuba's "revolution." This disparity of treatment between Haitian and Cuban refugees continued throughout the 1990s, most sharply during the violent coup years from 1991 to 1994 in which individuals, especially Lavalas supporters, were routinely politically persecuted. And, in the most recent crisis in Haiti in 2004, in fact, the first response of the US government was once again to prepare additional camps and detention centers on the base, rather than intervene to stabilize the country or to prevent the second violent overthrow of democratically elected President Aristide. Detention seems to persist as a systemic *modus operandi* of US foreign policy (as further examined in this book's "Postface").

Racism and racialization, clearly and lamentably, form part of the diasporic experiences of international migrants worldwide. Discriminated against, barred entry, detained, expelled: diasporic communities profoundly suffer the consequences of racism and racial oppression. Diasporas and diasporic communities, however, are not merely victims of nation-state politics (both those of the sending "mother" country and of the receiving "host" country), international foreign policy and geopolitical shifts (such as European colonialism, anticolonial struggles, world wars, including the Cold War, civil warfare, "ethnic cleansing," and genocidal pogroms), international law, international regulatory bodies (such as the United Nations, World Bank, the International Monetary Fund, and the World Trade Organization), and the fracturing conjunctures and radical disjunctures of global capitalism: diasporas are inexorably produced by all of these historical movements, yet diasporas are also productive factors within the world. Diasporas and diasporic communities also write back to global capitalist, nationalist, and internationalist strictures and form myriad counterhegemonic narratives to the dominant narratives of nation and capital. And in the next chapter, we examine how diasporas become crucial sites of transnational activism, the struggle for global social justice, and how these communities produce important diasporic "arts of resistance."

Questions for Reflection and Discussion

- The increase in French anti-Maghrebi sentiments, particularly aimed at Franco-Algerian youths (or "Beurs"), and anti-Arab violence, targeted at citizens, migrants, and illegal aliens, also raises important questions about nation-states and the people dwelling within the territorial borders of these states. For example, how are definitions of nations (or nation-states), nationality, nationalism, citizenship, foreigners, immigrants, and migrants overlapping with a society's understanding of societal good and cultural threat?
- What factors influence the determination of both national interest and perceived threats to a nation's self-understanding?
- How are immigrants and migrants often scapegoated for societal ills that are actually larger sociocultural issues, such as economic recession and unemployment?
- How do race, ethnicity, religion, and nationality play into a nation's self-definition (whether on a political, juridical, or ideological level)?
- What forms the foundations – often conflicting, contradictory, or disjunct – for various definitions of nationality across the globe, in this case "French" nationality? Ethnicity? Geographical place of residence? Shared history, heritage, or tradition? Common cultural values? How do these elements enter into (often contentious) dialogues over what constitutes a "nation-state" and its "nationality" (its "nationalist" banner, *Geist* or *ésprit du corps*, if you will)?
- How do these conflicting ideas play out in books, films, television, and magazines?
- How do these conflicting ideas impact the ways in which artistic works of cultural production are designated (or marketed) within a national literature and within the global markets for such commodities?

Additional Research

Analyzing film and visual cultures

Watch Matthieu Kassovitz's film *La Haine* ("Hate") and then write a short essay (3–5 pages) that considers the ways that race inflects diaspora and shapes debates about immigration, citizenship, and cultural belonging in France.

Racialized conflicts between the migrant communities and their diasporic country of adoption (*société d'accueil*) are often violently depicted in literature, cinema, music, and other popular cultural media. According to Neil MacMaster, "The considerable impact of Kassovitz's film *La Haine*, which gives a powerful picture of anomie, frustration, rebellious minority youth and police violence in the *banlieue* was also symptomatic of widespread public interest and concern" (1997, 207). Kassovitz's film is extremely interesting for the myriad questions it raises about ethnic minorities within nationalist borders.

Questions to Consider about La Haine

- In what ways do Kassovitz's characterization of Saïd, Vinz, and Hubert – as "Arab," "Jew," and "African" – resist racist stereotypes? How, if at all, does it repeat French racist stereotypes?
- Why do you think Kassovitz cast the three protagonists as an "Arab," a "Jew," and an "African"? How does this choice emphasize the cultural, political, and social conflicts surrounding a nation and its minorities?
- How are these youth oppositionally juxtaposed to the institutional force of the "French" police, and to the "white" skinhead members of the neo-Nazi gang in the film?
- How does the film highlight the cultural differences in the ways that "French" teen gangs are treated and "non-French" gangs ar treated, although some members are clearly "French citizens"?

Thinking through writing

Neil MacMaster relates political strife, ethnic tensions, and migratory conflicts to French national anxiety – "an anxiety fuelled by the perceived loss of great power status, the erosion of French culture by American consumerism, the inroads of Anglo-Saxon terminology and related processes of globalization" (1997, 207). Do you agree or disagree? Read *Le Monde* (French edition or English translation edition) and follow articles and editorials reporting on immigration politics in France for a two-week period, reading those articles as "symptomatic" of what MacMaster identifies as French national anxiety; then evaluate the journalistic reporting on these topics in a short essay (3–5 pages).

6

Transnational Activism, Diasporic Arts of Resistance

In this chapter we will focus on diasporic activist forms of mobilization and everyday practices of resistance to oppression. Diasporic communities have been (and continue to be) vital sites for political resistance to globalization, global capitalism, and the "War on Terror." Public intellectuals and scholars have become increasingly interested in what has been defined as the "globalization of dissent" (Arundhati Roy), "transnational grassroots movements for social justice" (Nina Glick Schiller and George Fouron), and "cosmopolitical activism" (Paul Gilroy). This chapter thus sketches out the malleable and living contours of diasporas and political dissent. That does not mean, however, that diasporas – or some diasporic communities – cannot also be extremely conservative, nationalist voices for capitalist development in their home and host countries, as well as monetary funds for pro-business development projects, such as multinational free trade zones (to give but one example). Diasporas, like nations, are fractured, polyvocal sites of belonging, participation, disenfranchisement, identification, or disidentifications. So diasporas are necessarily sites of (anti-globalization) dissent and of (global capitalist) defense. In this chapter, we will foreground and focus our analysis on diasporas as sites of radical dissent.

Organized around the capitalist traffic between globalization and diasporas, this chapter operates on the premise that globalization is not a one-way street (from the West to the rest), nor even a two-way street, but a complex, congested, multiply-laned, and interchange-movement of ideas, products, and people. The chapter thus examines the myriad ways that diasporic communities are impacting global political discourses or transnational political debates (about environmentalism, social justice, labor rights, human rights) and even in some cases transforming international economic relations. To cite only one salient example: economic remittances made by diasporic communities to family members in their countries of origin have dramatically impacted the economies of those small nation-states (as in Cuba, the Dominican Republic, Haiti, Mexico, the Philippines, and elsewhere).

The chapter also explores the interrelations of homeland and diasporic forms of cultural production – from film and television to visual arts, music, or street arts (murals, graffiti, street theater) – as arts of resistance. After the implementation of structural adjustment plans (SAPs) in Argentina, for example, mothers took to the streets with pots and pans, banging music to express their discontent with the governmental capitulation to international financial institutions; and such homeland protests often mirrored those in diasporic locales. Protesters in Haiti and in its diaspora, for example, created carnival floats with *djabs* (devil masks) labeled "IMF" (the International Monetary Fund) and performed *Rara* songs about the impact of global capitalism on small economies such as Haiti's. Novelist Arundhati Roy, to isolate another exemplum, has been an outspoken, fearless, and indefatigable advocate not only for South Asian immigrants in North America, but also more broadly both on the behalf of exploited victims of international financial institutions and global capitalist policies across the third world and on the behalf of Muslim immigrants detained in military prisons as part of the "War on Terror." Writers, musicians, film directors, and visual artists increasingly use their artistic media to challenge the unfair treatment of immigrants in diasporic locations. We will thus pay critical attention to diaspora and transnational forms of cultural production (music, film, documentaries, carnival, street events) and the ways in which these vibrant cultural forms are being used as politicized forms of resistance.

While not all diasporic formations are resistant to the structures and structural forces of the nation-state and globalization, or to the delimiting strictures of nationalism or those of global capitalism as regulated through global regulatory bodies and international financial institutions, diasporas may be radicalized as sites of resistance; and diasporic forms of activism and cultural production may articulate resistance to nationalist abuses of power, or the national state-apparatus or regimes of power, as well as the infractions and human rights violations of multinational corporations, internationally funded development projects, or the deleterious impacts of global capitalism on the daily lives of citizens and immigrants from or in small developing countries. Diasporas, thus, may be active and activist sites for anti-globalization battles and places of vibrant dissent; likewise, diasporic cultural production may also directly and indirectly critique the inhumanity too often promulgated in the name of humanity, i.e., the human rights abuses ironically committed by those advocating (human) development. Diasporic forms of cultural production, then, may be powerful, counterhegemonic, and strategic "arts of resistance," a term that I borrow, but also modify, from anthropologist James C. Scott as he theorizes it in two of his books – *Weapons of the Weak: Everyday Forms of Peasant Resistance* (1985) and *Domination and the Arts of Resistance: Hidden Transcripts* (1990).

Examining thus the interrelated issues of transnational activism and diasporic "arts of resistance," we will contextualize our discussions within three distinct, but not unrelated case studies. First, we will consider Indian diasporic resistance (in collaboration with internally displaced persons and grassroots activists in India) to the Narmada Valley Development Plan – a World Bank-funded dam project along the Narmada River – in which diasporic scholars and writers, notably Amitava Kumar, Arundhati Roy, and Vijay Prashad have all been active. Second, we will look at Haitian diasporic activism around several key transnational issues that transpired in the post-Duvalier period: the Center for Disease Control (CDC) labeling of Haitians as HIV carriers and its impact on INS policy; the 1991 coup d'état in Haiti and the militaristic aborting of democracy; and the Emergency Economic Recovery Program in 1994. Third, we will focus on the transnational activist efforts of Filipino domestic workers in Hong Kong and their active, organized resistance to forced remittances (legislated by the Philippine government and mandated by Executive Order 857 under the administration of former President Ferdinand Marcos), and which ultimately led the government to end the policy during the administration of President Gloria Aquino.

Following Amitava Kumar's critical lead in *World Bank Literature* (2003), I propose that literature and other artistic forms of cultural production need to be read or analyzed alongside economic policy documents, legal case rulings, and other material-political texts by capitalist cultures during this moment of global or late capital. We thus need interdisciplinary approaches in order to better understand pressing capitalist "development" issues or profound material problems through literary or artistic forms of representation that reflect on the lived experiences of poverty and economic injustice. "The term 'World Bank Literature'," Kumar writes in his introduction to the collection of the same title, "is a provocation" (xvii) intended to prompt examinations of "the complex, highly mediated relationship between literary studies, [and] cultural value" (xviii), and "to cast the existence of what was traditionally called 'literature' in relation to the looming shadow of the World Bank" (xxx). One contributor to the volume, Phillip E. Wegener, further elaborates: "A similar set of imperatives are at work in the 'concept' of World Bank Literature being articulated in this volume, as it too grapples on a number of different fronts with the political task of constructing adequate representations of our own 'unrepresentable, imaginary global social reality'" (280–281). Kumar importantly asks, as Wegener explains, "Where is the literature of the New Economic Policy?" (284). Through the conglomerate "World Bank Literature," as Kumar urges, literary scholars need to further examine the interrelations of literature and political economy; his work thus builds upon, but also extends, materialist based scholarship undertaken by postcolonial literary and cultural theorists such as Bruce Robbins, E. San Juan, Jr., Arif Dirlik, Inderpal Grewal, Caren Kaplan, and others.

As negotiations for the Free Trade Agreement of the Americas (FTAA) proceed (and stall) among international financial institutions and individual nation-states within the hemisphere (in no small part due to national, regional, and transnational activitist resistance movements at the grassroots levels), we need to ask how American identities have shifted as a result of the presumed "death" of Marxist resistance and the "triumph" of capital in a post-1989 world. It thus becomes imperative for students and scholars to examine the import of "free trade" rhetoric in the humanities and other disciplines. Following Kumar's provocative suggestion that "'World Bank Literature' might well be a new name for postcolonial studies in the twenty-first century," I suggest that we might also want to consider (or at least reflect upon) the ways in which debates about "free trade" in the Americas may also have filtered into and informed the contemporary shift toward hemispheric American studies; and how, nevertheless, theoretical models such as John Carlos Rowe's important "postnational" model might offer space for resistance within American studies. With the spectral shadows of the North American Free Trade Agreement (NAFTA), passed in 1992, the Central American Free Trade Agreement passed in 2005, and the FTAA, in which negotiations set for completion in 2005 indefinitely stalled, looming in the global capitalist, yet near, distance, and as the imperialist backdrop of this chapter, we must remain vigilant in our efforts to reframe the ways in which colonial and neocolonial dependency not only persist in, but also become reinforced through, global capitalism in the contemporary historical context.

And while diasporic activism most definitely includes international lobbying efforts, massive letter-writing campaigns, cross-national petition drives, national and transnational mobilization, collaboration with grassroots and nongovernmental organizations at home, and organizing (often multiethnic) protests in metropolitan centers, or "global cities," worldwide, it should not be limited to these visible forms of diasporic resistance: in other words, we also need to recognize and examine the diasporic "arts of resistance" and the myriad forms of "everyday" resistance, or what James C. Scott calls the "weapons of the weak."

Arguing that violent revolutions are rare while subtle acts of resistance are a daily occurrence, Scott suggests in *Weapons of the Weak* (1985) and *Domination and the Arts of Resistance* (1990) that we need to pay far more attention to "*everyday* forms of peasant resistance – the prosaic but constant struggle between peasantry and those who seek to extract labor, food, taxes, rents, and interest from them" (1985, xvi). These forms of everyday resistance – "poaching, foot-dragging, pilfering, dissimulation, flight" (1990, xiii) – Scott argues, are crucial to understanding how disempowered individuals contest their abuse and exploitation, noting that "individual acts of foot-dragging and evasion, reinforced by a venerable popular culture of resistance and multiplied many thousand-fold, may, in the end, make an utter shambles of the policies dreamed up by their would-be superiors in the capital" (1985, xvii). Scott further develops his concept of *everyday* resistance in *Domination and the Arts of Resistance*, distinguishing in the later book between *public transcripts*, or the official forms of dominant discourse that transcribe and encode power, and *hidden transcripts*, which remain embedded within dominant discourses, yet "beyond direct observation by powerholders" (4). For Scott, *public transcripts* are "*self*-portrait[s] of dominant elites as they would have themselves seen" (1990, 18); they are, then, necessarily partial, subjective, and whitewashed accounts of historical relations of power, the powerful, and the powerless. For these reasons, Scott contends, "the analysis of the hidden transcripts of the powerful and of the subordinate offers us, I believe, one path to a social science that uncovers contradictions and possibilities, that looks well beneath the placid surface that the public accommodation to the existing distribution of power, wealth, and status often presents" (1990, 15). Jennie M. Smith, in "Melodic Machetes" from *When the Hands Are Many* (2001), builds on Scott's concepts of *everyday resistance* and *hidden transcripts* and applies these utilitarian theoretical concepts to daily acts of performed resistance in Haitian peasant culture; telling the story of a disgruntled young woman named Kami who composes pointed songs to protest her treatment by Eli, her demanding father-in-law, who is well within ear of her melody, Smith eloquently describes *chan pwen*, or "sung points," in Haitian peasant culture as performed modes of cultural resistance to power and oppression.

Within Scott's analysis of power and discourse, the more openly articulated the form of resistance, the greater the degree of power and access to privileged sectors of social, historical, and cultural resources. For Scott, the disenfranchised, or powerless, resist and formulate transcripts that rewrite power relations. Certainly in the case of the Haitian *peyizans andeyò*, or *moun andeyò*, rural peasants, everyday resistance or hidden transcripts offer vital means of surviving oppression and contesting it, if not openly and defiantly revolting against it (although that too occurs in Haiti, as its history and as the crisis in early 2004 starkly remind us). Yet, I want to suggest a third path that intervenes between *public* and *hidden* transcripts, that offers intermediary points of negotiation of power and exploitation, and that seeks to represent subaltern individuals who may not have access to written language, televisual media, video footage, or audiotape. Diasporic forms of cultural production are not quite dominant forms of social-cultural discourse, and yet they are *public transcripts*. Diasporic cultural production registers more audibly and visibly than *hidden transcripts*; as such, these art forms are *public transcripts*, but ones still marginalized within the larger field of social-cultural discourse: diasporic writers, artists, musicians, film directors, and performance artists create *public transcripts*, sometimes with open contestations of power and hegemony, but also with more subtly or nuanced *hidden* messages embedded within their cultural art forms. Diasporic literary texts, documentary films, and rap songs are thus "arts of resistance."

Diasporic writers, artists, musicians, and directors produce cultural forms that contest the relations of power between first and third worlds in the global economy, while also challenging imperialist foreign policies and the negative impact those policies often have on their home country. Just as we need to probe the transnational influences fostering national forms of state violence, similarly, we also need to insist on the interrelations of literature and political economy, rather than divorcing aesthetic and economic issues along rigidly policed disciplinary lines. In this chapter, I work toward those ends. Other forms of cultural production (music, art, cinema), similarly, need to be analyzed in relation to the material, economic, and political contexts in which they are produced. Diasporic writers, artists, musicians, and directors are not only deeply cognizant of audience, production, and political questions accompanying representation: they also participate culturally and artistically to resist the transnational forces that have contributed to political destabilization in their home country.

Diasporic writers – like Edwidge Danticat, Dany Laferrière, Arundhati Roy, and Jessica Hagedorn, among others – compose narratives that critique the damaging effects both of US foreign policy and the actions of international financial institutions on the poorest, most desperate citizens who remain behind in their home countries. Danticat, for example, has been a visible activist within the United States to protest the impact of US foreign policies, as well as state and local policies, on both Haitian Americans and on her home country Haiti, marching in New York, for instance, to protest police violence against Haitian American men (Patrick Dorismond, Abner Louima) by the NYPD. Roy, like Danticat, has been a courageous spokeswoman and dedicated nonfiction writer to raise awareness in the US and worldwide about issues impacting India and destitute, displaced tribal Indians in the subcontinent. By doing so, Danticat and Roy participate in transnational forms of social justice activism, wherein diasporic activists organize to protest global action or inaction about Haitian and Indian social, economic, and political problems, using the media, community resources, publishers, and the constitutionally protected rights of free speech and assembly to pressure federal, state, and local governments to alter policies and effectuate change both within the diasporic context and at home in Haiti or India. Nina Glick Schiller and Georges Fouron insightfully discuss such transnational forms of grassroots activism in *Georges Woke Up Laughing* (2001), asserting that long-distance nationalists create subaltern political forms through participation in "transnational movements for global justice" (272). Diasporic "arts of resistance" articulate honor and respect for those too often nameless, faceless individuals who, due to poverty, illiteracy, or disenfranchisement, cannot represent or agitate for political change; these writers and activists thus attempt to articulate resistance through written words for those who may not be able to read or write, and thus represent, their own lived experiences. Representation, of course, is not without its own perils; and diasporic activism may often miss the mark, despite well-intentioned motives, and unconsciously or inadvertently reinscribe class interests without intending to do so. Still, diasporic activists often hit the mark, and their efforts are important ones in the transnational struggle for global social justice. Diasporic artists and writers not only represent, but also transmute, lived historical experiences; and their diasporic "arts of resistance" are important forms of political critique worldwide.

So too do diasporic literary texts expose violences, power differentials, and injustices, while portraying, with dignity, those who suffer from these global infractions against humanity. These explorations are particularly important now given the current historical collision of military imperialism and global capitalism that has led to the global dominance of the US, which acts unilaterally and unapologetically so, and to the erosion of political sovereignty for small developing states such as Haiti, India, or the Philippines, the three developing countries foregrounded in this chapter. Diasporic forms of cultural production also utilize national resources and audiences to transnationally critique imperialism and suffering in homelands and in diasporas, and thereby contribute to and participate in "transnational" grassroots movements for social justice internationally or globally. Diasporic cultural forms thus challenge minority-dominant stratifications in the countries of adoption, not only exposing ideological presuppositions about race, class, nation, and economy, but also contesting those relations of power. Diasporic forms of cultural production, as "arts of resistance," also confront the dominance of wealthier, "developed" countries globally, critiquing the consequent erosion of sovereignty within smaller, "developing" states. Filipino, Haitian, and Indian diasporic writers, artists, musicians, directors, and performance artists thus use their performed arts of resistance as political protest.

Case Study 1: Troubled Waters, Dam Nation, Grassroots, and Transnational Indian Diasporic Resistance: Whence Narmada?

For some, it may be easy to forget: the Narmada is a river, not a dam.[1] Flowing westward from the Armarkantak mountains through the states of Madhya Pradesh, Maharashtra, and Gujarat to the Gulf of Khambat, or Cambay (which empties into the Arabian Sea), the Narmada River is – at 1,312 kilometers/815 miles, in length – the fifth-largest river in India, the largest in Gujarat. "There is, in the heart of India, a sacred pool surrounded by temples and shrines," as Catherine Caufield writes, and "from this pool rises India's holiest river, the Narmada" (1996, 8). According to legend, "Shiva himself named it Narmada, the 'ever-delightful.' As the old people say, you wash away all your sins by bathing several times in the Yamuna or three times in the Saraswati or once in the Ganges, but the mere sight of the Narmada has the same effect!" (Caufield 1996, 5). Forgetful of myth and legend, others see the Narmada as riverine water to be dammed, a reservoir created from submerged villages and the forest and hills dwelled in by the *adivasis*,[2] or indigenous tribes,[3] unassimilated to caste or Hinduism, the wretched of this earth and thus easily displaced; for these proponents of nationalist development, the Narmada is a major dam project – conceived by Jawaharlal Nehru, the first prime minister of an independent, post-Partition India before it actually existed in 1946; for these engineers, politicians, capitalist investors, and international lenders, the Narmada is irrigation, hydroelectric power, flood prevention and control, and potable drinking supply for an estimated 40 million people in the drought-ridden portions of Gujarat, like Saurashtra, Kachchh (or the Kutch), and North Gujarat.[4] From sacred temples to "modern temples," as Nehru proclaimed big dams, propelling national development. As Sardar Sarovar Narmada Nigam Ltd, the corporation constructing the largest dam of the Narmada Valley Dam Projects (NVDP), claims on its website, the construction of the dam fulfills part of the national plan for economic development: that is, to channel "the unharnessed natural resources – land, water, minerals, forests, sea wealth and so on and the idle manpower so as to transform them into productive wealth for the people" ("Need for Sardar Sarovar Project"). For the economists, engineers, and capital investors at Sardar Sarovar Narmada Nigam Ltd, the dams solve multiple development problems: poverty, unemployment, scarcity of arable agricultural land, lack of energy, and water deficits. But for Friends of the River Narmada, the dam projects will have and have already had "an extremely devastating effect on the riverine ecosystem and have rendered destitute large numbers of people (whose entire sustenance and modes of living are centered around the river)."[5]

Conceived by Nehru, yes, but born of India's early postcolonial decades of massive infrastructural development and nation-building, the NVDP experienced a long period of gestation, followed by excruciating birth pains: first conceptualized as the Broach Project, a large dam on the Narmada, "surveys for the construction of a high-level canal for increased irrigation delivery were undertaken in early 1961"; and "after more than three decades of investigations and planning, Indian authorities finally sanctioned the development initiative in 1978" (Khagram 2004, 71, 2): thus was the NVDP born. Planners of the NVDP propose constructing 30 large dams (10 on the Narmada River, the remainder on the river's tributaries), 165 medium-sized dams, and 3,000 small dams in the river valley. Four of the large dams under construction are the Sardar Sardovar, the Indira-Sagar, the Maheshwar, and the Maan dams. The Indira-Sagar Dam (also commonly referred to as the Narmada Sagar Dam), which has been under construction on the Narmada River since 1984 when former Prime Minister Indira Ghandi laid the foundation stone on the site, is located in the Khandwa District in the western part of the Indian state Madhya Pradesh. Like the Sardar Sarovar Dam, it has also been scrutinized by grassroots activists for its lack of resettlement and rehabilitation plan, its irresponsible submergence of rural villages, and its consequent displacement of families living in the area.[6] According to opponents of the Indira-Sagar, the dam will destroy 250 villages and displace approximately 175,000 people, submerging "91,348 hectares of land," including over 40,000 hectares of "deciduous forests."[7] The Maheshwar Dam, another big dam included in the NVDP, is a hydroelectric project predicted to generate 400 megawatts of electricity; first under the purview of the Narmada Valley Development Authority (NVDA), the Madhya Pradesh Electricity Board is now overseeing its construction. Initially attracting major international electropower corporations – notably, Siemens, Bayernwerk, and VEW Energie of Germany, and both Pacgen (or PacifiCorp) and Ogden of the United States – most of these multinational companies later fully divested from the project following local grassroots agitation and following widespread international resistance to the dam because of its harmful environmental effects, its human rights violations, and its seemingly callous disregard of indigenous rights.[8] According to an International Rivers Network Press Release (dated March 27, 2000), "the Maheshwar Dam would displace more than 35,000 farmers, wage laborers, fishers and crafts people in 61 villages and submerge about 1,100 hectares of rich agricultural land."[9] The Maan Dam, a big dam planned and now also under construction by the Government of Madhya Pradesh (GoMP), is also part of the NVDP, though not located on the Narmada River: on the Maan River, one of the Narmada's tributaries, the dam is primarily an "irrigation project" designed in order to provide needed agricultural water into the Dhar district.[10]

The Sardar Sarovar Project (SSP) is the largest of the big dams to be constructed on the Narmada River: at a proposed 138.68 meters/455 feet, the dam is currently 110.64 meters high with an authorization to build to 121.92 meters as of March 2006. Located 170 kilometers "upstream from where the river flows into the Gulf of Khambat," the SSP has been the site of fissiparous debates about costs and benefits, political controversy, and resistance activism.[11] As Catherine

Caufield explains in "The Holiest River" (the opening chapter of *Masters of Illusion: The World Bank and the Poverty of Nations*), "The centerpiece of the scheme is to be the Sardar Sarovar Dam, stretching 4,000 feet across the river and rising to the height of a 45-story building" (1996, 8). Water resources would be allocated among the three riparine states, as well as the state of Rajasthan. By governmental and project-generated estimates, the SSP, once completed, would irrigate more than 1.8 million hectares of cultivable land, including in the extremely arid regions of Saurasthra and Kachchh, or the Kutch, in the state, as well as some land in Rajasthan. According to government experts, the SSP will also generate 1,450 MW hydroelectricity (1,200 MW generated by the River Bed Power House and 250 MW generated by the Canal Head Power House) to be divided among the people of Madhya Pradesh (57 percent), Maharasthra (27 percent), and Gujarat (16 percent).[12] Proponents of the SSP also claim, even more compellingly, that the dam project would provide potable drinking water for people living in 135 towns and 8,215 villages in Gujarat and outside of its state borders, or for "over 2.35 million people."[13] Describing the SSP as a "vehicle for taking plentiful waters of Narmada basin which are today flowing down to the sea, to the water starved regions of Saurashtra, Kachchh, North Gujarat and Rajasthan," the Sardar Sarovar Narmada Nigam Ltd even avers, emphatically, that *not* building the Sardar Sarovar Dam would be an inexcusable national travesty; would, in effect, constitute an immoral act of social injustice:

> Such water transfer also enables optimum use of arable land and water when they are apart from each other. While land cannot be transferred, water can be flown to distant places. Otherwise land one side and water away at other place, both remain unused, unproductive. And if in face of hunger and poverty, water and land are allowed to remain separated and unused, it can be regarded as a crime against humanity![14]

Opponents of the SSP, however, claim not only that the projected benefits (irrigation, hydroelectric power, drinking water supply) are not only administratively exaggerated, but that these projected benefits are premised on flawed "trickle down" capitalist economics that rarely delivers – that is, rarely trickles down. Also, they argue, the projected benefits must be balanced against the inevitable costs (to the environment, to indigenous rights, to human rights) that the SSP manifests. Most problematically, the opponents maintain, neither the government of Gujarat, nor those of Maharashtra or Madhya Pradesh, have adequately provided for the "resettlement and rehabilitation" of those families to be displaced by the SSP. According to opponents of the SSP, the dam reservoir, if constructed to the proposed height, would result in the human displacement of an estimated 320,000 rural villagers, tribals, and *adivasis* who live in that part of the Narmada Valley. If raised to 121.92 meters as planned and authorized by the Narmada Control Authority (NCA) on March 8, 2006, an additional "24,421 families in 177 villages of Madhya Pradesh," according to estimates cited in a UN press release (dated April 13, 2006), will be displaced. Even the Sardar Sarovar Narmada Nigam Ltd estimates the number of Project Affected Families (PAFs) at just under 41,000 and moreover concedes that the SSP would, at Full Reservoir Level (FRL) of 138.68 meters/455 feet, inevitably submerge 245 villages (three fully and the remaining 242 partially), totaling 193 submerged villages in the state of Madhya Pradesh, 33 in Maharashtra, and 19 in Gujarat. In all, an expected 37,690 hectares of land – 13,542 hectares of forest lands; 11,279 hectares of arable agricultural lands; and 12,869 hectares of riverbed lands – would ultimately be submerged beneath the dam reservoir.[15] If one also accounts for human displacements due to the dam, the canal system, and other associated construction projects around the SSP dam area, then the figure increases to approximately 1 million impacted individuals, according to Friends of the River Narmada.[16] Despite the environmental, human rights, and indigenous rights problems with the NVDP, construction proceeds, though at times at an admittedly slow pace for a major national, multibillion dollar, infrastructural development project. When completed, or rather *if* completed, it will be the "single largest river valley project in India" (Baviskar 2004, 199).

Problems arose almost immediately, both among the three riparine states (Madhya Pradesh, Maharashtra, and Gujarat) who not only share the westward flowing river, but will also share the estimated costs and the projected benefits of the NVDP, and amidst mobilized grassroots active resistance to the dam projects.[17] To resolve interstate disputes, the Narmada Water Resources Development Committee (NWRDC), led by Dr. A. N. Khosla and unofficially known as the Khosla Committee, and which "ultimately formulated a set of recommendations based on a commitment to the intensive use of all the Narmada River Valley's water resources in the service of a top-down, technocratic vision of development as economic progress," was formed in 1964, following Nehru's death in 1963; and with continued and unresolved interstate conflicts over costs and benefits, the Narmada Water Disputes Tribunal (NWDT) was created in 1969, though the tribunal did not issue "its final award" until 1978, almost ten years after its conception and a near decade-long period of investigation, research, negotiation, and deliberation among representatives from the three states, economists, engineers, physicists, program developers, and the tribunal members (Khagram 2004, 74, 76–77).

Several elements are key to understanding transnational activism and diasporic arts of resistance in the case of India's Narmada River Valley: the two phases (first in the late 1970s, second in the early 1980s) of national grassroots resistance that led to the formation of the transnational anti-dam coalition in the late 1980s; the roles played by two Indian nationals, Medha Patkar and Arundhati Roy, in raising both international awareness about and Indian diasporic support for the Narmada cause; and finally the central role played by the SSP within the larger NVDP. The Sardar Sardovar, the largest dam on the Narmada River, has been the source of intense international scrutiny, radical grassroots mobilization, and extensive judicial review, as addressed more extensively below; and for these reasons, our discussions of the local grassroots organizations and the transnational and diasporic alliances for social justice in the Narmada River Valley will focus on the SSP.

Two Indian women have spearheaded grassroots, tribal, local, rural, regional, national, international, and transnational diasporic anti-dam efforts:

the sociologist Medha Patkar and writer Arundhati Roy. Patkar and Roy could be metaphorically likened to twin avengers of river and earth, lauded and revered by supporters, yet equally reviled by detractors. In an Op-Ed piece written for *The Indian Express* on April 22, 2006, Madhu Purnima Kishwar declaims:

> The spectacular success of Medha Patkar's Narmado Bachao Andolan in manipulating the media for over two decades is unparalleled in the history of social activism. I am no expert on the economic viability of big or small dams. Therefore, I have no verdict to pass on the Sardar Sarovar dam project. All I can say is that the mountains of propaganda material generated by the NBA, including the melodramatic tracts written by Arundhati Roy, convince me that their expertise cannot be trusted either.[18]

Inspiring highest praise and venomous attack, while instigating acrimonious public debate, they are clearly not without their vociferous detractors. While it risks eliding the valiant efforts and committed mobilization struggles by leaders in domestic nongovernmental organizations, such as Dr. Anil Patel of Arch-Vahini or Murlidhar Devidas ("Baba") Amte, also of the Andolan, many do attribute the successful grassroots mobilization of rural villagers and *adivasis* (if not exclusively, then overwhelmingly) to the indefatigable and indeed selfless work of sociologist-turned-activist Medha Patkar. As Caufield writes of Patkar: she arrived in the Narmada Valley from Bombay "a thirty-year-old social worker," who "wearing canvas sneakers and a faded sari, . . . traveled thousands of miles up and down the Narmada Valley," learning the "languages of the tribal people," eating "their food," and living "their Spartan life," until the culturally isolated tribals inexorably came to love and intuitively trust her (1996, 13, 14). From first efforts in the state of Maharashtra to organize villagers slated for "resettlement and rehabilitation" – R&R as it is often officially referenced, though the legalistic language serves to obscure the lived, human experiences of village submergence (beneath dam reservoirs) and human displacement – Patkar went on to become a founding member of the Narmada Bachao Andolan (NBA), or "Save the Narmada," also known as the Andolan, that ultimately mobilized rural villagers and *adivasis* throughout the entire Narmada Valley in the states of Maharashtra, Madhya Pradesh, and Gujarat; that galvanized anti-dam sentiments throughout the country, drawing crucial support from politicians, the media, scholars, activists, and other concerned citizens; and that successfully forged transnational alliances with international NGOs in order to force the issue of the NVDP and its indigenous, human, and environmental ramifications into myriad points of global political spotlight.

Grassroots resistance first emerged in 1978, proliferated around 1985 when the government of India became signatory to a $450 million loan extended by the World Bank to fund the NVDP, became transnationalized in the period from 1985 until 1993 when the World Bank withdrew from the project, and reentered a more nationally centered (and judicially determined) phase from 1995 to 2000 as domestic NGOs brought suits and legal cases intended to halt the dam project before the Indian Supreme Court, with initial successes from 1995 to 1999 but a major legal setback in 2000 with the court's ruling that the NVDP not only proceed but also be expedited. In this chapter, we will focus on the period from 1985 to 2000 – from the moment of World Bank funding of the project in 1985 through the late 1980s when indigenous grassroots resistance movements forged strategic transnational alliances with international NGOs, leading to the withdrawal of funding by international financial institutions in 1993 and favorable rulings by the Indian Supreme Court in 1995–6, and ending in 2000 with the ruling against the anti-dam resistance movement. We will, however, also review earlier resistance from 1978 to 1985 and resistance since the 2000 Supreme Court ruling in categorical favor of the NVDP. Throughout our sketch of the history of the NVDP, generally, and the SSP, specifically, we will highlight the roles played by Patkar and Roy. And in our focus on the transnational period, we will also emphasize the roles played by Patkar and Roy in forming strategic international alliances, in radicalizing sectors of the Indian diaspora or expatriate communities worldwide, and ultimately, and significantly, in raising global awareness about the Narmada Valley Dam Projects' violations of human and indigenous rights, as well as its environmental exploitations.

According to Sanjeev Khagram in *Dams and Development* (2004), the *first wave of indigenous resistance* to the NVDP emerged in the late 1970s with the "Save the Nimar Action Committee" headed by political candidate Arjun Singh. To resist both the unfair and inequitable compensation of displaced villagers and the failure by state governments to implement plans for R&R, a *second wave of indigenous resistance* emerged in the early 1980s "in opposition to the 1979 GoG resolution on 'resettlement and rehabilitation'" (2004, 87–88). In the state of Gujarat, domestic grassroots resistance emerged in early 1983 (Bharuch District) with the creation of the NGO Action Research in Community Health and Development, or Arch-Vahini, led by Dr. Anil Patel.[19] Similar grassroots resistance efforts were spearheaded in the state of Maharashtra by Medha Patkar. Our history of the NVDP, generally, and the SSP, specifically, will elaborate on and be organized around the domestic and transnational phases of resistance.

Popular domestic resistance in the state of Madhya Pradesh emerged almost immediately: in 1978, the Nimar Bachao Andolan ("Save the Nimar" Action Committee) was created under the political leadership of Arjun Singh as a coalition between "merchants and farmers" (Baviskar 2004, 202), between wealthy, large-landowning farmers, small landowners, and tribals opposed to the dam projects in the Nimar region of Madhya Pradesh, one of the first areas to be submerged once construction started; however, the coalition dissolved once Singh was elected Chief Minister under the Congress (I) Party, defeating the then-ruling Janata Party in Madhya Pradesh, the grassroots movement ending and simultaneously, but naively, funneling its hopes and objectives into Singh's political platform. Hopes were soon dashed: Singh abandoned the movement's demands for lowering the Sardar Sarovar Project dam height from 455 feet to "436 feet to prevent submergence of the Nimar area" and signed a compromise with Madhavasingh Solanki, Gujarat's Chief Minister, also a member of the Congress (I) Party, "to 'implement the decision of the Narmada Water Disputes Tribunal'

[and] ... to explore the possibility of reducing the distress of the displaced persons as much as possible" (Khagram 2002, 209, 210).

One year after the Tribunal Award of 1978, the government of Gujarat hosted "the first reconnaissance mission of the World Bank" in November 1979 (Khagram 2004, 85). To fund recommendations suggested by the World Bank, the Bank "secured $10 million from the United Nations Development Program to assist the government of Gujarat in implementing these recommendations (Khagram 2004, 86). From the beginning of dam construction, "resettlement and rehabilitation" of people displaced by the dam reservoir and canal channels were a perpetual problem. Although the Tribunal Award specifically stipulated that the state governments should offer land compensation for land submerged, the states offered cash for land and only then to deed-holding landowners, not to land-dwelling tribals who were legally dismissed as "encroachers" (2004, 87). On June 11, 1979, the GoG issued a resolution specifically excluding "landless" tribals from compensation, rendering them ineligible for R&R packages (Khagram 2004, 87).

Domestic grassroots agitation and actual cases of forced displacement in Gujarat also led to a 1980 statement issued by the World Bank condemning "involuntary resettlement" (Khagram 2004, 88). Initial efforts to "transnationalize" the cause were led by Dr. Anil Patel of Arch-Vahini who formed strategic alliances with John Clark, the director of Oxfam-UK in 1983; Clark was secondarily able to influence Tim Lancaster in the UK branch of the World Bank. Yet, as Khagram demonstrates, "the various tactics employed by the domestic opposition did not have much of an impact until a transnationally coordinated lobbying campaign targeted at the World Bank's involvement with the SSP supported by foreign nongovernmental organizations was organized" (Khagram 2004, 90). By the mid-1980s, however, "a transnational coalition was set up among Oxfam, Survival International, The Ecologist, Arch-Vahini, the civil rights nongovernmental organization Lok Adikar Sangh in Gujarat, the domestic environmental nongovernmental organization Kalpavriksh in New Delhi, and others" (2004, 91).

Leading up to the international Bank loan agreement between the GoI and the World Bank signed in 1985, the Bank sent Thayer Scudder to investigate problems related to dam displacement of rural villagers and stipulated that resettlement and rehabilitation policies be outlined as part of the loan agreement. Survival International, an international NGO based in the UK and advocating for the rights of indigenous people worldwide, also became involved in the NVDP: in 1985, Survival International wrote letters to both the International Labor Organization (ILO) and the World Bank inculpating the GoG for violating ILO Convention 107, which protected the rights of indigenous people. Plans for the World Bank loan agreement, despite protests, proceeded apace, and in February 1985, the institution published a World Bank Report entitled "Narmada River Development (Gujarat) Water Delivery and Drainage Project." In collaboration with Arch-Vahini and Oxfam-UK, Tim Lancaster (Executive Director of the UK World Bank office) leveled criticism against the Bank's plans in 1985, also raising the possibility that the GoG was in violation of ILO Covenant 107 in March 1985 (Khagram 2004, 93). Writing a letter of reply to Survival International in April 1985, the World Bank proceeded with loan negotiations with the GoI, and "the loan and credit agreements were signed with the federal government of India and project agreements with the state governments on May 10, 1985" (Khagram 2004, 94). Although the GoG signed the World Bank project agreement stipulating equitable compensation to all displaced families, including landless tribals, it also simultaneously filed a case with the Supreme Court of India to have "encroachers" ousted without compensation. According to Khagram, the Supreme Court, "based on arguments presented at the hearing . . . issued an interim stay order on construction of the rock filled dykes and appointed an inquiry commission to investigate the matter further" (2004, 96).

Following a reminder by the World Bank to the GoG to fulfill its "obligations" to compensate all oustees – not just deed-holding landowners – the GoG issued a resolution agreeing to compensate all those holding land titles as specified by the NWDT award of 1978, but still refused to compensate "encroachers" (Khagram 2004, 96). In the midst of recurrent complaints against the GoG's lack of adequate planning for and insufficient implementation of resettlement and rehabilitation, Medha Patkar began to mobilize domestic resistance in the state of Maharashtra, founding the Narmada Dharangrasta Samiti (Narmada Action Committee) and meeting with William Partride and Abdul Salam of the World Bank on their July 1986 supervisory mission in the Narmada Valley. Consequently, "the report they submitted to the World Bank on July 12, 1986 was extremely critical of the GoG's implementation of resettlement policies, observing that if changes were not soon made, the principles of the Bank's own policy of 1980 would be violated" (Khagram 2004, 98). The report led to a follow-up supervisory mission to ensure "implementation of resettlement policies for these projects" in the Narmada Valley in April 1987 (Khagram 2004, 98). These supervisory missions, moreover, led to three concessional resolutions (made on December 14–17, 1987) by the GoG on the issue of R&R: The GoG agreed to augment land compensation packages for "landed oustees"; increased "subsistence allowances . . . during the process of relocation"; and adopted, monumentally, the "same package for all landless oustees of Gujarat, not just those cultivating unauthorized lands" (Khagram 2004, 99).

At this point, domestic grassroots resistance splintered into NGOs (like Arch-Vahini and Anand Niketan Ashram) devoted primarily to monitoring and facilitating R&R of displaced families and those (like the Narmada Dharangrast Samiti and Kalpavriksh) which shifted efforts more comprehensively into an anti-dam campaign that became transnationalized in the late 1980s. In the summer and early autumn of 1988, "major demonstrations were launched all over India by the villagers and a coalition of domestic NGOs that supported the grassroots struggle against the project" (Khagram 2002, 222). Steeling anti-dam sentiments were the "repressive measures" exerted by the GoG, which ordered the state police to arrest "4,000 tribals" in the town of Waghadia and which impinged upon the rights of the "*dharna* activists" (Khagram 2002, 222). Unlike domestic NGOs cooperating with R&R efforts in Gujarat, these activists opposed the dam in its entirety. And in their anti-dam campaign, they "combined a number of critiques: that the resettlement reforms were not likely to be implemented, that the projects would cause irreparable environmental damage, and that the project's economic costs far outweighed their economic benefits" (Khagram 2004, 100). Domestic grassroots resistance in the Narmada Valley thus took on "massive multilevel, transnational" contours as "the Narmada Projects" became *the* "symbolic example of a destructive vision of development that had to be stopped, no matter what the cost" (Khagram 2004, 100). As Patkar urgently asked the people of Gujarat, Maharashtra, Madhya Pradesh, India, and the world, "Development? What sort of development is this? Development with destruction?" (quoted in Khagram 2004, 1). And in summer 1989, Patkar reenergized the domestic resistance into a transnational anti-dam campaign, founding the Narmada Bachao Andolan (NBA), or "Save the Narmada."

On September 28, 1989, the NBA (the Andolan) mobilized 300 NGOs and rallied 60,000 people in a massive demonstration against "destructive development" known as the Harsud Rally (Khagram 2004, 116–117). At Harsud, "the *sankap*, or resolve, taken was *Vikas chahiye, vinash nahin*, or 'We want development, not destruction'" (Khagram 2002, 222). The Andolan thus not only restricted "destructive development," but also envisioned alternative modes of sustainable development that did not violate the rights of human beings, particularly indigenous peoples, or degrade the environment. *Paryayi vikas-neetee* became the model of alternative development propounded by the NBA; and the principles of *paryayi vikas-neetee* were firmly grounded in protecting the human environment and the vital natural resources (water, earth, air, forests, rivers). *Paryayi vikas-neetee*, Subodh Wagle explains, is "an alternative development paradigm . . . essentially a broad framework and a set of norms which allow people to find their own definitions of human progress and work for them in ways that are commensurate with their aspirations, histories, cultures, social norms, and political choices" (2002, 76). Or, as Patkar herself articulates, "environmental issues 'were soon firmly rooted in the notion that environmentally sustainable resource use and control by local peoples, and the prevention against the encroachment on those resources by outsiders, was fundamental to our vision of participatory, socially just and equitable development" (quoted in Khagram 2002, 220). Patkar thus redefined the terms of development, environmental sustainability, and even "encroachment" – one of the key terms of contention in the Narmada debates. As Arundhati Roy later followed in her footsteps, Patkar herself insisted that the government and capitalist infrastructural developers were "encroaching" on tribal lands, not the other way around, as legal governmental documents maintained. Defining these terms and delimiting their material (moral) jurisdiction were the heart of the Narmada debates.

Seeds for a second transnational coalition had already been planted after Patkar met Bruce Rich of the Environmental Defense Fund (EDF) in 1986: three years after this fortuitous meeting of international activists in the Narmada Valley, a broader coalition emerged in October 1989 when Washington-based NGOs brought Patkar, representing the NBA, together with Peter Miller and Lori Udall, both representing the EDF, to testify before the Subcommittee on Natural Resources, Agricultural Research, and the Environment of the United States House of Representatives Hearing in October 1989. Testimony by Patkar, Miller, and Udall was successful in convincing Subcommittee Chairman James Scheuer "to organize a special oversight hearing to investigate the World Bank's support for the SSP" (Khagram 2002, 223). In fact, as Sanjeev Khagram writes, "the overwhelming evidence presented on the negative social and environmental impacts persuaded a number of representatives to ask for a suspension of World Bank support (US House 1989, 2002, 223). Subsequent to US HR hearings, a powerful transnational alliance consolidated around protecting the environment of the Narmada Valley and securing human rights and indigenous rights in the region. The transnational coalition amalgamated diverse international NGOs from across the globe: Kalpavriksh and the Narmada Bachao Andolan from India; the Rainforest Information Center from Australia; Survival International from England; the EDF and the International Rivers Network, both from the United States; Probe International from Canada; and Friends of Earth from Japan. From March 6–7, 1990, a major act of *satyagraha* (nonviolent resistance) was held in India, where "ten thousand people blocked the Bombay Agra highway, which passes through the Narmada Valley, for twenty-eight hours" (Khagram 2002, 223). Occupying the highway, or *chakka jam* ("blocking the road"), several activists, including Patkar, staged a hunger strike, and "hundreds of members of the Save the Narmada Movement protested for four days in front of the prime minister's residence" (Khagram 2002, 223; Wagle 2002, 87). One month later, in April 1990, the first International Narmada Symposium was held in Tokyo and hosted by Friends of Earth. The Symposium and the transnational coalition "ultimately resulted in the withdrawal of Japanese assistance from India for the SSP" (Khagram 2002, 223; Udall 1995, 212).

Success brought momentum, and with it broader coalitions: the transnational anti-dam campaign soon spawned a larger movement for alternative models of sustainable development. Eight months later, in December 1990, the Jan Vikras Sangarsh Yatra (or "March of the Struggle for People's Development") was organized, which brought together "thousands of villagers, activists, and supporters [who] walked for six days through the Narmada Valley from Madhya Pradesh toward the dam site in Gujarat" (Khagram 2002, 224). The GoG responded by coordinating a pro-dam counter-protest and by barricading the dam site "to prevent the marchers from getting to their destination" (Khagram 2002, 224). Patkar and others again staged an "indefinite fast" to protest Gujarat's violent state tactics.

International "noise" created by the transnational coalition against the Sardar Sarovar Dam led to an unprecedented move by the World Bank: in June 1991, the Bank commissioned an independent review of the SSP, appointing Bradford Morse, former executive director of the United Nations Development Program, and Thomas Berger, a human rights lawyer from Canada, to chair the review committee, which became known as the Morse Commission and which began investigating the SSP in September 1991. The same year, the GoG had "forcibly" resettled villagers in the Narmada Valley and "arrested hundreds of people who refused to resettle," which led to an Amnesty International Report documenting the government's "human rights violations" (Khagram 2002, 224); the Gujarat police also continued its brutal assault against *satyagraha* protesters, galvanizing international criticism against the dam project. Despite ongoing investigations by the Morse Commission and international criticism, construction of the SSP continued unabated. Radicalizing their protests against the GoG and the SSP, members of the Andolan vowed *doobenge par hartenge nahin* ("We will drown, but move we will not") and further declared *jal samarpan* ("suicide by drowning") as the "ultimate protest" against the dam (Khagram 2002, 225). In 1992, the Commission published the Morse Report criticizing the SSP and the GoG for its negative environmental actions, its violation of indigenous human rights (through "forcible" or involuntary resettlement as well as through its administrative neglect in designing and implementing an equitable, voluntary plan for "resettlement and rehabilitation"); to the shock and dismay of Gujarat and World Bank officials, but to the delight of Andolan members, Morse and Berger recommended that the Bank "step back" from the project and that the construction of the Sardar Sarovar Dam be halted. Despite these clear recommendations by the Morse Commission, the GoG and the World Bank attempted to "quick-fix" problems and proceed apace with the SSP, leading the Narmada International Action Committee to publish "an open letter" (signed by "250 NGOs from thirty-seven countries") to the World Bank in the *Financial Times* in 1992 that criticized the Bank's "duplicity and calling for a suspension of the SSP" (Khagram 2002, 225–226). Following massive demonstrations and growing international resistance to the SSP (not only by concerned citizens and publics, but also by government officials and financial lenders), the World Bank withdrew funding from the project on March 26, 1993; or rather, one day before the six-month deadline established by the Bank for the GoG to design and implement an equitable R&R policy and fix other problems associated with the SSP, the Bank allowed the GoI to state that construction of the Sardar Sarovar Dam would proceed independent of international financing (Khagram 2002, 226; Khan 1995, 425–427).

With the World Bank's withdrawal from the SSP in 1993, the resistance entered a primarily "national" phase once again with a series of Supreme Court cases filed and ruled upon from 1994 until 2000. The Narmada International Action Committee, spearheaded by the NBA, also led to the establishing of a "domestic Indian review group" of the project in June 1993, "less than three months after the World Bank's withdrawal" (Khagram 2002, 226). NBA activists filed two petitions with the Indian Supreme Court requesting cessation of building on the SSP dam site – the first requesting a stay "until the report of the domestic review, which had been completed in April 1994, was made public" (Khagram 2002, 227); and the second requesting a permanent halt in construction due to the "social and environmental costs" of the SSP (Khagram 2002, 227). In 1995, the Indian Supreme Court ruled in favor of the anti-dam campaign, ordering a halt to the construction of the Sardar Sarovar Dam at 80.3 meters. In essence, "India's Supreme Court found that the fundamental rights of the persons to be displaced under India's democratic constitution had been violated as well as that Indian law and international agreements on various environmental issues had not been fulfilled by project authorities" (Khagram 2002, 227). Judicial gains, however, were subsequently reversed in the Indian Supreme Court ruling in 1999 that allowed for construction of the Sardar Sarovar Dam up to 88 meters and again in the 2000 Supreme Court ruling that not only allowed for construction up to 90 meters, but also permitted for planned construction of the dam up to the originally planned height of 138 meters in 5-meter increments to allow for gradual "resettlement and rehabilitation" of "project-affected persons," yet administratively "subject to the Relief and Rehabilitation Subgroup of the Narmada Control Authority" (NCA) (www.narmada.org).

Still active in the resistance, the Andolan and Patkar's visionary role remained important; however, a new national actor, Arundhati Roy, took on the cause and was successful in forcing the issues back into global consciousness (and conscience) in 1999, after the Indian Supreme Court – reversing earlier rulings in 1995 and 1996 that halted construction of the Sardar Sarovar Dam – ruled that construction should not only proceed, but further, that it should be expedited. Born in Kerala, educated in Corpus Christi, and now residing in New Delhi, internationally acclaimed novelist, ardent anti-globalization activist, and rhetorically searing social justice nonfiction writer, Arundhati Roy has done more to raise public and popular awareness worldwide about the Narmada River Dam Projects, and especially the SSP, than any other Indian national. In two essays that seem to revisit the Caribbean feminist wish – "If I could write this as fire" – Roy rhetorically deconstructs and wryly, if also fiercely and angrily, unpacks the ideological presuppositions (modernist, nationalist, capitalist, developmentalist) that have fueled the NVDP since its inception and that have plagued its stop-again-start-again governmental and judicial and procedural mechanisms.[20] "Lies, Dam Lies, and Statistics," published in the *Guardian* in June 1999, is a terse, steel-plated literary bullet aimed at the government of India, generally, and the governments of Madhya Pradesh, Maharashtra, and Gujarat, specifically. "For the Greater Common Good," a longer version of the same essay, was also published simultaneously in two periodicals – *Frontline* and *Outlook* – in June 1999, and later reprinted in the book *The Cost of Living* (1999). In what follows, we will analyze some of Roy's rhetorical, textual, and political strategies in attacking the proponents of the dam projects and their negative presuppositions about land tenancy, land use, and human indigenous rights, as well as advocating on the behalf of the rights of displaced families (including dispossessed widows and minor children[21] who have no claim to compensation, resettlement, or rehabilitation as "oustees," as the government has bureaucratically defined them) and land-dwelling but not landowning or deed-holding *adivasis*, indigenous dwellers, whom the government has dismissively labeled "encroachers."

Following the February 1999 Supreme Court ruling lifting the four-year stay in construction and allowing for construction of the Sardar Sarovar Dam up to 88 meters, Roy visited the Narmada Valley to see first-hand and open-eyed the region slated for submergence: "In March," she writes in *The Cost of Living*, "I traveled to the Narmada Valley. I returned, numbed. I returned unable to ignore or accept what everybody (including myself) has, over the years, gradually accepted and successfully ignored" (1999, ix). Though India is the "third largest dam-builder in the world" – 3,300 big dams since Independence – and though "their reservoirs have uprooted millions of people," Roy laments, yet also incredulously disbelieves, "there are no government records of how many people have been displaced" (1999, ix). And this from a country that "has detailed figures for how many million tons of food grain or edible oils the country produces . . . how much bauxite is mined in a year or what the total surface area of the national highways adds up to," and even the daily fluctuations in "the value of the rupee . . . [or] how many cricket matches we've lost on a Friday in Sharjah," as well as "vasectomies in any given year"; in other words, for a country bureaucratically mired in figures, numbers, statistics, or quantifiable data, it is hard to believe that "the government of India does not have a figure for the number of peoples who have been displaced by dams or sacrificed in other ways at the altars of 'national progress'" (1999, 16).

Roy's essay "The Greater Common Good" articulates an anti-imperialist dissent, raging against the twentieth-century fetish for the "big" and praying for a twenty-first "century of the small." Following a century-long trajectory that worshiped the "big" – "Big bombs, big dams, big ideologies, big contradictions, big countries, big wars, big heroes, big mistakes" – Roy calls for a "dismantling of the Big" (1999, 12). Tabulating the capital "gains" and national "losses" comprising the "greater common good" arithmetically (as she also does in "The Algebra of Infinite Justice," an essay about the post-9/11 "War on Terror"), Roy deploys several rhetorical strategies – declamatory irony, sardonic wit, mathematical rage, moral accounting, narrative diatribe, and heartfelt plea – challenging notions of property, possession, dispossession, costs, gains, liabilities, profits, expenditure, and expendability. In the opening pages, Roy launches an ironic disclaimer, one that acknowledges her critics' beliefs about her, even as it disavows those claims on her politically, intellectually, and materially. Declaiming her reputation, even as she ironically acknowledges it, Roy writes, "Let me say at the outset that I'm not a city-basher. I've done my time in a village. I've had first-hand experience of the isolation, the inequity and the potential savagery of it. I'm not an anti-development junkie, nor a proselytiser for the eternal upholding of custom and tradition" (1999, 8). As the woman who boldly stated that the only thing that should be "globalized" is "dissent," Roy denies at the "outset" those who would dismiss the message with the messenger, before defining herself in a definitive, yet speculative, "pronoun-linking verb-predicate adjective" syntactically arranged sentence: "What I am, however, is curious" (1999, 8). She rhetorically invites her readers into her curiosity, into an inquisitive desire to know (or to seek) the truth about the Narmada. "Curiosity," Roy defends, "took me to the Narmada Valley" (1999, 8). Rejecting news reports and governmental documents about the NVDP, Roy appeals to her own sense of moral conviction and a guiding sense of intuition:

> Instinct told me that this was *the big one*. The one in which the battle-lines were clearly drawn, the warring armies massed along them. The one in which it would be possible to wade through the congealed morass of hope, anger, information, disinformation, political artifice, engineering ambition, disingenuous socialism, radical activism, bureaucratic subterfuge, misinformed emotionalism and, of course, the pervasive, invariably dubious, politics of International Aid. (1999, 8; emphasis added)

That the Narmada is *the big one* is part of the problem for Roy, even as it attracted her too – as if flies to shit. Even the concept of *the big one*, for Roy, obscures the small details of millions of anonymous lives displaced along the river.

Following her sense of instinct and inquisitiveness, Roy asks fundamental questions about human existence, the environment, and notions of property at the heart of "our democracy": "Who owns this land? Who owns its rivers? Its forests? Its fish?" (1999, 9). Roy flouts that the idea that the Narmada is a *big* dam with *big* ideological consequences – i.e., a debate between "Development" and "Anti-Development," or between the national descendants of Nehru v. Gandhi (1999, 10). For Roy, the "story" of the Narmada – though it attracted her, she admits, like a vulture "drawn to kills" (1999, 12) – is one of "small heroes" and not that of a Nehru or a Gandhi (1999, 12). Rather, the Narmada equals millions of small wars, each fought for dignity, honor, and sustainable lives. Weighing gains against losses, profits against liabilities, the "greater common good" against the countless small sacrifices that still seem to always already add up to an administrative "zero" in the national developmental ledger, Roy asks why in India – "the world's third largest dam-builder" (1999, 13), a fact that she twice repeats – "one fifth of our population – 200 million people – does not have safe drinking water, and two thirds – 600 million – lack basic sanitation" (1999, 14). Roy, noting the first world's end to big dam construction for ecological and human reasons, pointedly writes that "the Local Pain for National Gain myth has been blown wide open" (1999, 15). Yet, what the first world no longer wants, it exports; and the third world imports big dams "in the name of Development Aid, along with their other waste, like old weapons, superannuated aircraft carriers, and banned pesticides" (1999, 15). India, Roy cringes to think, "actually *pays* to receive their gift-wrapped garbage" (1999, 15).

Since the GoI has no documented data on such national development projects, Roy herself mathematically calculates the estimated costs of Big Dam construction in number of displaced persons. Based on an average of "10,000 people per Large Dam" and a total of 3,300 Large Dams built in India since 1947, Roy estimates that 33 million people have been displaced by big dams, and a modest estimate of 50 million people for those displaced by large dams plus medium-sized dams, small dams, canal networks, and "other Development projects" (1999, 17). As Roy intimates with wry satirical wit, if also lugubrious disbelief about hypocritical, circumloquacious governmental logic: "We daren't say so, because it isn't official. It isn't official because we daren't say so" (1999, 17). Displaced, erased from the books, forgotten in the national ledger: "The millions of displaced people don't exist anymore. When history is written they won't be in it" (1999, 20). Mathematical truth, statistical lies: "Numbers used to make my eyes glaze over," Roy writes: "Not anymore. Not since I began to follow the direction in which they point" (1999, 21). Vacillating between dismantling the data amassed and ignored through quantitative obfuscation and telling narrative truths, Roy implores: "Trust me. There's a story here" (1999, 21). Roy also deconstructs the ideological presuppositions fueling India's progress – vague notions with nevertheless real material costs, ideals about nation, development, modernity, and even about "progress." Still, questions persist, niggling her mind: "What kind of country is this? Who owns it? Who runs it? [and] what's going on?" (1999, 22). National neglect or deliberate strategic plan? "It's time to spill a few state secrets," Roy confides. "Let's not delude ourselves," she writes: "There is a method here, precise, relentless, and 100 percent manmade" (1999, 22). Clarity cuts through obfuscating state rhetoric – or "lies, dam lies, and statistics" – and incisively reveals an ugly national truth: "The Indian state," Roy clarifies, "is not a state that has failed. It is a state that has succeeded impressively in what it set out to do. It has been ruthlessly efficient in the way it has appropriated India's resources – its land, its water, its forests, its fish, its meat, its eggs, its air – and redistributed them to a favored few (in return, no doubt, for a few favors)" (1999, 22–23).

Yet, for Roy, nature has its limits, and even extensive and intensive capitalist expropriation and exploitation meet their marks (or measures) in nature itself: "We don't seem to know that the resources we're feasting on are finite and rapidly depleting" (1999, 23). And the state, "an overstretched State," is as Roy bitingly writes, "a giant poverty-producing machine" (1999, 24). Human costs, material losses, monetary profits: the state machine feeding on its own people that it has starved. "Already," Roy impugns and castigates, "50 million people have been fed into the development mill and have emerged as air conditioners and popcorn and rayon suits," or irrigation, hydroelectric power, modernized standards of living, modern luxuries, or late capital commodities to be discarded once consumed, used up, or simply unwrapped. To ensure that we do not miss the point, Roy explicitly concludes, "The international dam industry is worth $20 billion a year" (1999, 29) – no *small* gain to offset and compensate for the 50 million displaced; but rather, a *big* boon – for the "greater common good," of course. But "God forbid, you suggest that the human costs are perhaps too high"; as Roy wryly notes, "then you're history" (1999, 31). In a final rhetorical blow, Roy likens big dams to nuclear arms, "both weapons of mass destruction" (1999, 80). "Both," Roy argues, are "twentieth-century emblems that mark a point in time when human intelligence has outstripped its own instinct for survival" (1999, 80). For Roy, "they're both malignant indications of a civilization turning upon itself" (1999, 80). And while the logic of "destructive development" (too often veiled, packaged, and marketed to all-too eager and willingly consuming consumer-citizens as national "development" or even more universally and seemingly benignly as human "progress") may appear (amidst fetishizing capitalist smoke-and-mirrors) to entail no losses – a proverbial win-win for global capitalism in all its national economic localities – it comes at a price! At end, Roy asks that we simply "understand the price that's being paid for it" (1999, 81): she asks that we have "the courage to watch while the dues are cleared and the books are squared" (1999, 81). "Our dues. Our books. Not theirs," she concludes. "Be there," she demands.

Through her nonfiction rhetoric of dissent, then, Arundhati Roy, like Medha Patkar, has been a powerful agent and an extremely influential voice in the anti-dam campaign both to raise global consciousness (and political conscience) about the Narmada River Valley and its people and to rally Indian diasporic subjects

and sympathetic political activists in forging a transnational political coalition
against the NVDP. Successes of the anti-dam campaign (at least until the Indian
Supreme Court reversal in their 1999 ruling in favor of the NVDP and the GoG)
ultimately depended, as Khagram astutely demonstrates, on the political coalesc-
ing of "transnational grassroots movements for social justice" (Glick Schiller and
Fouron 2001), "cosmopolitical activism" (Gilroy 2004) in New Delhi, London,
Washington, DC, and other urban metropolitan centers of capital, or "global
cities" (Sassen 1988), and democratic institutions in India that "offered domestic
opponents a range of political opportunities that would not have existed in an
authoritarian regime" (Khagram 2002, 226–227).

The Patkar began working in the rural villages scheduled or zoned for submergence
in the Narmada Valley in the state of Maharashtra in 1985 (Baviskar 2004,
202–203). In 1987, Patkar also devoted time to reenergizing the grassroots protests against the SSP in the Nimar area of Madhya Pradesh. Leading rural grassroots efforts, the Andolan (NBA) centered through activist work around two
major dams in the NVDP – the Sardar Sarovar Dam and the Narmada Sagar
Dam (Baviskar 2004, 203). Initially protesting the lack of "resettlement and
rehabilitation" plans by the governments of Gujarat, Maharashtra, and Madhya
Pradesh, the Andolan soon channeled their efforts into opposing the entire SSP,
grounding their decision in ecological and human rights considerations. In fact,
the NBA sought to halt construction of the Sardar Sarovar Dam completely,
which it was able to do temporarily at least. Initial efforts by the NBA were primarily domestic and focused almost exclusively on displacement and forcing
better resettlement programs for displaced rural villagers in the valley; and the
grassroots organization was successful in prevailing upon the Gujarat government to provide land compensation for submerged land, not just cash disburse-
ment for land as the 1978 Tribunal had specified, as well as for lands dwelled
upon but not owned – i.e., without legal deeds of landownership and thus with
property rights. Despite these "concessions," many promised resettlement packages have yet to materialize (Baviskar 2004, 203n3). Both Amita Baviskar and
Sanjeev Khagram see this second phase of Andolan resistance – or the anti-dam
campaign – as one that successfully forged transnational alliances between local
grassroots organizations, international NGOs, and Indian diasporic communities
outside of the subcontinent.

The Andolan, organizing *dharnas*, or *dharanas* (sit-ins) and other acts of
satyagraha (nonviolent resistance) in the wake of the World Bank decision to
fund the NVDP in 1985, while forging strategic transnational alliances with
international NGOs, ultimately created enough world noise that it compelled the
World Bank into commissioning an independent review of the NVDP in 1991
under the leadership of Bradford Morse and Thomas Berger (the Morse Commission). The Morse Report (1992) published a scathing critique of the dam
projects, particularly indicting the national government of India and the state
governments of Gujarat, Maharashtra, and Madhya Pradesh for failing to create
and implement a rehabilitation policy for those families displaced by the project.
A year later, in 1993, following face-saving tactics that allowed the government
of India to announce that it would independently fund the NVDP without Bank

funds, the World Bank withdrew from the project. The Andolan was also successful at the national level, at least at first, in appealing to the Indian Supreme Court on behalf of tribal and *adivasi* rights. Given the failures of Gujarat, Madhya Pradesh, and Maharashtra to "resettle" and "rehabilitate" those impacted by the dam projects, the Supreme Court ruled in 1995 to halt construction of the Sardar Sarovar Dam at 80.3 meters until R&R policies could be designed and fully implemented by the states.

Patkar was also a founding member of the Narmada Bachao Andolan (NBA), a coalitional effort initially focused on fair "resettlement and rehabilitation" of *all people* affected by the dam projects – landowners as well as tribals,[22] and *adivasis*, who had dwelled on and agriculturally tilled land in the Narmada Valley for generations, but who did not hold deeds to the lands claimed and acquired first by the British colonial empire in the subcontinent and later by the government of India, and who were pejoratively referred to as "encroachers" in dam-planning documents. Strikingly, in legal documents, "resettlement and rehabilitaton" was restricted to deed-holding landowners and individuals whose lands were submerged to create the dam reservoir, or to those classified as PAPs: "project affected peoples"! *Dharnas* and other acts of *satyagraha* proliferated in the late 1980s, beginning in the years after India signed the World Bank loan agreement in 1985 until the Bank withdrew funding for the project in 1993. Following the World Bank decision to fund the NVDP to the amount of US$450 million in 1985, grassroots resistance among indigenous tribals, scholars, activists, and sympathetic Indian citizens not only proliferated domestically, but the effort became internationalized as Arch-Vahini, the NBA (or the Andolan), and other national NGOs reached out to and formed critical alliances with transnational NGOs, such as Oxfam-UK, the Environmental Defense Fund, the Environmental Policy Institute, the International Rivers Network, and the National Wildlife Federation.

Case Study 2: Haitian Diaspora and Transnational "Tenth Department" Activism

The Haitian diaspora in the United States has been a vocal, long-distance *department* of the homeland, working for political, economic, and democratic change in Haiti while also organizing to resist what many regard as US imperialism in the small developing country. Three historical moments in the post-Duvalier period of Haiti's history stand out as ones that galvanized Haitian diasporas – across class, racial, and political lines – and stirred a wide response from Haitian Americans who took to the streets, wrote Senators and Representatives, lobbied the Congressional Black Caucus, and inspired change. The first major moment of Haitian diasporic activism in the post-Duvalier period in the US, particularly in New York, occurred after the labeling of Haitians by the Center for Disease Control (CDC) in 1990 as one of the *4Hs*, or HIV carriers, along with heroin users, homosexuals, and hemophiliacs, which became the discriminatory basis for both denying Haitian refugees and immigrants entry into the United States and for segregating detained refugees at Guantánamo Naval Base by HIV sero-positive or seronegative status. The second major moment of Haitian American diasporic activism followed the 1991 military coup d'état that ousted democrati-cally elected President Jean-Bertrand Aristide and the consequent diasporic efforts to push both the United Nations and the US government to intervene in the three-year crisis from 1991 to 1994, popularly referred to as a "reign of terror." The third major moment of Haitian diasporic activism in the United States revolved around the diasporic responses (some of it very conservative and dis-tinctly pro-privatization and pro-business; some anti-capitalist, pro-socialist, and pro-social spending) to the 1994 Economic Emergency Recovery Program (EERP), dubbed by critics *plan lanmò* ("death plan"), which was the international devel-opment loan and structural adjustment program (SAP) requiring privatization of state utilities that was collectively designed by the IMF, the World Bank, and the Inter-American Development Bank (IADB).

After only seven months in office, on September 29, 1991, Aristide was ousted from office by a violent, right-wing military coup d'état led by Général Raoul Cédras (though many believe that the real man in power was Michel François, the chief of police in Port-au-Prince who was ironically nicknamed "Sweet Mickey," a tag he shares with the *konpa* star Michel Martelly); on September 30, Aristide fled the country. By October 3, the Organization of American States (OAS) recommended that the international community suspend all economic interactions with the Haitian state; consequently and unsurprisingly, the "embargo" only increased Haitian hardship, and floods of refugees – sadly, ironi-cally, itself a human *lavalas* – abandoned the country in makeshift boats. Fol-lowing the coup d'état and Aristide's exile from the country, massive waves of refugees boarded small boats and fled the war-torn country; many of those who had supported Lavalas and Aristide were viciously persecuted after the president went into exile. Within the first six months of 1991, for example, according to Marvin Dunn in *Black Miami in the Twentieth Century* (1997), "1,030 Haitians were interdicted, with only 17 being allowed to seek asylum. During the same six months, the Coast Guard rescued 1,081 Cubans at sea and brought them to south Florida. Few of the Cubans applied for asylum, since immigration law allowed them to become permanent US residents after a year in the country. However, this policy did not apply to Haitians" (1997, 325).

The Tenth Department, so coined by Aristide in October 1990, took to the streets of Manhattan in an act of political solidarity with the ousted leader on October 11, 1991: "over 60,000 blocked downtown Manhattan for hours to protest apparent tacit US support for the military coup" (Jean-Pierre 1995, 203). This was not the first political act organized by the Haitian diaspora in the US, which had marched across the Brooklyn Bridge in March 1990 to protest the erroneous and racist designation of Haitians by the Food and Drug Administra-tion (FDA) and the CDC as one of the four high (or "at-risk") carriers of the HIV virus – what Edwidge Danticat and others have sarcastically referred to as the targeted 4Hs: homosexuals, hemophiliacs, heroin users, and Haitians. It was, however, a decisive moment of diasporic activism that affected policies and poli-tics both within Haiti and the US. As Nina Glick Schiller and Georges Fouron note, "it was the political mobilization of the diaspora on behalf of Aristide . . . that firmly implanted the concept of the Haitian people as a transnational nation among Haitians in Haiti" (2001, 122).[23] It was also markedly different from earlier diasporic activism – not only in that it was directed toward both homeland and host country, but also in that it was open and public, rather than secretive and anonymous. As Jean-Pierre writes, "the new groups began to stage public demonstrations to denounce the US role in Haitian politics. Previously Haitians had protested with their faces hidden for fear of being recognized by the hundreds of spies working in the United States for Papa Doc" (1995, 199). Jean-Pierre also explains that the Tenth Department was responsible for a massive voter turnout, an estimated 260,000 to 300,000 Haitian American voters who voted "overwhelmingly" for Democratic candidate William Jefferson ("Bill") Clinton in the 1992 US presidential election (1995, 203).

Those who did, falsely believed that Clinton would end Bush's policy of interdiction and detention at Guantánamo Bay (decried as inhumane by activists), which the candidate vocally (and in the end, hypocritically) censured during his presidential campaign. Beginning in November 1991, under Bush's directive, the INS detained all Haitian refugees to be interviewed at Guantánamo Bay; the situation worsened in May 1992 when Bush issued the Kennebunkport Order requiring the US Coast Guard to intercept all Haitian refugees and return them directly and immediately to Haiti (Laguerre 1998, 83). Clinton proved to be an on-again, off-again friend to Haiti and its diasporic communities in the United States. Once elected, and profoundly disappointing the Haitian American community, Clinton implemented the Kennebunkport Order that he had earlier denounced during the presidential campaign: this broken campaign promise and regressive policy shift, unfortunately, had devastating material consequences for Haitian refugees, as "US cutters manned by the Coast Guard, under executive order from President Bush and then President Clinton, chased the boats in the high seas and placed refugees under US custody at the makeshift tent city in Guantanamo" (Laguerre 1998, 83, 27). (The racist and racializing INS policy of interception-detention-deportation toward Haitian refugees fleeing political persecution and detained at Guantánamo Bay Naval Base during the mid-1990s is discussed more extensively in chapter five, "Race and Diasporas.")

Perilous for Haitian refugees assail in small boats crossing the Atlantic Ocean, the period from 1991 to 1994 was also dangerous for those remaining in Haiti, and military and paramilitary violence in the country, as well as the exile of Aristide, also impelled the diaspora (businessmen, working-class taxi drivers, college professors, and even writers and artists) to activist resistance. In "The Missing Peace," from the short-story collection *Krik? Krak!*, for example, Haitian American fiction writer Edwidge Danticat takes up the figure of Emmanuel "Toto" Constant, founder and ruthless leader of a brutal paramilitary gang that slaughtered Haitian political supporters of "Titid" (as Jean-Bertrand Aristide was affectionately called by supporters). During the *defakto* military regime under the rule of Général Raoul Cédras, the CIA supported and funded the creation of *Révolutionnaire Front pour l'Avancement et le Progrès d'Haïti* (Revolutionary Front for Advancement and Progress in Haiti), more commonly known as

FRAPH, an acronym that homonymically sounds like the French word *frappe*, which means to hit, beat, or strike. Started in 1993 by Constant, who was on CIA payroll, FRAPH was ostensibly created as an anti-Lavalas conservative party intended to spy on Lavalas party members; however, FRAPH became one of the most violent military junta organizations that Haiti has even seen, killing an estimated 5,000 Lavalas supporters and committing brutal atrocities with impunity. Elizabeth McAlister refers to FRAPH as a "cocaine-trafficking network and death squad" (2002, 165). She further elaborates:

> FRAPH was meant to become a right-wing party alternative to Jean-Bertrand Aristide's party, and as such was given seed money by the United States Central Intelligence Agency. The group quickly became involved in cocaine trafficking, and its *ti nèg* foot soldiers carried out an unprecedented campaign of gang rape against poor women and children, often in front of family members, atrocities that will undoubtedly affect Haitian society for generations. (2002, 232n8)

Feminist scholar Terry Ray and Human Rights Watch/Americas have both discussed FRAPH's use of rape as a tactic of torture and control (McAlister 2002, 232n8).

The period of Aristide's exile from 1991 to 1994 was, quite literally, a "reign of terror": according to political activist and scholar Charles Arthur, "For three years, summary executions, arbitrary searches and arrests, disappearances, beatings, torture, and extortion were systematic and commonplace" (2002, 25). FRAPH alone was "responsible for massacres in poor neighborhoods, random shootings with dead bodies left in the street to spread terror, attacks on grassroots organizations of the poor, rapes and sexual terrors of women activists, and assassinations of political leaders" (Glick Schiller and Fouron 2001, 122). According to Beverly Bell in *Walking on Fire: Haitian Women's Stories of Survival and Resistance*, "A common tactic of FRAPH members – themselves largely recruited from slums and villages – was to slice off the faces of their victims before depositing them in open-field garbage dumps in Cité Soleil" (2001, 13). One of the most violent leaders of FRAPH, "Toto" Constant, was granted asylum in the United States and now lives in New York, and it is unlikely that he will be deported or extradited for trial for his crimes against humanity, though lawyers in Haiti are attempting to do so. Louis-Jodel Chamblain, an armed rebel leader in the 2004 crisis, and Jean-Pierre Baptiste (aka, "Tatoune") were also FRAPH members. In September 1993, Chamblain assassinated Antoine Izmery, who was dragged from church, made to kneel, and shot. Chamblain was tried *in absentia* for Izmery's murder and additional murders of individuals in Gonaïves in 1995; however, he lived in exile in the Dominican Republic for the decade-long period from 1994, the year of Aristide's return to power, until 2004, the year of Aristide's second exile. "Toto" Constant and "Tatoune" were both involved in the 1994 Raboteau Massacre, in which Lavalas and Aristide supporters were openly slaughtered; both were tried *in absentia* for the massacre. Tatoune was briefly imprisoned, receiving a life sentence for his crimes, but was later freed in a jail break.

In 1993, the CIA (in cooperation with Lynne Garrison, author of *Voodoo Politics*) also issued a damning, but incredible (literally) psychological profile of Aristide, describing the exiled leader as a "psychotic manic depressive with proven homicidal tendencies" (Dupuy 1997, 153; cf. Fatton 2002, 180). Whenever Aristide provoked disfavor in the US, as when frustrating efforts to privatize state utilities, the CIA recirculated the psychological profile. Paul Farmer, describing the "most likely scenario" for Haiti following Aristide's restoration in 1994, wryly notes, "the CIA continues to operate in Haiti (the agency has, reportedly, recently received a $5 million 'emergency grant' to counter Aristide's opponents – a novel project for the agency)" (1995, 228). In the 2004 crisis, speculations about CIA support, training, and arming of rebels – many of whom were former FRAPHists or CIA payrollees – again swirled in Haiti and in its diaspora. Diasporic writers, artists, and directors not only critiqued the military intervention by US and UN peacekeeping forces, but also the post-intervention economic plans for "rebuilding" Haiti through international loans.

Laferrière, in "Un Écrivain primitif" ("A Primitive Writer"), the opening chapter of *Pays sans chapeau* (1996) recounts the exhilaration and artistic palpitation experienced upon first returning home – after a 20-year absence – to Haiti, which he affectionately, yet despairingly refers to as "ce caillou au soleil auquel s'accrochent plus de sept millions d'hommes, de femmes et d'enfants affamés" (13) ("this sun-burnt stone that more than seven million starving men, women, and children cling to") (9). We need to contextualize Laferrière's wry opening line – indeed his entire autobiographical literary narrative *Pays sans chapeau* – I contend, in two historical events of 1994: the "inter-vasion"[24] (as it was satirically dubbed: somewhere between *intervention* and *invasion*) by US and UN troops and the signing of the Emergency Economic Recovery Program, the IMF-structured and World Bank-funded plan to "rebuild" Haiti, which significantly also imposed a global capitalist "structural adjustment plan" (SAP) on the country and required the privatization of state utilities, such as electricity and telephone services. During the period from 1991 to 1994, "while the junta leaders were being pressured to step down, Aristide was being pushed to accept an array of neoliberal fiscal policies to be implemented upon his return" (Smith 2001, 25). In efforts not only to resolve the constitutional and military crisis in Haiti and to end the *defakto* regime of Général Cédras, but to also plan for the economic development of the country, the United States and the World Bank arranged a meeting of international donors and governmental officials in Paris. Meeting in 1993, the group (exiled Haitian President Aristide, officials from the World Bank, the IMF, governmental administrators from the G7 and the US, as well as other international donors) agreed upon and signed the Emergency Economic Recovery Program (EERP) to the fiscal tune of $2.1 billion! According to Jennie M. Smith in *When the Hands are Many*, the plan required and imposed the "a strict structural adjustment plan (SAP) involving government downsizing, privatization of state enterprises, trade liberalization, the maintenance of low wages, and financial deregulation – policies now renowned in the Third World for virtually guaranteeing the increased immiseration of the poor" (2001, 34). When the EERP was signed, Mark Schneider, a USAID administrator, congratulated and thanked those present, stating, "Thanks to contributors from the United States Government and the Governments of Japan, Sweden, Mexico, Switzerland, France, Canada, Netherlands, Argentina, and Haiti – $81,474,605 in arrears to these three financial institutions [IMF, IADB, and World Bank] were cleared and, in so doing, removing the most serious obstacle to the use of $260 million in frozen funds from these institutions" (quoted in Glick Schiller and Fouron 2001, 223). Schneider also announced that $40 million in loans from the World Bank and an additional $70 million in loans from the Inter-American Development Bank (a bank funded by the United States government for development throughout the Americas) would be issued to Haiti for national "development" purposes (Glick Schiller and Fouron 2001, 223). While this was seemingly driven by generosity and charity alone, Glick Schiller and Fouron remain more skeptical about the interests served by such structural adjustment programs: "Translated into more straightforward language, this meant that the taxpayers of ten governments, including Haiti, repaid eighty-one million dollars in loan payments to banks that represent the richest governments in the world, including a US-financed development bank. These same banks would in return lend Haiti more money, which would also have to be repaid" (2001, 223). It is not difficult to envision the trajectory that straps most small developing countries: new loans obtained to pay interest on old debts. Also the international "aid" funds do not always aid those who most need assistance, but rather perpetuate the cycles of (third-world) indebtedness and (first-world) profit. Exemplary in this regard: USAID. "It is typical," Ira Kurzban (2001) writes, "for USAID officials to go to Capitol Hill and boast about how our foreign aid dollars 'are returned to the US' because they go mostly to US companies conducting studies or overseeing programs." Citing a USAID official, Smith similarly writes that "seventy-nine cents of every USAID dollar is actually spent in the United States," although some estimates are as high as 90 cents per dollar (2001, 36). Smith further indicts USAID as giving with one hand while taking with the other; this two-handed gesture reveals that USAID serves US interests as much, if not more than, those of the developing countries that it purportedly "aids." According to Smith, "while offering hundreds of thousands of impoverished Haitians food on a daily basis, [USAID] has repeatedly fought against efforts by the Haitian government to raise the minimum wage and discouraged price controls of basic foodstuffs" (37). Smith (2001, 37–38) and Bell (2001, 102) both document peasant grassroots activism in which rural Haitians are allying with diasporic Haitians and others throughout the Americas to protest the SAPs imposed on American countries by USAID, the IMF, the World Bank, the IADB, and other international donors wed to the so-called Washington Consensus.

Both sociologist Alex Dupuy and anthropologist Jennie M. Smith have described Haiti's condition as one of "grinding poverty."[25] According to Smith, "estimates of the average per capita income hover around $250, though the majority of the population (most of them peasants cultivating 'non-arable' land) are said to earn less than $100 a year, and live well below the World Bank's absolute poverty line" (2001, 26). Contrasting Haitian poverty with EuroAmerican wealth through interviews with well-known economic scholars of globalization (such as Immanuel Wallerstein) and through breath-taking cinematographic views of Port-au-Piment, Haitian diasporic director Raoul Peck's film *Profit and Nothing But! Impolite Thoughts on the Class Struggle* also powerfully addresses the stark disparities of equality, opportunity, and wealth created and sustained by global economic structures, which maintain affluent "first world" zones while destabilizing and impoverishing the masses or so-called "third world" citizens. Similarly, Haitian diasporic writer Dany Laferrière's texts offer searing and satirical critiques of how military capitalism is entangled in the "development" practices of international aid in *Pays sans chapeau* (1996). Predictably, *la plan lanmò* (an apt moniker for SAPs in most "developing" countries) prescribed the same generic Bretton Woods-designed plan that the World Bank and IMF routinely impose, making these countries free for the multinational movement of global capital, if not truly free. At political protests following the signing of *plan lanmò*, activist thespians took to the streets during Carnival costumed as Djabs, "three-horned demons," openly and satirically referred to by the name "IMF" (Bell 2001, 102).

As if satirizing *la plan lanmò* as appropriate measures for *un pays sans chapeau*, or a "country without hats" – literally, according to Vodou, one in which everyone is already dead – Laferrière runs into a shoeshine man on the streets of the capital who tells the writer that all Haitians are *zonbi*-s, the living dead or undead:

> Si on était vraiment des êtres humains, continue-t-il, vous croyez qu'on survivrait à cette famine, à tous ces tas d'immondices qu'on trouve à tous les coins de rue . . . Et puis, vous ne voyez pas que toutes les autres nations sont dans le pays? (Il fait référence aux soldats des Nations Unis qui occupent les rues de Port-au-Prince.) Que croyez-vous qu'ils sont en train de faire? Ils font des études, mon ami. Ils viennent ici pour étudier combien de temps l'être humain peut rester sans manger ni boire. Mais ils ne sauvent pas qu'on est déjà morts. (54)

> "If we were really human beings," he went on, "do you think we could survive this famine, and those heaps of garbage and trash you see at every corner? Do you see those other people in our country? He pointed out the United Nations soldiers who where occupying the streets of Port-au-Prince. "What do you think they're doing here? They're carrying out studies, my friend. They're here to find out how long a human being can last without eating or drinking. What they don't know is that we're already dead. (1996, 47–48)

A *death plan* for the *dead*: Laferrière's *pays natal, un pays sans chapeau*. Written in 1996, two years after the EERP was signed, Laferrière's alterbiographical novel suggests that little has changed, especially for the better. Later in the novel, Laferrière's *mère* – murmuring aloud to her son during a sleepless night like so many others wracked by fear, worry, and insomnia – laments,

> On a l'impression d'être déjà mort, ici. Tout le monde, je veux dire les justes et les méchants. Tu vois, on trouve des charniers un peu partout. Les tueurs ne sont pas plus vivants ques les tués. Nous sommes tous déjà morts" (93–94)

It's as if we're all dead here, already. Everybody, the virtuous and the wicked alike. The whole country's a killing ground. The killers aren't any more alive than their victims. We've all died, all of us. (83)

Case Study 3: Filipina Maids in Hong Kong

Like Indian diasporic and Haitian diasporic subjects, Filipina domestic workers in Hong Kong have staged diasporic resistance both to host and home, toward Hong Kong labor laws negatively impacting their work conditions and toward Philippine overseas labor policies negatively impacting their livelihood in material, monetary ways. In 1982, President Ferdinand Marcos issued Executive Order 857 requiring that Filipina migrant domestic workers remit 50 percent of their salaries through Philippine banks or financial institutions directly to the Philippine government; and the executive order also required some Filipino overseas workers to remit as much as 70 percent of their salaries directly to the government (Constable 1997, 164). To enforce E.O. 857, the Overseas Employment Development Board (OEDB) maintained a strict non-renewal policy for passports and overseas employment contracts for those Filipino migrant workers who failed to comply (for willful or negligent non-compliance). Two years after President Marcos issued E.O. 857, a group of ten Filipina migrant maids working in Hong Kong – a small, but unified collective! – formed the United Filipinos against Forced Remittances, writing, signing, and sending to the president a statement of protest. Their opposition, they explained, was not to the principle of diasporic development funds or to the ideas of sending remittances, but rather to the compulsory nature of the order and the punitive measures targeted against those who did not comply: "To force us to remit," they wrote, "is a curtailment of our freedoms and an intrusion into our private affairs" (McLean 1984; CIIR 1987, 8; quoted in Constable 1997, 165). In response, in 1984, the Philippine government "announced a 50 percent reduction of the amount," but did not reverse the order or make remittances non-compulsory (Constable 1997, 165). But, as a direct response to the Filipina maids' resistance to E.O. 857, which first spread into broad Filipino resistance throughout Hong Kong, and then into Filipino diasporic worker communities across the globe, the Philippine government lifted the executive order, ending forced remittances on May 1, 1985. According to anthropologist Nicole Constable, the "change in policy" was the result of Filipino diasporic activism among overseas workers in many countries of adoption working in concert with "growing opposition to the Marcos government in the Philippines and criticism of the executive order by the International Labor Organization" (1997, 165). Changing its name to the United Filipinos in Hong Kong (UNIFIL), the group expanded into a coalition of smaller activist groups in Hong Kong working and organizing for workers' rights. In 1987, UNIFIL and other diasporic workers' organizations together "successfully opposed a customs tax imposed by the Aquino government" (Constable 1997, 165). Following a ban on new overseas contracts for Filipino domestic workers under the age of 35 – ostensibly "to protect" these women "from abuse" – UNIFIL helped to form

United Filipinos against the Ban, an umbrella group representing "an alliance of twenty-two domestic worker groups" (Constable 1997, 165; Fan 1988); and after the organization organized extensive "letter-writing campaigns . . . the ban was lifted."

Filipina domestic workers in Hong Kong were also vocal and organized in advocating workers' rights in Hong Kong during the 1980s and 1990s. In 1987, the Governor in Council implemented the New Conditions of Stay – more commonly referred to as the "two-week rule" – stipulating that

> (a) once a contract has been terminated, the foreign domestic helper must either leave within two (2) weeks or before the date of expiration of her visa if it falls shorter than two weeks; (b) No change of employment will normally be allowed during the period of contract (two years); (c) Those who break their contracts will not be allowed to submit to a new and valid contract before they leave Hong Kong; and (d) Any foreign domestic helper who breaches a condition of stay (for example working for employers not mentioned in the contract) will be returned to her country of origin and will not be allowed to take up employment again in Hong Kong. (MFMW 1991, 25–26; quoted in Constable 1997, 150)

Implemented by the Governor of Council, designed to prevent "job hopping" (or quick succession of new employers to attain better work environment and salary), and enforced by the Hong Kong Immigration Department, the policy did little to protect domestic laborers from abusive working conditions or abusive employers. For example, the policy included "no provision to guarantee that the employer supply the worker with return airfare, remaining wages, or other monetary claims within the two-week period" (Constable 1997, 150). Moreover, "the two-week rule encourage[d] workers to endure poor working conditions, physical and emotional abuse, maltreatment and illegal work" in order to avoid deportation by the Labor Department and the Immigration Department in Hong Kong (1997, 150). In 1993, six years after the New Conditions of Stay were introduced and implemented, Filipina domestic migrants protested the two-week rule, as well as insufficient increases in the minimum salary, and also fought for limiting work hours (Constable 1997, 165). A protest march attended by almost 500 Filipina domestics, joined by Thai and South Asian domestic workers, was held at Chater Garden in the Central District of Hong Kong in August 1993. And while the turn out was impressive and managed to capture media attention, the outcomes were not so positive: the protest, in fact, did not result in any changes to labor law, immigration policy, work hours, or salary increases. Hong Kong's Central District, though, is not only the site of organized protests and activism, but also the high-traffic, weekly site of diasporic forms of "everyday" resistance to employer efforts to micromanage domestic workers' lives.

Like remittance offices and money wiring businesses in Rome, where Filipinas gather to send money home and to share information with one another (as discussed in chapter two, "Gender and Diasporas"), Statue Square in Hong Kong is a similar diasporic meeting place for Filipina domestics on Sunday afternoons, the typical day off for these women: diasporic domestics gather at the square to chat, complain about employers, share information, tell jokes, buy food in the open air market, protest work conditions, organize for better pay and labor standards, or just relax among other Filipinas in the city (Constable 1997, 111–124). Sunday afternoon gatherings at Statue Square or at Chater Garden – a weekly display of Tagalog chatter, or Pilipina banter, buying and selling at upstart Philippine food markets, and the peddling of imported goods from the Philippines – even when not worker-organized or actively political, Constable argues, also becomes a multilayered and outdoor public place of everyday diasporic resistance to employer controls over time, labor, space, body, and tasks. The Central District has been so transformed by the visible, audible, and multitudinous presence of Filipinas on the square on Sunday afternoon that Gary McDonough and Cindy Wong insist in *Global Hong Kong* that their presence is an indelible mark of the district as a global "downtown" and of Hong Kong as a "global city":

> A . . . striking transformation of this central space occurs on Sundays, when public spaces, the overhead passages connecting buildings, and even the open ground floor of the modern Hongkong and Shanghai Bank building teem with thousands of expatriate maids, mainly from the Philippines, who gather with their friends on their day off, feeling unwelcome in malls or other places that expect consumption. These women, nearly two hundred thousand in the new millennium, have become mainstays of dual career families but escape their demands at home one day a week to come together, sit on the ground, share food, gossip, play music, and domesticate public spaces. (2005, 14)

While Hong Kongers are plaintive about the Sunday afternoon transformation of the Central District into what they pejoratively regard as "a third-rate amusement park" (Constable 1997, 4), Filipinas relish the time off to spend privately, even in public, among friends from home, speaking in Tagalog or Pilipina, eating *adobo* or other Philippine dishes, and participating in everyday forms of resistance while simply living among themselves for an afternoon; not surprisingly, then, Filipinas regard Hong Kongers' "complaints as attempts to hide Hong Kong's dependence on their labor" (McDonough and Wong 2005, 15; Escoda 1994) or to keep them indoors and out of sight.

Rhacel Salazar Parreñas also details "everyday" forms of diasporic resistance among Filipina maids working in Rome and Los Angeles in her cultural ethnographic study *Servants of Globalization* (2001). For example, rather than merely adopting a subservient attitude, or an extreme display of deference revealing "an internalized sense of inferiority," as Constable argues, Filipina migrant maids more self-consciously negotiate emotional responses in their domestic work environments: "they are," Parreñas writes, "able to hold feelings of attachment and detachment from their employers simultaneously and in the process attempt to subvert the script within the routine of domestic work" (2001, 189). Parreñas, borrowing the theoretical distinction between tactics and strategies as articulated by Michel de Certeau, delineates that while "tactics occur in the place of oppression and involve the manipulation of time through key moments of intervention, . . . strategies require the source of a place, a space in which to strategize and retreat" (2001, 189). Drawing thus on Scott's distinction between public and hidden scripts and de Certeau's distinction between tactics and strategies, both of which underscore "the fluid operation of power" across lines of inequity rather than a centralized and unified flow of power from the top down, Parreñas asserts that "through tactics, domestic workers take advantage of opportune moments within the daily rituals of domestic work by creatively interjecting subversive acts in everyday routines so as to resist the tedium and disciplinary measures that normalize inequalities between employers and employees" (2001, 195, 189). Realizing that employers manipulate (or play upon) their emotions to "elicit additional labor," or make them "more willing to comply with substandard wages," Filipina migrant maids often tactically level the emotional and worker playing field through emotional displays or affective outbursts, "crying, showing anger, projecting a somber mood, becoming very quiet ... or by simply talking back"; however, for emotional outbursts – precisely because they represent a "tactical" deviation from the "public" script of subservient domestic helper that is expected and required of them – to be effective, they must also be rare (Parreñas 2001, 190). As Parreñas illustrates through her case study subjects, Filipina migrant maids in Rome and in Los Angeles find that such tactics are particularly effective when the emotional outbursts create "emotional discomfort in employers, such as unease and guilt" (2001, 191).

Other tactics of daily resistance to domestic labor (with its heavy work loads, long hours, low pay, and frequently demeaning treatment) include deliberately working at a slow pace, "banging pots and pans," or more direct forms of resistance like "talking back" or even "quitting" (2001, 192, 193), though these more confrontational behaviors proved less effective and were more like to anger employers than to emotionally manipulate them to the maid's work advantage. By resisting the public script that proscribes subservience, deference, and obsequiousness, these Filipina migrant maids are drawing on hidden scripts that form a collective, not individual act of resistance, "part of a shared struggle among domestic workers" (2001, 194). As Parreñas explains, "Domestic workers find the strength to incorporate tactics in the daily activities of domestic work from the 'hidden transcript' that they maintain with other domestic workers, those with whom they share experiences in migration and at work" (2001, 194). This "hidden script" is forged through domestic worker chatter during off-hours spent together in "churches, community centers, and buses," as well as remittance agencies and money wiring businesses, where these women "speak of difficulties encountered in the workplace and complain about the unreasonable demands and abusive behavior of employers," or in short, "reveal their true feelings ... [and] built-up frustrations ... accumulated in the workplace" (2001, 194). Patricia Baclayon, a Filipina migrant working in Los Angeles, openly expressed profound disappointment, in an interview with Parreñas, not only with her job as a live-in domestic in the US, but also with her host country, which she openly referred to as the "United Mistakes of America" (2001, 196). For Parreñas, these daily tactics of resistance, and the hidden transcript documenting that resistance, are not individual forms of diasporic everyday resistance, but rather are "collective" and become an important tool or "weapon of the weak" for contesting the disparities of wealth, power, and cultural capital between employee and employer, as well as between home and host countries (2001, 195).

Questions for Reflection and Discussion

- What are the parameters that support cultural production within global capitalist economies?
- What are the parameters that limit cultural production within global capitalist economies? And what are the limitations of literary or cultural resistance in the global capital marketplace?
- Is speech free? Was it ever?
- How, if at all, has "freedom of speech" been altered (even restricted) by political and economic discourses about "free trade"?
- What are the interrelations of rhetorical constructions of democracy and capital?
- How has political national sovereignty been eroded by global capitalist regulatory institutions?
- What is the relation of sovereignty to subjectivity? Of violence to representation?
- *Arts and Literatures*: How are we to grapple with the failures of metaphor in the face of torture?

Additional Research

Analyzing film and visual cultures

Visually breathtaking and rhetorically moving, Haitian American director Raoul Peck's *Le Profit et rien d'autre* (*Profit and Nothing But! Impolite Thoughts on the Class Struggle*) is a film both cerebral and aesthetic, intellectually arduous and yet starkly beautiful, a cinematic montage of his poor Haitian homeland adrift in a globe capitalistically striated. Known for bold political documentaries, such as the award-winning *Lumumba* about Patrice Emery Lumumba, the assassinated socialist leader of the Democratic Republic of Congo, Peck rarely shies from controversy or polemic; rather, he uses the screen to direct our gaze toward *les invisibles*, the world's colonized, exploited, enslaved, and oppressed. After viewing the documentary film *Profit and Nothing But!*, analyze Peck's film and examine the director's diasporic Marxist resistance to the impact of international financial institutions (IFIs) both on his homeland, Haiti, and on the Haitian diaspora.

Questions to consider about Profit and Nothing But!

- How does Peck use film as political protest? What are the implications of film as diasporic "art of resistance"?

- What is the role of the narrator in the film?
- How does the filmic narrative voice complement, supplement, or even complicate the visual iconography of the film?
- Where is the film set? What are the different locations filmed by Peck? How are the locations contrasted and why?

Thinking through debating

Conduct research on national, diasporic, and transnational political resistance (among individuals from Latin American and South American countries) to the Free Trade Agreement of the Americas (FTAA). In an informal debate, articulate the "affirmative" arguments for passing FTAA and the "negative" arguments against passing the free trade agreement.

Thinking through writing

Using research compiled for the above exercise, write a research paper that overviews the debate around free trade in the Americas and how grassroots activists have shaped this debate.

Postface
Diasporic Shifts Post-9/11

In this closing "Postface," we shall navigate the post-9/11 geopolitical landscape, seeking to understand how the terrorist attacks of September 2001 negatively impacted international migration and diasporic communities across the globe, focusing specifically on the partial closing of national borders, severe restrictions legislatively imposed on transborder movement across international boundaries, the emergence (or reconsolidation, as is the case in US military and central intelligence prisons) of detention, interrogation, trial by military tribunals, and/or deportation as regulatory mechanisms, and the waging of the US-led, global "War on Terror" as itself a deployed, transnational form of global violence. In the post-9/11 period, territorial borders of domestic "homelands" – particularly those in what Paul Gilroy and Stuart Hall refer to as the "overdeveloped" countries of North America and Europe – have entered a decisively "nervous" and restrictive period that coincided with legal maneuvering to allow for greater deportation of immigrants. These shifts inform this concluding postface. Finally, we shall also examine how the recently passed Central American Free Trade Agreement (CAFTA), the impending Free Trade Agreement of the Americas (FTAA), and the summer 2005 bombings in London may further impact diasporic communities, global migration patterns, and worldwide debates about citizenship, nationality, and political belonging.

September 11, 2001 marked a significant turning point in global geopolitical restructuring: loosely affiliated, transnationally operating, and globally scattered terrorist organizations, including Al Qaeda, masterminded by Osama bin Laden (who formed a loose-jihadi network in 1979 in Afghanistan shortly after the Soviet invasion and officially founded the political organization in 1988, declaring *jihad* against the "West" in 1990 after the Iraqi invasion of Kuwait, the deployment of US troops to Saudi Arabia, and the subsequent onset of the Gulf War in 1991), and other organizations like the Algerian-based Armed Islamic Group (GIA)[1] and the South East Asian network Jemaah Islamiah (JI),[2] have declared worldwide *jihad* against the United States and other allied countries, not only the overdeveloped states of Europe, North America, and the Pacific, like Australia and New Zealand, but also the oil-rich OPEC states of the Gulf region of the Middle East like Saudi Arabia and the United Arab Emirates, and perhaps especially the state of Israel, which is typically perceived or regarded by Al Qaeda as a militarized state responsible for first displacing and then oppressing Palestinian minorities, as a state predominantly ruled by an Ashkenazi European-descended population that perpetuates the European colonialist presence in or occupation of the Middle East.[3] A transnational "coalition of the willing" – led by the United States, fueled by a neoconservative political and foreign policy agenda, and globally deployed – has led a counterterrorist war against the fundamentalist jihadists.

While the terrorist acts need to be understood within a historical context that not only grounds notions of *jihad* within colonial resistance to European colonial occupation and geographical division (or carving up) of the region, but also links Cold War politics, the global trade in oil, the emergence of the Middle East as a third economic power (between Western capitalism and USSR communism) during the 1960s and 1970s, the events of September 11 have also undeniably come to define a new era of geopolitical realignment that forges emergent alliances, even as it too often relies on the rhetoric of a "clash of civilizations" promulgated by academic pundits-cum-presidential cabinet advisers like Samuel Huntington and his neoconservative ilk.[4] The language of the global terror war too often, however, serves only to obscure historical trajectories and to hyperbolize geopolitical divides, leading us to incredulously ask: "Clash of civilizations"? Battle between fundamentalists? A cosmic war between "good" and the so-called "Axis of Evil"? Before assuming such broad and reductive generalizations, rhetorically overblown by both warring factions, let's examine the twenty-first century conflict in more detail, placing the current global crisis within a historical material framework that attends to its twentieth-century precursors.

Fallout from 9/11 has had global ramifications: both through the continuation of "terror" and the War on Terror, although retaliatory violence can at times seem indiscernible and the rhetorical overdetermination of the terms often serves only to obfuscate the geopolitical and material realities fueling this "war": for example, historian Adam Roberts deconstructs the current deployments of the terms "terrorist" and "terrorism" by placing their contemporary uses within a longer history of terrorism, the etymological history of the word's meanings, and its legal codifications by nation-states and the United Nations ("The Changing Faces of Terrorism," BBC News). In another vein, Dr. S. Sayyid challenges the idea that the War on Terror can be neatly divided along axiomatic lines of good and evil, warriors against terrorism and terrorists, forcefully writing:

> Before the United States declared Saddam Hussein to be the most dangerous man alive (forgetting in passing that the use of weapons of mass destruction is not the prerogative of homicidal dictators alone – after all the first person to gas the Kurds was Winston Churchill and the only person to nuke two cities was Harry S. Truman, both democratically elected), it supported him in his invasion of Iran, ignored his use of chemical weapons against the Iranians and later his own people, and was

not too bothered about his human rights record until he invaded Kuwait. (Sayyid, "Crusades and Jihads in Postcolonial Times," BBC News)

"Terrorism" and the "War on Terror" are thus inexorably defined differently and through alternate terms depending on one's location (ideological as much as geopolitical, and perhaps more) – for others, these terms (terrorism and war on terror) may be defined alternately as revolutionary resistance fighters and global economic imperialists. While rhetorically, politically, and morally complicated, we cannot, however, simply deny the ways in which global power and local disempowerment, however transnationalized, as well as global capitalist economic wealth or possession, and inversely, dispossession, are internationally and legally defined terrains with real material impacts. In other words, the global terms of the debate – terrorism and War on Terror – cannot simply be willed away or intellectually deconstructed out of existence. We must, necessarily then, use these terms with caution and with the knowledge that they are inherently imprecise and subjectively overdetermined. So, of necessity, let's proceed with inexact, yet legally prescribed language, since it is a juridical reality if also a rhetorical conundrum too often delimiting not only the debate, but also the current geopolitical "clash."

Terrorist plans of attack (and actual attacks) carried out by Al Qaeda and other "terrorist" organizations against the United States and its allies have continued since 2001; and multinational armed conflicts have been waged in Afghanistan and Iraq. First, some historical gloss of the actual events may be necessary, so for the sake of clarity and memory, let's review several intertwined histories, those of 9/11 and the post-9/11 period of geopolitical realignment: to begin, we will recall the terrorist attacks of September 11, ongoing acts of violent terrorist attacks globally (planned, foiled, and unfortunately, also executed) since 2001, the onset of the US-led War on Terror and all major anti-terrorist initiatives that are part of the Global War on Terror, including the military wars of occupation currently being waged in Afghanistan and Iraq; and then we will sketch out and overview a brief historical timeline of anti-terrorism legislation, focusing primarily on the United States and the United Kingdom.

"Terror" and the "War on Terror": 9/11 and Post-9/11 Geopolitical Realignments

On the morning of September 11, 2001, 19 armed terrorists (from historically US-allied countries during the Gulf War in 1991 and the wealthier oil-rich states from the Gulf region of the Middle East: Saudi Arabia, Egypt, the United Arab Emirates, and Yemen), hijacked four airplanes all departing from airports along the metropolitan eastern seaboard of the United States (Boston's Logan International, Dulles in Washington, DC, and Newark International) and successfully initiated the largest attack ever led against the United States of America on its own soil. Egyptian-born and German-educated Mohamed Atta, regarded as the ringleader of the 9/11 attacks, led the hijackers who, according to Al Qaeda plans, abducted airplanes and flew them into the Twin Towers of the World Trade Center in Manhattan, New York and the Pentagon in the US national capital of Washington, DC. Waleed al Shehri, Wail al Shehri, Mohamed Atta, Abdul Aziz al Omari, and Satam al Suqami hijacked American Airlines Flight 11, scheduled to fly from Boston to Los Angeles, departing at 7:59 a.m. and crashing into the north tower of the World Trade Center between 8:46 a.m. and 8:47 a.m. EST. Fayez Banihammad, Mohand al Shehri, Marwan al Shehhi, Hamza al Ghamdi, and Ahmed al Ghamdi hijacked United Airlines Flight 175, scheduled to fly from Boston to Los Angeles, departing at 8:14 a.m. and crashing into the south tower of the World Trade Center at 9:03 a.m. EST. Hani Hanjour, Nawaf Hamzi, Salem al Hamzi, Majed Moqed, and Khalid al Mihdhar hijacked American Airlines Flight 77, scheduled to fly from Washington to Los Angeles, departing from Dulles Airport at 8:20 a.m. and crashing into the Pentagon at 9:37 a.m. EST. And Ziad Jarraj, Ahmed al Nami, Saeed al Ghamdi, and Ahmad al Haznawi hijacked United Airlines Flight 93, scheduled to fly from Newark to San Francisco, departing at 8:42 a.m. and crashing in a field over central Pennsylvania at 10:02 a.m. EST having failed to hit its intended target, the White House in Washington, DC ("The Four Hijacks," BBC News). Over 3,000 US citizens, permanent residents, immigrants, and foreign visitors died that day in New York, Pennsylvania, and Washington, DC. The violence reached beyond those whose lives were directly impacted through death and injury, however, with the entire country and all of its people – fervent "patriots" and patriotic dissenters alike – entering a "nervous" and volatile period of "terror," war, and "war on terror."

Following the September 2001 terrorist attacks against the United States, the US initiated its War on Terror, leading a broad coalition, though not without national and international dissenters, in waging warfare against the Taliban regime (believed to be "harboring" leaders from Al Qaeda and other terrorist organizations) in October 2001. Two months later, in December 2001, two significant events transpired: the reputed twentieth hijacker Zacarias Moussaoui, a Moroccan French citizen, was arrested and charged with "conspiring" against the United States, intended terrorism against the US, and political alliance with Al Qaeda on December 12 (subsequently being found guilty of conspiracy and sentenced to life imprisonment on May 6, 2006); and Richard Reid, a Jamaican Briton swearing allegiance to Osama bin Laden, and better known as the "shoe bomber," was arrested after rigging his shoes with explosive devices and boarding a flight from Paris to Miami on December 23. In January 2002, President George W. Bush delivered his presidential State of the Union address before the country, declaring Iraq, Iran, and North Korea the "Axis of Evil," a declaration that paved the way to war in Iraq and that fueled anti-American sentiments and public opinion in Iran and North Korea. Not surprisingly, the US has entered a period of tense conflict with both Iran and North Korea since declaring the two countries part of a three-pronged Axis of Evil with Iraq. Three months later, on April 11, 2002, a suicide bomber carried out a mission in Djerba, an island off the coast of Tunisia in North Africa, bombing a synagogue and killing 19 people. In fall 2002, on October 12, a suicide bomber set off an explosion in a Bali nightclub in Kuta; according to "Indonesian authorities . . . the attacks were carried out by the South East Asian militant network Jemaah Islamiah which is said to have links to al-Qaeda" ("Timeline: Al-Qaeda," BBC News). On November 28, 2002, "a simultaneous suicide car bomb and the firing of air-to-air missiles" set off an explosive firestorm in an Israeli-owned resort, the Paradise Hotel, in the Indian Ocean coastal city of Mombasa, Kenya, with two groups claiming responsibility for the terrorist attack: Al Qaeda operatives ("Timeline: Al-Qaeda," BBC News) and the relatively unknown organization the Army of Palestine, who proclaimed on Hezbollah TV in Lebanon that the group planned the attack to coincide with the "55th anniversary of the United Nations resolution which on 29 November 1947 called for the division of Palestine, as it was then called, into Jewish and Arab states," a partition rejected by Palestinians and other Arabs (Reynolds, "Al-Qaeda Suspected in Kenya Attacks," BBC News).

Fifteen months after Bush's notorious 2002 State of the Union address, the United States and its cobbled "coalition of the willing" (that included Spain, Italy, and Britain, but notably did not include traditional US European allies like France, as well as Germany) initiated air strikes over Baghdad that marked the beginning of the war in Iraq, though many countries and even dissident citizens in the US opposed to waging the war challenged the US claim, unsubstantiated and later disproved though widely circulated, that the dictatorship of Sadam Hussein was stockpiling "weapons of mass destruction" (WMDs) and further determined that the "preemptive strikes" by the US on March 20, 2003 was an aggressive act of unilateralism. (The Anti-War movement, though vibrant and widespread throughout the US and globally, leading up to the US war against Iraq – initiated in March 2003 in an air missile bombing campaign – was largely ignored by the US media and the administration.) On May 12, 2003, 11 days after President George W. Bush, speaking from the deck of the USS *Abraham Lincoln*, peremptorily declared victory in Iraq on May 1, a series of suicide bomb attacks were carried out in Riyadh, Saudi Arabia ("Timeline: Al-Qaeda," BBC News). Four days later, suicide bombers set off explosions in Casablanca, Morocco, targeting a "Spanish restaurant, a fivestar hotel, a Jewish community centre and the Belgian consulate" ("Timeline: Al-Qaeda," BBC News). In late 2003, two terrorist attacks were waged in Turkey: on December 15, suicide bombers carried out attacks against two synagogues in the Turkish capital Istanbul; and five days later, on December 20, two bombs were detonated at the British consulate and the HSBC bank offices, also in Istanbul ("Timeline: Al-Qaeda," BBC News).

In March 2004, almost exactly one year after the war in Iraq began, terrorist groups bombed the railroads in Madrid, Spain, which was, according to the BBC, likely the actions of the Islamic Combatant Group, a Moroccan organization with affiliations and support for Al Qaeda (though many initially believed it to be the work of ethnic Basque militant separatists), and which ultimately led to the withdrawal of Spanish troops from Iraq. On July 7, 2005, three Pakistani Britons and one Jamaican Briton, all UK citizens born and raised in Britain, planned, organized, and executed bomb attacks against London's metropolitan public transportation system, including major attacks on the "tube" (metropolitan subway system) and city bus lines near the University of London and Tavistock Square. Nearly five years after the 9/11 attacks, planned terrorist attacks were prevented in Canada, Germany, and the US during summer 2006. Seventeen suspected terrorists (who had planned to bomb sites in Toronto and even to behead the prime minister) were arrested in Ontario on June 3, 2006. In July 2006, terrorist plans to bomb transportation systems in both Germany and the US were also obstructed. Attacks were planned on German railways and on tunnels across the Hudson River from New Jersey into Manhattan, New York.

US and UK Anti-Terrorism Legislation and the Impact on Diasporic Communities

International migratory flows have been profoundly impacted by the terrorist attacks against the Pentagon, the Twin Towers of the World Trade Center, and the attempted attack on the White House in Washington, DC, as well as continued terrorist attacks since 9/11 in Bali, Turkey, Tunisia, Madrid, London, and elsewhere. Diasporic shifts post-9/11 have witnessed the proliferation of extraterritorial sites of detention and interrogation, increased detention for asylees and illegal border crossers, expanded ground for legal deportation of immigrants, and the tightening of international boundaries and the restriction of transborder migrations in the name of "homeland security." Supported and sanctioned by the USA Patriot Act (first legislatively passed and executively signed into law on October 2001 and then renewed in March 2006), as discussed below, fueled by the nefariously named if nebulously aimed War on Terror, and further promulgated by the transnational "coalition of the willing" in wars being waged in Afghanistan and Iraq, these post-9/11 shifts have had global ramifications, not limited to the US, North America, or even the so-called Global North or former first-world countries.

Introduced to the US House of Representatives as H.R. 3162 by Representative F. James Sensenbrenner, Jr. from Wisconsin on October 23, 2001, passed by the House on October 24 and the Senate on October 25, and signed into law by President George W. Bush just three days after the bill was introduced on October 26, and only weeks after the September 11 terrorist attacks in the US, and without substantive congressional debate or even extensive legal review, the USA Patriot Act[5] imposes draconian measures for surveying, tracking, and regulating citizens, as well as their financial transactions, internet searches, international telephone calls, purchases, and even library records, and authorizing arrest, search, interrogation, and detention of immigrants. A separate security bill passed by US Congress administratively created the Department of Homeland Security (DHS) as a cabinet under the Executive Branch of the US government with former Pennsylvania governor Tom Ridge serving as its first secretary. Both the former Immigration and Naturalization Service (INS), now called the US Citizenship and Immigration Services (USCIS), and the Federal Emergency Management Association (FEMA), were brought under the control of the new DHS, which has been a controversial move from the beginning, with concerns over federal distribution of emergency funds and services following natural disasters increasing after the crushing blow (of high-speed wind, torrential rain, and massive levee flooding) to New Orleans by Hurricane Katrina in September 2005. On a cautionary note, we might also be concerned that the US government so readily conflates citizens, immigrants, disaster, emergency, and terrorism on administrative and bureaucratic levels.

Anti-terrorism laws were being legislated and enforced in most Western states after the 1993 bombing by Ramzi Yousef of the World Trade Center in New York on February 26 of that year and the 1996 bombing of the US military base near Dhahran, Saudi Arabia on June 25, with the US Congress subsequently passing anti-terror legislation in 1996 (Antiterrorism and Effective Death Penalty Act) and the UK following suit after 1997 under Tony Blair's leadership. Following the 1998 bombing of both the US embassy in Kenya and the US embassy in Tanzania, and following the October 12, 2000 attack on the *USS Cole*, a warship docked at Aden Port in Yemen, the British parliament passed the Terrorism Act 2000 in the year preceding the terrorist attacks of September 2001. Terrorism Act 2000 included measures to broaden the legal definitions of terrorism, ban organizations identified as terrorist groups ("from Irish paramilitaries to militant Islamist organizations"), expand the legal ground for prosecuting individuals for both committing terrorist acts and for inciting them, and extend police powers to hold and question those suspected of terrorist affiliations ("Q&A: Terror Laws Explained," BBC News). More restrictive legislation – authorizing widespread use of surveillance technologies, including face recognition devices, wiretapping, and proposals to issue national identification cards, to maintain national citizen and immigrant registry databases, and to detain suspected terrorists without warrant, the most controversial proposal in the US and the UK, since it violates the long-protected, common law rule of *habeas corpus*,[6] the right to know the charge on which one is being held – has been passed since 2001. The British parliament has passed two additional major anti-terrorism laws since 2001, both largely judicially authored and administratively promulgated by Home Secretary David Blunkett (journalistically referred to as the "hard-line, scandal-plagued . . . architect of much of Britain's post-9/11 anti-terror policy"):[7] the Anti Terror Crime and Security Act 2001 (ATCSA) and the Prevention of Terrorism Act 2005 (PTA). ATCSA, passed immediately following the events of 9/11, was ostensibly "designed to prevent terrorist suspects from using the immigration system to prevent their detention and removal" ("Q&A: Terror Laws Explained," BBC News). ATCSA also legislated other controversial and fiercely debated surveillance and detention measures, including:

- The use of phone taps as evidence in court.
- Intensive surveillance of terror suspects after release.
- The introduction of security-cleared prosecutors who would be able to view material from intelligence sources.
- New "civil restriction orders" – such as curfews or tagging – to limit the activities of people thought to be linked to terrorism, but not themselves considered serious suspects. ("Terror Detention Law Must Go," BBC News)

Specifically, Part IV of ATCSA authorized "the Home Secretary to detain international terrorists indefinitely and without trial" (Upton 2004; "Q&A: Terror Laws Explained," BBC News). In passing the law, the British derogated Article 5 of the European Convention on Human Rights, which allows countries to detain individuals "in time of war or other public emergency threatening the life of the nation," though no other European country has derogated Article 5 as part of the War on Terror during the post-9/11 period ("Terror Detention Law Must Go," BBC News; Upton 2004). Finally, ATSCA also allowed the British government to freeze the assets not only of known terrorist organizations, but also individual suspected terrorists ("Q&A: Terror Laws Explained," BBC News). Initially set to expire in 2006, but either legally extended or juridically overridden and replaced by provisions legislated in the Prevention of Terrorism Act 2005, Secretary Blunkett renewed the "powers set out" by ATCSA in autumn 2004.

In the United States, the USA Patriot Act – with temporary provisions also initially scheduled to "sunset," or expire, and despite voluble, vociferous opposition, spearheaded in the US Senate by Senator Russ Feingold of Wisconsin, and amid ongoing debates about infractions against civil liberties – was renewed in March 2006 and signed into law by President Bush as Public Law 107-56. Immigration laws, and particularly refugee laws, have also become increasingly restrictive in the wake of 9/11. This is true for the United States, as well as other historically immigrant-receiving countries like Canada, Britain, Australia, and New Zealand, and more closed countries like Austria, Germany, France, and other parts of Europe. As Edward Newman avers, writing in a study on "Refugees, International Security, and Human Vulnerability," published by the United Nations University Press in 2003, "the terrorist attacks" of September 2001 "have accelerated the move towards more restrictive asylum and refugee policies" (2003, 9). As he further explains, in the wake of the "terrorist attacks" and the onset of the War on Terror, "refugee movements and asylum seekers have been regarded by some with a heightened wariness as sources of instability and even potential sources of terrorism" (2003, 9–10). And in the US, the "most affected immigrant group in terms of admissions policies has been resettled refugees," and this despite the fact that the 19 terrorist hijackers who planned, orchestrated, and carried out the 9/11 attacks had entered the US on foreign student visas, not as refugees (2003, 10).

Secret Prisons, Detentions of Suspected Terrorists, and Debates about Civil Liberties

One of the most troubling consequences of the War on Terror has been the global increase of detention of suspected terrorists, those believed to "aid and abet" terrorists through funding or other forms of material support, and even those affiliated with terrorist groups. Extra-territorial detention sites, discussed at greater length below, have further served to imperil civil liberties and circumscribe the hegemonic dominance of the US militaristically, even as the sites have openly flouted international guidelines established by the Geneva Conventions. Acts of torture, sexual humiliation, debasement, and physical abuse – as documented in digital photographs that surfaced in April 2004 and circulated in the news media – at Abu Ghraib, a prison associated with Sadam Hussein's own excesses of state violence and torture of political prisoners, not only unsettled concerned citizens in the US and worldwide, but also raised speculation about similar forms of abuse operative in detention centers at the US Naval Base in Guantánamo and the Airforce Base at Baghram, and rumored torture sites in Syria and other countries. Despite the initial shock and awe incited by photographs detailing horrific abuses and prisoner torture at the Abu Ghraib prison in Iraq, and precisely because of the ongoing and even defiant nature of extra-legal interrogation and detention as well as gross, determined, deliberate circumvention of international law at the US Naval Base at Guantánamo Bay, Cuba, international concern and fierce public citizen outcry has consequently centered most on the detention center known as the Delta Camp housed in Guantánamo, or "Gitmo," as it is frequently dubbed by the media. Abu Ghraib and Guantánamo, however, are only two sites within a proliferating system of extra-territorial "secret prisons" maintained by the US military and the CIA and must be comparatively examined as part-and-parcel of the same US imperial system of transnational incarceration of terrorists, terrorist suspects, and so-called "enemy combatants."

Since September 11, 2001, the Guantánamo Bay Naval Base has also become notorious worldwide for the initial detention in 2002 of more than 700 men (comprised of more than 40 nationalities, including Afghans, Australians, Bosnia-Herzegovinians, Brits, Kuwaitis, Pakistanis, and US citizens) who were arrested during the US-led military offensive against the Taliban regime in Afghanistan and bordering regions of Pakistan in 2001 and 2002; and who have been defined not as prisoners of war, but rather as "enemy combatants."[8] Amnesty International led the charge against the US government and US military for unlawful detention of so-called "enemy combatants" without legal counsel, and it openly critiqued the US policy of circumventing the Geneva Conventions by denying these detainees "prisoner of war" status, which would grant them protection under international law.[9] Since the implementation of the War on Terrorism Detainee Mission, the naval base has constructed a new maximum security facility known as Camp Delta, which can hold up to 100 men in solitary confinement. Potentially detained for an indefinite length of time, the 660+ men held in isolation were interrogated through "stress and duress" tactics, and until recently denied legal representation; consequently, many men suffered mental health deterioration, attempted suicide in a vain effort to escape the deplorable conditions and to end their uncertain futures, and staged ongoing and widespread hunger strikes. The USA Patriot Act has indeed had deleterious effects not only on US foreign policy, but also on the nation's domestic policy, allowing for unprecedented levels and modes of surveillance, as well as broadly and loosely defined latitude with respect to the detention, interrogation, and prosecution of US citizens and immigrants within the US; in fact, the Patriot Act has significantly eroded the cumulative and hard-won efforts of a more than four-decades-long struggle for the establishment of civil rights in this country.[10]

We must see these post-9/11 political shifts, however, not as new forms of domestic and transnational imperialism, but rather in continuum with the decades-earlier forms of US military imperialism in the Americas. These geopolitical, geoeconomic, and transnational military shifts are thus a global extension of the Monroe Doctrine onto other hemispheric terrains. Detention seems to persist as a systemic *modus operandi* of US foreign policy.

A petition for writ of *habeas corpus* was filed on the behalf of detainees in March 2002, with *amicus curiae* ("friend of the court") briefs being filed by numerous individuals and organizations, including Amnesty International, the American Civil Liberties Union, diplomats, British parliamentarians, former prisoners of war, military officers, Fred Korematsu, who filed the appeal to challenge Executive Order #9066 that ordered the internment of Japanese Americans during World War II, and even Guantánamo officials. In an *amicus curiae* brief filed by 175 British parliamentarians, they write, "the exercise of executive power without possibility of judicial review jeopardises the keystone of our existence as nations – namely the rule of law" (quoted in Goldberg 2004). Two cases were ultimately filed with the courts: *Rasul v. Bush*, No. 03-334 and *Al Odah v. United States*, No. 03-343. The former was filed on the behalf of two British citizens and two Australian detainees by the Center for Constitutional Rights (CCR); the latter was filed on the behalf of 16 Kuwaiti detainees by the law firm of Shearing & Sterling. Both appeals were denied. As Michael Ratner explains, the appeals were denied "not because the federal district court decided that what the government is doing is right, but because the court decided it could not even hear the case and determine whether the detentions were legal" (2003, 132–133). Writing a statement for the Center for Constitutional Rights, subsequently published in longer form in *Lost Liberties: Ashcroft and the Assault on Personal Freedom*, Ratner details what he regards as the three "most worrisome" measures operative in the War on Terror: first, the "indefinite detentions at the United States Naval Base, Guantanamo Bay, Cuba"; second, "the lack of any judicial review of those detentions"; and third, the "plan to employ military commissions to try some of those detained" (2003, 133). Ratner complains that Guantánamo may as well be on "another planet," since the US naval base essentially functions like a "permanent United States penal colony floating in another world" (2003, 133).

In November 2003, the Supreme Court agreed to hear the legal cases brought against the US government by detainees, though the Bush administration contended that the US Judiciary had no jurisdiction over Guantánamo Bay, Cuba.[11] The Supreme Court case combined the two briefs filed at the lower court levels (*Rasul v. Bush*, No. 03-334 and *Al Odah v. United States*, No. 03-343), as had the Federal District Court of the District of Columbia. Relying on the precedence of *Johnson v. Eisentrager* (1950),[12] the Federal District Court ruled that the detainees were not under the jurisdiction of US constitutional law, since they were being detained outside of the US. In April 2004, the Supreme Court hearings of the case began. Legally, lawyers for the US government argued that Guantánamo is a liminal no-man's land; critics contended that it is a "lawless zone" – one not subject to judicial surveillance. As the hearings ensued on April 20, protesters outside marched with signs reading "No Concentration Camps!" Solicitor

General Theodore Olson, whose wife Barbara Olson (a journalist) died in the plane that struck the Pentagon on September 11, argued that the detention of the men at Guantánamo – uniformly and unequivocally defined by the government as Al-Qaeda conspirators and terrorists, a claim that remains disputed by claimants and critics – is necessary to prevent future terrorist attacks in the United States. John Gibbons, the attorney representing the detainees, openly challenged the literal interpretations of the language of the Guantánamo lease, arguing that "Cuban law has never had any application inside that base," and further asserting that "it's totally artificial to say that because of this provision in the lease, the executive branch can create a 'no-law' zone where it is not accountable to any judiciary anywhere" (quoted in Greenhouse, "Court Hears").[13] Since the precedence of *Johnson v. Eisentrager* (1950) establishes that US federal law has no jurisdiction over foreign territories, Gibbons' legal argument hinged (and the Supreme Court's ruling also later hinged) on the status of Guantánamo and whether or not it is "functionally, if not formally, part of the United States" (Greenhouse, "Court Hears"). The major issue, as Linda Greenhouse writes in the *New York Times* article, "Court Hears Arguments about Guantánamo Bay Detainees," published on April 20, 2004, "is how to characterize the United States role in the Cuban outpost, which it has occupied since 1903 under a perpetual lease that gives it 'complete jurisdiction and control' while preserving Cuba's 'ultimate sovereignty'."

While Justice Breyer articulated concern about "unchecked executive power" and allegations of "lawlessness," Supreme Court Chief Justice Antonin Scalia quite incredibly argued (as the Federal District Court had already ruled based on the Guantánamo lease and its preservation of Cuba's "ultimate sovereignty") that the US government could not subject Guantánamo Bay to federal law since doing so would violate the sovereignty of the Cuban government, a government that the US has not even recognized as "legitimate," much less sovereign, since the 1958 revolution. The "sovereignty" argument rang hollow to many observers:[14] the US government routinely undermines the sovereignty of small island states throughout the Caribbean, as it did most recently in Haiti in 2004 when it militarily intervened in the crisis and pressured Aristide to resign the presidency. This legal argument is also ironic given the deliberative, sustained, complex, and myriad ways that the US has wielded its own sovereignty (checked by none, not least the United Nations) to undermine small island sovereignty through "shiprider" agreements, economic trade agreements, and other military measures in the region.

In her presidential address to the American Studies Association, "Violent Belongings and the Question of Empire Today," Amy Kaplan describes Guantánamo as an "imperial location, close to home, in the ambiguous border between the domestic and the foreign" (2004, 12).[15] Kaplan argues that Guantánamo is a liminal, militarized zone where "contemporary empire building in the Middle East meets the history of imperialism in the Americas" (12). Even its "location," Kaplan reasons, is difficult to define: "Where is Guantánamo? In America, yes; in the United States, yes and no; in Cuba, well, sort of" (12). Kaplan also argues that Guantánamo's liminality makes it, regrettably, the site *par excellence* for imperialist abuses, since "the courts . . . [had thus far] ruled that the US ha[d] no sovereignty over Guantánamo, even though it exerts total control there" (13).[16] In a press release denouncing the treatment of detainees held at Guantánamo, Amnesty International called upon the Supreme Court to retrieve the detainees from "the legal black hole into which they have been thrown in the name of national security" and to end the executive "logic of lawlessness" that had thus far been supported in the lower courts ("Supreme Court"). According to ACLU Director Steven R. Shapiro, "The Guantánamo detainees have been placed in a legal limbo with no law to protect them and with no court to hear their pleas" (ACLU press release). In contrast with the US governmental labeling of them as "enemy combatants," many detainees conversely argue that they are "innocent noncombatants," alleging that they were inadvertently or even mercenarily turned into the US military by bounty hunters; some claim that they were humanitarian volunteers. These counter-claims are potentially significant (if provable), since the US policy of "indefinite detention" hinges on the classification of the individuals as "enemy combatants" during wartime (Greenhouse, "Court Hears"). The Supreme Court hearing of the briefs filed on behalf of Guantánamo detainees, along with two other related cases (*Hamdi v. Rumsfeld*, No. 03-6696 and *Rumsfeld v. Padilla*, No. 03-1027) filed respectively on behalf of Yaser Hamdi and José Padillo, US citizens who are also being detained as "enemy combatants," may be crucial to determining the balance not only "between civil liberties and national security, but [also] between the executive branch and the judiciary" (Greenhouse, "Court Hears"). Ultimately, the Supreme Court ruled that the detainees are entitled to legal counsel, though it also determined that each case must be individually tried and decided.

The transnational, "imperial tendrils" of US American Empire have also, regrettably, passed through military *routes* from Guantánamo Bay to US-occupied Iraq: the human rights violations by US soldiers, and in all probability, by military intelligence officers as well, have *roots* in detentions and "stress and duress" procedures affiliated with the Guantánamo Bay Naval Base. In a provocative and deeply disturbing article, "The Gray Zone," published in *The New Yorker* (May 24, 2004), Seymour M. Hersch details "special access programs" (SAPs) covertly run by the Department of Defense and former Secretary of Defense Donald Rumsfeld with the assistance of Stephen Cambone, Under-Secretary of Defense for Intelligence. As Hersch writes in the opening paragraph of the article:

> The roots of the Abu Ghraib prison scandal lie not in the criminal inclinations of a few Army reservists but in a decision, approved last year by Secretary of Defense Donald Rumsfeld, to expand a highly secret operation, which had been focused on the hunt for Al Qaeda, to the interrogation of prisoners in Iraq. Rumsfeld's decision embittered the American intelligence community, damaged the effectiveness of elite combat units, and hurt America's prospect in the war on terror.

According to "past and present" intelligence officials, the program authorized the use of "physical coercion" and "sexual humiliation" to compel responsiveness from the detained Iraqis and to obtain information about armed insurgencies. Could it be merely coincidental that a program that wrecks so much havoc and creates ruinous material effects shares an acronym – SAP – with the structural adjustment programs of the IMF and World Bank? Initially, the scope of SAP was limited to Al Qaeda and other "terrorist" detainees, such as those captured in Afghanistan in 2001 and 2002 and detained at Guantánamo, who were – according to the Bush administration and Rumsfeld's Defense Department – not protected under the Geneva Conventions. Later, however, the scope of the SAP, at Rumsfeld's authorization, was broadened to include Iraqi detainees at Abu Ghraib. "The commandos were to operate in Iraq as they had in Afghanistan," Hersch writes: "The male prisoners could be treated roughly, and exposed to sexual humiliation." Not only the rules, but also military intelligence officers of the SAP, were brought into Abu Ghraib.

The human rights violations at Abu Ghraib, the notorious prison where Baathist soldiers committed horrific atrocities under the rule of Sadam Hussein, occurred at the now US-run prison after the August 2003 visit to Abu Ghraib of Major General Geoffrey Miller, who then oversaw the detention camps at the Guantánamo Bay Naval Base, to "Gitmoize" the prison and the interrogation procedures. The stepped-up "Gitmo" procedures were to be implemented in order to obtain more "actionable intelligence." Ironically, Major General Miller was sent back to Abu Ghraib in April 2004 at the behest of the Defense Department in order "clean it up" following the human rights violations documented in sadistic, pornographic photographs that scandalized the world (*60 Minutes*; *Washington Post*). During Rumsfeld's and Cambone's testimony before Congress about the Abu Ghraib violations, Senator Hillary Rodham-Clinton, Democrat of New York, questioned the Defense Secretary and the Under-Secretary about Major General Miller's role in the prison scandal:

> If, indeed, General Miller was sent from Guantánamo to Iraq for the purpose of acquiring more actionable intelligence from detainees, then it is fair to conclude that the actions that are at point here in your report [on abuses at Abu Ghraib] are in some way connected to General Miller's arrival and his specific orders, however they were interpreted, by those MPs and the military intelligence that were involved. . . . Therefore, I for one don't believe I yet have adequate information from Mr. Cambone and the Defense Department as to exactly what General Miller's orders were . . . how he carried out those orders, and the connection between his arrival in the fall of '03 and the intensity of the abuses that occurred afterward.

The implications of Senator Clinton's line of questioning is clear: the human rights abuses at the notorious Abu Ghraib, we may logically infer, are connected to the efforts of Major General Miller to "Gitmoize" the prison. These inferences, Hersch also reasons, are consistent with Secretary Rumsfeld's "lack of alarm . . . and curiosity" upon finding out about the abuses at Abu Ghraib. In a May 26, 2004 article, the *Washington Post* alleges that Miller specifically urged the use of ferocious dogs against Iraqi detainees.

"The Gray Zone," Hersch's title, reflects the murky, yet racialized terms defining the "special access program" of the Defense Department: the title reveals not only the morally ambiguous scope of the program, but also allusively suggests the shockingly racialized terms of the "SAPs," which are referred to as "black" programs. The covert "black" programs, according to Hersch, contrast with the overt "white" world. The objective of the "black special-access program" is to get "the intelligence flowing into the white world." The SAP is highly secretive, very few people being "read" into – as Hersch's informant, a former intelligence official, told him – "our heart of darkness." To be "read" into the program means to be given clearance or access; and yet, such a literary metaphor is difficult to ignore, particularly since those "read" into the program were indeed actively reading academic scholarship on the "Arab" psyche to determine the best ways to obtain "actionable intelligence." Their determination: sexual humiliation and non-lethal (?) violence. Literary critics may find it deeply disturbing, though perhaps not surprising, that individuals "read" into the "black" SAP, as well as neoconservatives in the "white" world, relied upon and exploited academic "knowledge production" to further advance such infractions against humanity. According to Hersch,

> The notion that Arabs are particularly vulnerable to sexual humiliation became a talking point among pro-war Washington conservatives in the months before the March, 2003 invasion of Iraq. One book that was frequently cited was "The Arab Mind," a study of Arab culture and psychology, first published in 1973, by Raphael Patai, a cultural anthropologist who taught at among other universities, Columbia and Princeton, and who died in 1996. The book includes a twenty-five page chapter on Arabs and sex, depicting sex as a taboo vested with shame and repression.

According to another academic informant, Patai's book was "the bible of the neocons on Arab behavior" (quoted in Hersch). Dialogues among neoconservatives, the informant continued, revolved around two themes: force and sexual shame. The idea that all Arab psychological and sexual behavior could be neatly, reductively, and homogenously defined (across ethnicity, class, nationality, and gender) by one now-deceased US American academic in 1973 is too ludicrous to even comment upon, and the fact that neoconservatives not only used, but also believed, Patai's "knowledge" reveals immensely more about the "neoconservative" mind, whatever that might be, than it ever could about the so-called "Arab" mind. Further evidence attests that many neoconservatives – notably Army Lieutenant General William G. Boykin – regard the War on Terror in ultrareligious terms (*Arab v. Judeo-Christian*). Boykin scandalized many, and even embarrassed some neoconservatives, by equating "the Muslim world with Satan." Boykins' moral maligning of Muslims, in Christomythic terms, evokes centuries-long pejorative portrayals of Islam as well as most African and African diasporic religions; Haitian Vodou, for example, was historically regarded by Christian colonizers as "devil worship": the propagandistic tactics of vilifying enemies, and the deadly role that religion so often plays in that vilification, seem to have varied remarkably little across highly divergent geographical spaces and historical times.

The "imperial tendrils" of US American Empire indeed travel in circuitous *routes*. Terry Stewart, a partner in the private securities corporation Advanced

Correction Management, who worked at Abu Ghraib in 2003, was assigned during summer 2004 to report to Haiti in order to reform the country's prison system. Stewart has been a figure plagued by scandal and allegations of prisoner abuse, not just implicitly by association in Abu Ghraib, but also more directly in the continental United States. Former Director of the prison system for the State of Arizona, Stewart was involved in a 1997 Justice Department suit that charged that male prison guards assaulted, raped, and sodomized female inmates, although the suit was settled after the state agreed to implement court-ordered reforms.

While most US wars have remained remote to the shores of the continental US – in Iraq, Vietnam, Korea, Western Europe, North Africa, East Asia, or within the Caribbean and closer to home – the US Naval Base at Guantánamo Bay has been the militarized center for other rhetorically determined, yet still materially destructive "wars": notably, the War on Drugs and the War on Terror; but I would also add the War against Refugees. These administrative and militarized attacks – against drugs, "enemy combatants," and refugees – have distinctly transnational and overtly racialized dimensions. In the last chapter on transnational forms of diasporic political activism, we discussed the "wars" against Haitian refugees during the 1990s that preceded the detention of "enemy combatants," although both are partially and rhetorically entangled with the military base's involvement in the War on Drugs – ever popular with the legislative branches of the US government and the US American pubic alike, and thus a perennial favorite capable of rallying unwavering, nearly unquestioned political support and exorbitant amounts of budgetary funding. For example, Haitian refugees who were detained at the Guantánamo Bay Naval Base during the early to mid-1990s were routinely and rhetorically aligned with illegal drug traffickers: all boats containing Haitian passengers intercepted at sea were immediately suspected of twofold unforgivable crimes: illegal narcotics transshipment and illegal refugee transportation: in effect, a double indemnity. Similarly, as Afghan men were detained as "enemy combatants" at the Guantánamo Naval Base in 2002, the Bush administration stepped up its US media campaign in the ever-ready blitz of the War on Drugs, warning American consumers of "black market" illegal substances that dealing, buying, and using heroin was tantamount to "supporting terrorism" (since, it was reasoned, opium dollars could be, almost ineluctably would be, diverted to terrorist organizations), and the media campaign even went so far as to reductively conflate chemical substances and geopolitical territories, eliding their differences and implying that marijuana, like heroin, could be connected to potential terrorist acts against the United States. Threats of potential terrorist acts, of course, incited fear in the US American public and sustained steadfast, though not unchallenged support, for military interventions as part of the War on Terror.

"The US," journalists reporting for the Associated Press (AP) write, "has created a global network of overseas prisons, its islands of high security keeping 14,000 detainees beyond the reach of established law" ("US Detainees Abroad Face a Legal Vacuum"). Identified as a global "US prison network abroad," an article published by the AP reported that the number of detainees (labeled as "enemy combatants" and not "prisoners of war" as a way of legally circumventing the Geneva Conventions) exceeds 14,000 – more than 13,000 detainees in Iraq, 500 in Afghanistan, and 455 now in Guantánamo, down from 770 detainees initially held there in 2002. In the article entitled "US Detainees Abroad Face a Legal Vacuum," the AP also reported: "The secret prisons – unknown in number and location – remain available for future detainees," and while recent legislation passed by the US Congress in late September 2006 and signed into law by President George W. Bush in October 2006 ostensibly protects detainees from acts of torture, "the new manual banning torture doesn't cover CIA interrogators. And thousands of people still languish in a limbo, deprived of one of common law's oldest rights, habeas corpus, the right to know why you are imprisoned." In military prisons and Central Intelligence Agency prisons, the US has established an extra-territorially located, transnationally operated "prison network": violations of civil liberties, legal due process, and allegations of human rights violations have swirled around military and immigrant detentions at the Delta Camp located in Guantánamo, as well as in US-based immigration prisons (as documented by Mark Dow in *American Gulag*) or at detention centers in the countries where the "coalition of the willing" is currently waging war, as in Iraq – with military prisons Abu Ghraib, now closed, Camp Bucca located in the southern desert, and Camp Cropper located at the Baghdad airport, newly reconstructed as a $60 million "state-of-the-art detention center" ("US Detainees Abroad Face a Legal Vacuum") – or in Afghanistan (the Bagram Airforce Base), and myriad CIA-operated "secret prisons" in Middle Eastern countries like Syria and newly independent states (formerly part of the USSR) in Central Asia and Eastern Europe.

Britain, which sought and won release of four Britons held by the US military in the Delta Camp at Guantánamo Bay, faced its own detention scandal as 11 terrorist suspects (initially there were 17), many held since December 2001, were being "indefinitely" detained ("under emergency powers" authorized by the Anti-Terrorism and Security Act 2001 following 9/11) at three institutions – Broadmoor Hospital; Woodhill High Security Prison; and HM Prison Belmarsh located in southeast London – despite voluble public outcry, political dissent, and legal criticism by Liberty, a civil liberties organization in the UK, which consistently maintained that "detention without trial is alien to our democracy," as director Shami Chakrabarti articulated. Solicitor Gareth Peirce, who represented several UK detainees, also warned the British government that the policy violated the European Convention on Human Rights and that "if there is no swift government action on the issue, detainees [w]ould ask the European Court of Human Rights to get involved" ("Britain's Guantanamo," BBC News). Following a legal appeal to challenge the legality of the UK detentions, initially rejected by the British Court of Appeal, Peirce also impugned the British government, inculpating its collaboration with the US-led global War on Terror, noting that the detentions violated *habeas corpus*, and further suggesting that the court decision was not only legally questionable, but also immoral: the lawyer openly stated, "It shows that we have completely lost our way in this country legally and morally" ("Terror Suspects' Appeal Rejected," BBC News). According to a BBC report, critics of the British detention policy referred to "Belmarsh as 'Britain's Guanta-namo'" ("Terror Suspects' Appeal Rejected"). In March 2004, the British govern-ment released one detainee due to insufficient evidence in the state case against the individual suspected of terrorism, followed by a second detainee release in April 2004. In August 2004, Liberal Democrat and British Judge Lord Carlyle pushed dissenting public opinion onto the country's legal terrain, when he stated, "It's contrary to our tradition to hold people without charge" ("Terror Detention Law Must Go," BBC News). A third detainee was released in September 2004.

Activist critics also claimed that even as arrests and detentions increased, legal charges and indictments did not necessarily follow: "Between the New York attacks and last month," according to the BBC News, by 2004, "there ha[d] been 561 arrests in the UK under the Terrorism Act. But up to the end of January, only 98 of these had faced charges under this legislation, leading to six convic-tions" ("Too Many Arrests, Too Few Charges?" BBC News). The BBC News reported in January 2005 that the number of arrests and detentions from Sep-tember 2001 until December 2004 had totaled 701, resulting in only 119 people being "charged with terrorist-related offences" and a paltry 17 convictions ("Q&A: Terror Laws Explained," BBC News). BBC news journalists weighed alternative rationales for the disparity in the high number of arrests and low number of indictments: "This could be interpreted as a sign that intelligence-led raids are difficult to convert into prosecutions. It could be argued that the urgency of guarding against terror means it is worth risking mistakes. But it could also be argued that the authorities are unjustly casting their net too widely" ("Too Many Arrests, Too Few Charges?" BBC News). The Institute of Race Relations, who conducted a survey or study of "stop and search" arrests, allowed under Section 44 of the Terrorism Act 2000,[17] in the UK (which has increased among Asian Britons by 300 percent, or about 3,000 people in "absolute terms"), more bluntly indicted the British police and detention policy: "the majority of those being arrested are Muslim – but the majority being convicted are not," meaning, scholars writing the report for the think tank assert, that "the wrong people are being targeted" ("Q&A: Terror Laws Explained," BBC News).

Following the rejection of the Court of Appeal hearing in August 2004, legal solicitors defending and representing the legal rights of the detainees presented their case before the Law Lords, part of the House of Lords and the "highest judges in the land" ("Q&A: 'Terror' Detainee Release," BBC News) in October 2004. In December 2005 the Law Lords ruled that "the measures which allowed foreign terror suspects to be detained indefinitely without trial were . . . unlaw-ful" ("Terror Suspect Freed from UK Jail," BBC News).

Londonistan? Transnational Divides, Symmetry, and the "Clash" (Within and Without)

In a 2004 article published in the *London Review of Books* British lawyer John Upton queried the abrogation of law and the infractions against civil liberties occurring "In the Streets of Londonistan." Intended as a rhetorical troubling of the Manichaean logic dividing jihadist terrorists from democratic defenders, or the Islamic Shariah "-stan-states" from the supposed democracies of the West, Upton deploys the neologism "Londonistan" as a deconstruction of the so-called "clash of civilizations" promulgated by Huntington and neocon company, in order to strikingly point out the structural similarities of the "clash of fundamentalisms," as Tariq Ali diagnoses terror and war on terror. Defusing the rhetoric of both the Al-Muhajiroun, whose spokespersons have asserted, as if echoing Huntington, "The world is now split into two camps," and that of the British National Police, who Upton overheard identifying the organization in derisive racist terms ("Fucking Pakis"), the lawyer-journalist questions the language of the war on terror that threatens to further divide those already materially, politically, and rhetorically one from the other. Upton also questions the governmental language used in promoting legislation that supports the global War on Terror:

> A black cloud of Islamist terror is said to be hanging over the Western world; and specific causes of violence and discontent have disappeared into it. Instead, we promote the idea that all acts of political violence involving Arabs or Muslims, if seen from the correct (that is to say US-inspired) angle, will fit together like a jigsaw to form an image of Osama bin Laden. (Upton 2004)

While not questioning the reality of airstrikes against Kabul in October 2001 or against Baghdad in March 2003, nor the undeniable if grievous reality of the deployment of ground troops in both Afghanistan and Iraq post-9/11 and post-air bombing campaigns, Upton avers that the War on Terror is as much ideological as it is militaristic:

> If this is a war, as the neocons and Blairite hawks would have us believe, it is being fought as much in the realm of ideology and words as in the realm of explosive shoes and ricin laboratories. It is a propaganda war of shadowy unprovables, in which the absence of an attack is claimed as a victory by the police and intelligence services. A war in the course of which the security services will gain and our civil liberties suffer. A war in which the dilemmas of counter-terrorist policing have begun to express some of the most sensitive cultural irresolutions in British society. (Upton 2004)

For Upton, what is most troubling is the "Manichean nature of the struggle," the declaration of a state of emergency that heightens the fear of terrorist threats as an administrative means of totalizing executive control in the country, and the parliamentary signing of "emergency legislation" that threatens the rule of law and order, violates due process, and violates civil liberties. Citing "maître-penseur" and director of the Centre for the Study of Terrorism in St. Andrews, Dr. Magnus Ranstorp, Upton writes that British and US neocons now regard Al-Qaeda "as a strategic innovator of Clausewitzian skill," one "attempting to destroy the state from within"; and with regressive and repressive anti-terrorist legislation like the USA Patriot Act and the Anti-Terrorism Crime and Security Act, both of which graft "anti-terrorist provisions onto immigration law," and both passed in 2001 by the US Congress and the British parliament, respectively, it may be tempting, as Upton himself intimates, to acknowledge the validity of this neoconservative argument, but not without also conceding the direct complicity of both nation-states in their own legislative and executive efforts to destabilize the rule of law and civil liberties. In short, Upton hints, terrorists and counter-terrorists both collude in eroding law and in fueling war. Such repressive legislation, Upton writes in language that will certainly inspire virulent detractors, "would be a powerful weapon in any totalitarian state's armoury."

With a cover headline posing the question "Jihadtropolis?," *The New York Times Magazine* (June 25, 2006) features Christopher Caldwell's provocatively entitled article "The Lessons of Londonistan," which echoes Upton's title while more conservatively and less questioningly problematizing the ideological parameters of such an imagined metro-locale (i.e., for Caldwell, it is the 1.6 million Muslim Britons who have transformed London into Londonistan, and not the abrogation of law that mirrors the logic of the fundamentalist terrorists that the War on Terror supposedly opposes that renders it so, which seems to beg the question: have we not already become, and even deliberately self-refashioned ourselves, into the presumed nemesis that we phantasmagorically imagine out there in the Middle East, North Africa, and in the newly independent "-stan-states" of Central Asia, as well as the illegal alien enemy within who somehow managed to surreptitiously cross our borders, enter into our country, and now perilously, conspiratorily dwells among us waiting for the opportunity to bring us down?). In one such rhetorical move, Caldwell notes that Al Qacda operatives have seemingly hunkered (or bunkered) down in the mountainous border region between Afghanistan and Pakistan, before noting that the latter country has been "one of Britain's major sources of immigration since the '50s" (2006, 46) and further noting that two of the July 7 London bombers had not only recently visited Pakistan, but had also done so with the explicit purpose of contacting Al Qaeda figures in the country. In language that seems to censure transborder migration and diasporic transnational affiliations, Caldwell also concludes: "Like most modern 'diaspora' immigrants, the Pakistani-British visit their native country with little difficulty" (46). Pointing out that "there were 400,000 British visitors to Pakistan in 2004," the year preceding the July 7 bombings in London, Caldwell concludes that "all countries with large Muslim diasporas are vulnerable to the worldwide Wahhabi radicalization fomented at mosques and cultural centres financed by Saudi Arabia's government and its private charities," that "Britain is [also] vulnerable to radicalizing trends of South Asia – India, Bangladesh and Pakistan," and that "these trends risk becoming Britain's own, particularly among its socially isolated minorities" (46–47). Within a short paragraph Caldwell manages to conflate Pakistani Britons with Pakistani nationals (presumably, he reasons, "their native country," no matter where they may have been born or hold citizenship), to conflate radical Islamism with all "large Muslim diasporas" in Britain (or France or Australia or the US, Caldwell dangerously suggests), and to conflate a continental geographical expanse – that slippery region somewhere between the Middle East, North Africa, Central Asia, and the South Asian subcontinent – with *jihad* against the "democracies" of the West.

Similar debates have played out internationally and nationally (in the US) on the infractions of human rights in the global War on Terror. In May 2006, a United Nations panel called on the US to shut down the "detention camps at Guantánamo Bay" (Golden, "US Should Close Prison in Cuba, UN Panel Says"). International critics, including a prominent Spanish judge, and international nongovernmental organizations like Amnesty International and Human Rights Watch also called for the US to close the detention center at Guantánamo. Following international outcry against the violation of legal rights and alleged abuses of human rights for "enemy combatants" detained at the US Naval Base at Guantánamo Bay, during early summer 2006, the US Supreme Court ruled on June 29, 2006 that proposed military tribunals planned for enemy combatants at Guantánamo were unconstitutional. Recent legislation passed during the fall 2006 session of the US Congress codified into law detainee rights and their delimitations of rights.

On September 28, 2006, the Senate approved – by a 65-to-34 vote – a "detainee bill" that will allow the executive branch to "set up rules for the military commissions that will allow the government to proceed with prosecutions of high-level detainees, including Khalid Shaik Mohammed" (Zernike 2006). While the bill protects detainees held in military prisons from torture and "stress and duress" interrogation tactics, previously routine at Guantánamo, Abu Ghraib, and Baghram, it does not guarantee these same protections and rights to enemy combatants detained at the numerous CIA-operated secret prisons covertly scattered across the globe. The bill also strips detained enemy combatants of their *habeas corpus* rights, a long-held tenet and protected right under international law. Dissenting Senator Carl Levin of Michigan maintained that depriving detainees of the right of *habeas corpus* was "as legally abusive of the rights guaranteed in the Constitution as the actions at Abu Ghraib, Guantanamo and secret prisons were physically abusive of detainees" (Zernike 2006). While advocates of the bill argue that it legally protects detainees from "torture, rape, murder and any act intended to cause 'serious' physical or mental pain or suffering," and in accord with Article 3 of the Geneva Conventions, would "bar cruel and inhumane treatment," the bill also broadens the legal "definition of enemy combatants beyond the traditional definition used in wartime, to include noncitizens living in the United States as well as those in foreign countries and anyone determined to be an enemy combatant under criteria defined by the president or secretary of defense" (Zernike 2006), making the legal expansiveness of the definition broad indeed! In other words, the bill – now signed into law by President Bush – allows the president (i.e., George W. Bush) to designate anyone an enemy combatant by criteria established by the executive branch of the US government (i.e., George W. Bush). And *so it goes*, to echo the late Kurt Vonnegut, ironic political novelist and wry American satirist of the late twentieth century. In a *New York Times* article by Tim Golden entitled "Detainee Memo Created Divide in White House" (October 1, 2006), the author notes how the executive branch pressures Republicans in the legislative branch to "accept a broad definition of 'unlawful enemy combatants' whom the government can hold indefinitely, to maintain some of the president's control over CIA interrogation methods and to allow the government to present some evidence in military tribunals that is based on hearsay or has been coerced from witnesses" (A14).

In September 2006, Senate also passed a Pentagon budget bill (in the staggering amount of $448 billion) – "including $70 billion for the wars in Iraq and Afghanistan" (A. Taylor 2006), bringing the "total spent for Iraq, Afghanistan and other anti-terrorism efforts since the Sept. 11, 2001, attacks" to $507 billion (Abrams, "Security Bills"). In a radio broadcast debate on National Public Radio's "Market Place" between Robert Reich and David Fromm over the cost of military defense, homeland security, and the War on Terror, Fromm suggested that the exorbitant defense budget was necessary for "underwriting the military architecture of the planet"! Fromm conjectured that the expenditure was not only a necessary, but moreover worthwhile investment needed to protect the global economic trade in goods and services, from which the US economy dramatically benefits, profits that would, in his estimation, more than compensate for the costs of protecting global capitalism. Such bald economic rhetorical spin on the global War on Terror may be rare, though increasingly common and commonplace, yet it still truly manifests capitalism "with its clothes off," to evoke a never-more apropos phrase first articulated about the transatlantic slave trade by British cultural critic and sociologist Paul Gilroy.

Suffice it to say, and sadly: certain elements not only loom on the future horizon, but are *the* present reality of geopolitical realignments in the post-9/11 era and in the wake of volatility, unpredictability, turbulence, and chaos created by both transnational terrorist organizations and the violent mechanisms operative in the global War on Terror: astronomical defense and military spending; technological surveillance of citizens and immigrants; detention of suspected terrorists or enemy combatants, however the executive branch wishes to define, designate, and then indefinitely detain these individuals; the closing of international borders, or the guarded erection of fences and walls along them; the strict regulation of transborder migrations and cross-border movements for individuals, even persecuted refugees seeking political asylum, if not the goods and services commonly traded across those very borders under regional and transnational free trade agreements; the political repression and even racist, pejorative vilification of Muslim and non-Muslim diasporic communities (of Middle Eastern, North African, Central Asian, and South Asian origin) in Europe, North America, Australia, New Zealand, and elsewhere. Such diasporic shifts are, regrettably, those that have occurred post-9/11. And we will likely, and lamentably, be living in the wake of these geopolitical shifts for years, if not decades to come.

Question for Reflection

Caveat: Since this question pertains to "legal" or "official" documents that are government issued, the author strongly suggests this question as one for reflection only, not for class discussion. Also, students should, of course, evaluate these official documents in privacy, not in public.

Examine your driver's license, social security card, passport, or other governmentally issued photograph identification card. What information is included about you? What does this information reveal? What may an individual learn by simply evaluating this basic data (name, birth date, height, weight, etc.)? What purpose does this data serve?

Questions for reflection and discussion

- How are terms like *terror, terrorist, enemy combatant, jihad, jihadist,* and *war* ones that are culturally determined and differentially defined in varying geographical regions, linguistic registers, religious traditions, historical parameters, and geopolitical contexts?
- How do these differences impact global understanding and misunderstanding?
- How, if at all, may these differences be bridged through translation or diplomacy?
- What, if any, are the limits of translation? Of diplomacy?
- How are the same terms (as those enumerated in the first question) ones that are also rhetorically, politically, legally, and judicially defined, and thus malleable terms that may rapidly shift in meaning, valence, or effect?
- How, for example, have the terms *terror* and *enemy combatant* taken on new denotations (legally, juridically, politically, materially) and connotations (culturally, historically, popularly) since 2001?

Additional Research

Thinking through writing (1)

Read Antonio Negri and Michael Hardt's *Empire* (2001). After reflecting on the questions enumerated below, select one question as the basis for an analytical essay.

Questions to consider about Empire

- How might the forces of modern imperial nation and transnational Empire operate in tandem, simultaneously, yet in discordant friction (the former reterritorializing on the latter even as the latter deterritorializes the first)?
- Do you agree with Negri and Hardt's theorizations of "resistance" *within* Empire? What are the implications (epistemologically? morally? structurally?) for a theorization of resistance to Empire that only further compels a more efficient evolution of the capitalist imperial machine?
- What, according to Negri and Hardt, is the "crisis" in the construction of modern sovereignty?
- How, according to Negri and Hardt, does a dialectic of colonial sovereignty reveal the subversive underside of modern sovereignty (though it too remains

wed to the Hegelian dialectic in its political reversal as "revolutionary anti-thesis") (113)?

- How, according to Negri and Hardt, are poststructuralist theory (against Enlightenment) and postcolonialist theory (against imperialist epistemologies and colonialist domination) both *symptomatic* of the passage from imperialism to Empire, from modern sovereignty to imperial capitalist sovereignty?
- What is "imperial racism," according to Negri and Hardt? How are the imperial forms of racism divergent from the modern racialized logics? They write, "Difference is not written in law" (194). Is this true of modernity? Is this true of postmodernity? How, if at all, might a critical race theorist trouble this statement?

Thinking through debating

Read the two articles by John Upton and Christopher Caldwell that use the term "Londonistan" to reference demographic, citizenship, and immigrant shifts in the British capital since the end of World War II. In an informal debate, compare the rhetorical strategies of the two authors, Caldwell writing for a predominantly US-based readership, and Upton for a UK-based audience. How, for example, do the two writers differently understand and historically contextualize the neologism "Londonistan" in relation to terror and the global terror war?

Thinking through writing (2)

Write a short essay that offers a rhetorical analysis of the articles by Upton and Caldwell and that interprets the reporters' divergent uses and meanings of the term "Londonistan" in their journalistic writings about immigration, immigrants, terrorism, and the global terror war.

Sources

Caldwell, Christopher. "The Lessons from Londonistan." *New York Times Magazine* (June 25, 2006).

Upton, John. "In the Streets of Londonistan." *London Review of Books* 26.2 (January 22, 2004): www.lrb.co.uk/v26/n02/print/upto01.html.

Notes

PREFACE

1 See Haines and Rosen, *Illegal Immigration in America* (1999).
2 Kingma 2001, 207. See also UN, "Summary of the Report" (2005).
3 See Appadurai in *Theorizing Diaspora* (2002).
4 Tazreiter 2004, 45–46.
5 Tazreiter 2004, 46; Haines and Rosen 1999; Newman and van Selm 2003.
6 Smith 1997; Chin 1999; Kyle and Koslowski 2001.
7 Tazreiter 2004, 48. Given the massive upsurge in anti-immigrant sentiments and legislative policies in European and North American countries since 1980, and escalating in the post-Cold War period – a transnational phenomenon in the "developed" (or "overdeveloped") countries of the West and global North that has negatively impacted not only economic migrants, but also and more deleteriously, refugees – the United Nations High Commission for Refugees (UNHCR) has also shifted its administrative and global recommendations from refugee-admittance to "repatriation and temporary protection" (Tazreiter 2004, 48), while insisting that such policy shifts do not violate the 1951 Convention on Refugees' rule against *refoulement*. More recently, even in literature produced by the UNHCR, there has been a notable shift in the language and rhetorical constructions surrounding global asylees and refugees with the international organization moving away from the term "refugees" toward a nebulous classification "people of concern," particularly in documents written during the 1990s. While "people of concern" intends to administratively broaden the classification of "de facto refugees" (Tazreiter 2004, 49) to include individuals of gender discrimination, sexual persecution, children, and victims of ethnocidal violence who may not fall within the precise legal definitions of "refugee" as codified in the 1951 UN Convention that established the contemporary refugee regime, the expansive and vague classification also inadvertently reinscribes the boundaries of "refugees" and those guaranteed legal protection under the 1951 Convention. According to Tazreiter, "The provision of international law, including the Refugee Convention, as well as the UN Convention on Human Rights, indicate a contradiction in that the right to leave is provided with no complementary right to admission anywhere else" (2004, 50).

8 Tazreiter 2004, 50.
9 Tazreiter 2004, 51.

INTRODUCING DIASPORA: KEY TERMS

1 On Jews in Russia, generally, and on anti-Jewish pogroms in Russia beginning in 1881–2, specifically, see the following: Haberer 1995; Ro'i 1995; Strauss 1993; Klier and Lambroza 1992; Orbach 1984; and Klier 1984.
2 Kniesmeyer and Brecher, "Beyond the Pale: The History of Jews in Russia" (n.d.).
3 Kniesmeyer and Brecher, "Beyond the Pale: The History of Jews in Russia."
4 Kniesmeyer and Brecher, "Beyond the Pale: The History of Jews in Russia."
5 On Jewish languages, see Myhill 2004; Terrell 2001; Spolsky and Shohamy 1999; Díaz Más 1992; and Prager and Greenbaum 1982.
6 Kniesmeyer and Brecher, "Beyond the Pale: The History of Jews in Russia."
7 Despite the obvious import of the Haitian Revolution in the Americas and in the larger Atlantic world, its history has been too often undervalued and silenced within historical studies, as Michel-Rolph Trouillot persuasively argues in *Silencing the Past: Power and the Production of History* (see chapter three, "An Unthinkable History," 70–107). As Trouillot writes, the Haitian Revolution "entered history with the peculiar characteristic of being unthinkable even as it happened" (73); and he further reasons that "neither a single great book nor even a substantial increase in slave resistance studies will fully uncover the silence that surrounds the Haitian Revolution. For the silencing of that revolution has less to do with Haiti or slavery than it has to do with the West" (106). In the final paragraph of this chapter, Trouillot thus concludes that the "silencing of the Haitian Revolution is only a chapter within a narrative of global domination" (107).
8 See Geggus 2001 and 2002, as well as Gaspar and Geggus 1997.
9 Hugo published a story under the title "Bug-Jargal" in 1820, which is a precursor to the novel.
10 Gopinath 2005, 10.
11 On international policies related to global refugees, consult *Migration and Refugee Policies*, edited by Berstein and Weiner 1999. For the refugee crises of the 1990s, see the following: Goodwin-Gill 1996; Loescher 1994; van Selm 1998, 2000; Buckley and Cummings 2001; Helton 2002; Ogata 2005; and Opitz 2004. For more general post-1989 discussions of refugees and humanitarianism, see Zolberg et al. 1989; Zolberg and Benda 2001; UNHCR 2000. For a comparative analysis of US and German policies on refugees, see Münz and Weiner 1997.
12 See the website for the United Nations High Commissioner for Refugees: www.unhcr.ch/cgi-bin/texis/vtx/news/opendoc.htm?tbl=NEWS&id=4395c3354.

CHAPTER 1   DIASPORIC WORKERS, NEW GLOBAL ECONOMY

1 Migrant nurses and domestic workers are discussed in chapter two, "Gender and Diasporas."
2 See Jorge Duany 2005, 247.
3 The impact of the Haitian and Filipino diasporas on homeland politics in Haiti and the Philippines is further discussed in chapter six, "Transnational Activism, Diasporic Arts of Resistance."
4 See La 2004.

5   United Nations Department of Economic and Social Affairs 2005.

6   Cited in Brown 2006.

7   See Rosales 1999, 49–74.

8   See Johnson 2003. On race, labor, and political enfranchisement and disenfranchisement in Texas, also see Foley 1997.

9   See Acuña 2000, 219.

10 Havemann 2006.

11 Secure Fence Act of 2006 (H.R. 6061) is available through the searchable online database for the Library of Congress. All in-text quotations or citations are from the version of H.R. 6061 passed by Senate on September 29, 2006.

12 See Summary of H.R. 6061, Secure Fence Act of 2006, available online at www.gop. gov/Committeecentral/bills/hr6061.asp.

13 Swarns, "Senate Moves Toward Action on Border Fence." *New York Times* (29 Sept. 2006): A18. Hereafter cited as Swarns, "Senate Moves."

14 Swarns, "Senate Moves."

15 Ibid.

16 Turnbow 2006.

17 Hulse and Swarns 2006.

18 Ibid.

19 Ibid.

20 Hurt 2006.

21 Rodriguez 2006.

22 Lipton 2006. Newspaper coverage of the 2006 Congressional Debates on immigration reform, generally, and S. 2611 and H.R. 4427, specifically, has been extensive; see, among other articles, the following published in the *New York Times*: Lipton 2006; Bumiller 2006.

23 Sharp 2006.

CHAPTER 2   GENDER AND DIASPORAS

1   On power differentials and the political negotiation of power between migrant domestics and their employers – or among women, citizen employer and migrant employee – see Romero 1992, 97–133; Constable 1997, 83–124; Anderson 2000, 5–8; Chang 2000, 70–80; and Parreñas 2001, 150–196.

2   As Mireille Kingma, consultant for the International Council of Nurses and author of *Nurses on the Move: Migration and the Global Health Care Economy*, citing Oyowe (1996), writes: "Political instability in Sub-Saharan Africa (conflicts in Nigeria, Zaire [Congo], Sierra Leone, Somalia, etc.) is said to have forced thousands of qualified professionals into exile, and the majority of those left behind (in countries often facing severe economic crises) are now engaged in unskilled pursuits – in petty trading and taxi-driving – no longer practicing their professional skills" (2001, 209).

3   As a region, the entire Caribbean has been profoundly impacted by international economic migration since the end of World War II. As Kingma writes, "The migration outflows of the Caribbean are not limited to nurses. They affect every level of the regional labor market. The fact remains that the region has lost more than five million people over the last fifty years. The trigger for the mass exodus of professionals is said to be the rising demand for highly qualified people in North America and the United Kingdom" (2006, 182).

4   Traditionally an "exporter" of nurses, Ireland is now a major "importer" country, a consequence of global capital investment and the economic boom in the country during the 1990s. See Kingma 2006 and Buchan and Sochalski 2004.

5   According to Kingma, "The US is often depicted as the final destination in the ever-present migration pattern of health professionals – invoking the image of a prize at the end of a global treasure hunt" (2001, 208). See Kingma 2001, 205–208; 2006, 182–183.

6   Referring to the "exploitation of nurses" as "unethical and a violation of human rights," Kingma documents (through extensive case studies of and interviews with nurses worldwide) examples of exploitation, discrimination, and labor rights viola-tions: "Some nurses reported that when they arrived in a destination country, they were told that the contract they had signed at home was no longer valid. They were pressured to accept new terms of employment with lower pay and different working conditions. Some nurses were bullied into giving up their travel documents, making them even more dependent on their employer, while others were threatened with deportation if they told anyone about their situation" (2004, 196). According to Kingma, "exploita-tion also occurs because of gender and racial discrimination already present in a society. For example, the Royal College of Nursing, UK found in a recent study that black nurses as compared to white nurses in the UK were more often placed in acting manage-ment positions without financial compensation, and thus were denied the salary increase that would accompany a permanent promotion. Black nurses also tended to have more difficult access to continuing and further education" (2004, 197).

7   Kingma 2006, 177. Kingma further clarifies that "brain drain has also been defined as 'the emigration or flight of skilled human capital from one country to the other in search of better returns to one's knowledge, skills, qualifications and competencies" (ibid).

8   On the impact of GATS on international nurse migration and the global market and competition for healthcare providers, see Stilwell et al. 2004, 598–599 and Kingma 2006, 144–160.

9   "The Official Employment Contract for a Domestic Helper Recruited outside of Hong Kong is the only contract recognized by Hong Kong law (HK-LD 1992a, b, c; HK-ID 1993a, b, c, d)" (Constable 1997, 31).

10 The Philippine contract "ban" with Hong Kong was also meant as a punitive gesture toward Filipinas living and working as domestics there who had actively opposed a customs tax, planned but later aborted by the Aquino administration on their over-seas earnings.

CHAPTER 3   GLOBAL TRAFFIC

1   Amber L. Hollibaugh, self-identified (in *My Dangerous Desires*) as "a lesbian sex radical, ex-hooker, incest survivor, gypsy child, poor-white-trash, high-femme dyke," more forcefully raises the question of feminism and sex workers' rights (and to boot, in an in-your-face manner impossible to simply ignore!): "Why did it take so long for the women's movement to genuinely consider the needs of whores, of women in the sex trades? And why did it take so long for the movement to produce writings by those women? Maybe because it's hard to listen to – I mean really pay attention to – a woman who, without other options, could easily be cleaning your toilet? Maybe because it's intolerable to listen to the point of view of a woman who makes her living sucking off your husband?" (2000, 181).

2 See Kempadoo and Doezema, 1998, 20; and Law 2000, 98–99.

3 On sex tourism, see Truong 1990; Brennan 2004; Kempadoo 2004; Cabezas 2005; and the chapters in the edited collection by Kempadoo 1999.

4 The World Charter for Prostitutes' Rights, ratified by the International Committee for Prostitutes' Rights at the 2005 Congress held in Amsterdam, advocates for regulation of sex industries through national and international laws protecting sex workers (their human rights, working conditions, healthcare access, and provision of welfare services, as well as through taxation, educational programs, and the right to organize as workers). The Charter may be read in "Sex Workers and Sex Work," a special issue of *Social Text* edited by McClintock (1993, 183–185).

5 Brennan 2004, 103.

6 Abolitionist campaigns have been particularly ineffective in the Mekong region, especially Thailand, where the sex industry – based on long historical foundations and late capital economic strategy – flourishes. Dating to the fifteenth century, the Thai sex industry rapidly proliferated in the mid-1960s when the national government actively promoted the country and its capital city Bangkok as an enticing and exotic destination for affluent sex tourists worldwide (Bao 2005, 81; Muecke 1992, 892). Not surprisingly, some of its first tourists were also on active tours of duty as US soldiers fighting the Vietnam War (Truong 1990, 81–82; quoted in Bao 2005, 81). In the post-Vietnam War period following the fall of Saigon in 1975 and the withdrawal of US troops from the Southeast Asian country, "sex package tours were marketed in the Netherlands, Norway, West Germany, the United Kingdom, the Middle East, and elsewhere throughout the 1970s and 1980s" as the country sought to dominate "a wider international market" (Bao 2005, 81). Strategic national "selling" of sex and sex tours fueled explosive economic growth for the country, "with income from tourism rising from approximately 200 million baht in 1960 to more than 37 billion baht in 1986" (81). Thailand's sex industry was, by 1995, its "largest source of foreign exchange," and in 2002 alone, "10.8 million came to Thailand and spent US$7.7 billion, amounting to 6 percent of the country's gross domestic profit" (81; citing Mydans 2003). The Philippines, with its own history of US military occupation and prostitution in service of US soldiers stationed there, has also actively promoted sex tourism, as well as labor exportation, as a national economic "development" strategy.

7 Kevin Bales, "Working Paper," freetheslaves.org.

CHAPTER 4   QUEER DIASPORAS

1 For theorizations of queer diaspora, see the following: Manalansan 1993, 1994, 1995, 2000; Eng 1994, 1997, 2001; Puar 1994, 1995, 1998, 2001, 2002; Cruz-Malavé 1995, 1997; Gopinath 1995, 1996, 1997, 1998, 2000, 2002; Muñoz 1995, 1999; Muñoz and Barrett 1996; Watney 1995; Leong 1996; Sinfield 1996; Eng and Hom 1998; Rosello 1999; Grossman 2000; Holland 2000; Patton and Sánchez Eppler 2000; Cruz-Malavé and Manalansan 2002; Rodriguez 2003. For early theoretical explorations into the imbrications of race, nationality, sexuality, and gender, see the special issue of *Social Text*: "Queer Transexions of Race, Nation, and Gender," edited by Harper, McClintock, and Muñoz. See also the special issues of *GLQ* on issues related to queer diasporas and queer globalization: "Thinking Sexuality Transnationally," edited by Muñoz and Barrett; and "Queer Tourism: Geographies of Globalization," edited by Puar.

2 Gopinath 1997, 266.

3 In the Tagalog glossary appendix to *Global Divas* (2003), Manalansan defines *bakla* as "homosexual, effeminate person, hermaphrodite gay" (200); a more comprehensive definition and the range of its queer sexual identity practices and performances may be found in chapter one (see 2003, 25, especially).

4 On homonormativity, see Warner 2000 and Duggan 2002; reprinted in Duggan 2003.

5 Sikes, "Social Protest and the Performance of Gay Identity."

6 Goldie, "Queer Nation?"

7 For an intellectually framed analysis of "Queer Nation," see Berlant and Freeman 1993. For related theorizations of queerness, nationality, and citizenship, see also Berlant 1991, 1992, 1993; Berlant, Warner, et al. 1994; Rosello 1994, 1997; Berlant and Warner 1998.

8 Plummer 1992.

9 See, for example, Altman 1996 and 1997. For the theoretical intersections of postcolonial and queer terrains, see Hayes 1996 and 2000, as well as Hawley 2001a and 2001b.

10 Patton and Sánchez-Eppler 2000, 3.

11 Patton and Sánchez-Eppler 2000, 3.

12 Patton and Sánchez-Eppler 2000, 4. Later in the editors' introduction to *Queer Diasporas*, they elaborate the "slippage" between bodies and places: "Bodies do not rest stably in a place until a discourse overtakes, agitates, and names their desires. Rather, bodies pack and carry tropes and logics from their homelands; they seek out an 'imagined community' of intrinsic queerness, which they read about between the lines of international media and policy. But traveling the paths of international policy, global media, academic disciplines, and nationalist ideologies, discourses themselves may travel even faster. Dislocated bodies may refind their native discourses when they get 'there,' as if they have 'discovered' that the Other elsewhere is 'naturally' the same. By the same token, the intrusive discourses may construct as unnatural a queerness that had always lain in want of a recategorizing discourse" (10–11).

13 Patton and Sánchez-Eppler 2000, 8.

14 See Berlant 1997 and Manalansan 2003.

15 See Solomon 2004, 3–29; on immigration prisons and abuses within immigration detention centers, see Dow 2004.

16 On queer *disidentification* with nationality and citizenship, see Berlant and Freeman 1993; Gopinath 1996, 125; Muñoz 1999; and Binnie 2004, 70.

CHAPTER 5   RACE AND DIASPORAS

1 See Young and Braziel, "Cultural Amnesia and the Academy," editor's introduction to *Race and the Foundations of Knowledges* (2006).

2 See Associated Press, "Australian Racial Violence Spills into 2nd Night."

3 See Hudson 2003; Bell-Fialkoff 1996.

4 Sciolino and Bernard 2006.

5 For the chronology of the fall 2005 unrest, I have relied heavily on "Chronologie: Les violences urbaines au jour le jour," published by *Le Monde*. Unless otherwise referenced, all internal quotations within the chapter's prose chronology of events from October 27, 2005 to November 12, 2005 are from the online "Chronologie" published on the *Le Monde* website.

6   Hopquin 2006.
7   Hopquin 2006.
8   Jérôme 2005.
9   Bronner 2006.
10 "Une Saint-Sylvestre sous haute surveillance."
11 Ridet 2006.
12 "AC le feu fait remonter 'la parole des citoyens' à l'Assemblée."
13 "Immigrants March, Present Complaints."
14 Bernard, "Attackers Set Fire to Bus in Marseille, Wounding One."
15 Patrice de Beer, "France's Incendiary Crisis."
16 Ibid.
17 I am heavily indebted to Neil MacMaster's *Colonial Migrants and Racism: Algerians in France, 1900–62* (1997).
18 Bousquet 1991, 73.
19 Begag 1990, 6.
20 Bousquet 1991, 74.
21 Hargreaves and McKinney, "Introduction," 19.
22 Begag 1990, 5.
23 Begag 1990, 10.
24 Holt 1995, quoted in MacMaster 1997, 210.
25 MacMaster 1997, 275n8.
26 MacMaster 1997, 1.
27 Hargreaves 1991, 66.
28 Hargreaves 1987, 108–109.
29 Poinsot 1993.
30 As Jean-Pierre writes, "In December 1972, a group of Haitian refugees landed on the shores of Miami after braving the high seas in a flimsy craft" (1995, 196).
31 See Dash 2001, 45.
32 According to Dash, "A second phase of migration to the United States was inaugurated in 1972, when the first boatload of Haitians arrived in Florida. This meant that poorer Haitians, who could not afford visas and airfares, were able to buy a seat on these boats by selling their possessions and leave for the 700-mile trip to Florida. This was the beginning of the Haitian 'boat people' phenomenon, which grew in intensity because of the intensifying economic crisis that plagued the regime of Jean-Claude Duvalier" (2001, 46).
33 See Nicholls 1979, 179.
34 I place "democracy" in quotation marks to suggest that American democracy has often failed its own ideals, or to keep us mindful of the fact that some Haitians believe "Americans Don't Have Democracy!" as Jennie Smith reminds us in *When the Hands Are Many* (2001). In a political meeting in the southwestern peninsula of Haiti, Smith was told that Americans lack the democracy that they espouse: "The Americans, they come here to tell us what democracy is, but as for me, I don't see that they truly understand the thing. American democracy, that's not real democracy! How can you have democracy if you don't have respect? Hmmph. . . . *Demokrasi? Se pa demokrasi, sa se demokrache?* [Democracy? That's not democra-*cy*. That's democra-*spit!*]" (2001, 5).
35 See Farmer 1992, especially part five. See also by Farmer: "On Guantanamo" and "Pestilence and Restraint: Guantanamo, AIDS, and the Logic of Quarantine" in Farmer 2003.

36 See Dow's important study, *American Gulag* (2004). Two of the most notorious prisons are Miami's Krome Detention Center, where Haitian refugees are currently being detained, and Houston's Corrections Corporation of America Processing Center.

37 According to Glick Schiller and Fouron, "Demonstrations, statements of protest placed as paid advertisements in the *New York Times*, patient lobbying with US congresspeople, and the press of Haitian refugees seeking to enter the United States did keep the issue of Aristide's presidency alive in the United States" (2001, 122). One interviewee identified as Franck said of the *Dizyèm Depatman* (Tenth Department): "The *Dizyèm* [Tenth Department] is a leta [state] that the Haitians occupy, and that is where they collaborate together to help Haiti. . . . The people of the diaspora are the ones who made it possible for Aristide to return after the Haitian people became martyrs. They stood up, they shook up the leadership of the American government to take action to save Haiti" (202–203).

CHAPTER 6   TRANSNATIONAL ACTIVISM, DIASPORIC ARTS OF RESISTANCE

1 "After independence," Ashish Chadha writes, "India embarked, under the leadership of Jawaharlal Nehru, on an ambitious plan to wrench the country free of British imperialism and to assert its autonomy. Greatly impressed by Stalinist reforms in the Soviet Union, Nehru introduced similar five-year plans in order to develop and modernize the country by building huge dams, power plants, steel plants and, later, nuclear power plants. These development projects have made India one of the most powerful countries in the Third World but have caused the displacement and dislocation of about 5 million people, a number equal to the population displaced during partition of the subcontinent in 1947. The victims were never party to the planning of the projects that would render them homeless and dispossess them of a landscape that they had held for generations. Among the worst culprits were the big dams, proclaimed as 'Secular Temples' of the independent country by Nehru, of which India is the largest manufacturer in the world" (1999, 146).

2 According to Chadha, land-dwelling tribals "have been called *adivasi*, *admijati*, *vanyajatis*, *girijans*, or *pahadia*. Most of these early terms explicity mean the settler, the forest settler or just the outsider. The term *adivasi*, in particular, denotes one who is an inhabitant from the earliest times and who still lives as people lived in earliest times" (1999, 151).

3 As Chadha explains, "The various tribal groups, Tadvi, Vasvi, Paura, Bhailala, Rattawa and Nayar, speak different languages, though most of the men understand the official language of their respective states. So the Tadvis in Gujarat speak Gujarati along with Bhili, whereas the Vasava of Maharashtra speak Marathi along with Bhili. Women in these communities are, however, unable to understand the non-tribal languages, due to the infrequent contact with outside cultures" (1999, 150). Chadha also informs us that "the constitution of India includes these populations among the 'Scheduled Tribes' which encompass 700 different groups of people comprising a population of 60 million, living in various socio-economic conditions (Ghurye 1962)," noting that "the framers of the constitution provided these groups with special privileges and concessions, in order to integrate them into national life" (1999, 150). Although "there has been continuous debate, particularly since 1947, over the extent

to which these tribal groups can be considered indigenous," Chadha also clarifies by offering a definition for *indigenous*, which he defines, "in the Indian context, as a population who, prior to the *Pax Britannica*, had from time immemorial maintained a symbiotic physical and cultural relationship with a particular landscape, who were largely outside of the caste system of the mainstream Hindu society and who were politically independent of this system." And while "cultural and economic contact did occur between these two groups, the indigenous one maintained its distinctive character" (1999, 150).

4   See Chadha 1999, 148; Alagh et al. 1995, 156; and Wagle 2002, 73.

5   See "A Brief Introduction to the Narmada Issue," Friends of the Narmada Website; available online at www.narmada.org/introduction.html.

6   "The Indira-Sagar Dam," Friends of the River Narmada: www.narmada.org/nvdp. dams/indira-sagar/index.html.

7   Ibid.

8   "Maheshwar Dam," Friends of the River Narmada: www.narmada.org/maheshwar. html.

9   International Rivers Network 2000.

10 "Maan Dam," Friends of the River Narmada <narmada.org/nvdp.dams/maan/>.

11 McCully 1994.

12 See "Power House," Sardar Sarovar Narmada Nigam Ltd website: www. sardarsarovardam.org.

13 McCully 1994. See also "Benefits," Sardar Sarovar Narmada Nigam Ltd website: www.sardarsarovardam.org.

14 See "Need for Sardar Sarovar Project," on the Sardar Sarovar Narmada Nigam Ltd website: www.sardarsarovardam.org.

15 "Sardar Sarovar Reservoir," Sardar Sarovar Narmada Nigam Ltd website: www. sardarsarovardam.org. See also Yadan 2006.

16 See "Sardar Sarovar Dam" on the Friends of the River Narmada website: www. narmada.org/sardarsarovar.html. Updates on the Narmada Valley Dam Project, including the individual Sardar Sarovar Project, may be accessed online at the Friends of the River Narmada website: www.narmada.org.

17 On the projected economic benefits of the NVDP, particularly the SSP, as researched and published by proponents of the development project in the midst of the Indian Supreme Court cases on the matter, see the contributions in Alagh, Desai, et al. 1995. On the potential environmental costs of the dam project, as researched and published by anti-dam detractors, see Alagh et al. 1995. See Sen 1995 for a discussion of private interest versus public interest, the case for the dam projects, and the case against based on "loss of land and livelihoods" (191); "poor quality governmental plans" (193); "uneven distribution of costs and benefits" (195); and "ecological impact" (197). Khan 1995, Maiti 2001, Roy 1999, Wagle 2002, and Parasuraman 1997 all also explore the environmental impact of the NVDP, as well as critique the nationalist and capitalist developmental notions subtending its plans for construction, as do Khagram 2002, 2004, and Baviskar 2004. The scholarly contributions by Baviskar and Khagram, however, focus more centrally on the resistance – indigenous grass-roots and transnational, respectively – to the NVDP. The human impact through displacement of the NVDP is detailed extensively in the collection edited by Drèze et al. 1997 and the monograph by Parasuraman (1997).

18 Kishwar 2006.

19 For a statement in his own words, see Patel 1997.

20 As Chadha explains, the mobilized grassroots resistance to the NVDP not only challenges the dam projects itself, but also raises "larger questions ... pertaining to human rights, the State's ecological ethics, the Nehruvian paradigm of development, and involvement of the local population at the decision-making level about their own landscape" (1999, 149).

21 On the particular plights suffered by displaced Indian widows, see Bhatia 1997, 1998. On the larger feminist implications of the NVDP, see Silliman 2001.

22 On tribal displacements caused by the NVDP and their grassroots resistance to preserve land, culture, and livelihood, see Baviskar 2004.

23 Glick Schiller and Fouron define a *transnational nation-state* as the "reconstitution of the concept of the state so that both the nation and the authority of the government it represents extend beyond the state's territorial boundaries and incorporate dispersed populations" (2001, 20–21).

24 For very divergent perspectives on the US "inter-vasion" of Haiti in 1994, see Ballard 1998, whose dedication refers to "military service" as "the ultimate form of patriotism"; Shacochis 1999; and former US army soldier (Special Forces) Stan Goff's scathing insider-turn-outsider critique of US militarism in *Hideous Dream* (2000).

25 Dupuy 1997, 43; Smith 2001, 26.

POSTFACE: DIASPORIC SHIFTS POST-9/11

1 The Armed Islamic Group (GIA) is an Algerian-based organization with transnational contacts in France and other European countries.

2 The exact nature of the organization Jemaah Islamiah (JI) is unknown, some maintaining that the group hopes to "overthrow governments in the region and replace them with a pan-South East Asian Islamic state" and others that it is merely a "loose affiliation of like-minded people, many of whom have no interest in terrorism." JI has also been charged with a failed "plot to blow up the US embassy in Singapore" in December 2001 ("The Bali Bombers' Network of Terror," BBC News).

3 "Timeline: Al-Qaeda," BBC News.

4 See Huntington 1996. For an alternate account of the "clash," see Ali 2002.

5 The full title of the bill is "United and Strengthening America by Providing Appropriate Tools Required to Intercept and Obstruct Terrorism" (USA PATRIOT).

6 *Habeas corpus* has been a roundly recognized component of European civil liberties and common law protection of rights since 1679.

7 Caldwell 2006.

8 Following the 9/11 attacks, Joint Task Force 160 assumed the role as executors of the "War on Terrorism Detainee Mission," authorized as a "wartime" measure (www.nsgtmo.navy.mil), later joined by Joint Task Force 170. The two JTFs were then merged into the Joint Task Force Guantanamo (www.nsgtmo.navy.mil).

9 For more information about alleged US violations of international law and human rights abuses at the Guantánamo Bay Naval Base, see the many publications by Amnesty International included in the bibliography at the end of this book. For a scholarly critique of the US policy of detaining "enemy combatants," see Elsea 2003.

10 For scholarly critiques of the post-9/11 US American landscape, focusing on alleged human rights violations at Guantánamo Bay, in Afghanistan, and on federal executive

and judicial infringements on civil liberties within the US, see Brown 2003; Leone and Anrig 2003.

11   "In accepting the cases," Linda Greenhouse writes in an article published on November 10, 2003 in the *New York Times*, "the court moved from the sidelines to the center of the debate over whether the administration's response to the terrorist attacks of Sept. 11, 2001, reflects an appropriate balance between national security and individual liberty."

12   *Johnson v. Eisentrager* (1950) was a case brought by German intelligence agents who had been arrested by US military officers in China during World War II, who were later charged with committing espionage for the Japanese government, and who were being detained at US military bases in Germany at the time of their appeal. In the 1950 ruling, the Supreme Court determined that federal law had no jurisdiction over the case since the detainees were outside of the United States territory.

13   Gibbons also argued that the detention of over 600 men at Guantánamo Bay without "legal adjudication" was "unconstitutional." To establish this point, Gibbons further contended that the US government was treating the Guantánamo Bay Naval Base like a "no-law zone," alleging that the government was holding prisoners at Gitmo as a "legal keep-away," and thereby insulating, shielding, or protecting the orders of the executive branch from judicial review or scrutiny. Violations against the constitutional checks and balances at the foundational core of the constitutionally defined US tripartite government, then, were central to Gibbons' legal arguments against that very government: the attorney thus argued that the executive branch acts as unilaterally at home as it does in the world.

14   To many, arguing against judicial review of executive orders implemented at Guantánamo based on the "ultimate sovereignty" of Cuba was the height of rhetorical sophistry: for critics, it was regarded as a legal argument devoid of substantive effect or consequence for Cuba and its presumptive "sovereignty," but pregnant with dangerous precedence and deleterious consequences for US legally sanctioned lawlessness. Questions of sovereignty recur throughout this study, and I briefly address how the sovereignty of small states is eroded by US imperialism, the strictures of international financial institutions, and other regulatory bodies in chapters two, four, and five.

15   Similarly, see Radway's 1998 presidential address to the ASA, "What's in a Name?"

16   In contrast with the legal, juridical, and military (i.e., "official") histories of Guantánamo, Kaplan suggests that American studies scholars tell alternative stories about the region. Counter-narratives would, for example, connect the contemporary detention of "enemy combatants" at the naval base with the imperialist acquisition of the region by the US at the end of the Spanish-American War; tell "a related story of immigration, bodies, and borders, a narrative of the Haitian refugees in the 1990s for whom the cages of Camp X-ray were originally built, and to whom the courts initially deemed the Bill of Rights inapplicable" (14); tell how "earlier internments," such as the internment of Japanese Americans during World War II, "haunt the legal grounds to Guantánamo" (14); and tell *telling* stories of mistranslation. According to Kaplan, "this empire fears translation; it views all translation as potential sabotage" (15). She cites the cases of Captain Yussef Yee and Senior Airman Ahmad I. al-Halabi who were charged with "conveying information out of Guantánamo" and with deliberate, surreptitious mistranslation.

17   Caldwell 2006.

Bibliography

"A Few Good Men." *Economist* 370.8358 (2004): 26.

"A Few Good Men." *Harper's Magazine* 311.1866 (2005): 23–24.

"A Second Group of Detainees Arrives at Base." *New York Times* 151.51998 (2002): A8.

"'Abolish Torture Now,' Religious Leaders Say." *Christian Century* 123.13 (2006): 14–15.

Abrams, Elliott. "The Shiprider Solution: Policing the Caribbean." *National Interest* 43 (Spring 1996): 86–92.

Abrams, Jim. The Associated Press. "Security Bills Pass Congress." *Cincinnati Enquirer* (1 Oct. 2006).

"Abu Ghraib, Caribbean Style." *New York Times* 1 Dec. 2004: A30+.

Abu-Lughod, ed. *Sociology for the Twenty-First Century: Continuities and Cutting Edges.* Chicago: University of Chicago Press, 1999.

"AC le feu fait remonter 'la parole des citoyens' à l'Assemblée. " *Le Monde* 25 Oct. 2006. www.lemonde.fr/web/article/0,1-0@2-706693,36-827244,0.html.

Ackerman, Frank, et al. *The Changing Nature of Work.* Washington, DC: Island Press, 1998.

Ackerman, Spencer. "Cross to Bear." *New Republic* 230.19 (2004): 13–14.

Acuña, Rodolfo. *Occupied America: A History of Chicanos.* New York: Longman, 2000.

Adams Jr., Richard H., and John Page. "Poverty, Inequality and Growth in Selected Middle East and North Africa Countries, 1980–2000." *World Development* 31.12 (2003): 2027.

Adams, Richard H., and John Page. "Do International Migration and Remittances Reduce Poverty in Developing Countries?" *World Development* 33.10 (2005): 1645–1669.

Adler, Emanuel. *Communitarian International Relations: The Epistemic Foundations of International Relations.* New York: Routledge, 2005.

Adler, Leonore Loeb, and Uwe P. Gielen, eds. *Migration: Immigration and Emigration in International Perspective.* Westport, CT: Praeger, 2003.

"Administration Says It Will Adhere To Geneva Conventions." *Congress Daily* (2006): 14.

African Network for the Prevention and Protection against Child Abuse and Neglect and Anti-Slavery International. "Report of the Eastern and Horn of Africa Conference on Human Trafficking and Forced Labor." Conference on Human Trafficking and Forced Labor. Nairobi, Kenya: Nairobi Safari Club, 2005.

"After Geneva. Africa?" *Nursing Standard* 19.42 (2005): 20–21.

Aggleton, Peter, ed. *Men Who Sell Sex: International Perspectives on Male Prostitution and HIV/AIDS.* Philadelphia: Temple University Press, 1999.

Agnew, Vijay, ed. *Diaspora, Memory, and Identity: A Search for Home.* Toronto: University of Toronto Press, 2004.

Agustín, Laura. "The Disappearing of a Migration Category: Migrants Who Sell Sex." *Journal of Ethnic and Migration Studies* 32.1 (January 2006): 29–47.

Ahmad, Natasha. "Trafficked Persons or Economic Migrants? Bangladeshis in India." *Trafficking and Prostitution Reconsidered: New Perspectives on Migration, Sex Work, and Human Rights.* Ed. Kamala Kempadoo, Jyoti Sanghera, and Bandana Pattanaik. Boulder: Paradigm Publishers, 2005. 211–228.

Ahmed, Aftab. "Using a Dynamic, Interactive, and Participatory Process to Develop and Redefine the Human Trafficking Paradigm in Bangladesh." *Trafficking and Prostitution Reconsidered: New Perspectives on Migration, Sex Work, and Human Rights.* Ed. Kamala Kempadoo, Jyoti Sanghera, and Bandana Pattanaik. Boulder: Paradigm Publishers, 2005. 199–210.

Ahmed, Nilufar. "Women in Between: The Case of Bangladesi Women Living in London." *Transnational Migration and the Politics of Identity.* Ed. Meenakshi Thapan. Thousand Oaks, CA: Sage, 2005. 99–129.

Aiken, Linda H., et al. "Trends in International Nurse Migration." *Health Affairs* 23.3 (2004): 69–77.

Akokpari, John. "Globalization, Migration, and the Challenges of Development in Africa." *Perspectives on Global Development & Technology* 5.3 (2006): 125–153.

Al Odah v. United States, No. 03–343 (2004).

Alagh, Y. K., Mahesh Pathak, and D. T. Buch, eds. *Narmada and Environment.* New Delhi: Har-Anand Publications, 1995.

Alagh, Y. K., R. D. Desai, G. S. Guha, and S. P. Kashyap, eds. *Economic Dimensions of the Sardar Sarovar Project.* New Delhi: Har-Anand Publications, 1995.

Al-Ali, Nadje, and Khalid Koser, eds. *New Approaches to Migration? Transnational Communities and the Transformation of Home.* New York: Routledge, 2002.

"Algeria's Top GIA Rebel Captured." British Broadcasting Corporation (29 April 2005). BBC News Online. www.news.bbc.co.uk/go/pr/fr/-/2/hi/africa/4500171.stm.

Ali, Tariq. *Clash of Fundamentalisms: Crusades, Jihad and Modernity.* New York: Verso, 2002.

Alidio, Kimberly. "Empire of Care: Nursing and Migration in Filipino American History (Book)." *Journal of American Ethnic History* 23.1 (2003): 119–121.

"All We Said Was that the Red Cross Was There." *New Republic* 231.24 (2004): 10–11.

Allen, S. "Personal Reflections on the 23rd Quadrennial Congress of the International Council of Nurses: 'Nursing on the Move: Knowledge, Innovation and Vitality' (Taipei Taiwan 21–27 May 2005)." *International Nursing Review* 53.1 (2006): 19–20.

Al-Shahi, Ahmed, and Richard Lawless, eds. *Middle East and North African Immigrants in Europe.* New York: Routledge, 2005.

Al-Sheik, Ameen Sa'eed. "Sworn Statement." Baghdad Correctional Facility, Abu Ghraib, Iraq APO AE 09335 (January 16, 2004). Available in pdf format online from the *Washington Post* at www.media.washingtonpost.com/wp-srv/world/iraq/abughraib/151362.pdf.

Altman, Dennis. "Global Gaze/Global Gays." *GLQ: A Journal of Lesbian and Gay Studies* 3 (1997): 417–436.

Altman, Dennis. "Rupture or Continuity? The Internationalization of Gay Identities." *Social Text* 14.3 (Fall 1996): 77–94.

Altman, Dennis. "The New World of 'Gay Asia'." *Asian and Pacific Inscriptions: Identities, Ethnicities, Nationalities.* Ed. Suvendrini Perera. Victoria, Australia: Meridian, 1995. 121–138.

"America on Trial: Inside the Legal Battles That Transformed Our Nation – from the Salem Witches to the Guantánamo Detainees (Book)." *Publishers Weekly* 251.15 (2004): 56.

American Civil Liberties Union (ACLU). Press Release. "In Historic Arguments, Supreme Court Considers Legal Rights of Guantanamo Detainees." April 20, 2004. www.aclu.org/SafeandFree/SafeandFree.cfm?ID=15506&c=206.

"Americans and Torture." *Columbia Journalism Review* 45.3: 19–31.

Amery, Hussein A., and William P. Anderson. "International Migration and Remittances to a Lebanese Village." *Canadian Geographer* 39.1 (1995): 46.

Amnesty International. "Supreme Court Must End Lawlessness in Guantánamo Bay." Date accessed: May 20, 2004. www.amnesty.nl.persberichten/NK-PB0454.shtml.

Amnesty International. *Bosnia-Herzegovina, Unlawful Detention of Six Men from Bosnia-Herzegovina in Guantánamo Bay.* London: Amnesty International, International Secretariat, 2003.

Amnesty International. *United States of America – The Threat of a Bad Example: Undermining International Standards as "War on Terror" Detentions Continue.* London: Amnesty International, International Secretariat, 2003.

Amnesty International. *United States of America – Beyond the Law: Update to Amnesty International's April Memorandum to the US Government on the Rights of Detainees held in US Custody in Guantánamo Bay and Other Locations.* London: Amnesty International, International Secretariat, 2002.

Amnesty International. *United States of America – Memorandum to the US Government on the Rights of People in US Custody in Afghanistan and Guantánamo Bay.* London: Amnesty International, International Secretariat, 2002.

Amuedo-Dorantes, Catalina, and Susan Pozo. "On the Use of Differing Money Transmission Methods by Mexican Immigrants." *International Migration Review* 39.3 (2005): 554–576.

"An Introduction from the Guest Editors." *Feminist Review* (2004): 4–6.

Anderson, Bridget. "Just Another Job? The Commodification of Domestic Labor." *Global Woman: Nannies, Maids, and Sex Workers in the New Economy.* Ed. Barbara Ehrenreich and Arlie Russell Hochschild. New York: Metropolitan Books, Henry Holt, 2002. 104–114.

Anderson, Bridget. "Different Roots in Common Ground: Transnationalism and Migrant Domestic Workers in London." *Journal of Ethnic & Migration Studies* 27.4 (2001): 673–683.

Anderson, Bridget. *Doing the Dirty Work? The Global Politics of Domestic Labour.* New York: Zed Books, 2000.

Anderson, Bridget. "Servants and Slaves: Europe's Domestic Workers." *Race & Class* 39.1 (1997–1998): 37.

Anderson, David E. "NCC Hails Court Rebuff of Bush's Detainee Policy." *Christian Century* 123.15 (2006): 14.

Anderson, Joan M. "Migration and Health: Perspectives on Immigrant Women." *Sociology of Health & Illness* 9.4 (1987): 410–438.

Anderson, Kenneth. "What to do with Bin Laden and Al Qaeda Terrorists? A Qualified Defense of Military Commissions and United States Policy on Detainees at Guantanamo Bay Naval Base." *Harvard Journal of Law & Public Policy* 25.2 (2002): 593.

Andersson, Ruben. "The New Frontiers of America." *Race & Class* 46.3 (2005): 28–38.

Andrade-Eekhoff, Katharine. "The Untapped Riches of Remittances?" *NACLA Report on the Americas* 38.4: 47.

Andreas, Peter, and Timothy Snyder, eds. *The Wall Around the West: State Borders and Immigration Controls in North America and Europe*. Lanham, MD: Rowman & Littlefield, 2000.

Andrews, Thomas C., and David L. Cull. "Self-mutilation and Malingering among Cuban Migrants Detained at Guantanamo Bay." *New England Journal of Medicine* 336.17 (1997): 1251.

Annas, George J. "Hunger Strikes at Guantanamo – Medical Ethics and Human Rights in a 'Legal Black Hole.'" *New England Journal of Medicine* 355.13 (2006): 1377–1382.

Anthias, Floya, and Gabriella Lazaridis, ed. *Gender and Migration in Southern Europe*. New York: Berg, 2000.

Apap, Joanna. *The Rights of Immigrant Workers in the European Union: An Evaluation of the EU Public Policy Process and the Legal Status of Labour Immigrants from the Maghreb Countries in the New Receiving States*. New York: Kluwer Law International, 2002.

Appadurai, Arjun. "Disjuncture and Difference in the Global Cultural Economy." *Theorizing Diaspora: A Reader*. Ed. Jana Evans Braziel and Anita Mannur. Blackwell, 2002. 25–48.

Appadurai, Arjun, ed. *Globalization*. Durham, NC: Duke University Press, 2001.

Appadurai, Arjun. *Modernity at Large: Cultural Dimensions of Globalization*. Minneapolis: University of Minnesota Press, 1996.

Appadurai, Arjun. "Disjuncture and Difference in the Global Cultural Economy." *Public Culture* 2.2 (1990): 1–24.

Applebaum, Richard P., and William I. Robinson, eds. *Critical Globalization Studies*. New York: Routledge, 2005.

Aral, Sevgi O., et al. "The Social Organization of Commercial Sex in Moscow, Russia." *Sexually Transmitted Diseases* 30.1 (2003): 39.

Arango, Joaquin, and Philip Martin. "Best Practices to Manage Migration: Morocco-Spain." *International Migration Review* 39.1 (2005): 258–269.

Arends-Kuenning, Mary. "The Balance of Care: Trends in the Wages and Employment of Immigrant Nurses in the US between 1990 and 2000." *Globalizations* 3.3 (2006): 333–348.

Arendt, Hannah. *The Origins of Totalitarianism*. New York: Harvest Books, 2005.

Arias, Donya C. "Experts Address Global Nursing Shortage, Put Forth Suggestions." *Nation's Health* 35.8 (2005): 14.

Armstrong, Fiona. "Migration of Nurses: Finding a Sustainable Solution (Cover story)." *Australian Nursing Journal* 11.3 (2003): 24–26.

Armstrong, Fiona. "Walking Away: Leaving Home and Leaving Nursing." *Australian Nursing Journal* 12.6: 18–19.

Aronson, Bernard W., and William D. Rogers. "Helping Cuban Families is in America's Interest." *Migration World Magazine* 28.1/2 (2000): 5.

Arthur, Charles. *Haiti: A Guide to the People, Politics and Culture*. Northampton, MA: Interlink Books; London: Latin American Bureau, 2002.

Arthur, John A. *Invisible Sojourners: African Immigrant Diaspora in the United States.* Westport, CT: Praeger, 2000.

Asante, Molefi Kete. *The Afrocentric Idea.* Philadelphia: Temple University Press, 1998.

Asante, Molefi Kete. *Afrocentricity.* Trenton, NJ: Africa World Press, 1987.

Asis, Maruja Milagros B., Huang, Shirlena, and Brenda S. A. Yeoh. "When the Light of the Home is Abroad: Unskilled Female Migration and the Filipino Family." *Singapore Journal of Tropical Geography* 25.2 (2004): 198–215.

Associated Press. "Remains of Guantanamo Suicides Sent Home." *Cincinnati Enquirer* (17 June 2006): A11.

Associated Press. "Gitmo, Insanity Defense Cases on Docket Today." *Cincinnati Enquirer* (29 June 2006): A5.

Associated Press. "Justices Say Bush Went Too Far at Guantanamo." *MSNBC* (29 June 2006). www.msnbc.msn.com/id/13592908/?GT1=8211&print=1&displaymode=1098.

Associated Press. "US Detainees Abroad Face a Legal Vacuum." *MSNBC* (18 Sept. 2006). www.msnbc.msn.com/id/14887908/print/1/displaymode/1098/.

Associated Press. "Accused Terrorist Wins Canadian Rights Case." *MSNBC* (24 Oct. 2006). www.msnbc.com/id/15400887/print/1/displaymode/1098.

Associated Press. "House Renews Patriot Act, But Senate Could Balk." *MSNBC* (14 Dec. 2005). www.msnbc.msn.com/id/10467408/.

Associated Press. "Australian Racial Violence Spills into 2nd Night." *MSNBC* (12 Dec. 2005). www.msnbc.msn.com/id/10430528/.

Augarde, J. "La Migration Algérienne. " *Hommes et Migrations*, 1970. 99–100.

Auster, Bruce B., and Kevin Whitelaw. "Terror's Cellblock." *US News & World Report* 134.16 (2003): 21.

Ayoub, Nina C. "Nota Bene." *Chronicle of Higher Education* 52.22 (2006): A20.

Azam, Farooq-i. "Emigration Dynamics in Pakistan." *International Migration* 33.3/4 (1995): 729.

B. K. "Cuba Libre." *New York* 37.29 (2004): 166.

Bacevich, Andrew. *American Empire: The Realities and Consequences of US Diplomacy.* Cambridge, MA: Harvard University Press, 2002.

"Background Information on Haiti." School of the Americas Watch. Available online at: www.soaw.org/new/article.php?id=750.

Bade, Klaus J., and Myron Weiner, eds. *Migration Past, Migration Future: Germany and the United States.* Providence: Berghahn, 1997.

Baernholdt, Marianne, and Hayley Mark. "An Internship at the International Council of Nurses." *American Journal of Nursing* 101.11 (2001): 81.

Bain, Irene. "South-East Asia." *International Migration* 36.4 (1998): 553.

Balderrama, Francisco E., and Raymond Rodríguez. *Decade of Betrayal: Mexican Repatriation in the 1930s.* Albuquerque: University of New Mexico Press, 1995.

Baldoz, Rick. "Empire of Care: Nursing and Migration in Filipino American History." *Contemporary Sociology* 34.1 (2005): 52–53.

Bales, Kevin. "Because She Looks Like a Child." *Global Woman: Nannies, Maids, and Sex Workers in the New Economy.* Ed. Barbara Ehrenreich and Arlie Russell Hochschild. New York: Metropolitan Books, Henry Holt, 2002. 207–229.

Bales, Kevin. "Working Paper" freetheslaves.org.

Ballard, John R. *Upholding Democracy: The United States Military Campaign in Haiti, 1994–1997.* Westport, CT: Praeger, 1998.

Bannon, Ian, and Paul Collier, eds. *Natural Resources and Violent Conflict: Options and Actions.* Washington, DC: International Bank for Reconstruction and Development, 2003.

Bao, Jiemin. *Marital Acts: Gender, Sexuality, and Identity among the Chinese Thai Diaspora*. Honolulu: University of Hawai'i Press, 2005.

Barbassa, Juliana. "Female Immigrants Earn Less, But Send More Home." Associated Press. September 7, 2006.

Barber, Benjamin. *Fear's Empire: War, Terrorism, and Democracy*. W. W. Norton, 2003.

Barber, Benjamin. *McWorld vs. Jihad*. New York: Ballantine Books, 1996.

Barlas, Dilek. *Etatism and Diplomacy in Turkey*. New York: Brill, 1998.

Barrett, Christopher B., and Daniel G. Maxwell. *Food Aid After Fifty Years: Recasting Its Role*. New York: Routledge, 2005.

Barry, John, et al. "Abu Ghraib and Beyond." *Newsweek* 143.20 (2004): 32–38.

Basch, Linda, Nina Glick Schiller, and Cristina Szanton Blanc. *Nations Unbound: Transnational Projects, Postcolonial Predicaments, and Deterritorialized Nation-States*. Langhorne, PA: Gordon & Breach, 1994.

Basok, Tanya. "Migration of Mexican Seasonal Farm Workers to Canada and Development: Obstacles to Productive Investment." *International Migration Review* 34.1 (2000): 79–97.

Bauböck, Rainer. *Transnational Citizenship: Membership and Rights in International Migration*. Aldershot: Edward Elgar Publishing, 1994.

Baver, Sherri L. "Including Migration in the Development Calculus: The Dominican Republic and other Caribbean . . ." *Latin American Research Review* 30.1 (1995): 191.

Baviskar, Amita. *In the Belly of the River: Tribal Conflicts over Development in the Narmada Valley*. Oxford: Oxford University Press, 2004.

Beauregard, Robert A., and Sophie Body-Gendrot, eds. *The Urban Moment: Cosmopolitan Essays on the Late-20th-Century City*. Thousand Oaks, CA: Sage, 1999.

Begag, Azouz. "The 'Beurs', Children of North African Immigrants in France: The Issue of Integration." *Journal of Ethnic Studies* 18.1 (1990).

Begg, Moazzam. "Tortured Truth." *New Statesman* 135.4798 (2006): 19.

Bell, Beverly. *Walking on Fire: Haitian Women's Stories of Survival and Resistance*. Ithaca: Cornell University Press, 2001.

Bell, David. "'Perverse Dynamics, Sexual Citizenship and the Transformation of Intimacy." *Mapping Desire: Geographies of Sexualities*. Ed. David Bell and Gill Valentine. New York: Routledge, 1995. 304–318.

Bell-Fialkoff, Andrew. *Ethnic Cleansing*. New York: St. Martin's Press, 1996.

Belza, M. J. "Risk of HIV Infection among Male Sex Workers in Spain." *Sexually Transmitted Infections* 81.1 (2005): 85–88.

Benchellali, Mourad. "Detainees in Despair." *New York Times* (14 June 2006): A 23, Op-Ed.

Berggren, Vanja, Staffan Bergström, and Anna-Karin Edberg. "Being Different and Vulnerable: Experiences of Immigrant African Women Who Have Been Circumcised and Sought Maternity Care in Sweden." *Journal of Transcultural Nursing* 17.1 (2006): 50–57.

Beriss, David. *Black Skins, French Voices: Caribbean Ethnicity and Activism in Urban France*. Boulder: Westview Press, 2004.

Berlant, Lauren. "The Queen of America Goes to Washington City: Harriet Jacobs, Frances Harper, Anita Hill." *Feminisms: An Anthology of Literary Theory and Criticism*. New Brunswick, NJ: Rutgers University Press, 1997. 931–950.

Berlant, Lauren. "The Theory of Infantile Citizenship." *Public Culture* 5.3 (1993): 395–410.

Berlant, Lauren. "Queer Nationality." *Boundary 2: An International Journal of Literature and Culture* 19.1 (Spring 1992): 149–180.

Berlant, Lauren. "National Brands/National Body: Imitation of Life." *Comparative American Identities: Race, Sex, and Nationality in the Modern Text.* Ed. Hortense Spillers. New York: Routledge, 1991. 110–140.

Berlant, Lauren, and Elizabeth Freeman. "Queer Nationality: The Political Logic of Queer Nation and Gay Activism." *Fear of a Queer Planet: Queer Politics and Social Theory.* Ed. Michael Warner. Minneapolis: University of Minnesota Press, 1993. 193–229.

Berlant, Lauren, and Michael Warner. "Sex in Public." *Critical Inquiry* 24.2 (Winter 1998): 547–566.

Berlant, Lauren, Michael Warner, et al. "Forum: On the Political Implications of Using the Term 'Queer,' as in 'Queer Politics,' 'Queer Studies,' and 'Queer Pedagogy'." *Radical Teacher* 45 (Winter 1994): 52–57.

Berman, Jacqueline. "(Un)Popular Strangers and Crises (Un)Bounded: Discourses of Sex-Trafficking, the European Political Community and the Panicked State of the Modern State." *European Journal of International Relations* 9.1 (2003): 37–86.

Bernard, Ariane. "Attackers Set Fire to Bus in Marseille, Wounding One." *New York Times* (30 Oct. 2006): A6.

Bernard, Ariane. "In Paris Suburbs, Worrying Attack by Youths." *New York Times* (1 June 2006): A6.

Bernstein, Ann, and Myron Weiner, eds. *Migration and Refugee Policies: An Overview.* New York: Pinter, 1999.

Berrgmann, Emilie L., and Paul Julia Smith, eds. *¿Entiendes? Queer Readings, Hispanic Writings.* Durham, NC: Duke University Press, 1995.

Bertram, Geoff. "Introduction: The MIRAB Model in the Twenty-First Century." *Asia Pacific Viewpoint* 47.1 (2006): 1–13.

Bhatia, Bela. "Widows, Land Rights and Resettlements in the Narmada Valley." *Widows in India: Social Neglect and Public Action.* Ed. Martha Alter Chen. Thousand Oaks, CA: Sage, 1998. 257–260.

Bhatia, Bela. "Forced Evictions in the Narmada Valley." *The Dam and the Nation: Displacement and Resettlement in the Narmada Valley.* Ed. Jean Drèze, Meera Samson, and Satyajit Singh. Oxford: Oxford University Press, 1997. 267–321.

Bialke, Joseph P. "'Dutch': Al-Qaeda and Taliban Unlawful Combatant Detainees, Unlawful Belligerency, and the International Laws of Armed Conflict." *Air Force Law Review* 55 (2004): 1–85.

Bigo, Didier, and Elspeth Guild, eds. *Controlling Frontiers: Free Movement Into and Within Europe.* Aldershot: Ashgate, 2005.

Bilsborrow, R. E., Graeme Hugo, A. S. Oberai, and Hania Zlotnik, eds. *International Migration Statistics: Guidelines for Improving Data Collection Systems.* Geneva: International Labor Office, 1997.

Binford, Leigh. "Migrant Remittances and (Under)Development in Mexico." *Critique of Anthropology* 23.3 (2003): 305–336.

Binnie, Jon. *The Globalization of Sexuality.* Thousand Oaks, CA: Sage, 2004.

Bischoff, Henry. *Immigration Issues.* Westport, CT: Greenwood Press, 2002.

Bishop, Ryan, and Lillian S. Robinson. *Night Market: Sexual Cultures and the Thai Economic Miracle.* New York: Routledge, 1998.

Blatt, David. "Immigrant Politics in a Republic Nation." *Post-Colonial Cultures in France.* Ed. A. G. Hargreaves and M. McKinney. New York: Routledge, 1997. 40–58.

"Blistering Fight." *CQ Researcher* 16.29 (2006): 691.

Bloch, Alice. "Emigration from Zimbabwe: Migrant Perspectives." *Social Policy & Administration* 40.1 (2006): 67–87.

Bloche, M. Gregg, and Jonathan H. Marks. "Doctors and Interrogators at Guantanamo Bay." *New England Journal of Medicine* 353.1 (2005): 6–8.

Boeri, Tito, Gordon Hanson, and Barry McCormick, eds. *Immigration Policy and the Welfare System*. A Report for the Fondazione Rodolfo Debenedetti in Association with the William Davidson Institute. Oxford: Oxford University Press, 2002.

Bonner, Raymond. "Detainee Says He Was Tortured in US Custody (Cover story)." *New York Times* 154.53124 (2005): 1–15.

Bookman, Milicia Z. *Ethnic Groups in Motion: Economic Competition and Migration in Multiethnic States*. London: Frank Cass, 2002.

"Books received." *Ethnic & Racial Studies* 27.3 (2004): 528–532.

Boontinand, Jan. "Feminist Participatory Action Research in the Mekong Region." *Trafficking and Prostitution Reconsidered: New Perspectives on Migration, Sex Work, and Human Rights*. Ed. Kamala Kempadoo, Jyoti Sanghera, and Bandana Pattanaik. Boulder: Paradigm Publishers, 2005. 175–198.

Booth, Kim, and Tim Dunne, eds. *Worlds in Collision: Terror and the Future of Global Order*. New York: Palgrave Macmillan, 2002.

Borjas, George J., ed. *Issues in the Economics of Immigration*. Chicago: University of Chicago Press, 2000.

Borjas, George J. *Heaven's Door: Immigration Policy and the American Economy*. Princeton: Princeton University Press, 1999.

Borovnik, Maria. "Working Overseas: Seafarers' Remittances and their Distribution in Kiribati." *Asia Pacific Viewpoint* 47.1 (2006): 151–161.

Bose, Christine E., and Edna Acosta-Belen, eds. *Women in the Latin American Development Process*. Philadelphia: Temple University Press, 1995.

Bose, Meena, and Rosanna Perotti, eds. *From Cold War to New World Order: Foreign Policy of George Bush*. Westport, CT: Greenwood Press, 2002.

Bosman, Julie. "Evictions Raise the Tension Level at Guantánamo." *New York Times* (19 June 2006): C3.

Boswell, Christina. *European Migration Policies in Flux: Changing Patterns of Inclusion and Exclusion*. Oxford: Blackwell, 2003.

Bousquet, Gisèle L. *Behind the Bamboo Hedge: The Impact of Homeland Politics in the Parisian Vietnamese Community*. Ann Arbor: University of Michigan Press, 1991.

Boyle, Frances M., Shirley Glennon, Jake M. Najman, Gavin Turrell, John S. Western, and Carole Wood, eds. *The Sex Industry: A Survey of Sex Workers in Queensland, Australia*. Aldershot: Ashgate, 1997.

Boyle, Paul. "Population Geography: Transnational Women on the Move." *Progress in Human Geography* 26.4 (2002): 531–543.

Bradshaw, York W., and Michael Wallace. *Global Inequalities*. Thousand Oaks, CA: Pine Forge Press, 1996.

Brah, Avtar, Mary J. Hickman, and Maírtín Mac an Ghaill, eds. *Global Futures: Migration, Environment and Globalization*. Basingstoke: Macmillan; New York: St. Martin's Press, 1999.

Bras, Hilde. "Maids to the City: Migration Patterns of Female Domestic Servants from the Province of Zeeland, the Netherlands (1850–1950)." *History of the Family* 8.2 (2003): 217.

Braverman, Paul. "The Loneliest Cause." *American Lawyer* 24.12 (2002): 89.

Bravin, Jess. "Guantanamo Bay Detainees Seek Hearings." *Wall Street Journal – Eastern Edition* 240.3 (2002): A4.

Bravin, Jess. "Judge Says Courts Have No Power Over Guantanamo Bay Detainees." *Wall Street Journal – Eastern Edition* 240.23 (2002): B8.

Bravin, Jess. "Panel Says US Policy on Detainees In Cuba Breaks International Law." *Wall Street Journal – Eastern Edition* 239.51 (2002): B2.

Bravin, Jess. "Guantanamo Defense Lawyers Are Barred From Status Hearings." *Wall Street Journal – Eastern Edition* 244.55 (2004): A8.

Bravin, Jess. "US to Unveil Review System for Guantanamo Detainees." *Wall Street Journal – Eastern Edition* 243.120 (2004): B1–B3.

Bravin, Jess. "Critics of Tribunals Gain Unlikely Allies: Lawyers in Uniform." *Wall Street Journal – Eastern Edition* 243.54 (2004): A1–A6.

Bravin, Jess. "Lawyers for Saudi Prisoner Ask Court to Throw Out Roberts Ruling." *Wall Street Journal – Eastern Edition* 246.42 (2005): A4.

Bravin, Jess. "Justices Hear Challenge to Plan For Guantanamo-Prisoner Trials." *Wall Street Journal – Eastern Edition* 247.73 (2006): A6.

Bravin, Jess, and Alex Frangos. "Who's Held at Guantanamo?" *Wall Street Journal – Eastern Edition* 244.86 (2004): B1–B2.

Bravin, Jess, Jackie Calmes, and Carla Anne Robbins. "Status of Guantanamo Bay Detainees Is Focus of Bush Security Team's Meeting." *Wall Street Journal – Eastern Edition* 239.19 (2002): A16.

Bravin, Jess, David S. Cloud, and Laurie P. Cohen. "US Dismisses Queries About Cuba Detainees." *Wall Street Journal – Eastern Edition* 239.16 (2002): B12.

Braziel, Jana Evans, and Anita Mannur, eds. *Theorizing Diaspora: A Reader*. Oxford: Blackwell, 2002.

Braziel, Jana Evans, and Anita Mannur. "Nation, Migration, Globalization: Points of Contention in Diaspora Studies." *Theorizing Diaspora: A Reader*. Ed. Braziel and Mannur. Oxford: Blackwell, 2002.

Brecher, Jeremy, John Brown Childs, and Jill Cutler, eds. *Global Visions: Beyond the New World Order*. Boston: South End Press, 1993.

Brennan, Denise. *What's Love Got to Do With It? Transnational Desires and Sex Tourism in the Dominican Republic*. Durham, NC: Duke University Press, 2004.

Brennan, Denise. "Selling Sex for Visas: Sex Tourism as a Stepping-stone to International Migration." *Global Woman: Nannies, Maids, and Sex Workers in the New Economy*. Ed. Barbara Ehrenreich and Arlie Russell Hochschild. New York: Metropolitan Books, Henry Holt, 2002. 154–168.

Brenner, Michael. *The Renaissance of Jewish Culture in Weimar Germany*. New Haven: Yale University Press, 1996.

Brettell, Caroline B., and James F. Hollifield, eds. *Migration Theory: Talking across Disciplines*. New York: Routledge, 2000.

Brewis, Joanna, and Stephen Linstead. *Sex, Work and Sex Work: Eroticizing Organization*. New York: Routledge, 2000.

Bridge, Gary, and Sophie Watson, eds. *A Companion to the City*. Oxford: Blackwell, 2000.

Brinkley, Joel. "From Afghanistan to Saudi Arabia, via Guantánamo." *New York Times* 154.53004 (2004): A4.

"Britain's Guantanamo." British Broadcasting Corporation (26 Jan. 2005). BBC News Online. www.news.bbc.co.uk/go/pr/fr/-/2/hi/programmes/breakfast/4207875.stm.

Brock, Deborah R. *Making Work, Making Trouble: Prostitution as a Social Problem*. Toronto: University of Toronto Press, 1998.

Bronner, Luc. "Crise des banlieues, l'onde de choc. " *Le Monde* (5 Jan. 2006).

Brown, Cynthia, ed. *Lost Liberties: Ashcroft and the Assault on Personal Freedom*. New York: New Press, 2003.

Brown, Mary Elizabeth, ed. *Shapers of the Great Debate on Immigration: A Biographical Dictionary*. Westport, CT: Greenwood Press, 1999.

Brown, Richard P. C. "Estimating Remittance Functions for Pacific Island Migrants." *World Development* 25.4 (1997): 613.

Brown, Richard P. C., and John Connell. "Occupation-specific Analysis of Migration and Remittance Behaviour: Pacific Island Nurses in Australia and New Zealand." *Asia Pacific Viewpoint* 47.1 (2006): 135–150.

Brown, Richard P. C., and John Connell. "The Migration of Doctors and Nurses from South Pacific Island Nations." *Social Science & Medicine* 58.11 (2004): 2193.

Brown, Richard P. C., and Bernard Poirine. "A Model of Migrants' Remittances with Human Capital Investment and Intrafamilial Transfers." *International Migration Review* 39.2 (2005): 407–438.

Brown, Stuart S. "Can Remittances Spur Development? A Critical Survey." *International Studies Review* 8.1 (2006): 55–75.

Browne, Ray. "Convict Maids: The Forced Migration of Women to Australia (Book)." *Journal of Popular Culture* 33.4 (2000): 153.

Browning, Gary, Abigail Halcli, and Frank Webster, eds. *Understanding Contemporary Society: Theories of the Present.* Thousand Oaks, CA: Sage, 2000.

Brush, Barbara L., and Rukmini Vasupuram. "Nurses, Nannies and Caring Work: Importation, Visibility and Marketability." *Nursing Inquiry* 13.3 (2006): 181–185.

Bryant, Nancy H. *Women in Nursing in Islamic Societies.* Oxford: Oxford University Press, 2003.

Buchan, James. "Nurse Migration and International Recruitment." *Nursing Inquiry* (1 Dec. 2001a): 203+.

Buchan, James. "Guest Editorial." *International Nursing Review* (1 June 2001b): 65+.

Buchan, James, and Sochalski. "The Migration of Nurses: Trends and Policies." *Bulletin of the World Health Organization* 82.8 (August 2004): 587–594.

Buchan, James, Ian Seccombe, and Gabrielle Smith. *Nurses Work: An Analysis of the UK Nursing Labour Market.* Aldershot: Ashgate, 1998.

Buckley, Mary, and Sally Cummings, eds. *Kosovo: Perceptions of War and Its Aftermath.* London: Continuum, 2001.

Budman II, Jan L. "Rasul v. Bush: Exhorting Extrication of Executive Detainees from Camp X-Ray, Guantanamo Bay." *Widener Law Journal* 15.1 (2005): 175–229.

Budryte, Dovile. *Taming Nationalism? Political Community Building in the Post-Soviet Baltic States.* Aldershot: Ashgate, 2005.

Bumiller, Elisabeth. "Bush Now Favors Some Fencing Along Border." *New York Times* (19 May 2006): A19.

Burbach, Roger, Orlando Núñez, and Boris Kagarlitsky. *Globalization and Its Discontents: The Rise of Postmodern Socialisms.* London: Pluto Press, 1997.

Burg, Steven L., and Paul S. Shoup. *The War in Bosnia-Herzegovina: Ethnic Conflict and International Intervention.* Armonk, NY: M. E. Sharpe, 1999.

Burger, Timothy J. "At Gitmo, the Wait Goes On." *Time* 165.5 (2005): 18.

"Bush Signs Bill Allowing Prosecution Of Detainees In Cuba." *Congress Daily* (2006): 9.

Bush, George W. "The President's News Conference With Chancellor Angela Merkel of Germany." *Weekly Compilation of Presidential Documents* 42.2 (2006): 64–69.

Bush, George W., and Vicente Fox. "The President's News Conference With President Vicente Fox of Mexico in Monterrey, Mexico." *Weekly Compilation of Presidential Documents* 40.3 (2004): 54–60.

Bustamante, Jorge A., Clark W. Reynolds, and Raul A. Hinojosa Ojeda, eds. *US–Mexico Relations: Labor Market Interdependence.* Stanford: Stanford University Press, 1992.

"Busted Flush (Cover story)." *National Review* 57.10 (2005): 14.

Busza, Joanna, Sarah Castle, and Aisse Diarra. "Trafficking and Health." *BMJ: British Medical Journal* 328.7452 (2004): 1369–1371.

"But Is It Theatre?" *Economist* 372.8382 (2004): 71–72.

Butler, Judith. "Guantanamo Limbo." *Nation* 274.12 (2002): 20–24.

Butler, Kim D. "Abolition and the Politics of Identity in the Afro-Atlantic Diaspora: Toward a Comparative Approach." *Crossing Boundaries: Comparative History of Black People in Diaspora*. Ed. Darlene Clark Hine and Jacqueline McLeod. Bloomington: Indiana University Press, 1999. 121–32.

Buxton, Nick. "Debt Cancellation and Civil Society: A Case Study of Jubilee 2000." *Fighting for Human Rights*. Ed. Paul Gready. New York: Routledge, 2004. 54–77.

Cabezas, Amalia Lucía. "Accidental Crossings: Tourism, Sex Work, and Women's Rights in the Dominican Republic." *Dialogue and Difference: Feminisms Challenge Globalization*. Ed. Marguerite Waller and Sylvia Marcos. Basingstoke: Palgrave Macmillan, 2005. 201–230.

Caglar, Ayse. "Hometown Associations, the Rescaling of State Spatiality and Migrant Grassroots Transnationalism." *Global Networks* 6.1 (2006): 1–22.

Calabrese, Andrew, and Jean-Claude Burgelman, eds. *Communication, Citizenship, and Social Policy: Rethinking the Limits of the Welfare State*. Lanham, MD: Rowman & Littlefield, 1999.

Caldwell, Christopher. "The Lessons from Londonistan." *New York Times Magazine* (25 June 2006).

Calhoun, Craig, Paul Price, and Ashley Timmer, eds. *Understanding September 11*. New York: New Press, 2002.

Calliste, Agnes. "Race, Gender and Canadian Immigration Policy: Blacks from the Caribbean, 1900–1932." *Journal of Canadian Studies* 28.4 (1993): 131.

Campbell, Susan. "Responding to International Disasters." *Nursing Standard* 19.21 (2005): 33–36.

Campesino, Maureen, and Gary E. Schwartz. "Spirituality among Latinas/os: Implications of Culture in Conceptualization and Measurement." *Advances in Nursing Science* 29.1 (2006): 69–81.

Campt, Tina. *Other Germans: Black Germans and the Politics of Race, Gender, and Memory in the Third Reich*. Ann Arbor: University of Michigan Press, 2004.

"Can Migration Cure Nurse Shortages? Should It?" *Health Affairs* 23.3 (May/June 2004): 68.

Cannon, Angie. "A Bit of Clarity from the Court." *US News & World Report* 137.1 (2004): 36.

Cantú, Lionel, Jr. "A Place Called Home: A Queer Political Economy." *Sexuality and Gender*. Ed. Christine L. Williams and Arlene Stein. Oxford: Blackwell, 2002. 382–394.

Caplan, Richard. *Europe and the Recognition of New States in Yugoslavia*. Cambridge: Cambridge University Press, 2005.

Carling, Jørgen. "Cartographies of Cape Verdean Transnationalism." *Global Networks* 3.4 (2003): 533.

Carter, Terry. "New Defense Measures Ok'd." *ABA Journal* 90.4 (2004): 68.

Castles, Stephen. *Ethnicity and Globalization: From Migrant Worker to Transnational Citizen*. Thousand Oaks, CA: Sage, 2000.

Castles, Stephen, and Mark J. Miller. *The Age of Migration: International Population Movements in the Modern World*. New York: Guilford Press, 2003.

Castro, Max J., ed. *Free Markets, Open Societies, Closed Borders? Trends in International Migration and Immigration Policy in the Americas.* Coral Gables, FL: North-South Center Press; Boulder: Lynne Rienner, 1999.

Catanese, Anthony. *Haitians: Migration and Diaspora.* Boulder: Westview Press, 1999.

Caufield, Catherine. "The Holiest River." *Masters of Illusion: The World Bank and the Poverty of Nations.* New York: Henry Holt, 1996. 5–29.

Cave, Damien. "US Says Inmate Legal Notes May Have Aided Suicide Plot." *New York Times* (9 July 2006): A15.

Ceniza Choy, Catherine. *Empire of Care: Nursing and Migration in Filipino American History.* Durham, NC: Duke University Press, 2003.

Chadha, Ashish. "The Anatomy of Dispossession: A Study in the Displacement of the Tribals from their Traditional Landscape in the Narmada Valley due to the Sardar Sarovar Project." *The Archaeology and Anthropology of Landscape.* Ed. Peter J. Ucko and Robert Layton. New York: Routledge, 1999. 147–158.

Chang, Grace. *Disposable Domestics: Immigrant Women Workers in the Global Economy.* Cambridge, MA: South End Press, 2000.

Chang, Iris. *The Chinese in America: A Narrative History.* New York: Viking, 2003.

Chang, Leslie T. "At 18, Min Finds A Path to Success In Migration Wave." *Wall Street Journal – Eastern Edition* 244.91 (2004): A1–A10.

"Checklist of White House Press Releases." *Weekly Compilation of Presidential Documents* 42.36 (2006): 1593–1594.

Cheever, Susan. "The Nanny Dilemma." *Global Woman: Nannies, Maids, and Sex Workers in the New Economy.* Ed. Barbara Ehrenreich and Arlie Russell Hochschild. New York: Metropolitan Books, Henry Holt, 2002. 31–38.

Cheng Sim, Hew. "Singles, Sex and Salaries: The Experiences of Single Bidayuh Women Migrants in Kuching." *Asian Studies Review* 25.3 (2001): 361.

Chew, Lin. "Reflections by an Anti-Trafficking Activist." *Trafficking and Prostitution Reconsidered: New Perspectives on Migration, Sex Work, and Human Rights.* Ed. Kamala Kempadoo, Jyoti Sanghera, and Bandana Pattanaik. Boulder: Paradigm Publishers, 2005. 65–82.

Chikanda, Abel. "Nurse Migration from Zimbabwe: Analysis of Recent Trends and Impacts." *Nursing Inquiry* 12.3 (2005): 162–174.

Child, Nick. "Guantanamo Controversy Rumbles On." British Broadcasting Corporation (18 Oct. 2004). BBC News Online: www.news.bbc.co.uk/2/hi/americas/3754238.stm.

Chin, Christine B. N. "Walls of Silence and Late Twentieth Century Representations of the Foreign Female Domestic Worker: The Case of Filipina and Indonesian Female Servants in Malaysia." *International Migration Review* 31.2 (1997): 353–385.

Chin, Ko-Lin. *Smuggled Chinese: Clandestine Immigration to the United States.* Philadelphia: Temple University Press, 1999.

Chomsky, Noam. "Democracy Enhancement, part 2: The Case of Haiti." *Z Magazine* (July/August 1994). Electronic journal. Date accessed: October 2003. www.zmag.org/chomsky/articles/z9407–dem-enhance-2.html.

Chomsky, Noam, Paul Farmer, and Amy Goodman, eds. *Getting Haiti Right This Time: The US and the Coup.* Monroe, ME: Common Courage Press, 2004.

Choo, Vivien. "Philippines Losing Its Nurses, and Now Maybe Its Doctors." *The Lancet* 361.9366 (2003): 1356.

Christian, Louise. "Cowboy Courts." *Lawyer* 17.30 (2003): US5.

Christopher, Kimberly A. "Determinants of Psychological Well-Being in Irish Immigrants." *Western Journal of Nursing Research* 22.2 (2000): 123.

"Chronologie: Les violences urbaines au jour le jour." *Le Monde.* www.lemonde.fr/web/module_chrono/0,11–0@2-3226,32-705641,0.html.

Chu, Jeff, and Sue Cullinan. "World Watch." *Time Europe* 159.7 (2002): 12.

"Church Delegation Barred from Guantanamo." *National Catholic Reporter* 40.14 (2004): 7.

Cleary, Joe, and Claire Connolly, eds. *The Cambridge Companion to Modern Irish Culture.* Cambridge: Cambridge University Press, 2005.

Cleveland, David A. "Migration in West Africa: A Savanna Village Perspective." *Africa* 61.2 (1991): 222–246.

Clifford, James. "Diasporas." *Cultural Anthropology* 9.3 (1994): 302–338.

Clifford, James. "Traveling Cultures." *Cultural Studies.* Ed. Lawrence Grossberg, Cary Nelson, and P. Treichler. New York: Routledge, 1992. 96–116.

Cliggett, Lisa. "Gift Remitting and Alliance Building in Zambian Modernity: Old Answers to Modern Problems." *American Anthropologist* 105.3 (2003): 543–552.

Cloud, David S. "State Dept. Disavows Statement on Suicides." *New York Times* (13 June 2006): A19.

Cloud, David S. "Guantánamo Reprimand Was Sought, An Aide Says." *New York Times* 154.53274 (2005): A16.

Cloud, David S., and Neil A. Lewis. "Prisoner's Ruse is Inquiry Focus at Guantánamo." *New York Times* 155.53608 (2006): A1–A14.

Cloud, David S., Sheryl Gay Stolberg, and Kate Zernike. "White House Bill Proposes System to Try Detainees (Cover story)." *New York Times* 155.53652 (2006): A1–A15.

Cockburn, Alexander. "Chickens in a Darkening Sky." *Nation* 276.14 (2003): 9.

Cohen, Jeffrey H. "Remittance Outcomes and Migration: Theoretical Contests, Real Opportunities." *Studies in Comparative International Development* 40.1 (2005): 88–112.

Cohen, Jeffrey H. *The Culture of Migration in Southern Mexico.* Austin: University of Texas Press, 2004.

Cohen, Jeffrey H., Richard Jones, and Dennis Conway. "Why Remittances Shouldn't Be Blamed for Rural Underdevelopment in Mexico: A Collective Response to Leigh Binford." *Critique of Anthropology* 25.1 (2005): 87–96.

Cohen, Jon. "HIV and Heroin: A Deadly International Affair." *Science* 301.5640 (2003): 1657–1658.

Cohen, Nick. "Can Judges Restore America's Honour?" *New Statesman* 133.4689 (2004): 23–24.

Cohen, Richard E., and Peter Bell. "Congressional Insiders Poll." *National Journal* 38.28 (2006): 6–8.

Cohen, Robin. *Global Diasporas: An Introduction.* Seattle: University of Washington Press, 1997.

Cohen, Robin, ed. *The Sociology of Migration.* Brookfield, VT: Edward Elgar, 1996.

Cohen, Robin, ed. *The Cambridge Survey of World Migration.* Cambridge: Cambridge University Press, 1995.

Cohen, Stanley. "Post-Moral Torture: From Guantanamo to Abu Ghraib." *Index on Censorship* 34.1 (2005): 24–30.

Cohen, Steve. *Deportation is Freedom! The Orwellian World of Immigration Controls.* Philadelphia: Jessica Kingsley Publishers, 2006.

Cohen, Steve, Beth Humphries, and Ed Mynott, eds. *From Immigration Controls to Welfare Controls.* New York: Routledge, 2002.

Coicaud, Jean-Marc, Michael W. Doyle, and Anne-Marie Gardner, eds. *The Globalization of Human Rights*. New York: United Nations University Press, 2003.

Cole, David. "Bad Guys." *Nation* 278.18 (2004): 24.

Cole, David. "Guantánamo, Revisited." *Nation* 3 May 2004: 7+.

Cole, David. "Korematsu II?" *Nation* 277.19 (2003): 6–7.

Cole, David. "Defending Show Trials." *Nation* 276.23 (2003): 6.

Cole, David. "Guantánamo Gulag." *Nation* 276.22 (2003): 5–6.

Cole, Phillip. *Philosophies of Exclusion: Liberal Political Theory and Immigration*. Edinburgh: Edinburgh University Press, 2000.

"Confused by Law, Nursing Homes Bar Legal Immigrant." *Migration World Magazine* 25.4 (1997): 12.

Connell, John. "Losing Ground? Tuvalu, the Greenhouse Effect and the Garbage Can." *Asia Pacific Viewpoint* 44.2 (2003): 89–107.

Connell, John, and Dennis Conway. "Migration and Remittances in Island Microstates: A Comparative Perspective on the South Pacific and the Caribbean." *International Journal of Urban & Regional Research* 24.1 (2000): 52–78.

Conover, Ted. "In the Land of Guantánamo." *New York Times Magazine* 152.52529 (2003): 40.

Constable, Nicole. "Filipina Workers in Hong Kong Homes: Household Rules and Relations." *Global Woman: Nannies, Maids, and Sex Workers in the New Economy*. Ed. Barbara Ehrenreich and Arlie Russell Hochschild. New York: Metropolitan Books, Henry Holt, 2002. 115–141.

Constable, Nicole. *Maid to Order in Hong Kong: Stories of Filipina Women*. Ithaca: Cornell University Press, 1997.

"Continuing Embarrassment." *America* (13 Mar. 2006): 4+.

Cooper, Christopher, and Jess Bravin. "US Studies How Detainees' Status Might Be Changed." *Wall Street Journal – Eastern Edition* 245.120 (2005): A6.

Cooper, Christopher. "Pentagon Is Set to Convene First Guantanamo Tribunals." *Wall Street Journal – Eastern Edition* 244.16 (2004): A9.

Copjec, Joan, and Michael Sorkin, eds. *Giving Ground: The Politics of Propinquity*. New York: Verso, 1999.

Cornelius, Wayne A., Takeyuki Ysuda, Philip L. Martin, and James F. Hollifield, eds. *Controlling Immigration: A Global Perspective*. Stanford: Stanford University Press, 2004.

Corpuz-Brock, Jane. "Gospel, Cultures, and Filipina Migrant Workers." *International Review of Mission* 85.336 (1996): 63.

Corrin, Chris. "Traffic in Women in War and Peace: Mapping Experiences in Southeast Europe." *Journal of Contemporary European Studies* 12.2 (2004): 177–192.

Coulter, Ann. "Guantanamo Loses Five-Star Rating." *Human Events* 61.22 (2005): 6.

Coulter, Ann. "Losing Their Heads Over Gitmo." *Human Events* 61.21 (2005): 6.

Coulter, Ann. "Lookin' For Love in All the Wrong Places." *Human Events* 58.5 (2002): 6.

"Court Rules Against War Crimes Trials For Guantanamo Detainees." *Congress Daily* (2006): 10.

Cowan, David T., and Ian Norman. "Cultural Competence in Nursing: New Meanings." *Journal of Transcultural Nursing* 17.1 (2006): 82–88.

Cowell, Alan. "Panels Say Britain Underrated Threat Before July Attacks." *New York Times* (12 May 2006): A16.

Cowell, Alan. "A Year Later, Homegrown Terror Still Baffles Britons." *New York Times* (6 July 2006): A3.

Crahan, Margaret E., and Alberto Vourvoulias-Bush, eds. *The City and the World: New York's Global Future*. New York: Council on Foreign Relations, 1997.

Craige, John Houston. *Black Baghdad*. New York: Minton, Balch, 1933.

Crane, Stephen. *Wounds in the Rain: War Stories*. Plainview, NY: Books for Libraries Press, 1976.

"Crime and Punishment." *Economist* 371.8374 (2004): 43–44.

Crook, John R., ed. "Contemporary Practice of the United States Relating to International Law." *American Journal of International Law* 99.2 (2005): 479–503.

Cruickshank, Dan. "Afghanistan: At the Crossroads of Ancient Civilisations." British Broadcasting Corporation. BBC News Online: www.bbc.co.uk/history/recent/sept_11/afghan_culture_print,html .

Cruz-Malavé, Arnaldo. "Toward an Art of Transvestism: Colonialism and Homosexuality in Puerto Rican Literature." *Queer Representations: Reading Lives, Reading Cultures*. Ed. Martin Duberman. New York: New York University Press, 1997. 226–244.

Cruz-Malavé, Arnaldo. "Toward an Art of Transvestism: Colonialism and Homosexuality in Puerto Rican Literature." *¿Entiendes? Queer Readings, Hispanic Writings*. Ed. Emilie L. Bergmann and Paul Julian Smith. Durham, NC: Duke University Press, 1995. 137–167.

Cruz-Malavé, Arnaldo, and Martin F. Manalansan IV, eds. *Queer Globalizations: Citizenship and the Afterlife of Colonialism*. New York: New York University Press, 2002.

Cruz-Malavé, Arnaldo, and Martin F. Manalansan IV. "Introduction: Dissident Sexualities/Alternative Globalisms." *Queer Globalizations: Citizenship and the Afterlife of Colonialism*. New York: New York University Press, 2002. 1–10.

"Cuba Abandons Vote on Detainees Held by US at Guantánamo." *New York Times* 153.52828 (2004): A13.

Cueva, Susan. "Susan Cueva Talks to Caroline Sweetman About Migrant Workers." *Gender & Development* 3.3 (1995): 55–59.

Cwickel, Julie, and Elizabeth Hoban. "Contentious Issues in Research on Trafficked Women Working in the Sex Industry: Study Design, Ethics, and Methodology." *Journal of Sex Research* 42.4 (November 2005): 306–316.

Dahlstrom, K. Elizabeth. "The Executive Policy Towards Detention and Trial of Foreign Citizens at Guantanamo Bay." *Berkeley Journal of International Law* 21.3 (2003): 662.

Dao, James. "Detainees Stage Protest at Base Over Turban." *New York Times* 151.52044 (2002): A12.

Dash, J. Michael. *Culture and Customs of Haiti*. Westport, CT: Greenwood Press, 2001.

Davidson, Cynthia, ed. *Anytime*. Cambridge, MA: MIT Press, 1999.

Davidson, Cynthia C., ed. *Anywise*. Cambridge, MA: MIT Press, 1996.

Davidson, Julia O'Connell, and Jacqueline Sanchez Taylor. "Fantasy Islands: Exploring the Demand for Sex Tourism." *Sexuality and Gender*. Ed. Christine L. Williams and Arlene Stein. Oxford: Blackwell, 2002. 355–368.

Day, Sophie, and Helen Ward, eds. *Sex Work, Mobility and Health in Europe*. London: Kegan Paul, 2004.

Dayan, Joan. "Paul Gilroy's Slaves, Ships, and Routes: The Middle Passage as Metaphor." *Research in African Literatures* 27.4 (Fall 1996): 7–14.

De Bardeleben, Joan. *Soft or Hard Borders? Managing the Divide in an Enlarged Europe*. Aldershot: Ashgate, 2005.

de Beer, Patrice. "France's Incendiary Crisis." www.opendemocracy.net/globalization-institutions_government/justice_2827.jsp.

De Feyter, Koen. *Human Rights: Social Justice in the Age of Market*. New York: Zed Books, 2005.

De Greiff, Pablo, and Ciaran Cronin, eds. *Global Justice and Transnational Politics*. Cambridge, MA: MIT Press, 2002.

de Haas, Hein. "International Migration, Remittances and Development: Myths and Facts." *Third World Quarterly* 26.8 (2005): 1269–1284.

de Haas, Hein, and Roald Plug. "Cherishing the Goose with the Golden Eggs: Trends in Migrant Remittances from Europe to Morocco 1970–2004." *International Migration Review* 40.3 (2006): 603–634.

De Vries, Petra. "'White Slaves' in a Colonial Nation: The Dutch Campaign against the Traffic in Women in the Early Twentieth Century." *Social & Legal Studies* 14.1 (2005): 39–60.

Dedman, Bill. "Gitmo Interrogations Spark Battle Over Tactics." *MSNBC* (23 Oct. 2006). www.msnbc.msn.com/id/15361458/print/1/displaymode/1098.

Dedman, Bill. "Can the '20th Hijacker' of Sept. 11 Stand Trial?" *MSNBC* (24 Oct. 2006). www.msnbc.msn.com/id/15361462/1/displaymode/1098.

Delacoste, Frédérique, and Priscilla Alexander, eds. *Sex Work: Writings by Women in the Sex Industry*. San Francisco: Cleis Press, 1987.

DeLaet, Debra L. *US Immigration Policy in an Age of Rights*. Westport, CT: Praeger, 2000.

Delphy, Christine. "Gender, Race and Racism: The Ban of the Islamic Headscarf in France." *Transnational Migration and the Politics of Identity*. Ed. Meenakshi Thapan. Thousand Oaks, CA: Sage, 2005. 228–251.

Deneulin, Séverine. "Individual Well-being, Migration Remittances and the Common Good." *European Journal of Development Research* 18.1 (2006): 45–58.

Derderian, Richard L. *North Africans in Contemporary France: Becoming Visible*. Basingstoke: Palgrave Macmillan, 2004.

"Despite Ruling, Tribunals Continue in Cuba." *New York Times* 154.53029 (2004): A17.

"Detainees to Receive Protections." *Cincinnati Enquirer* (12 July 2006): A1.

DeWind, Josh, and David H. Kinley III. *Aiding Migration: The Impact of International Development Assistance on Haiti*. Boulder: Westview Press, 1986.

Díaz Más, Paloma. *Sephardim: The Jews from Spain*. Trans. George K. Zucker. Chicago: University of Chicago Press, 1992.

Díaz-Briquets, Sergio, and Jorge Pérez-López. "Refugee Remittances: Conceptual Issues and the Cuban and Nicaraguan Experiences." *International Migration Review* 31.2 (1997): 411–437.

Dickinson, Tim. "The Briefing." *Rolling Stone* (2005): 48.

Ding Ying. "'Black Sites' Blacken The White House." *Beijing Review* 49.26 (2006): 14–15.

Dirlik, Arif. *The Postcolonial Aura*. Boulder: Westview Press, 1998.

Dirlik, Arif. "The Postcolonial Aura: Third World Criticism in the Age of Global Capitalism." *Dangerous Liaisons: Gender, Nation and Postcolonial Perspectives*. Ed. Anne McClintock, Aamir Mufti, and Ella Shohat. Minneapolis: University of Minnesota Press, 1997.

Dirlik, Arif, and Malcolm Yeung, eds. *Chinese on the American Frontier*. Lanham, MD: Rowman & Littlefield, 2001.

Ditmore, Melissa. "Trafficking in Lives: How Ideology Shapes Policy." *Trafficking and Prostitution Reconsidered: New Perspectives on Migration, Sex Work, and Human*

Rights. Ed. Kamala Kempadoo, Jyoti Sanghera, and Bandana Pattanaik. Boulder: Paradigm Publishers, 2005. 107–126.

"Dodd Loses Bid To Block Civilians From Becoming Interrogators." *Congress Daily* (2004): 8–9.

"Does the Treatment of Prisoners at the Detention Facility in Guantánamo Bay Violate International Law? Pro." *International Debates* 4.4 (2006): 106–108.

Djajić, Slobodan, ed. *International Migration: Trends, Policies and Economic Impact*. New York: Routledge, 2001.

Dladla, A. N., et al. "Speaking to Rural Women: The Sexual Partnerships of Rural South African Women whose Partners are Migrants." *Society in Transition* 32.1 (2001): 79–82.

Doezema, Jo. "Who Gets To Choose? Coercion, Consent, and the UN Trafficking Protocol." *Gender & Development* 10.1 (2002): 20–27.

Donnelly, John M. "Detainee Treatment Debate Simmering." *CQ Weekly* 63.44 (2005): 3064.

Donovan, Gill. "The US Military." *National Catholic Reporter* 38.13 (2002): 6.

Doomernik, Jeroen, and Hans Knippenberg, eds. *Migration and Immigrants: Between Policy and Reality: A Volume in Honor of Hans van Amersfoort*. Amersterdam: Aksant, 2003.

Doorley, Michael. *Irish-American Diaspora Nationalism: The Friends of Irish Freedom, 1916–1935*. Dublin: Four Courts, 2005.

Dow, Mark. *American Gulag: Inside US Immigration Prisons*. Berkeley: University of California Press, 2004.

"Down at Gitmo." *National Review* 58.19 (2006): 26–28.

Drainville, Andre C., ed. *Contesting Globalization: Space and Place in the World Economy*. New York: Routledge, 2004.

Dreazen, Yochi J. "Report Says Pentagon Violated Medical Ethics at Guantanamo." *Wall Street Journal – Eastern Edition* 245.122 (2005): A4.

Drèze, Jean, Meera Samson, and Satyajit Singh, eds. *The Dam and the Nation: Displacement and Resettlement in the Narmada Valley*. Oxford: Oxford University Press, 1997.

Duany, Jorge. "Dominican Migration to Puerto Rico: A Transnational Perspective." *Centro Journal* 17.1 (2005): 243–268.

Dubois, H. F. W., G. Padovano, and G. Stew. "Improving International Nurse Training: An American–Italian Case Study." *International Nursing Review* 53.2 (2006): 110–116.

Duffin, Christian. "Unions Urge Ministers to Combat UK Nurse Exodus." *Nursing Standard* 18.20 (2004): 5.

Duffin, Christian, and Colin Parish. "Africa Faces Apocalypse as AIDS and Migration Decimate Key Staff." *Nursing Standard* 19.38 (2005): 9.

Duggan, Lisa. *The Twilight of Equality: Neoliberalism, Cultural Politics, and the Attack on Democracy*. Boston: Beacon Press, 2003.

Duggan, Lisa. "The New Homonormativity: The Sexual Politics of Neoliberalism." *Materializing Democracy: Toward a Revitalized Cultural Politics*. Ed. Russ Castronovo and Dana D. Nelson. Durham, NC: Duke University Press, 2002. 175–194.

Duggan, Lisa. "Queering the State." *Social Text* 39 (1994): 1–14.

Dummet, Michael. *On Immigration and Refugees*. New York: Routledge, 2001.

Dunn, Marvin. *Black Miami in the Twentieth Century*. Gainesville: University of Florida Press, 1997.

Dupuy, Alex. "The New World Order, Globalization and Caribbean Politics." *New Caribbean Thought: A Reader.* Ed. Brian Meeks and Folke Lindahl. Jamaica: University of the West Indies Press, 2001. 521–536.

Dupuy, Alex. *Haiti in the New World Order: The Limits of the Democratic Revolution.* Boulder: Westview Press, 1997.

Dupuy, Alex. *Haiti in the World Economy: Class, Race, and Underdevelopment since 1700.* Boulder: Westview Press, 1989.

Durand, Jorge, and Douglas S. Massey. "Mexican Migration to the United States: A Critical Review." *Latin American Research Review* 27.2 (1992): 3.

Durand, Jorge, et al. "International Migration and Development in Mexican Communities." *Demography* 33.2 (1996): 249–264.

Dyer, Owen. "Force Feeding at Guantanamo Breaches Ethics, Doctors Say." *British Medical Journal* 332.7541 (2006): 569.

Edgar, Bill, Joe Doherty, and Henk Meert, eds. *Immigration and Homelessness in Europe.* Bristol: Policy Press, 2004.

Editorial. "A Victory for the Rule of Law." *New York Times* (30 June 2006): A22.

Editorial. "Degrading America's Image." *New York Times* (6 June 2006): A22.

Editorial. "Guantanamo Ruling Protects Us." *Cincinnati Enquirer* (1 July 2006): B12.

Editorial. "The Deaths at Gitmo." *New York Times* (12 June 2006): A20.

Editorial. "The Rule of Law." *New York Times* (12 July 2006): A22.

Ehrenreich, Barbara. "Maid to Order." *Global Woman: Nannies, Maids, and Sex Workers in the New Economy.* Ed. Barbara Ehrenreich and Arlie Russell Hochschild. New York: Metropolitan Books, Henry Holt, 2002. 85–103.

Ehrenreich, Barbara, and Arlie Russell Hochschild. "Introduction." *Global Woman: Nannies, Maids, and Sex Workers in the New Economy.* Ed. Barbara Ehrenreich and Arlie Russell Hochschild. New York: Metropolitan Books, Henry Holt, 2002. 1–13.

Eisenberg, Daniel, and Timothy J. Burger. "What's Going On at Gitmo?" *Time* 165.23 (2005): 30–31.

Ellerman, David. "Labour Migration: A Developmental Path or a Low-level Trap?" *Development in Practice* 15.5 (2005): 617–630.

Ellingwood, Ken. *Hard Line: Life and Death on the US-Mexico Border.* New York: Pantheon Books, 2004.

Elliott, Michael, and Mark Thompson. "Camp X-Ray." *Time Europe* 159.4 (2002): 24.

Elsea, Jennifer. *Treatment of Battlefield Detainees in the War on Terrorism.* New York: Novinka Books, 2003.

"*Empire of Care: Nursing and Migration in Filipino American History* (Book)." *American Historical Review* 108.4 (2003): 1173–1174.

"Empty Beds, Empty Stomachs." *Economist* 376.8445 (2005): 38.

Eng, David. "A Dialogue on Racial Melancholia" (with Shinhee Han). *Loss: The Politics of Mourning.* Ed. David L. Eng and David Kazanjian. Berkeley: University of California Press, 2003. 343–371.

Eng, David L. *Racial Castration: Managing Masculinity in Asian America.* Durham, NC: Duke University Press, 2001.

Eng, David L. "Melancholia in the Late Twentieth Century." *Feminisms at a Millennium.* Ed. Judith A. Howard and Carolyn Allen. Chicago: University of Chicago Press, 2000. 265–271.

Eng, David L. "Out Here and Over There: Queerness and Diaspora in Asian American Studies." *Social Text* 15.3–4 (1997): 31–52.

Eng, David L. "In the Shadows of a Diva: Committing Homosexuality in David Henry Hwang's M. Butterfly." *Amerasia Journal* 20.1 (1994): 93–116.

Eng, David L., and Alice V. Hom, eds. *Q&A: Queer in Asian America*. Philadelphia: Temple University Press, 1998.

Eng, David L., and David Kazanjian. "Introduction: Mourning Remains." *Loss: The Politics of Mourning*. Ed. Eng and Kazanjian. Berkeley: University of California Press, 2003. 1–28.

Eng, David L., and David Kazanjian, eds. *Loss: The Politics of Mourning*. Berkeley: University of California Press, 2003.

"Entertainment, of a Kind." *Economist* 374.8416 (2005): 44.

Entzinger, Han, Marco Martiniello, and Catherine Wihtol de Wenden, eds. *Migration between States and Markets*. Aldershot: Ashgate, 2004.

Epps, Brad, Keja Valens, and Bill Johnson González, eds. *Passing Lines: Sexuality and Immigration*. Cambridge, MA: Harvard University Press, 2005.

Epstein, Richard A. "Produce the Body." *Wall Street Journal – Eastern Edition* (7 Oct. 2006): A7.

Escobar, Arturo. *Encountering Development: The Making and Unmaking of the Third World*. Princeton: Princeton University Press, 1995.

Escoda, Isabel. *Letters from Hong Kong*. Hong Kong: Media Mark, 1994.

Espinoza, Robert. "Migration Trends: Maps and Chart." *Global Woman: Nannies, Maids, and Sex Workers in the New Economy*. Ed. Barbara Ehrenreich and Arlie Russell Hochschild. New York: Metropolitan Books, Henry Holt, 2002. 275–280.

Eun-Ok Im, and Kyeongra Yang. "Theories on Immigrant Women's Health." *Health Care for Women International* 27.8 (2006): 666–681.

Europol. "Legislation on Trafficking in Human Beings and Illegal Immigrant Smuggling." Europol Public Information, 2005.

Evans, Tony. *The Politics of Human Rights: A Global Perspective*. Ann Arbor: Pluto Press, 2005.

"Ex-G.I. Writes About Use of Sex In Guantánamo Interrogations." *New York Times* 154.53108 (2005): A21.

"Excerpts From Supreme Court Arguments on Detainees at Guantánamo." *New York Times* 153.52826 (2004): A20.

"Executive Power – Military Commissions – DC Circuilt Upholds the Constitutionality of Military Commissions for Guantanamo Bay Detainees – *Hamdan v. Rumsfeld*, 415 F.3d 33 (D.C. Cir.), cert. granted, 126 S. Ct. 622 (2005)." *Harvard Law Review* 119.5 (2006): 1606–1613.

Fahrmeir, Andreas, Oliver Faron, and Patrick Weil, eds. *Migration Control in the North Atlantic World: The Evolution of State Practices in Europe and the United States from the French Revolution to the Inter-War Period*. New York: Berghahn Books, 2003.

Fainstein, Susan S., and Scott Campbell, ed. *Readings in Urban Theory*. Cambridge, MA: Blackwell, 1996.

Fainstein, Susan S., Ian Gordon, and Michael Harloe, eds. *Divided Cities: New York and London in the Contemporary World*. Oxford: Blackwell, 1992.

Faist, Thomas. *The Volume and Dynamics of International Migration and Transnational Social Spaces*. Oxford: Clarendon Press; New York: Oxford University Press, 2000.

Fan, Cheuk-wan. "Maids Unite to Battle Manila." *Hong Kong Standard* (February 28, 1988).

Farmer, Paul. *Pathologies of Power: Health, Human Rights, and the New War on the Poor*. Berkeley: University of California Press, 2003.

Farmer, Paul. "The Significance of Haiti." *Haiti: Dangerous Crossroads*. Ed. Deidre McFadyen, Pierre LaRamée, Mark Fried, and Fred Rosen. North American Congress on Latin America (NACLA). Boston: South End Press, 1995. 217–230.

Farmer, Paul. *The Uses of Haiti.* Monroe, ME: Common Courage Press, 1994.

Farmer, Paul. *AIDS and Accusation: Haiti and the Geography of Blame.* Berkeley: University of California Press, 1992.

Farmer, Paul. *Infections and Inequalities: The Modern Plagues.* Berkeley: University of California Press, 1999.

Fatton, Jr., Robert. *Haiti's Predatory Republic: The Unending Transition to Democracy.* Boulder: Lynn Rienner Publishers, 2002.

Featherstone, Mike, and Scott Lash, eds. *Spaces of Culture: City, Nation, World.* London: Sage, 1999.

Feingold, David A. "Human Trafficking." *Foreign Policy* (September/October 2005): 26–32.

Feingold, Russell. "Does the Treatment of Prisoners at the Detention Facility in Guantánamo Bay Violate International Law? Pro." *International Debates* 4.4 (2006): 124–126.

Fekete, Liz, and Frances Webber. *Inside Racist Europe.* London: Institute of Race Relations, 1994.

Ferguson, Yale H., and R. J. Barry Jones, eds. *Political Space: Frontiers of Change and Governance in a Globalizing World.* Albany: State University of New York Press, 2002.

Ferrer, Ada. *Insurgent Cuba: Race, Nation, and Revolution, 1868–1898.* Chapel Hill: University of North Carolina Press, 1999.

Ferrer, Ada. "Rethinking Race and Nation in Cuba." *Cuba, the Elusive Nation: Interpretations of National Identity.* Ed. Damián J. Fernández and Madeline Cámara Betancourt. Gainesville: University Press of Florida, 2000. 60–78.

Ferri, Richard S. "Sometimes the Grass Is Greener." *American Journal of Nursing* 103.9 (2003): 20.

Feuer, A. B. *The Spanish-American War at Sea: Naval Action in the Atlantic.* Westport, CT: Praeger, 1995.

Fields, A. Belden. *Rethinking Human Rights for the New Millennium.* Basingstoke: Palgrave Macmillan, 2003.

Fields-Meyer, Thomas, and Don Sider. "Keeper of the Peace." *People* 57.15 (2002): 127.

Fisher, William F. *Toward Sustainable Development? Struggling over India's Narmada River.* Armonk, NY: M. E. Sharpe, 1995.

Fitzpatrick, Joan. "Jurisdiction of Military Commissions and the Ambiguous War on Terrorism." *American Journal of International Law* 96.2 (2002): 345.

Fleck, Fiona. "Should I Stay or Should I Go?" *Bulletin of the World Health Organization* 82.8 (2004): 634.

Fogarty, Gerard P. "Guantanamo Bay: Undermining the Global War on Terror." *JFQ: Joint Force Quarterly* (2005): 59–67.

Fogarty, Gerard P. "Is Guantanamo Bay Undermining the Global War on Terror?" *Parameters: US Army War College* 35.3 (2005): 54–71.

Foley, Neil. *The White Scourge: Mexicans, Blacks, and Poor Whites in Texas Cotton Culture.* Berkeley: University of California Press, 1997.

Foo, A. F., and Belinda Yuen, eds. *Sustainable Cities in the 21st Century.* Singapore: Faculty of Architecture, Building and Real Estate, National University of Singapore, 1999.

"For Immigrant Maids, Not A Job But Servitude." *Migration World Magazine* 24.3 (1996): 12.

Ford, Norman D. "Retiring in Mexico." *Atlantic Monthly* 209.6 (1962): 98.

Fortier, Anne-Marie. "Making Home: Queer Migrations and Motions of Attachment." *Uprootings/Regroundings: Questions of Home and Migration.* New York: Berg, 2003. 115–136.

Fox, Ben. The Associated Press. "Suicides at Gitmo Might Have Been Part of Bigger Plot." *Cincinnati Enquirer* (9 July 2006): A3.

Fox, Ben. The Associated Press. "Media Shown the Door at Gitmo." *Cincinnati Enquirer* (16 June 2006): A17.

Fox, Ben. The Associated Press. "Guantanamo Bay Hunger Strike Grows to about 75." *Cincinnati Enquirer* (30 May 2006): A4.

Fraenkel, Jon. "Beyond MIRAB: Do Aid and Remittances Crowd Out Export Growth in Pacific Microeconomies?" *Asia Pacific Viewpoint* 47.1 (2006): 15–30.

"France Detains GIA Suspect." British Broadcasting Corporation (23 Dec. 1997). BBC News Online: www.news.bbc.co.uk/2/hi/europe/41954.stm.

France, David, Sarah Downey, and Craig Nelson. "Slavery's New Face." *Newsweek* 136.25 (December 18, 2000): 60–66.

Frank, Mitch. "A Pattern of Abuse?" *Time* 163.20 (2004): 45.

Frayne, Bruce. "Rural Productivity and Urban Survival in Namibia: Eating Away from Home." *Journal of Contemporary African Studies* 23.1 (2005): 51–76.

Frederick, John. "The Myth of Nepal-to-India Sex Trafficking: Its Creation, Its Maintenance, and Its Influence on Anti-Trafficking Interventions." *Trafficking and Prostitution Reconsidered: New Perspectives on Migration, Sex Work, and Human Rights.* Ed. Kamala Kempadoo, Jyoti Sanghera, and Bandana Pattanaik. Boulder: Paradigm Publishers, 2005. 127–148.

Friberg, Emil, Schaefer, Kendall, and Leslie Holen. "US Economic Assistance to Two Micronesian Nations: Aid Impact, Dependency and Migration." *Asia Pacific Viewpoint* 47.1 (2006): 123–133.

Friedman, Jonathan, ed. *Globalization, the State, and Violence.* Walnut Creek, CA: AltaMira Press, 2003.

Friedman, Jonathan, and Shalini Randeria, eds. *Worlds on the Move: Globalization, Migration, and Cultural Security.* New York: I. B. Tauris, 2004.

Friends of the Narmada Website: www.narmada.org.

"From Terror to Torture." *America* (31 Jan. 2005): 3+.

Fukuyama, Francis. *The End of History and the Last Man.* New York: Free Press, 1992.

Fuller, Graham E. *Migration and Social Cohesion.* Boulder: Westview Press, 1995.

Furman, Frida Kerner, Elizabeth A. Kelly, and Linda Williamson Nelson. *Telling Our Lives: Conversations on Solidarity and Difference.* Lanham, MD: Rowman & Littlefield, 2005.

Gabaccia, Donna R., and Colin Wayne Leach, eds. *Immigrant Life in the US: Multidisciplinary Perspectives.* New York: Routledge, 2004.

Gall, Carlotta. "Delegation Seeks Release of Afghans Being Held at Guantánamo." *New York Times* (15 June 2006): A10.

Gall, Carlotta. "Rights Group Reports Afghanistan Torture." *New York Times* 155.53433 (2005): A14.

Gall, Carlotta, and Neil A. Lewis. "Tales of Despair from Guantánamo (Cover story)." *New York Times* 152.52517 (2003): A1.

Gamburd, Michele Ruth. "Money That Burns Like Oil: A Sri Lankan Cultural Logic of Morality and Agency." *Ethnology* 43.2 (2004): 167–184.

Gammage, Sarah. "Exercising Exit, Voice and Loyalty: A Gender Perspective on Transnationalism in Haiti." *Development & Change* 35.4 (2004): 743–771.

Gammeltoft, Peter. "Remittances and Other Financial Flows to Developing Countries." *International Migration* 40.5 (2002): 181.

Gangoli, Geetanjali. "Sex Work, Poverty and Migration in Eastern India." *Poverty, Gender and Migration*. Ed. Sadhna Arya and Anupama Roy. Thousand Oaks, CA: Sage, 2006. 214–235.

Ganin, Zvi. *An Uneasy Relationship: American Jewish Leadership and Israel, 1948–1957.* Syracuse: Syracuse University Press, 2005.

Gardiner, Beth. "Reminders of Attack Persist within London." *New York Times* (7 July 2006): A2.

Gardner, K., and R. Grillo. "Transnational Households and Ritual: An Overview." *Global Networks* 2.3 (2002): 179.

Geddes, Andrew. *Immigration and European Integration: Towards Fortress Europe?* Manchester: Manchester University Press, 2000.

Geddes, Andrew. *The Politics of Migration and Immigration in Europe.* Thousand Oaks, CA: Sage, 2003.

Geggus, David. *Haitian Revolutionary Studies.* Bloomington: Indiana University Press, 2002.

Geggus, David, ed. *The Impact of the Haitian Revolution in the Atlantic World.* Columbia: University of South Carolina Press, 2001.

Geggus, David, and David Barry Gaspar, eds. *A Turbulent Time: The French Revolution and the Greater Caribbean.* Bloomington: Indiana University Press, 1997.

Geisen, Thomas, Anthony Andrew Hickey, and Allen Karcher, eds. *Migration, Mobility, and Borders: Issues of Theory and Policy.* Frankfurt am Main: IKO-Verlag für Interkulturelle Kommunikation, 2004.

"Geneva Conventions." *International Law Update* 12 (2006): 124–127.

Gerrish, Kate. "Guest Editorial." *International Nursing Review* (1 June 2004): 65+.

Ghatak, Subrata, and Anne Showstack Sassoon, eds. *Migration and Mobility: The European Context.* New York: Palgrave, 2001.

Gibbs, Nancy, et al. "Inside 'The Wire.'" *Time* 162.23 (2003): 40–45.

Gibney, Matthew J. *Globalizing Rights.* The Oxford Amnesty Lectures 1999. Oxford: Oxford University Press, 2003.

Gibson, Katherine, Lisa Law, and Deirdre McKay. "Beyond Heroes and Victims: Filipina Contract Migrants, Economic Activism and Class Transformations." *International Feminist Journal of Politics* 3.3 (2001): 365–386.

Gibson-Graham, J. K. *The End of Capitalism (As We Knew It).* Oxford: Blackwell, 1996.

Giddens, Anthony, ed. *The Global Third Way Debate.* New York: Polity Press, 2001.

Giddens, Anthony. *Runaway World: How Globalization is Reshaping Our Lives.* New York: Routledge, 2000.

Giddens, Anthony. *The Third Way and Its Critics.* New York: Polity Press, 2000.

Giddens, Anthony. *The Consequences of Modernity.* Stanford: Stanford University Press, 1991.

Giddens, Anthony, and William Hutton, eds. *Global Capitalism.* New York: New Press, 2000.

Gilpin, Robert, and Jean M. Gilpin. *Global Political Economy: Understanding the International Economic Order.* Princeton: Princeton University Press, 2001.

Gilpin, Robert, and Jean M. Gilpin. *The Challenge of Global Capitalism: The World Economy in the 21st Century.* Princeton: Princeton University Press, 2000.

Gilroy, Paul. *After Empire.* New York: Routledge, 2004.

Gilroy, Paul. *Against Race: Imagining Political Culture beyond the Color Line.* Cambridge, MA: Harvard University Press, 2000.

Gilroy, Paul. "Diaspora." *Paragraph* 17.1 (March 1994): 207–212.

Gilroy, Paul. *The Black Atlantic: Modernity and Double Consciousness.* Cambridge, MA: Harvard University Press, 1993.

Gilroy, Paul. *There Ain't No Black in the Union Jack: The Cultural Politics of Race and Nation.* Chicago: University of Chicago Press, 1991.

Gitlin, Todd. "MIA: News of Prison Toll." *Nation* (4 July 2005): 6+.

"Global Resource on Nurse Migration." *American Nurse* 37.4: 5.

Glick Schiller, Nina, and Georges Fouron. *Georges Woke Up Laughing: Long-Distance Nationalism and the Search for Home.* Durham, NC: Duke University Press, 2001.

Glick Schiller, Nina, and Georges Fouron. "Transnational Lives and National Identities: The Identity Politics of Haitian Immigrants." *Transnationalism from Below.* Ed. Michael Peter Smith and Luis Eduardo Guarnizo. New Brunswick, NJ: Transaction Publishers, 1999. 130–161.

Glick Schiller, Nina, Linda Basch, and Cristina Blanc-Szanton. *Towards a Transnational Perspective on Migration: Race, Class, Ethnicity, and Nationalism Reconsidered.* New York: New York Academy of Sciences, 1992.

Global Fund for Women. www.globalfundforwomen.org/faq/trafficking.html.

Glytsos, Nicholas P. "Determinants and Effects of Migrant Remittances: A Survey." *International Migration: Trends, Policies and Economic Impact.* Ed. Slobodan Djajif. London: Routledge, 2001.

Glytsos, Nicholas P. "The Role of Migrant Remittances in Development: Evidence from Mediterranean Countries." *International Migration* 40.1 (2002): 5.

Goff, Stan. *Hideous Dream: A Soldier's Memoir of the US Invasion of Haiti.* Winnipeg: Soft Skull Press, 2000.

Gold, Stephen J. *The Israeli Diaspora.* Seattle: University of Washington Press, 2002.

Goldberg, Suzy. "Guantánamo Cases Go to Supreme Court." *Guardian* (April 20, 2004). www.guardian.co.uk/guantanamo/story/0,13743,1195723,00.html.

Golden, Tim. "After Ruling, Uncertainty Hovers at Cuba Prison (Cover story)." *New York Times* 155.53626 (2006): A1–A21.

Golden, Tim. "Detainee Memo Created Divide in White House." *New York Times* (1 Oct. 2006): A1.

Golden, Tim. "After Ruling, Uncertainty Looms at Cuba Prison." *New York Times* (30 June 2006): A1, A18, A19.

Golden, Tim. "Jihadist or Victim: Ex-Detainee Make a Case." *New York Times* (15 June 2006): A1, A10.

Golden, Tim. "The Battle for Guantánamo." *New York Times Magazine* 155.53705 (2006): 60–145.

Golden, Tim. "Tough US Steps in Hunger Strike at Camp in Cuba." *New York Times* 155.53485 (2006): A1–A18.

Golden, Tim. "US Says It Fears Detainee Abuse in Repatriation." *New York Times* 155.53565 (2006): 1–6.

Golden, Tim. "US Should Close Prison in Cuba, UN Panel Says." *New York Times* (20 May 2006): A1.

Golden, Tim. "Voices Baffled, Brash and Irate in Guantanamo." *New York Times* 155.53510 (2006): A1–A11.

Golden, Tim, and Eric Schmitt. "A Growing Afghan Prison Rivals Bleak Guantánamo." *New York Times* 155.53502 (2006): 1–4.

Golden, Tim, and Don Van Natta, Jr. "US Said to Overstate Value of Guantáamo Detainees (Cover story)." *New York Times* 153.52887 (2004): A1–A12.

Goldie, Terry. "Queer Nation?" Eleventh Annual Robarts Lecture. March 4, 1997. York University, Toronto. www.yorku.ca/robarts/projects/ lectures/pdf/rl_goldie.pdf.

Goldie, Terry, and Robert Gray, eds. Special Issue on "Postcolonial and Queer Theory and Praxis." *ARIEL: A Review of International English Literature* 30.2 (April 1999).

Goldin, Liliana R., ed. *Identities on the Move: Transnational Processes in North America and the Caribbean Basin*. Albany: Institute for Mesoamerican Studies, University at Albany, 1999.

Goldring, Luin. "Family and Collective Remittances to Mexico: A Multi-dimensional Typology." *Development & Change* 35.4 (2004): 799–840.

Gonzales, Alberto R. "The Rule of Law and the Rules of War." *New York Times* 153.52850 (2004): A17.

Gonzales, Alberto R., and Thomas L. Hemingway. "Does the Treatment of Prisoners at the Detention Facility in Guantánamo Bay Violate International Law? Con." *International Debates* 4.4 (2006): 107–127.

Goodin, Emily. "A Tale of Two Senators." *National Journal* 38.28 (2006): 70.

Goodley, Jo. "Migration, Crime and Victimhood." *Punishment & Society* 5.4 (2003): 415–431.

Goodman, Benny. "World of Opportunity." *Nursing Standard* 20.28 (2006): 69.

Goodman, Benny. "Overseas Recruitment and Migration." *Nursing Management – UK* 12.8 (2005): 32–37.

Goodman, Brenda. "National Briefing." *New York Times* 155.53444 (2005): A23.

Goodstein, Laurie, Sarah Kershaw, and Neil A. Lewis. "Army Chaplain in Detention Sought to Teach About Islam (Cover story)." *New York Times* 152.52617 (2003): A1–A21.

Goodwin-Gill, Guy S. *The Refugee in International Law*. Oxford: Oxford University Press, 1996.

Gopinath, Gayatri. *Impossible Desires: Queer Diasporas and South Asian Public Cultures*. Durham, NC: Duke University Press, 2005.

Gopinath, Gayatri. "Local Sites, Global Contexts: The Transnational Trajectories of Deepa Mehta's Fire." *Queer Globalization/Local Homosexualities: Citizenship, Sexualities, and the Afterlife of Colonialism*. Ed. Arnaldo Cruz Malave and Martin Manalansan. New York: New York University Press, 2002.

Gopinath, Gayatri. "Queering Bollywood: Alternative Sexualities in Popular Indian Cinema." *Journal of Homosexuality* 39.3–4 (2000): 283–297.

Gopinath, Gayatri. "Homo-Economics: Queer Sexualities in a Transnational Frame." *Burning Down The House: Recycling Domesticity*. Ed. Rosemary Marangoly George. Boulder: Westview Press, 1998. 102–124.

Gopinath, Gayatri. "Nostalgia, Desire, Diaspora: South Asian Sexualities in Motion." *positions* 5.2 (1997): 467–489.

Gopinath, Gayatri. "Funny Boys and Girls: Notes on A Queer South Asian Planet." *Asian American Sexualities: Dimensions of the Gay and Lesbian Experience*. Ed. Russell Leong. New York: Routledge, 1996. 119–127.

Gopinath, Gayatri. "'Bombay, UK, Yuba City': Bhangra Music and the Engendering of Diaspora." *Diaspora* 4.3 (1995): 303–322.

Gormley, Lisa. "Visiting Detainees to Prevent Torture." *The Lancet* 361.9368 (2003): 1557.

Gothard, Jan. *Blue China: Single Female Migration to Colonial Australia*. Melbourne: Melbourne University Press, 2001.

Gowricharn, Ruben. "Moral Capital in Surinamese Transnationalism." *Ethnic & Racial Studies* 27.4 (2004): 607–621.

Goyette, Kimberly A. "In Service and Servitude: Foreign Female Domestic Workers and the Malaysian Modernity Project (Book)." *International Migration Review* 33.4 (1999): 1124–1125.

Graham, David T., and Nana K. Poku, eds. *Migration, Globalization and Human Security*. New York: Routledge, 2000.

Graham, Otis L., Jr. *Unguarded Gates: A History of America's Immigration Crisis*. Lanham, MD: Rowman & Littlefield, 2004.

Graham, Stephen, ed. *The Cybercities Reader*. New York: Routledge, 2004.

Grande, Edgar, and Louis W. Pauly, eds. *Complex Sovereignty: Reconstituting Political Authority in the Twenty-First Century*. Toronto: University of Toronto Press, 2005.

Grant, Richard, and John Rennie Short. *Globalization and the Margins*. New York: Palgrave Macmillan, 2002.

Gray, John. *False Dawn: The Delusions of Global Capitalism*. New York: New Press, 2000.

Gready, Paul, ed. *Fighting for Human Rights*. New York: Routledge, 2004.

Greenberger, Robert S., and Jess Bravin. "High Court Backs Detainees' Right To Challenge US (Cover story)." *Wall Street Journal – Eastern Edition* 243.126 (2004): A1–A6.

Greenhouse, Linda. "Justices, 5–3, Broadly Reject Bush Plan to Try Detainees (Cover story)." *New York Times* 155.53626 (2006): A1–A20.

Greenhouse, Linda. "Justices to Rule on a Challenge to US Tribunals (Cover story)." *New York Times* 155.53392 (2005): A1–A20.

Greenhouse, Linda. "Court Hears Arguments about Guantánamo Bay Detainees." *New York Times* (April 20, 2004). www.newyorktimes.com.

Greenhouse, Linda. "Justices Affirm Legal Rights of 'Enemy Combatants' (Cover story)." *New York Times* 153.52895 (2004): A1–A14.

Greenhouse, Linda. "Court Hears Case on US Detainees (Cover story)." *New York Times* 153.52834 (2004): A1–A18.

Greenhouse, Linda. "Supreme Court Hears the Case of Guantánamo (Cover story)." *New York Times* 153.52826 (2004): A1–A20.

Greenhouse, Linda. "Finding Common Ground In Asking the Court to Act." *New York Times* 153.52664 (2003): A14.

Greenhouse, Linda. "Justices to Hear Case of Detainees at Guantánamo." *New York Times* 153.52664 (2003): A1–A14.

Greenhouse, Linda. "Supreme Court to Hear Case of Detainees at Guantánamo." *New York Times* (November 10, 2003). www.newyorktimes.com.

Grewal, Inderpal. *Home and Harem: Nation, Gender, Empire and the Cultures of Travel*. Durham, NC: Duke University Press, 1996.

Grewal, Inderpal, and Caren Kaplan, eds. *Scattered Hegemonies: Postmodernity and Transnational Feminist Practices*. Minneapolis: University of Minnesota Press, 1994.

Grosby, Steven. *Nationalism: A Very Short Introduction*. Oxford: Oxford University Press, 2005.

Grossman, Andrew, ed. *Queer Asian Cinema: Shadows in the Shade*. New York: Harrington Park Press, 2000.

"Guantánamo Bay Detainees Geneva Conventions in the Age of Terrorism." *International Debates* 4.4 (2006): 97.

"Guantáanamo Bay Detainees Overview Current Status and Legal Challenges." *International Debates* 4.4 (2006): 98–128.

"Guantánamo Detainees Begins Hearings." *New York Times* 153.52933 (2004): A10.

"Guantánamo-on-Thames?" *Economist* 369.8353 (2003): 49.

"Guantanamo Press Restrictions Increase." *Quill* 90.8 (2002): 35.

"Guantánamo Prosecutor Challenges Impartiality." *New York Times* 153.52974 (2004): A23.

"Guantánamo: A Sad Anniversary." *National Catholic Reporter* 42.12 (2006): 28.

Guarnizo, Luis Eduardo. "The Economics of Transnational Living." *International Migration Review* 37.3 (2003): 666–699.

Gubert, Flore. "Do Migrants Insure Those Who Stay Behind? Evidence from the Kayes Area (Western Mali)." *Oxford Development Studies* 30.3 (2002): 267–287.

Guild, Elspeth, and Joanne van Selm, eds. *International Migration and Security: Opportunities and Challenges.* New York: Routledge, 2005.

Guiraudon, Virginie, and Christian Joppke, eds. *Controlling a New Migration World.* New York: Routledge, 2001.

Gundel, Joakim. "The Migration-Development Nexus: Somalia Case Study." *International Migration* 40.5 (2002): 255.

Gutierrez, David G., ed. *Between Two Worlds: Mexican Immigrants in the United States.* Wilmington, DE: Scholarly Resources, 1996.

Gutman, Roy, and Sami Yousafzai. "The Madman of Guantánamo." *Newsweek* 139.21 (2002): 50.

Haberer, Erich. *Jews and Revolution in Nineteenth-Century Russia.* Cambridge: Cambridge University Press, 1995.

Haberman, Clyde. "But in London, the Foreigners Are Us." *New York Times* (9 May 2006): A23.

Habermas, Jürgen (interviewed by Michael Haller). *The Past as Future.* Trans. and ed. Max Pensky. Lincoln: University of Nebraska Press, 1994.

Hacohen, Dvora. *Immigrants in Turmoil: Mass Immigration to Israel and Its Repercussions in the 1950s and After.* Trans. Gila Brand. Syracuse: Syracuse University Press, 2003.

Hagen, Jonas. "Migration and Remittances." *UN Chronicle* 42.4 (2005): 12.

Hailbronner, Kay, David A. Martin, and Hiroshi Motomura, eds. *Immigration Controls: The Search for Workable Policies in Germany and the United States.* Providence: Berghahn Books, 1997.

Haine, W. Scott. *The History of France.* Westport, CT: Greenwood Press, 2000.

Haines, David W., and Karen E. Rosen, eds. *Illegal Immigration in America: A Reference Handbook.* Westport, CT: Greenwood Press, 1999.

Hakesley-Brown, Roswyn. "Nurses on the Move – Migration and the Global Health Care Economy." *Nursing Standard* 20.29 (2006): 36.

Hall, Rodney Bruce, and Thomas J. Biersteker, eds. *The Emergence of Private Authority in Global Governance.* Cambridge: Cambridge University Press, 2002.

Hall, Stuart. "Cultural Identity and Diaspora." *Identity: Community, Culture, Difference.* Ed. Jonathan Rutherford. London: Lawrence & Wishart, 1990. 222–237. Reprinted in *Theorizing Diaspora: A Reader.* Ed. Jana Evans Braziel and Anita Mannur. Blackwell, 2002. 233–246.

Haller, William, and Patricia Landolt. "The Transnational Dimensions of Identity Formation: Adult Children of Immigrants in Miami." *Ethnic & Racial Studies* 28.6 (2005): 1182–1214.

Halloran, Liz. "Clarity for Combatants?" *US News & World Report* 140.24 (2006): 36–37.

Hamdi v. Rumsfeld, No. 03–6696 (2004).

Hamilton, Annette. "Primal Dream: Masculinism, Sin and Salvation in Thailand's Sex Trade." *Sites of Desire, Economies of Pleasure: Sexualities in Asia and the Pacific.* Chicago: University of Chicago Press, 1997. 145–165.

Hammer, Juliane. *Palestinians Born in Exile: Diaspora and the Search for a Homeland.* Austin: University of Texas Press, 2005.

Hammerton, A. James, and Alistair Thomson. *Ten Pound Poms: Australia's Invisible Migrants. A Life History of Postwar British Emigration to Australia.* Manchester: Manchester University Press, 2005.

Hampshire, James. *Citizenship and Belonging: Immigration and the Politics of Demographic Governance in Postwar Britain.* Basingstoke: Palgrave Macmillan, 2005.

Hanley, Delinda C. "Redgraves Demand Justice for Guantanamo Bay Detainees." *Washington Report on Middle East Affairs* 23.4 (2004): 75–76.

Hansen, Jonathan M. "Making The Law In Cuba." *New York Times* 153.52825 (2004): A19.

Hansen, Randall. *Citizenship and Immigration in Post-War Britain.* Oxford: Oxford University Press, 2000.

Hanson, Gordon H. *Why Does Immigration Divide America? Public Finance and Political Opposition to Open Borders.* Washington, DC: Institute for International Economics, 2005.

Harcourt, Wendy, and Arturo Escobar, eds. *Women and the Politics of Place.* Bloomfield, CT: Kumarian Press, 2005.

Hargreaves, Alec G. *Immigration, "Race" and Ethnicity in Contemporary France.* New York: Routledge, 1995.

Hargreaves, Alec G. *La Littérature Beur. Un guide bio-bibliographique.* CELFAN Edition Monographs, New Orleans, LA: Tulane University, 1992.

Hargreaves, Alec G. *Voices from the North African Immigrant Community in France: Immigration and Identity in Beur Fiction.* New York: St. Martin's Press, 1991.

Hargreaves, Alec G., ed. *Immigration in Post-War France: A Documentary Anthology.* London: Methuen, 1987.

Hargreaves, Alec G., and Mark McKinney, eds. *Post-Colonial Cultures in France.* New York: Routledge, 1997.

Hargreaves, Alec G., and Mark McKinney. "Introduction: The Post-Colonial Problematic in Contemporary France." *Post-Colonial Cultures in France.* New York: Routledge, 1997.

Harper, Dean, Bobby Milis, and Ronald Parris. "Exploitation in Migrant Labour Camps." *British Journal of Sociology* 25.3 (1974): 283–295.

Harper, Marjory, ed. *Emigrant Homecomings: The Return Movement of Emigrants, 1600–2000.* Manchester: Manchester University Press, 2005.

Harper, Phillip Brian, Anne Mc Clintock, and José Esteban Muñoz, eds. Special Issue on "Queer Transexions of Race, Nation, and Gender." *Social Text* (1997): 52–53.

Harrington, Carol. "The Politics of Rescue." *International Feminist Journal of Politics* 7.2 (2005): 175–206.

Harris, Joanne. "20 Essex Street Duo Plays Part in Guantanamo Detainees' Victory." *Lawyer* 20.27 (2006): 14.

Harris, Joanne. "Guantanamo Detainee's Lawyers Want Statement Ignored after Torture Claim." *Lawyer* 18.38 (2004): 3.

Harris, Nigel. *Thinking the Unthinkable: The Immigration Myth Exposed.* New York: I. B. Tauris, 2002.

Harzig, Christiane. "Domestics of the World (Unite?): Labor Migration Systems and Personal Trajectories of Household Workers in Historical and Global Perspective." *Journal of American Ethnic History* 25.2/3: 48–73.

Hassner, Pierre. *The United States: The Empire of Force or the Force of Empire*, Chaillot Papers, no. 54. Paris: Institute for Security Studies, European Union, 2002. www. iss-eu.org/chaillot/chai54e.pdf.

Hatton, Timothy J., and Jeffrey G. Williamson. *The Age of Mass Migration: Causes and Economic Impact*. Oxford: Oxford University Press, 1998.

Havemann, Joel. "Senate Advances Fence Bill." *LA Times* (20 Sept. 2006). www.latimes. com.

Hawley, John C., ed. *Postcolonial, Queer: Theoretical Intersections*. Albany: State University of New York Press, 2001a.

Hawley, John C., ed. *Postcolonial and Queer Theories: Intersections and Essays*. Westport, CT: Greenwood Press, 2001b.

Hawthorne, Lesleyanne. "Qualifications Recognition Reform for Skilled Migrants in Australia: Applying Competency-based Assessment to Overseas-qualified Nurses." *International Migration* 40.6 (2002): 55–91.

Hawthorne, Lesleyanne. "The Globalization of the Nursing Workforce: Barriers Confronting Overseas Qualified Nurses in Australia." *Nursing Inquiry* 8.4 (2001): 213–229.

Hawthorne, Lesleyanne, Julie Toth, and Graeme Hawthorne. "Patient Demand for Bilingual Bicultural Nurses in Australia." *Journal of Intercultural Studies* 21.2 (2000).

Hayes, Jarrod Landin. *Queer Nations: Marginal Sexualities in the Maghreb*. Chicago: University of Chicago Press, 2000.

Hayes, Jarrod Landin. "Something Queer About the Nation: Sexual Subversions of National Identity in Maghrebian Literature of French Expression." Doctoral Thesis: City University of New York, 1996.

Hayter, Teresa. *Open Borders: The Case Against Immigration Controls*. London: Pluto Press, 2004.

Healy, Margaret. "Domestic Workers in Britain, 1996 (Cover story)." *Migration World Magazine* 25.1/2 (1997): 18.

Healy, Patrick D. "I'm Shocked And Outraged." *New York Times* 154.53257 (2005): 2.

Hedges, Chris. "An Actor's Craft and His Faith Intersect." *New York Times* 158.52965 (2004): B2.

Heffernan, John. "US Health Professionals' Call to Prevent Torture and Abuse of Detainess in US Custody." *Journal of Ambulatory Care Management* 28.4 (2005): 366–367.

Hegland, Corine. "Foggy Crystal Ball for Detainees." *National Journal* 38.27 (2006): 51–52.

Hegland, Corine. "Empty Evidence (Cover story)." *National Journal* 38.5 (2006): 28–31.

Hegland, Corine. "Who Is at Guantanamo Bay (Cover story)." *National Journal* 38.5 (2006): 33–35.

Heilmann, Conrad. "Remittances and the Migration-Development Nexus – Challenges for the Sustainable Governance of Migration." *Ecological Economics* 59.2 (2006): 231–236.

Held, David, and Anthony G. McGrew, eds. *The Global Transformations Reader*. Oxford: Blackwell, 2000.

Held-Warmkessel, Jean. "How to Make a PICC Line Stick." *Nursing* 31.5 (2001): 42–44.

"Hell-hole or paradise?" *Economist* 370.8367 (2004): 30–33.

"Help From Above." *Economist* 369.8350 (2003): 33.

Helton, Arthur C. *The Price of Indifference: Refugees and Humanitarian Action in the New Century.* Oxford: Oxford University Press, 2002.

Herbert, Bob. "Our Battered Constitution." *New York Times* 154.53115 (2005): A19.

Herbert, Bob. "Stories From The Inside." *New York Times* 154.53118 (2005): A21.

Herbert, Bob. "The Law Gets a Toehold." *New York Times* (13 July 2006): A23.

Herbert, Bob. "With the Gloves Off." *New York Times* 154.53226 (2005): A29.

"Here's to you, Mr Robertson." *Economist* 373.8401 (2004): 35.

Hernandez-Truyol, Berta Esperanza, ed. *Moral Imperialism: A Critical Anthology.* New York: New York University Press, 2002.

Hersch, Seymour M. "Torture at Abu-Ghraib." *The New Yorker* (May 10, 2004). www.newyorker.com/fact/content/?040510fa_fact. Date posted: April 30, 2004.

Hersch, Seymour M. "The Gray Zone." *The New Yorker* (May 24, 2004). www.newyorker.com/printable/?fact/040524fa_fact.

Herzog, Todd, and Sander L. Gilman, eds. *A New Germany in a New Europe.* New York: Routledge, 2001.

Hess, Sabine, and Annette Puckhaber. "'Big Sisters' are Better Domestic Servants?! Comments on the Booming *Au Pair* Business." *Feminist Review* (2004): 65–78.

Hewison, Kevin. "Thai Migrant Workers in Hong Kong." *Journal of Contemporary Asia* 34.3 (2004): 318–335.

Heyzer, Noeleen and Vivienne Wee. "Domestic Workers in Transient Overseas Employment: Who Benefits, Who Profits?" *The Trade in Domestic Workers: Causes, Mechanisms, and Consequences of International Migration.* Kuala Lumpur: APDC; Atlantic Highlands, NJ: Zed Books, 1994. 31–102.

Heyzer, Noeleen, Geertje Lycklama à Nijeholt, and Nedra Weerakoon, eds. *The Trade in Domestic Workers: Causes, Mechanisms and Consequences of International Migration.* London: Zed Books, 1994.

Higham, Scott, and Joe Stephens. "New Details of Prison Abuse Emerge. Abu Ghraib Detainees' Statements Describe Humiliation and Savage Beatings." *Washington Post* (May 21, 2004). www.washingtonpost.com.

Higman, B. W. *Domestic Service in Australia.* Victoria: Melbourne University Press, 2002.

Hine, Darlene Clark, and Jacqueline McLeod, eds. *Crossing Boundaries: Comparative History of Black People in Diaspora.* Bloomington: Indiana University Press, 1999.

Hirsh, Michael. "New War, Old Tactics?" *Newsweek* 145.4 (2005): 8.

"History of Guantanamo Bay" [electronic resource]. A compilation of The history of Guantanamo Bay (1953) by M. E. Murphy, its 1964 update, and articles recounting the base's recent history. Guantanamo Bay, Cuba: US Naval Station, 2001. www.nsgtmo.navy.mil. (GOVT. DOC# D 201.2:2002010542).

Ho, Christine G. T., and Keith Nurse, eds. *Globalization, Diaspora and Caribbean Popular Culture.* Kingston: Ian Randle, 2005.

Ho, Josephine. "From Anti-Trafficking to Social Discipline; Or, the Changing Role of 'Women's' NGOs in Taiwan." *Trafficking and Prostitution Reconsidered: New Perspectives on Migration, Sex Work, and Human Rights.* Ed. Kamala Kempadoo, Jyoti Sanghera, and Bandana Pattanaik. Boulder: Paradigm Publishers, 2005. 83–106.

Hochschild, Arlie Russell. "Love and Gold." *Global Woman: Nannies, Maids, and Sex Workers in the New Economy.* Ed. Barbara Ehrenreich and Arlie Russell Hochschild. New York: Metropolitan Books, Henry Holt, 2002.

Hoganson, Kristin. "Empire of Care: Nursing and Migration in Filipino American History (Book)." *Journal of American History* 90.4 (2004): 1548–1549.

Hoge, Warren. "Investigators for UN Urge US to Close Guantánamo." *New York Times* 155.53493 (2006): A6.

Hoge, Warren. "Hometown of British Prisoners Known for Tranquil Diversity." *New York Times* 151.52013 (2002): A14.

Holland, Gina. Associated Press. "Bush Dealt Gitmo Setback." *Cincinnati Enquirer* (20 June 2006): A1, A8

Holland, Sharon Patricia. "Bill T. Jones, Tupac Shakur and the (Queer) Art of Death." Special section: "Plum Nelly: New Essays in Black Queer Studies." Ed. Dwight A. Mc Bride and Jennifer DeVere Brody. *Callaloo* 23.1 (2000): 384–393.

Hollibaugh, Amber L. *My Dangerous Desires: A Queer Girl Dreaming Her Way Home.* Durham, NC: Duke University Press, 2000.

Hollibaugh, Amber L. "Sex Work Notes: Some Tensions of a Former Whore and a Practising Feminist." *My Dangerous Desires: A Queer Girl Dreaming Her Way Home.* Durham, NC: Duke University Press, 2000. 181–186.

Holston, James, ed. *Cities and Citizenship.* Durham, NC: Duke University Press, 1999.

Holt, Thomas C. "Marking: Race, Race-making and the Writing of History." *American Historical Review* 100, 1 (February 1995): 1–20.

Holt, Thomas C. "Slavery and Freedom in the Atlantic World: Striving to Be Free." *Crossing Boundaries: Comparative History of Black People in Diaspora.* Ed. Darlene Clark Hine and Jacqueline McLeod. Bloomington: Indiana University Press, 1999. 33–44.

"Home Soon." *Economist* 374.8409 (2005): 52.

Hondagneu-Sotelo, Pierrette, ed. *Gender and US Immigration: Contemporary Trends.* Berkeley: University of California Press, 2003.

Hood, Rory T. "Guantanamo and Citizenship: An Unjust Ticket Home?" *Case Western Reserve Journal of International Law* 37.2/3 (2006): 555–578.

Hooper, Michael. "Model Underdevelopment." *Haiti: Dangerous Crossroads.* Ed. North American Congress on Latin America (NACLA). Boston: South End Press, 1995. 133–145.

Hopkins Tanne, Janice. "Muslim Chaplain Speaks Out Over Guantanamo Hunger Strike." *British Medical Journal* 331.7521 (2005): 866.

Hopquin, Benoît. "Tué il y a un an à Epinay, après s'être déclaré 'flic.'" *Le Monde* (26 Oct. 2006). www.lemonde.fr/web/article/0,1–0@2–706693,36–827821@51–824202,0. html.

Hornby, Richard. "War Fever." *Hudson Review* 57.4 (2005): 647–654.

"How Complicit are Doctors in Abuses of Detainees?" *Lancet* (21 Aug. 2004): 267+.

Hudson, Kate. *Breaking the South Slav Dream: The Rise and Fall of Yugoslavia.* London: Pluto Press, 2003.

Hughes, Donna M. "The 'Natasha' Trade: The Transnational Shadow Market of Trafficking in Women." *Journal of International Affairs* 53.2 (2000): 625-651.

Hugo, Victor. *Bug-Jargal* [1826]. Trans. Christopher Bongie. New York: Broadview Press, 2004.

Hulse, Carl, and Rachel L. Swarns, "Senate Passes Bill on Building Border Fence." *New York Times* (30 Sept. 2006): A10.

Hulse, Carl, and Kate Zernike. "House Passes Detainee Bill As It Clears Senate Hurdle." *New York Times* (28 Sept. 2006): A20.

Huntington, Samuel. *The Clash of Civilizations and the Remaking of World Order.* New York: Simon & Schuster, 1996.

Hurst, Steven. *The Foreign Policy of the Bush Administration: In Search of a New World Order.* London: Cassell, 1999.

Hurt, Charles. "Senate Set to Consider Fence Bill." *Washington Times* (19 Sept. 2006). www.washingtontimes.com.

Ifekwunigwe, Jayne O. "Recasting 'Black Venus' in the New African Diaspora." *Women's Studies International Forum* 27.4 (2004): 397–412.

Ignacio, Emily Noelle. *Building Diaspora: Filipino Community Formation on the Internet.* New Brunswick, NJ: Rutgers University Press, 2005.

Ignatieff, Michael. "The American Empire: The Burden." *New York Times Magazine* (5 Jan. 2003): 22.

"I'm Still Here." *Harper's Magazine* 312.1872 (2006): 28–30.

"Immigrants March, Present Complaints." *Cincinnati Enquirer* (26 Oct. 2006).

Innes, Joanna. "Convict Maids: The Forced Migration of Women in Australia (Book)." *Labour History Review* 62.3 (1997): 365.

"Inside Washington." *National Journal* 38.37 (2006): 3–4.

International Committee for Prostitutes' Rights. "World Charter and World Whores' Congress Statements." *Sex Work: Writings by Women in the Sex Industry.* Ed. Frédérique Delacoste and Priscilla Alexander. San Francisco: Cleis Press, 1987. 305–321.

International Rivers Network. "US Company Signs Deal for Notorious Indian Dam" (Press Release) (March 27, 2000). Friends of the River Narmada Website. www.narmada.org/maheswar/ogden/irn.pr.html.

Ireland, Patrick. *Becoming Europe: Immigration, Integration, and the Welfare State.* Pittsburgh: University of Pittsburgh Press, 2004.

Isaac, Julius. *Economics of Migration.* London: K. Paul, Trench, Trubner, 1947.

Isikoff, Michael. "Pressure to Close the Facility." *Newsweek* 147.25 (2006): 9.

Isikoff, Michael. "Detainees' Rights: Scalia Speaks His Mind." *Newsweek* 147.14 (2006): 6.

Isikoff, Michael. "Secret Memo: Send to Be Tortured." *Newsweek* 146.6 (2005): 7.

Isikoff, Michael. "Unanswered Questions." *Newsweek* 145.3 (2005): 36.

Isikoff, Michael, and Daniel Klaidman. "The Road to the Brig." *Newsweek* 143.17 (2004): 26–28.

Isin, Engin F., ed. *Democracy, Citizenship, and the Global City.* New York: Routledge, 2000.

Isin, Engin F., and Bryan S. Turner, eds. *Handbook of Citizenship Studies.* London: Sage, 2002.

"Island Mentality." *New Republic* (13 Sep. 2004): 7+.

Itzigsohn, José. "Immigration and the Boundaries of Citizenship: The Institutions of Immigrants' Political Transnationalism." *International Migration Review* 34.4 (2000): 1126–1154.

Itzigsohn, José. "Migrant Remittances, Labor Markets, and Household Strategies: A Comparative Analysis of Low-Income Household Strategies in the Caribbean Basin." *Social Forces* 74.2 (1995): 633–655.

Iyer, Ramaswamy R. *Water: Perspectives, Issues, Concerns.* Thousand Oaks, CA: Sage, 2003.

Jackson, Robert H. *"Empire of Care: Nursing and Migration in Filipino American History* (Book)." *History: Reviews of New Books* 31.3 (2003): 104.

Jacobs, Stevenson. Associated Press. "Guantanamo Likely to Stay Open." *Cincinnati Enquirer* (30 June 2006): A1, A8.

Jagori. "Migration, Trafficking, and Sites of Work: Rights and Vulnerabilities." *Trafficking and Prostitution Reconsidered: New Perspectives on Migration, Sex Work, and Human Rights.* Ed. Kamala Kempadoo, Jyoti Sanghera, and Bandana Pattanaik. Boulder: Paradigm Publishers, 2005. 159–174.

James, Peter. *Modern Germany: Politics, Society and Culture*. New York: Routledge, 1998.

Jayyusi, Salma Khadra, and Zafar Ishaq Ansari, eds. *My Jerusalem: Essays, Reminiscences, and Poems*. Northampton: Olive Branch Press, 2005.

Jazayery, Leila. "The Migration-Development Nexus: Afghanistan Case Study." *International Migration* 40.5 (2002): 231.

Jean-Pierre, Jean. "The Tenth Department." *Haiti: Dangerous Crossroads*. Ed. Deirdre McFadyen and Pierre LaRamée with Mark Fried and Fred Rosen from the North American Congress on Latin America (NACLA). Boston, MA: South End Press, 1995. 195–204.

Jeffrey, Leslie Ann. *Sex and Borders: Gender, National Identity, and Prostitution Policy in Thailand*. Vancouver: University of British Columbia Press, 2002.

Jeffreys, Elaine. *China, Sex and Prostitution*. New York: Routledge Curzon, 2004.

Jeffries, Ian. *The Former Yugoslavia at the Turn of the Twenty-first Century: A Guide to the Economies in Transition*. New York: Routledge, 2002.

Jehl, Douglas. "Pentagon Seeks to Shift Inmates from Cuba Base." *New York Times* 154.53150 (2005): A1–A10.

Jérôme, Béatrice. "L'État refuse de payer les dégâts des violence urbaines." *Le Monde* (25 Dec. 2005).

Johnson v. Eisentrager 339 U.S. 763 (1950).

Johnson, Benjamin Heber. *Revolution in Texas: How A Forgotten Rebellion and Its Bloody Suppression Turned Mexicans into Americans*. New Haven: Yale University Press, 2003.

Johnson, Chalmers. *Blowback: The Costs and Consequences of American Empire*. New York: Holt, 2000.

Johnson, Chalmers. *The Sorrows of Empire: Militarism, Secrecy, and the End of the Republic*. New York: Henry Holt, 2004.

Johnston, David, and Neil A. Lewis. "Officials Describe Secret CIA Center at Guantánamo." *New York Times* 154.53067 (2004): A15.

Johnston, David. "Attack is Possible in US or Yemen, the FBI Warns (Cover story)." *New York Times* 151.52027 (2002): A1.

Joly, Danièle, ed. *International Migration in the New Millennium: Global Movement and Settlement*. Burlington, VT: Ashgate, 2004.

Joppke, Christian, ed. *Challenge to the Nation-State: Immigration in Western Europe and the United States*. Oxford: Oxford University Press, 1998.

Joppke, Christian, and Ewa Moraska, eds. *Toward Assimilation and Citizenship: Immigrants in Liberal Nation-States*. Basingstoke: Palgrave Macmillan, 2003.

Jordan, Bill, and Franck Düvell. *Migration: The Boundaries of Equality and Justice*. Cambridge: Polity Press, 2003.

Jordan, Bill, and Franck Düvell. *Irregular Migration: The Dilemmas of Transnational Mobility*. Northampton, MA: Edward Elgar, 2002.

Jordan, Jan. "Feminism and Sex Work: Connections and Contradictions." *Feminist Voices: Women's Studies Texts for Aotearoa/New Zealand*. Ed. Phillida Bunkle, Kathie Irwin, Alison Laurie, and Sue Middleton. Auckland: Oxford University Press, 1992. 180–196.

Jost, Kenneth. "Better Late Than Never." *CQ Weekly* (17 July 2006): 1952+.

Jost, Kenneth. "Government Secrecy." *CQ Researcher* 15.42 (2005): 1007–1013.

"Judge Blocks Repatriation of Cuban Detainees." *New York Times* 144.49867 (1994): A24.

Junod, Tom. "The Gospel of Gitmo." *Esquire* 144.1 (2005): 94–138.

Jureidini, Ray, and Nayla Moukarbel. "Female Sri Lankan Domestic Workers in Lebanon: A Case of 'Contract Slavery'?" *Journal of Ethnic & Migration Studies* 30.4 (2004): 581–607.

"Just A Few Bad Apples?" *Economist* 374.8410 (2005): 29–30.

Kachka, Boris. "The Tutu Monologues." *New York* 37.36 (2004): 20.

Kalb, Don, et al. *The Ends of Globalization: Bringing Society Back In*. Lanham, MD: Rowman & Littlefield, 2000.

Kalra, Virinder S., Raminder Kaur, and John Hutnyk, eds. *Diaspora and Hybridity*. Thousand Oaks, CA: Sage, 2005.

Kaplan, Amy. "Violent Belongings and the Question of Empire Today." Presidential Address to the American Studies Association, October 17, 2003. *American Quarterly* 56.1 (2004): 1–18.

Kaplan, Amy. *The Anarchy of Empire in the Making of US Culture*. Cambridge, MA: Harvard University Press, 2003.

Kaplan, Amy. "Homeland Insecurities: Transformations of Language and Space." *September 11 in History: A Watershed Moment?* Ed. Mary Dudziak. Durham, NC: Duke University Press, 2003. 55–69.

Kaplan, Amy, and Donald Pease, eds. *Cultures of United States Imperialism*. Durham, NC: Duke University Press, 1993.

Kaplan, Caren. *Questions of Travel: Postmodern Discourses of Displacement*. Durham, NC: Duke University Press, 1996.

Kaplan, Caren. "Deterritorializations: The Rewriting of Home and Exile in Western Feminist Discourse." *The Nature and Context of Minority Discourse*. Ed. JanMohamed and Lloyd. Oxford: Oxford University Press, 1990. 357–368.

Kaplan, Robert D. "Supremacy by Stealth: Ten Rules for Managing the World." *Atlantic Monthly* (July-August 2003): 68–69.

Kapur, Devesh, and John McHale. "Migration's New Payoff." *Foreign Policy* (2003): 49–57.

Kapur, Ratna. "Cross-Border Movements and Law: Renegotiating the Boundaries of Difference." *Trafficking and Prostitution Reconsidered: New Perspectives on Migration, Sex Work, and Human Rights*. Ed. Kamala Kempadoo, Jyoti Sanghera, and Bandana Pattanaik. Boulder: Paradigm Publishers, 2005. 25–42.

Karafolas, Simeon. "Migrant Remittances in Greece and Portugal: Distribution by Country of Provenance and the Role of . . ." *International Migration* 36.3 (1998): 357.

Katel, Peter, and Kenneth Jost. "Treatment of Detainees." *CQ Researcher* (25 Aug. 2006): 675+.

Katyal, Sonia K. "Sexuality and Sovereignty: The Global Limits and Possibilities of *Lawrence*." *William & Mary Bill of Rights Journal* 14.4 (April 2006): 1429–1492.

Katyal, Sonia K. "Exporting Identity." *Yale Journal of Law and Feminism* 14.1 (2002): 97–176.

Kay, Jonathan. "Outmaneuvering Terror: Redefining the Terrorist." *National Interest* (2004): 87–93.

Kelly, Karen. "Nurses on the Move: Migration and the Global Health Care Economy." *Nursing Education Perspectives* 27.5: 274–275.

Kelly, Liz, and Linda Regan. "Stopping Traffic: Exploring the Extent of, and Responses to, Trafficking in Women for Sexual Exploitation in the UK." Police Research Series, Paper 125. Home Office, Policing and Reducing Crime Unit. London: Crown Publishers, 2000.

Kelson, Gregory A., and Debra L. DeLaet, eds. *Gender and Immigration*. New York: New York University Press, 1999.

Kempadoo, Kamala. "Introduction: From Moral Panic to Global Justice: Changing Perspectives on Trafficking." *Trafficking and Prostitution Reconsidered: New Perspectives on Migration, Sex Work, and Human Rights*. Ed. Kamala Kempadoo, Jyoti Sanghera, and Bandana Pattanaik. Boulder: Paradigm Publishers, 2005. vii–xxxiv.

Kempadoo, Kamala, ed. "Sex Workers' Rights Organizations and Anti-Trafficking Campaigns." *Trafficking and Prostitution Reconsidered: New Perspectives on Migration, Sex Work, and Human Rights*. Ed. Kamala Kempadoo, Jyoti Sanghera, and Bandana Pattanaik. Boulder: Paradigm Publishers, 2005. 149–158.

Kempadoo, Kamala. *Sexing the Caribbean: Gender, Race, and Sexual Labor*. New York: Routledge, 2004.

Kempadoo, Kamala, ed. *Sun, Sex, and Gold: Tourism and Sex Work in the Caribbean*. Lanham, MD: Rowman & Littlefield, 1999.

Kempadoo, Kamala, and Jo Doezema, ed. *Global Sex Workers: Rights, Resistance, and Redefinition*. New York: Routledge, 1998.

Kempadoo, Kamala, Jyoti Sanghera, and Bandana Pattanaik, eds. *Trafficking and Prostitution Reconsidered: New Perspectives on Migration, Sex Work, and Human Rights*. Boulder: Paradigm Publishers, 2005.

Khagram, Sanjeev. *Dams and Development: Transnational Struggles for Water and Power*. Ithaca: Cornell University Press, 2004.

Khagram, Sanjeev. "Restructuring the Global Politics of Development: The Case of India's Narmada Valley Dams." *Restructuring World Politics: Transnational Social Movements, Networks, and Norms*. Minneapolis: University of Minnesota Press, 2002. 206–230.

Khan, Arfan. "International and Human Rights Aspects of the Treatment of Detainees." *Journal of Criminal Law* 69.2 (2005): 168–187.

Khan, Rahmatullah. "Sustainable Development, Human Rights and Good Governance – A Case Study of India's Narmada Dam." *Sustainable Development and Good Governance*. Ed. Konrad Ginther, Erik Denters, and Paul J. I. M. de Waart. Dordecht: Martinus Nijhoff Publishers, 1995. 420–428.

Kilvington, Judith, Sophie Day, and Helen Ward. "Prostitution Policy in Europe: A Time of Change?" *Feminist Review* (2001): 78–93.

Kim Il Rhan, and Cho Hyeyoung. "Mamasang: Remember Me This Way." *Inter-Asia Cultural Studies* 7.2 (2006): 348–352.

King Jr., Neil. "Lawyers File Suits To Set Categories In Detainee Cases." *Wall Street Journal – Eastern Edition* 244.3 (2004): A4.

King, Russell. "Albania as a Laboratory for the Study of Migration and Development." *Journal of Southern Europe & the Balkans* 7.2 (2005): 133–155.

King, Russell, and John Connell, eds. *Small Worlds, Global Lives: Islands and Migration*. New York: Pinter, 1999.

King, Russell, and Julie Vullnetari. "Orphan Pensioners and Migrating Grandparents: The Impact of Mass Migration on Older People in Rural Albania." *Ageing & Society* 26.5 (2006): 783–816.

King, Russell, Nicola Mai, and Mirela Dalipaj. *Exploding the Migration Myths: Analysis and Recommendations for the European Union, the UK, and Albania*. London: Fabian Society and Oxfam, 2003.

Kingma, Mireille. *Nurses on the Move: Migration and the Global Health Care Economy*. Ithaca: Cornell University Press, 2006.

Kingma, Mireille. "Nurse Migration is Only a Symptom, Not the Disease." International Council of Nurses. *International Nursing Review* 51 (2004): 196–199.

Kingma, Mireille. "Violence against Nurses: Violation of Human Rights." *Women in Nursing in Islamic Societies*. Oxford: Oxford University Press, 2003. 135–158.

Kingma, Mireille. "Nursing Migration: Global Treasure Hunt or Disaster-in-the-Making?" *Nursing Inquiry* 8.4 (2001): 205–212.

Kirkpatrick, David D. "Senators Laud Treatment Of Detainees In Guantánamo." *New York Times* 154.53259 (2005): A15.

Kishwar, Madhu Purnima. "Twenty Years on the Banks of the Narmada." *Indian Express*, Op-Ed Section (April 2, 2006). www.sardarsarovardam.org/news/news179.htm.

Kleinman, Mark. "The Economic Impact of Labour Migration." *Political Quarterly* 74 (2003): 59–74.

Klier, John D. *The Times of London, the Russian Press, and the Pogroms of 1881–1882*. Pittsburgh: Russian and East European Studies Program, University of Pittsburgh, 1984.

Klier, John D., and Shlomo Lambroza, eds. *Pogroms: Anti-Jewish Violence in Modern Russian History*. Cambridge: Cambridge University Press, 1992.

Kniesmeyer, Joke, and Daniel Cil Brecher. "Beyond the Pale: The History of Jews in Russia." www.friends-partners.org/partners/beyond-the-pale/.

Knörr, Jacqueline, and Barbara Merier, eds. *Women and Migration: Anthropological Perspectives*. Frankfurt: Campus; New York: St. Martin's Press, 2000.

Knowlton, Brian. "Cheney Backs Handling Of Detainees At Cuba Base." *New York Times* 154.53231 (2005): A15.

Knox, Paul, and Peter J. Taylor, eds. *World Cities in a World-System*. Cambridge: Cambridge University Press, 1995.

Koc, Ismet, and Isil Onan. "International Migrants' Remittances and Welfare Status of the Left-Behind Families in Turkey." *International Migration Review* 38.1 (2004): 78–112.

Kofman, Eleonore. "Gendered Global Migrations." *International Feminist Journal of Politics* 6.4 (2004): 643–665.

Kofman, Eleonore, Annie Phizacklea, Parvati Raghuram, and Rosemary Sales, eds. *Gender and International Migration in Europe: Employment, Welfare and Politics*. New York: Routledge, 2000.

Koikari, Mire. "Book review: *Empire of Care: Nursing and Migration in Filipino American History*." *Women's Studies International Forum* 28.1 (2005): 106–107.

Kokot, Waltraud, Khachig Tölöyan, and Carolin Alfonso, eds. *Diaspora, Identity and Religion: New Direction in Theory and Research*. New York: Routledge, 2004.

Kolb, Patricia J. "A Stage of Migration Approach to Understanding Nursing Home Placement in Latino Families." *Journal of Multicultural Social Work* 7.3/4 (1999): 95–112.

Kolker, Caryln. "Summer in Sana." *American Lawyer* 27.9 (2005): 28.

Kolker, Carlyn. "Touching the Untouchables." *American Lawyer* 26.12 (2004): 26–29.

Kondo, Atsushi. *Citizenship in a Global World: Comparing Citizenship Rights for Aliens*. Basingstoke: Palgrave, 2001.

Koopmans, Ruud, Paul Statham, Marco Giugni, and Florence Passy. *Contested Citizenship: Immigration and Cultural Diversity in Europe*. Minneapolis: University of Minnesota Press, 2005.

Korematsu v. United States 323 U.S. 214 (1944).

Koser, Khalid, ed. *New African Diasporas*. New York: Routledge, 2003.

Kremer, Michael, and Seema Jayachandran. "Odious Debt." International Monetary Fund. www.imf.org. Date Accessed: August 5, 2002.

Krishnadas, Jane. "The Sexual Subaltern in Conversations 'Somewhere in Between': Law and the Old Politics of Colonialism." *Feminist Legal Studies* 14.1 (2006): 53–77.

Kristof, Nicholas D. "Bush Takes on the Brothels." *New York Times* (May 19, 2006): A27.

Kudo, Kei. "Migration of Health Professionals." *The Lancet* 366.9481 (2005): 200.

Kulig, Judith C. "Family Life Among El Salvadorans, Guatemalans and Nicaraguans: A Comparative Study." *Journal of Comparative Family Studies* 29.3 (1998): 469–479.

Kumar, Amitava. "Introduction." *World Bank Literature*. Ed. Kumar. Minneapolis: University of Minnesota Press, 2003. xvii–xxxiii.

Kumar, Amitava, ed. *World Bank Literature*. Minneapolis: University of Minnesota Press, 2003.

Kumar, Amitava. "World Bank Literature: A New Name for Post-colonial Studies in the Next Century." *College Literature* 26.3 (Fall 1999): 125–134.

Kupchan, Charles A. *The End of the American Era: US Foreign Policy and the Geopolitics of the Twenty-First Century*. New York: Knopf, 2002.

Kuper, Andrew, ed. *Global Responsibilities: Who Must Deliver on Human Rights?* New York: Routledge, 2005.

Kurzban, Ira. "A Rational Foreign Policy Toward Haiti." NY Transfer News. www.blythe.org/nytransfer-subs/2001–Caribbean-Vol-1/A_Rational_Foreign_Policy_Toward_Haiti.

Kyle, David, and Rey Koslowski, eds. *Global Human Smuggling: Comparative Perspectives*. Baltimore: Johns Hopkins University Press, 2001.

La, John. "Forced Remittances in Canada's Tamil Enclaves." *Peace Review* 16.3 (2004): 379–385.

La Ferla, Ruth. "Retirees Come Full Circle." *New York Times* 154.53047 (2004): 1–6.

Labrianidis, Lois, and Brikena Kazazi. "Albanian Return-Migrants from Greece and Italy: Their Impact upon Spatial Disparities within Albania." *European Urban & Regional Studies* 13.1 (2006): 59–74.

Laferrière, Dany. *Down Among the Dead Men*. Trans. David Homel. Toronto: Douglas & McIntyre, 1997.

Laferrière, Dany. *Pays sans chapeau: roman*. Outremont, Québec: Lanctôt Éditeur, 1996.

Laguerre, Michel S. *Diasporic Citizenship: Haitian Americans in Transnational America*. New York: St. Martin's Press, 1998.

Lahav, Gallya. *Immigration and Politics in the New Europe: Reinventing Borders*. Cambridge: Cambridge University Press, 2004.

Lai, Him Mark. *Becoming Chinese American: A History of Communities and Institutions*. Lanham, MD: Rowman & Littlefield, 2004.

Laliotou, Ioanna. *Transatlantic Subjects: Acts of Migration and Cultures of Transnationalism between Greece and America*. Chicago: University of Chicago Press, 2004.

Lam, Andrew. *Perfume Dreams: Reflections on the Vietnamese Diaspora*. Berkeley, CA: Heyday Books, 2005.

Lancaster, Pat. "The Guantanamo Nightmare." *Middle East* (2005): 66.

Landman, James H. "Executive Power in an Age of Terror." *Social Education* 70.2 (2006): 93–98.

Langberg, Laura. "A Review of Recent OAS Research on Human Trafficking in the Latin American and Caribbean Region." *International Migration* 43.1/2 (2005): 129–139.

Lapham, Lewis H. "Notebook." *Harper's Magazine* 309.1855 (2004): 9–11.

Laplagne, Patrick, and Malcolm Treadgold. "A Model of Aid Impact in Some South Pacific Microstates." *World Development* 29.2 (2001): 365.

Latham, Robert, and Saskia Sassen, ed. *Digital Formations: IT and New Architectures in the Global Realm.* Princeton: Princeton University Press, 2005.

"Latina Nannies Care for American Childern." *Migration World Magazine* 27.5 (1999): 10.

Lavenex, Sandra. *The Europeanisation of Refugee Policies: Between Human Rights and Internal Security.* Aldershot: Ashgate, 2001.

Lavie, Smadar, and Ted Swedenburg. "Introduction: Displacement, Diaspora, and Geographies of Identity." *Displacement, Diaspora, and Geographies of Identity.* Ed. Lavie and Swedenburg. Durham, NC: Duke University Press, 1996. 1–25.

"Law Against Sex Trafficking." *Off Our Backs* 32.7/8: 5.

Law, Lisa. "Home Cooking: Filipino Women and Geographies of the Senses in Hong Kong." *ECUMENE* 8.3 (2001): 264–283.

Law, Lisa. *Sex Work in Southeast Asia: The Place of Desire in a Time of AIDS.* New York: Routledge, 2000.

Lazaridis, Gabriella. "Filipino and Albanian Women Migrant Workers in Greece: Multiple Layers of Oppression." *Gender and Migration in Southern Europe.* Ed. Anthias and Lazaridis. New York: Berg, 2000. 49–80.

Lazin, Fred A. *The Struggle for Soviet Jewry in American Politics: Israel versus American Jewish Establishment.* Lanham, MD: Lexington Books, 2005.

Leather, Andrew, et al. "Working Together to Rebuild Health Care in Post-conflict Somaliland." *The Lancet* 368.9541 (2006): 1119–1125.

Lechner, Frank J., and John Boli, eds. *The Globalization Reader.* Oxford: Blackwell, 2001.

Lee, Erika. *At America's Gates: Chinese Immigration during the Exclusion Era, 1882–1943.* Chapel Hill: University of North Carolina Press, 2003.

Lee, Helen. "'Second Generation' Tongan Transnationalism: Hope for the Future?" *Asia Pacific Viewpoint* 45.2 (2004): 235–254.

LeGates, Richard T., and Frederic Stout, eds. *The City Reader.* New York: Routledge, 2000.

Lelyveld, Joseph. "In Guantánamo." *New York Review of Books* 49.17 (2002): 62.

LeMay, Michael C. *US Immigration: A Reference Handbook.* Santa Barbara: ABC-CLIO, 2004.

Lenzer, Jeanne. "Teenager Held in Guantanamo Denied Medical Evaluation." *British Medical Journal* 329.7474 (2004): 1066.

Leone, Richard C., and Greg Anrig, Jr. eds. *The War on Our Freedoms: Civil Liberties in an Age of Terrorism.* New York: Public Affairs, 2003.

Leong, Russell, ed. *Asian American Sexualities: Dimensions of the Gay and Lesbian Experience.* New York: Routledge, 1996.

León-Ledesma, Miguel, and Matloob Piracha. "International Migration and the Role of Remittances in Eastern Europe." *International Migration* 42.4 (2004): 65–83.

Leopold, Evelyn. "Migrants Spur Economic Growth, But Treated Harshly." Reuters UK. October 6, 2005.

Levitt, Peggy. "Social Remittances: Migration Driven Local-Level Forms of Cultural Diffusion." *International Migration Review* 32.4 (1998): 926–948.

Lewis, Anthony. "Guantánamo's Long Shadow." *New York Times* 154.53252 (2005): A21.

Lewis, Anthony, Jennifer Hahn, and Wasim Salfiti. "One Liberty at a Time." *Mother Jones* 29.3: 72–78.

Lewis, Laura A. "Home Is Where the Heart Is: Afro-Latino Migration and Cinder-Block Homes on Mexico's Costa Chica." *South Atlantic Quarterly* 105.4 (2006): 801–829.

Lewis, Neil A. "Detainees May Test Reach of Guantánamo Ruling." *New York Times* (1 July 2006): A10.

Lewis, Neil A. "Freed From Guantánamo but Stranded Far From Home." *New York Times* 155.53672 (2006): A15.

Lewis, Neil A. "Military Lawyers Prepare To Speak on Guantánamo." *New York Times* (11 July 2006): A14.

Lewis, Neil A. "Red Cross Interviews 14 Qaeda Terrorism Suspects at Guantánamo." *New York Times* 156.53731 (2006): A18.

Lewis, Neil A. "Red Cross Officials to Visit Prisoners at Guantánamo." *New York Times* 156.53708 (2006): A18.

Lewis, Neil A. "US to Seek Dismissal of Guantámano Suits." *New York Times* 155.53449 (2006): A11.

Lewis, Neil A. "2 Prosecutors Faulted Trials For Detainees (Cover story)." *New York Times* 154.53293 (2005): A1–A12.

Lewis, Neil A. "At Guantánamo, Refueling With Java and Windmills." *New York Times* 154.53166 (2005): 23.

Lewis, Neil A. "Detainee's Lawyer Says Captors Foment Mistrust." *New York Times* 155.53421 (2005): A24.

Lewis, Neil A. "Documents Say Detainees Cited Abuse of Koran (Cover story)." *New York Times* 154.53226 (2005): A1–A19.

Lewis, Neil A. "Federal Judge Deals Setback To Detainees." *New York Times* 154.53100 (2005): A20.

Lewis, Neil A. "Guantánamo Detainees Gain in Ruling." *New York Times* 155.53380 (2005): A22.

Lewis, Neil A. "Guantánamo Detainees Make Their Case." *New York Times* 154.53163 (2005): A21.

Lewis, Neil A. "Head of Hospital At Guantánamo Faces Complaint." *New York Times* 154.53276 (2005): A13.

Lewis, Neil A. "Hunger Strike By Detainees Goes to Court." *New York Times* 155.53345 (2005): A29.

Lewis, Neil A. "In Raising Numbers, Lawyers Head for Guantánamo Bay." *New York Times* 154.53230 (2005): A10.

Lewis, Neil A. "Interrogators Cite Doctors' Aid at Guantánamo (Cover story)." *New York Times* 154.53255 (2005): A1–A17.

Lewis, Neil A. "Judge Extends Legal Rights For Guantánamo Detainees." *New York Times* 154.53112 (2005): A12.

Lewis, Neil A. "Ruling Lets US Restart Trials at Guantánamo (Cover story)." *New York Times* 156.53277 (2005): A1–A10.

Lewis, Neil A. "Some Held at Guantánamo Are Minors, Lawyers Say." *New York Times* 154.53244 (2005): A14.

Lewis, Neil A. "US Eroding Inmate's Trust At Cuba Base, Lawyers Say." *New York Times* 154.53147 (2005): A18.

Lewis, Neil A. "US Lawyer Is Questioned Over Rights Of Detainees." *New York Times* 154.53332 (2005): A16.

Lewis, Neil A. "Australian May Face US Tribunal." *New York Times* 153.52868 (2004): A16–A16.

Lewis, Neil A. "Broad Use of Harsh Tactics Is Described at Cuba Base." *New York Times* 154.53005 (2004): 1–21.

Lewis, Neil A. "Bush's Power To Plan Trial of Detainees Is Challenged." *New York Times* 153.52730 (2004): A16.

Lewis, Neil A. "Disagreement Over Detainees' Legal Rights Simmers." *New York Times* 154.53020 (2004): A15.

Lewis, Neil A. "Fate of Guantánamo Detainees Is Debated in Federal Court." *New York Times* 154.53051 (2004): A36.

Lewis, Neil A. "Freedom for Chinese Detainees Hinges On Finding a New Homeland." *New York Times* 154.53027 (2004): A17.

Lewis, Neil A. "General Takes Three Officers Off Tribunal At Cuba Base." *New York Times* 154.53010 (2004): A21.

Lewis, Neil A. "Guantánamo Prisoners Getting Their Day, but Hardly in Court (Cover story)." *New York Times* 154.53027 (2004): A1–A17.

Lewis, Neil A. "Lawyer Says Detainees Face Unfair System." *New York Times* 153.52736 (2004): A25.

Lewis, Neil A. "Military's Lawyers For Detainees Put Tribunals on Trial (Cover story)." *New York Times* 153.52839 (2004): A1–A24.

Lewis, Neil A. "Red Cross President Plans Visit to Washington on Question of Detainees' Treatment." *New York Times* 154.53050 (2004): A27.

Lewis, Neil A. "Relatives of Prisoners at Guantánamo Bay Tell of Anger and Sadness at Detentions." *New York Times* 153.52782 (2004): A13.

Lewis, Neil A. "Scrutiny of Review Tribunals As War Crimes Trials Open." *New York Times* 153.52951 (2004): A12.

Lewis, Neil A. "US Charges Two at Guantánamo with Conspiracy." *New York Times* 153.52770 (2004): A1–A14.

Lewis, Neil A. "US Is Readying Review For Detainees in Cuba." *New York Times* 153.52913 (2004): A10.

Lewis, Neil A. "US Judge Halts War-Crime Trial at Guantánamo (Cover story)." *New York Times* 154.53028 (2004): A1–A16.

Lewis, Neil A. "US Military Describes Findings at Guantánamo." *New York Times* 153.52795 (2004): 8.

Lewis, Neil A. "Detainees From the Afghan War Remain in a Legal Limbo in Cuba (Cover story)." *New York Times* 152.52463 (2003): A1.

Lewis, Neil A. "Lawyer Upset By Treatment of Ex-Chaplain For Detainees." *New York Times* 153.52647 (2003): A14.

Lewis, Neil A. "Red Cross Criticizes Indefinite Detention In Guantánamo Bay." *New York Times* 152.52632 (2003): A1–A24.

Lewis, Neil A. "Try Detainees or Free Them, 3 Senators Urge." *New York Times* 153.52696 (2003): A14.

Lewis, Neil A. "US in Talks To Return Scores Held At Cuba Site." *New York Times* 153.52684 (2003): A7.

Lewis, Neil A. "Guantánamo Prisoners Seek To See Families and Lawyers." *New York Times* 152.52321 (2002): A22.

Lewis, Neil A. "Judge Rebuffs Detainees at Guantánamo." *New York Times* 151.52197 (2002): A20.

Lewis, Neil A., and Julia Preston. "US Allows Lawyers To Meet Detainees." *New York Times* 153.52899 (2004): A16.

Lewis, Neil A., and Eric Schmitt. "Cuba Detentions May Last Years (Cover story)." *New York Times* 153.52758 (2004): A1–A21.

Li, Peter S. "Not One of the Family (Book)." *Journal of Ethnic & Migration Studies* 24.4 (1998): 795.

Lianos, Theodore P. "Factors Determining Migrant Remittances: The Case of Greece." *International Migration Review* 31.1 (1997): 72–87.

Lichtblau, Eric. "Justice Dept. Opens Inquiry Into Abuse of US Detainees." *New York Times* 154.53094 (2005): A20.

Lindorff, Dave. "Chertoff and Torture." *Nation* (14 Feb. 2005): 6+.

Liptak, Adam. "Scholars Agree That Congress Could Reject Conventions, but Not That It Should." *New York Times* 155.53641 (2006): A10.

Liptak, Adam, and Michael Janofsky. "Scrappy Group of Lawyers Shows Way for Big Firms." *New York Times* 153.52896 (2004): A14.

Lipton, Eric. "Seeking to Control Borders, Bush Turns to Big Military Contractors." *New York Times* (18 May 2006): A1.

Lo, Fu-chen, and Yue-man Yeung, eds. *Globalization and the World of Large Cities* [electronic resource]. Tokyo: United Nations University Press, 1998.

Loescher, Gil. *Beyond Charity: International Cooperation and the Global Refugee Crisis.* Oxford: Oxford University Press, 1994.

Long, Lynellyn D., and Ellen Oxfeld, eds. *Coming Home? Refugees, Migrants, and Those who Stayed Behind.* Philadelphia: University of Pennsylvania Press, 2004.

Louie, Andrea. *Chineseness across Borders: Renegotiating Chinese Identities in China and the United States.* Durham, NC: Duke University Press, 2004.

Lovink, Geert. *Uncanny Networks: Dialogues with the Virtual Intelligentsia.* Cambridge, MA: MIT Press, 2002.

Lowe, Lisa. *Immigrant Acts: On Asian American Cultural Politics.* Durham, NC: Duke University Press, 1996.

Lowell, B. Lindsay, and Stefka Georgieva Gerova. "Immigrants and the Healthcare Workforce: Profiles and Shortages." *Work & Occupations* 31.4 (2004): 474–498.

Lowell, B. Lindsay, and Mike Hogg. "Remittances, US Latino Communities, and Development in Latin American Countries." *Migration World Magazine* 28.5 (2000): 13.

Lowenstein, Roger. "The Immigration Equation." *New York Times Magazine* (9 July 2006): 36–43, 69–71.

Lowenstein, Steven M. *The Jewish Cultural Tapestry: International Jewish Folk Traditions.* New York: Oxford University Press, 2000.

Lucas, Robert E. B. *International Migration and Economic Development: Lessons from Low-Income Countries.* Northampton, MA: Edward Elgar, 2005.

Lucassen, Jan, and Leo Lucassen, eds. *Migration, Migration History, History: Old Paradigms and New Perspectives.* New York: Peter Lang, 1997.

Lucassen, Leo. *The Immigrant Threat: The Integration of Old and New Migrants in Western Europe since 1850.* Urbana: University of Illinois Press, 2005.

Luibhéid, Eithne. "Introduction: Queering Migration and Citizenship." *Queer Migrations: Sexuality, US Citizenship, and Border Crossings.* Ed. Luibhéid and Cantú. Minneapolis: University of Minnesota Press, 2005. ix–xlvi.

Luibhéid, Eithne. *Entry Denied: Controlling Sexuality at the Border.* Minneapolis: University of Minnesota Press, 2002.

Luibhéid, Eithne, and Lionel Cantú, Jr., eds. *Queer Migrations: Sexuality, US Citizenship, and Border Crossings.* Minneapolis: University of Minnesota Press, 2005.

Luxner, Larry. "Do As We Say, Not As We Do." *Middle East* (2003): 16.

Lydersen, Kari. *Out of the Sea and Into the Fire: Latin American-US Immigration in the Global Age.* Monroe, ME: Common Courage Press, 2005.

McAlister, Elizabeth. *Rara! Vodou, Power, and Performance in Haiti and Its Diaspora.* Berkeley: University of California Press, 2002.

McCarthy, Andrew C. "The New Juristocracy." *New Criterion* 25.1 (2006): 65–70.

McClintock, Anne, ed. "Sex Workers and Sex Work." Special edition of *Social Text* 37 (Winter 1993).

McCorkle, Bajeera. "Law, Politics and the US Policy of Detentions in Guantanamo Bay." *Conference Papers – American Political Science Association* (2004): 1–22.

McCully, Patrick. "Sardaar Sarovar Project (SSP): An Overview." International Rivers Network (May 25, 1994). Friends of the River Narmada Website: www.narmada.org/sardar-sarovar/irnoverview940525.html.

McDonald, David A., ed. *On Borders: Perspectives on International Migration in Southern Africa.* New York: Southern African Migration Project, St. Martin's Press, 2000.

McDonough, Gary, and Cindy Wong. *Global Hong Kong.* New York: Routledge, 2005.

McElroy, Jerome L. "Small Island Tourist Economies Across the Life Cycle." *Asia Pacific Viewpoint* 47.1 (2006): 61–77.

McGuire, Sharon, and Jane Georges. "Undocumentedness and Liminality as Health Variables." *Advances in Nursing Science* 26.3 (2003): 185.

McKay, Deirdre. "Cultivating New Local Futures: Remittance Economics and Land-Use Patterns in Ifugao, Philippines." *Journal of Southeast Asian Studies* 34.2 (2003): 285.

Mackell, Jan. *Brothels, Bordellos, and Bad Girls: Prostitution in Colorado, 1860–1930.* Albuquerque: University of New Mexico Press, 2004.

McLaughlin, James. "Status Review." *News Media & the Law* 28.3 (2004): 27–28.

McLellan, Faith. "Doing Justice – Justly." *The Lancet* 359.9304 (2002): 372.

McLeod, Mark Christian. "Undesirable Aliens: Haitian and British West Indian Immigrant Workers to Cuba, 1898 to 1940." PhD Dissertation: University of Texas-Austin, 2000.

McLeod, Mark Christian. "Undesirable Aliens." *Journal of Social History* 21 (1998): 599–624.

McMaster, Don. *Asylum Seekers: Australia's Response to Refugees.* Victoria: Melbourne University Press, 2001.

MacMaster, Neil. "Torture: From Algiers to Abu Ghraib." *Race & Class* 46.2 (2004): 1–21.

MacMaster, Neil. *Colonial Migrants and Racism: Algerians in France, 1900–62.* London: Macmillan; New York: St. Martin's Press, 1997.

McNeil-Walsh, Colleen. "Widening the Discourse: A Case for the Use of Post-colonial Theory in the Analysis of South African Nurse Migration to Britain." *Feminist Review* (2004): 120–124.

"Madrid Blasts: Who is to Blame?" British Broadcasting Corporation. BBC News Online: www.newsvote.bbc.co.uk/mpapps/pagetools/news.bbc.co.uk/2/hi/europe/3512748.stm.

Maggard, Kasey Q. "The Role of Social Capital in the Remittance Decisions of Mexican Migrants from 1969 to 2000." *Working Paper Series (Federal Reserve Bank of Atlanta)* 2004.29 (2004): 1–41.

Maher, Kristen Hill, and Silke Staab. "Nanny Politics." *International Feminist Journal of Politics* 7.1 (2005): 71–89.

Mahler, Jonathan. "The Bush Administration vs. Salim Hamdan (Cover story)." *New York Times Magazine* 155.53453 (2006): 44–90.

Mahler, Jonathan. "Commander Swift Objects." *New York Times Magazine* 153.52879 (2004): 42–47.

Maira, Sunaina, and Elisabeth Soep, eds. *Youthscapes: The Popular, The National, The Global*. Philadelphia: University of Pennsylvania Press, 2005.

Maiti, Prasenjit. "'Till the Rivers All Run Dry': A Human Ecological Analysis of the Narmada Bachao Andolan." *Electronic Green Journal* 14 (Spring 2001). www.egj.lib. uidaho.edu/egj14/index.html.

Malkin, Brendan. "Lovells Resigns Guantanamo Case." *Lawyer* 18.16 (2004): 3–3.

Manalansan IV, Martin F. *Global Divas: Filipino Gay Men in the Diaspora*. Durham, NC: Duke University Press, 2003.

Manalansan IV, Martin F. "Diasporic Deviants/Divas: How Filipino Gay Transmigrants 'Play with the World'." *Queer Diasporas*. Ed. Cynthia Patton and Benigno Sánchez-Eppler. Durham, NC: Duke University Press, 2000. 183–203.

Manalansan IV, Martin F. "In the Shadows of Stonewall: Examining Gay/Lesbian Transnational Politics and the Diasporic Dilemma." *GLQ: A Journal of Lesbian and Gay Studies* 2.4 (1995): 425–438. Reprinted in *Theorizing Diaspora: A Reader*. Ed. Jana Evans Braziel and Anita Mannur. Oxford: Blackwell, 2002. 207–227.

Manalansan IV, Martin F. "(Dis)Orienting the Body: Locating Symbolic Resistance among Filipino Gay Men." *positions* 2.1 (Spring 1994): 73–90.

Manalansan IV, Martin F. "(Re)Locating the Gay Filipino: Resistance, Postcolonialism, and Identity." *Critical Essays: Gay and Lesbian Writers of Color*. Ed. Emmanuel S. Nelson. New York: Haworth, 1993. 53–72.

"Mandatory Detention: Protection or Punishment (Cover story)." *Australian Nursing Journal* 9.8 (2002): 26–28.

Manderson, Lenore. "Parables of Imperialism and Fantasies of the Exotic: Western Representations of Thailand – Place and Sex." *Sites of Desire, Economies of Pleasure: Sexualities in Asia and the Pacific*. Chicago: University of Chicago Press, 1997. 123–144.

Mann, Michael. *Incoherent Empire*. London: Verso, 2003.

Marcelli, Enrico A., and B. Lindsay Lowell. "Transnational Twist: Pecuniary Remittances and the Socioeconomic Integration of Authorized and Unauthorized Mexican Immigrants in Los Angeles County." *International Migration Review* 39.1 (2005): 69–102.

Marek, Angie C. "The First to Face Tribunals." *US News & World Report* 136.8 (2004): 35.

Marguiles, Joseph. "A Prison Beyond the Law." *Virginia Quarterly Review* 80.4 (2004): 37–55.

"Marine Defends Guantánamo Detainee, and Surprises Australians." *New York Times* 153.52802 (2004): 13.

Markowitz, Fran, and Anders H. Stefansson, eds. *Homecomings: Unsettling Paths of Return*. Lanham, MD: Lexington Books, 2004.

Maroukis, Thanos. "Albanian Migrants in Greece: Transcending 'Borders' in Development." *Journal of Southern Europe & the Balkans* 7.2 (2005): 213–233.

Marquis, Christopher. "Pentagon Will Permit Captives At Cuba Base to Appeal Status (Cover story)." *New York Times* 153.52904 (2004): A1–A11.

Marshall, Phil, and Susu Thatun. "Miles Away: The Trouble with Prevention in the Greater Mekong Sub-Region." *Trafficking and Prostitution Reconsidered: New Perspectives on Migration, Sex Work, and Human Rights*. Ed. Kamala Kempadoo, Jyoti Sanghera, and Bandana Pattanaik. Boulder: Paradigm Publishers, 2005. 43–64.

Martí, José. *José Martí: Selected Writings*. Trans. Esther Allen. New York: Penguin Putnam, 2002.

Martin, Philip. "Migration and Development in Mexico." *Social Science Quarterly (University of Texas Press)* 79.1 (1998): 26–32.

Martin, Philip. "Migration and Trade: The Case of the Philippines." *International Migration Review* 27.3 (1993): 639–645.

Martin, Philip, Manolo Abella, and Elizabeth Midgley. "Best Practices to Manage Migration: The Philippines." *International Migration Review* 38.4 (2004): 1544–1559.

Martin, Philip, Susan Martin, and Ferruccio Pastore. "Best Practice Options: Albania." *International Migration* 40.3 (2002): 103.

Martin, Philip, Susan Martin, and Patrick Weil. "Best Practice Options: Mali." *International Migration* 40.3 (2002): 87.

Martin, Philip, Elizabeth Midgley, and Michael S. Teitelbaum. "Best Practice Options: Turkey." *International Migration* 40.3 (2002): 119.

Martin, Philip, Elizabeth Midgley, and Michael S. Teitelbaum. "Migration and Development: Whither the Dominican Republic and Haiti?" *International Migration Review* 36.2 (2002): 570–592.

Martin, Philip, Elizabeth Midgley, and Michael S. Teitelbaum. "Migration and Development: Focus on Turkey." *International Migration Review* 35.2 (2001): 596–605.

Martin, Susan. "Best Practice Options: Yugoslavia." *International Migration* 40.3 (2002): 59.

Martyr, Philippa. "Convict Maids (Book Review)." *H-Net Reviews in the Humanities & Social Sciences* (1998).

Maschke, Karen J., ed. *Gender and American Law: The Impact of the Law on the Lives of Women.* New York: Garland, 1997.

Masci, David. "The Issues." *CQ Researcher* 12.43 (2002): 1015.

Massey, Douglas S., and J. Edward Taylor, eds. *International Migration: Prospects and Policies in a Global Market.* Oxford: Oxford University Press, 2004.

Massey, Douglas S., and Lawrence C. Basem. "Determinants of Savings, Remittances, and Spending Patterns among US Migrants in Four Mexican Communities." *Sociological Inquiry* 62.2 (1992): 185–207.

Masud-Piloto, Felix Roberto. *From Welcomed Exiles to Illegal Immigrants: Cuban Migration to the US, 1959–1995.* Lanham, MD: Rowman & Littlefield, 1996.

Mathews, Paul W. "Book Reviews." *Journal of Contemporary Asia* 23.4 (1993): 570.

Mazzetti, Mark. "Combative Bush Releases Parts of Terror Study." *New York Times* (27 Sept. 2006): A1, A6.

Mazzetti, Mark, et al. "Inside the Iraq Prison Scandal (Cover story)." *US News & World Report* 136.18 (2004): 18–28.

Mazzucato, Valentina, Mirjam Kabki, and Lothar Smith. "Transnational Migration and the Economy of Funerals: Changing Practices in Ghana." *Development & Change* 37.5 (2006): 1047–1072.

Meeropol, Rachel, ed. *America's Disappeared: Secret Imprisonment, Detainees, and the "War on Terror."* New York: Seven Stories Press, 2005.

Meier, Viktor. *Yugoslavia: A History of Its Demise.* Trans. Sabrina Ramet. New York: Routledge, 1999.

Meilaender, Peter C. *Toward a Theory of Immigration.* New York: Palgrave, 2001.

Menjívar, Cecilia, et al. "Remittance Behavior Among Salvadoran and Filipino Immigrants in Los Angeles." *International Migration Review* 32.1 (1998): 97–126.

"Mexico Seeks Lower Fees on Funds Sent from US." *Migration World Magazine* 29.3 (2001): 10.

Meyer, Birgit, and Peter Geschiere, eds. *Globalization and Identity: Dialectics of Flow and Closure.* Oxford: Blackwell, 1999.

Meyers, Eytan. *International Immigration Policy: A Theoretical and Comparative Analysis.* New York: Palgrave Macmillan, 2004.

Michaelsen, Scott, and Scott Cutler Shershow. "Beyond and Before the Law at Guantánamo." *Peace Review* 16.3 (2004): 293–303.

Micollierr, Evelyne, ed. *Sexual Cultures in East Asia: The Social Construction of Sexuality and Sexual Risk in a Time of AIDS*. New York: Routledge Curzon, 2004.

"Migration, Remittances and Gender in the Context of Development: The Case of Thailand (Book)." *International Migration Review* 37.3 (2003): 927.

"Migration Threatens Health Systems in Developing Countries." *Australian Nursing Journal* 13.6: 10.

Miles, Malcolm, Tim Hall, and Iain Borden, eds. *The City Cultures Reader*. New York: Routledge, 2000.

Miles, Steven H. "Abu Ghraib: Its Legacy for Military Medicine." *The Lancet* 364.9435 (2004): 725–729.

Miller, Alice M. "Gay Enough: Some Tensions in Seeking the Grant of Asylum and Protecting Global Sexual Diversity." *Passing Lines: Sexuality and Immigration*. Ed. Brad Epps, Keja Valens, and Bill Johnson González. Cambridge, MA: Harvard University, David Rockefeller Center for Latin American Studies, 2005. 137–188.

Millman, Joel. "Mexicans Are Home for Holidays, Bearing Gifts for Rural Economy." *Wall Street Journal – Eastern Edition* 232.127 (1998): A7.

Mills, Charles W. *The Racial Contract*. Ithaca: Cornell University Press, 1997.

Minca, Claudio. "The Return of the Camp." *Progress in Human Geography* 29.4 (2005): 405–412.

Mingione, Enzo, ed. *Urban Poverty and the Underclass: A Reader*. Oxford: Blackwell, 1996.

"Ministering to the Enemy." *New York Times Magazine* 152.52634 (2003): 54.

Miriam, Kathy. "Stopping the Traffic in Women: Power, Agency and Abolition in Feminist Debates over Sex-Trafficking." *Journal of Social Philosophy* 36.1 (2005): 1–17.

Mitchell, Peter. *African Connections: Archaeological Perspectives on Africa and the Wider World*. Lanham, MD: AltaMira, Rowman & Littlefield, 2005.

Mittelman, James H., ed. *Globalization: Critical Reflections*. Boulder: Lynne Rienner Publishers, 1996.

Mobrand, Erik. "Politics of Cityward Migration: An Overview of China in Comparative Perspective." *Habitat International* 30.2 (2006): 261–274.

Moch, Leslie Page. *Moving Europeans: Migration in Western Europe since 1650*. Bloomington: Indiana University Press, 2003.

Momsen, Janet. *Gender, Migration and Domestic Service*. New York: Routledge, 1999.

Money, Jeanette. *Fences and Neighbors: The Political Geography of Immigration Control*. Ithaca: Cornell University Press, 1999.

Mooney, Margarita. "Migrants' Social Ties in the US and Investment in Mexico." *Social Forces* 81.4 (2003): 1147–1170.

Moors, Annelies. "Migrant Domestic Workers: Debating Transnationalism, Identity Politics, and Family Relations. A Review Essay." *Comparative Studies in Society & History* 45.2 (2003): 386.

Morales, Rebecca, and Frank Bonilla, eds. *Latinos in a Changing US Economy: Comparative Perspectives on Growing Inequality*. Newbury Park, CA: Sage, 1993.

"More Countries Plan 'Export' Programmes." *Nursing Standard* 18.40 (2004): 4.

Moreno, Jonathan D. "Detainee Ethics: Terrorists Subjects as Research." *American Journal of Bioethics* 3.4 (2003): 32–33.

"Morocco Tries Ex-Guantánamo Prisoners." *New York Times* 154.53056 (2004): A9.

Morris, Meaghan, and Brett de Bary, eds. *"Race" Panic and the Memory of Migration.* Trans. Bernard Prusak et al. Hong Kong: Hong Kong University Press; Banbury: Drake, 2001.

Muecke, Marjorie. "Mother Sold Food, Daughter Sells Her Body: The Cultural Continuity of Prostitution." *Social Science and Medicine* 35.7 (1992): 891–901.

Munger, Frank, ed. *Laboring Below the Line: The New Ethnography of Poverty, Low-wage Work, and Survival in the Global Economy.* New York: Russell Sage Foundation, 2002.

Muñoz, José Esteban. *Disidentifications: Queers of Color and the Performance of Politics.* Minneapolis: University of Minnesota Press, 1999.

Muñoz, José Esteban. "The Autoethnographic Performance: Reading Richard Fung's Queer Hybridity." *Screen* 36.2 (1995): 83–99.

Muñoz, José Esteban, and Amanda Barrett. Special Issue on "Queer Acts." *Women and Performance: A Journal of Feminist Theory* 8.2 (1996).

Munro, Martin. "Can't Stand Up for Falling Down: Haiti, Its Revolutions, and Twentieth-Century Negritudes." Special Issue: "Haiti, 1804–2004: Literature, Culture, and Art." *Research in African Literatures* 35.2 (Summer 2004): 2–17.

Münz, Rainer, and Rainer Ohliger, eds. *Diasporas and Ethnic Migrants: Germany, Israel and Post-Soviet Successor States in Comparative Perspective.* London: Frank Cass, 2003.

Münz, Rainer, and Myron Weiner, eds. *Migrants, Refugees, and Foreign Policy: US and German Policies toward Countries of Origin.* Providence: Berghahn Books, 1997.

Murdock, Deroy. "Gitmo Legal." *National Review* 57.22 (2005): 28–29.

Murphy, Rachel. "Migration and Inter-household Inequality: Observations from Wanzai County, Jiangxi." *China Quarterly* (2000): 965.

Murray, Elizabeth. "Russian Nurses: From the Tsarist Sister of Mercy to the Soviet Comrade Nurse: A Case Study of Absence of Migration of Nursing Knowledge and Skills." *Nursing Inquiry* 11.3 (2004): 130–137.

Musalo, Karen, Jennifer Moore, and Richard A. Boswell. *Refugee Law and Policy: A Comparative and International Approach.* Durham, NC: Carolina Academic Press, 2002.

Myers, Steven Lee, et al. "World Briefing." *New York Times* 155.53485 (2006): A8.

Myhill, John. *Language in Jewish Society: Towards a New Understanding.* Buffalo: Multilingual Matters, 2004.

Na He, et al. "Sexual Behavior among Employed Male Rural Migrants in Shanghai, China." *AIDS Education & Prevention* 18.2 (2006): 176–186.

Nackerud, Larry, et al. "The End of the Cuban Contradiction in US Refugee Policy." *International Migration Review* 33.1 (1999): 176–192.

Nagle, Jill, ed. *Whores and Other Feminists.* New York: Routledge, 1997.

Nagourney, Adam. "Dispute on Intelligence Report Disrupts Republicans' Game Plan." *New York Times* (28 Sept. 2006): A20.

Nairn, Alan. "Haiti Under the Gun: How US-Backed Paramilitaries Rule through Fear." *Nation* (8–15 Jan. 1996).

Nairn, Alan. "Behind Haiti's Paramilitaries." *Nation* (24 Oct. 1994).

Nairn, Alan. "He's our SOB." *Nation* (31 Oct. 1994): 481–482.

Nairn, Alan. "Our Man in FRAPH." *Nation* (24 Oct. 1994): 458–461.

Narayanan, Suresh, and Yew-Wah Lai. "The Causes and Consequences of Immigrant Labour in the Construction Sector in Malaysia." *International Migration* 43.5 (2005): 31–57.

Nathan, Debbie. "Oversexed." *The Nation* (29 Aug. 2005). Electronic copy available online at *The Nation* Website: www.thenation.com/doc/20050829/nathan.

"National Briefing." *New York Times* 154.53316 (2005): A14.

National Labor Committee (NLC). *The US in Haiti: How to Get Rich on 11¢ an Hour.* Washington, DC: National Labor Committee Education Fund, 1996.

National Security Council, The White House. "The National Security Strategy of the USA." Date posted: September 2002. Date accessed: March 2003. www.whitehouse.gov/nsc/nss.html.

"NCC Joins in Brief on Prison Detainees." *Christian Century* 121.3 (2004): 15.

Negri, Antonio, and Michael Hardt. *Empire.* Cambridge, MA: Harvard University Press, 2001.

Nethersole, Reingard. "Models of Globalization." *PMLA* 116.3 (May 2001): 638–649.

Nevins, Joseph. *Operation Gatekeeper: The Rise of the "Illegal Alien" and the Remaking of the US-Mexico Boundary.* New York: Routledge, 2002.

"New Round of Hearings at Guantánamo." *New York Times* 154.53065 (2004): A36.

"New Threats Said to Be From Qaeda Figure." *New York Times* 152.52564 (2003): 5.

"New US Legislation Prohibits Cruel, Inhuman, or Degrading Treatment, Restricts Habeas Corpus Petitions by Guantánamo Detainees, and Establishes Limited Judicial Review of Military Commissions." *American Journal of International Law* 100.2 (2006): 455–459.

Newhouse, John. *Imperial America: The Bush Assault on the World Order.* New York: Knopf, 2003.

Newitt, Malyn D. D. *A History of Portuguese Overseas Expansion, 1400–1668.* New York: Routledge, 2005.

Newman, Edward, and Joanne van Selm, eds. *Refugees and Forced Displacement: International Security, Human Vulnerability, and the State.* New York: United Nations University Press, 2003.

Newman, Edward. "Refugees, International Security, and Human Vulnerability: Introduction and Survey." *Refugees and Forced Displacement: International Security, Human Vulnerability, and the State.* Ed. Edward Newman and Joanne van Selm. New York: United Nations University Press, 2003. 3–30.

"News." *Nursing Ethics* 13.1 (2006): 91–93.

"News." *Nursing Ethics* 6.6 (1999): 541–543.

Nicholl, David J., et al. "Forcefeeding and Restraint of Guantanamo Bay Hunger Strikers." *The Lancet* 367.9513 (2006): 811.

Nicholls, David. *From Dessalines to Duvalier: Race, Colour, and National Independence in Haiti.* Cambridge: Cambridge University Press, 1979.

Nichols, Barbara, and Judith Oulton. "Developing a New Resource on International Nurse Migration: The International Centre on Nurse Migration." *Policy, Politics & Nursing Practice* 6.3 (2005): 168–170.

Nishigaya, Kasumi. "Female Garment Factory Workers in Cambodia: Migration, Sex Work and HIV/AIDS." *Women & Health* 35.4 (2002): 27.

"North Korea and Cuba Censured." *New York Times* 153.52821 (2004): A6.

"Not Good Enough." *Economist* 372.8382 (2004): 12.

"Notable and Quotable." *Wall Street Journal – Eastern Edition* 246.27 (2005): D8.

"Notable Supreme Court Decisions, 2003–2004." *World Almanac & Book of Facts* (2005): 43.

"Notice Board." *Nursing Standard* 20.18 (2006): 71.

Novak, Viveca. "A Thaw in the Legal War on Terrorism?" *Time* 163.17 (2004): 18.

Novak, Viveca. "The Detainees' New Friends." *Time* 163.3 (2004): 18.

Novak, Viveca. "The Guantanamo Detainees: Getting Heard." *Time* 164.2 (2004): 20.

Novak, Viveca. "A Softer Approach?" *Time* 162.24 (2003): 17.

Novak, Viveca, and Sally B. Donnelly. "Impure Tactics." *Time* 165.8 (2005): 33.

"Numbers." *Time* 166.13 (2005): 18.

Nyberg-Sørensen, Ninna, Nicholas Van Hear, and Poul Engberg-Pedersen. "The Migration-Development Nexus: Evidence and Policy Options." *International Migration* 40.5 (2002): 49.

Nye, Joseph S. *The Paradox of American Power: Why the World's Only Superpower Can't Go It Alone*. New York: Oxford University Press, 2002.

Nye, Joseph S., and John D. Donahue, eds. *Governance in a Globalizing World: Visions of Governance for the 21st Century*. Washington, DC: Brookings Institution Press, 2000.

Ogata, Sadako. *The Turbulent Decade: Confronting the Refugee Crises of the 1990s*. New York: W. W. Norton, 2005.

Öger, Vural. *Mein Deutschland, Meine Türkei: Leben zwischen Bosporus and Elbe*. Berlin: Rowohlt, 2002.

Okamura, Jonathan. "*Empire of Care*: Nursing and Migration in Filipino American History." *Amerasia Journal* 31.2 (2005): 193–196.

Olesen, Henrik. "Migration, Return, and Development: An Institutional Perspective." *International Migration* 40.5 (2002): 125.

O'Meara, Patrick, Howard D. Mehlinger, and Matthew Krain, eds. *Globalization and the Challenges of the New Century: A Reader*. Bloomington: Indiana University Press, 2000.

Omelaniuk, Irena. "Best Practices to Manage Migration: China." *International Migration* 43.5 (2005): 189–206.

Omeri, Akram, Christopher Lennings, and Lynnette Raymond. "Beyond Asylum: Implications for Nursing and Health Care Delivery for Afghan Refugees in Australia." *Journal of Transcultural Nursing* 17.1 (2006): 30–39.

Ong, Aihwa. *Flexible Citizenship: The Cultural Logics of Transnationality*. Durham, NC: Duke University Press, 1998.

Ong, Aihwa. "On the Edge of Empires: Flexible Citizenship among the Chinese in Diaspora." *positions* 1.3 (1993): 745–778.

"Opening Shots." *News Photographer* 61.9 (2006): 3.

Opitz, Götz-Dietrich. *Haitian Refugees Forced to Return: Transnationalism and State Politics, 1991–1994*. Münster: LIT; New Brunswick: Transaction Publishers, 2004.

Orbach, Alexander. *The Pogroms of 1881–1882: The Response from St. Petersburg Jewry*. Pittsburgh: Russian and East European Studies Program, University of Pittsburgh, 1984.

Orozco, Manuel. "Globalization and Migration: The Impact of Family Remittances in Latin America." *Latin American Politics & Society* 44.2 (2002): 41.

Orozco, Manuel. "Migrant Hometown Associations: Putting a Face to Globalization." *Harvard Journal of Hispanic Policy* 17 (2005): 79–86.

Osborn, Meredith B. "*Rasul v. Bush*: Federal Courts Have Jurisdiction over Habeas Challenges and Other Claims Brought by Guantanamo Detainees." *Harvard Civil Rights-Civil Liberties Law Review* 40.1 (2005): 265–276.

Østergaard-Nielsen, Eva, ed. *International Migration and Sending Countries: Perceptions, Policies and Transnational Relations*. London: Palgrave Macmillan, 2003.

Østergaard-Nielsen, Eva. *Transnational Politics: Turks and Kurds in Germany*. New York: Routledge, 2003.

Ouaked, Said. "Transatlantic Roundtable on High-skilled Migration and Sending Countries Issues." *International Migration* 40.4 (2002): 153–166.

Oulton, Judith A. "Human Resources – We Need New Ideas." *International Nursing Review* 51.4 (2004): 200.

Oulton, Judith A. "Inside View." *International Nursing Review* 51.3 (2004): 137–138.

Outshoorn, Joyce. "Debating Prostitution in Parliament." *European Journal of Women's Studies* 8.4 (2001): 472.

Outshoorn, Joyce. *The Politics of Prostitution: Women's Movements, Democratic States and the Globalization of Sex Commerce.* Cambridge: Cambridge University Press, 2004.

"Outward bound." *Economist* 364.8292 (2002): 24–26.

"Overseas Nurses to be Surveyed." *Nursing Standard* 19.5 (2004): 5.

Özden, Çaglar, and Maurice Schiff, eds. *International Migration, Remittances and the Brain Drain.* Washington DC: World Bank; London: Palgrave Macmillan, 2005.

Özveren, Eyüp, and Thomas Faist, eds. *Transnational Social Spaces: Agents, Networks and Institutions.* Aldershot: Ashgate, 2004.

Paddison, Ronan, ed. *Handbook of Urban Studies.* London: Sage, 2001.

Papademetriou, Demetrios G. "International Migration in a Changing World." *International Social Science Journal* 36.3 (1984): 409.

Papadopoulos, Irena, and Irena Papadopoulos. "Health and Illness Beliefs of Greek Cypriots Living in London." *Journal of Advanced Nursing* 29.5 (1999): 1097–1104.

Papastergiadis, Nikos. *The Turbulence of Migration: Globalization, Deterritorialization and Hybridity.* Cambridge: Polity Press, 2000.

Parasuraman, S. "The Anti-Dam Movement and Rehabilitation Policy." *The Dam and the Nation: Displacement and Resettlement in the Narmada Valley.* Ed. Jean Drèze, Meera Samson, and Satyajit Singh. Oxford: Oxford University Press, 1997. 26–65.

Parish, Colin. "Africa: The Case for More Nurses." *Nursing Standard* 19.41 (2005): 14–16.

Parish, Colin. "Poland and Latvia Sound Alarm on Staff Poaching." *Nursing Standard* 18.32 (2004): 4.

Parish, Colin. "Welcome to Planet Nursing." *Nursing Standard* 18.30 (2004): 15.

Park Edward J. W., and John S. W. Park. *Probationary Americans: Contemporary Immigration Policies and the Shaping of Asian American Communities.* New York: Routledge, 2005.

Parrado, Emilio A. "International Migration and Men's Marriage in Western Mexico." *Journal of Comparative Family Studies* 35.1 (2004): 51–71.

Parrado, Emilio A., Chenoa A. Flippen, and Chris McQuiston. "Migration and Relationship Power among Mexican Women." *Demography* 42.2 (2005): 347–372.

Parrado, Emilio A., Chris McQuiston, and Chenoa A. Flippen. "Integrating Community Collaboration and Quantitative Methods for the Study of Gender and HIV Risks Among Hispanic Migrants." *Sociological Methods & Research* 34.2 (2005): 204–239.

Parreñas, Rhacel Salazar. *Children of Global Migration: Transnational Families and Gendered Woes.* Stanford: Stanford University Press, 2005.

Parreñas, Rhacel Salazar. "The Care Crisis in the Philippines: Children and Transnational Families in the New Global Economy." *Global Woman: Nannies, Maids and Sex Workers in the New Economy.* Ed. Barbara Ehrenreich and Arlie Russell Hochschild. New York: Metropolitan Books, Henry Holt, 2002. 39–54.

Parreñas, Rhacel Salazar. *Servants of Globalization: Women, Migration and Domestic Work.* Stanford: Stanford University Press, 2001.

Parsons, Jeffrey T., ed. *Contemporary Research on Sex Work*. Binghamton: Haworth Press, 2005.

Passavant, Paul A., and Jodi Dean. *Empire's New Clothes: Reading Hardt and Negri*. New York: Routledge, 2004.

Patel, Anil. "Resettlement Politics and Tribal Interests." *The Dam and the Nation: Displacement and Resettlement in the Narmada Valley*. Ed. Jean Drèze, Meera Samson, and Satyajit Singh. Oxford: Oxford University Press, 1997. 66–92.

Patkar, Medha (in conversation with Smitu Kothari). "The Struggle for Participation and Justice: A Historical Narrative." *Toward Sustainable Development? Struggling over India's Narmada River*. Ed. William F. Fisher. Armonk, NY: M. E. Sharpe, 1995. 157–178.

Patterson, Margot. "US Under Fire for Treatment of Detainees." *National Catholic Reporter* 38.13 (2002): 3.

Patton, Cynthia, and Benigno Sánchez-Eppler, eds. *Queer Diasporas*. Durham, NC: Duke University Press, 2000.

Pavlowitch, Stevan K. *Tito, Yugoslavia's Great Dictator: A Reassessment*. Columbus: Ohio State University Press, 1992.

Paye, Jean-Claude. "Guantánamo and the New Legal Order." *Monthly Review: An Independent Socialist Magazine* 57.1 (2005): 45–55.

Peabody, Sue, and Tyler Stovall, eds. *The Color of Liberty: Histories of Race in France*. Durham, NC: Duke University Press, 2003.

Pearson, Alan. "Nursing in the Developing World: Lessons for the Future." *International Journal of Nursing Practice* (1 Aug. 2000): 167+.

Pearson, Elaine. "The Mekong Challenge: Human Trafficking: Redefining Demand." International Labour Organization. Bangkok: International Labour Office, 2005.

Peck, Raoul. *Monsieur le ministre . . . jusqu'au bout de la patience*. Port-au-Prince: Éditions Velvet, 1999.

Penninx, Rinus, Karen Kraal, Marco Martinello, and Steven Vertovec, eds. *Citizenship in European Cities: Immigrants, Local Politics and Integration Policies*. Aldershot: Ashgate, 2004.

Pereira, A. W. "Military Justice Before and After September 11." *Constellations: An International Journal of Critical & Democratic Theory* 9.4 (2002): 477–491.

Perine, Keith. "Court Rulings Erode Base Of Imprisonment Policy." *CQ Weekly* 63.10 (2005): 554–555.

Perine, Keith, and Chris Lehmann. "A Full-Court Press on Detainee Abuse." *CQ Weekly* 63.24 (2005): 1548.

Perkins, Roberta, Garrett Prestage, Rachel Sharp, and Frances Lovejoy, eds. *Sex Work and Sex Workers in Australia*. Sydney: University of New South Wales Press, 1994.

Peterson, Molly M. "Specter Cool To Democratic Demands For Miers' Paper Trail." *Congress Daily* (2005): 3–4.

Pettman, Jan Jindy. "Women on the Move: Globalization and Labour Migration from South and Southeast Asian States." *Global Society: Journal of Interdisciplinary International Relations* 12.3 (1998): 389–405.

Pettman, Jan Jindy. "Body Politics: International Sex Tourism." *Third World Quarterly* 18.1 (March 1997): 93–109.

Philips, David. "Shorter Notices." *English Historical Review* 113.451 (1998): 494.

Philips, John Edward, ed. *Writing African History*. Rochester, NY: University of Rochester Press, 2005.

Phillips, Kevin. *American Dynasty: Aristocracy, Fortune, and the Politics of Deceit in the House of Bush*. New York: Viking Penguin, 2004.

Phongpaichit, Pasuk. *From Peasant Girls to Bangkok Masseuses*. Geneva: International Labor Office, 1982.

Pickup, Francine. "More Words but No Action? Forced Migration and Trafficking of Women." *Gender & Development* 6.1 (1998): 44–51.

Pike, Linnet. "Sex Work and Socialization in a Moral World: Conflict and Change in Bādī Communities in Western Nepal." *Coming of Age in South and Southeast Asia: Youth, Courtship and Sexuality*. Ed. Lenore Manderson and Pranee Liamputtong. Richmond, UK: Curzon, 2002. 228–248.

Pincus, Fred L., and Howard J. Ehrlich, eds. *Race and Ethnic Conflict: Contending Views on Prejudice, Discrimination, and Ethnoviolence*. Boulder: Westview Press, 1994.

Plummer, Anne. "A First Foray Into Detainees' Rights." *CQ Weekly* 63.25 (2005): 1622–1623.

Plummer, Ken. "Speaking Its Name: Inventing a Gay and Lesbian Studies." *Modern Homosexualities: Fragments of Lesbian and Gay Experience*. Ed. Ken Plummer. London: Routledge, 1992. 3–28.

Poinsot, Marie. "Competition for Political Legitimacy at Local and National Levels Among Young North Africans in France." *New Community* 20.1 (October 1993): 79–92.

Poirine, Bernard. "A Theory of Remittances as an Implicit Family Loan Arrangement." *World Development* 25.4 (1997): 589.

Poirine, Bernard. "Rent, Emigration and Unemployment in Small Islands: The MIRAB Model and the French Overseas . . ." *World Development* 22.12 (1994): 1997.

"Policies Challenged." *CQ Researcher* 14.44 (2004): 1063–1064.

Popkin, Eric. "Transnational Migration and Development in Postwar Peripheral States: An Examination of Guatemalan and Salvadoran State Linkages with Their Migrant Populations in Los Angeles." *Current Sociology* 51.3/4 (2003): 347–374.

Portes, Alejando, ed. *The Economic Sociology of Immigration: Essays on Networks, Ethnicity, and Entrepreneurship*. New York: Russell Sage Foundation, 1995.

Potts, Deborah. "Worker-peasants and Farmer-housewives in Africa: The Debate about 'Committed' Farmers, Access to Land and Agricultural Production." *Journal of Southern African Studies* 26.4 (2000): 807–832.

"Practise What You Preach." *Economist* 374.8411 (2005): 12.

Prager, Leonard, and A. A. Greenbaum. *Yiddish Literary and Linguistic Periodicals and Miscellanies: A Selective Annotated Bibliography*. Darby, PA: Published for the Association for the Study of Jewish Languages by Norwood Editions, 1982.

Prashad, Vijay. *Keeping Up with the Dow Joneses*. Cambridge, MA: South End Press, 2004.

Prashad, Vijay. *Fat Cats and Running Dogs: The Enron Stage of Capitalism*. Monroe, ME: Common Courage Press, 2002.

Pratt, Mary Louise. *Imperial Eyes: Travel Writing and Transculturation*. New York: Routledge, 1992.

Premnath, Guatam. "The Weak Sovereignty of the Postcolonial Nation-State." *World Bank Literature*. Ed. Amitava Kumar. Minneapolis: University of Minnesota Press, 2003. 253–264.

Preston, Julia. "ACLU Gains in Its Quest for CIA Documents on Detainees." *New York Times* 154.53114 (2005): A13.

Pribilsky, Jason. "'Aprendemos A Convivir': Conjugal Relations, Co-parenting, and Family Life Among Ecuadorian Transnational Migrants in New York and the Ecuadorian Andes." *Global Networks* 4.3 (2004): 313–334.

Pries, Ludger, ed. *New Transnational Social Spaces: International Migration and Transnational Companies in the Early Twenty-first Century.* New York: Routledge, 2001.

"Proceedings Halted In a Detainee's Case." *Wall Street Journal – Eastern Edition* 246.106 (2005): A4.

Procter, James, ed. *Writing Black Britain, 1948–1998: An Interdisciplinary Anthology.* Manchester: Manchester University Press, 2000.

Puar, Jasbir K. "Circuits of Queer Mobility: Tourism, Travel, and Globalization." *GLQ: A Journal of Lesbian and Gay Studies* 8.1–2 (2002): 101–137.

Puar, Jasbir K. "Global Circuits: Transnational Sexualities and Trinidad." *Signs* 26 (2001): 1039–1065.

Puar, Jasbir K. "Transnational Sexualities: South Asian (Trans)nation(alism)s and Queer Diasporas." *Q&A: Queer in Asian America.* Ed. David L. Eng and Alice V. Hom. Philadelphia: Temple University Press, 1998. 405–422.

Puar, Jasbir K. "Resituating Discourse of 'Whiteness' and 'Asianness' in Northern England: Second Generation Sikh Worm and Construction of Identity." *Socialist Review* 24.1–2 (1995): 21–53.

Puar, Jasbir K. "Writing My Way 'Home': Travelling South Asian Bodies and Diasporic Journeys." *Socialist Review* 24.4 (1994): 75–108.

Pyle, Jean. "Globalization, Transnational Migration, and Gendered Care Work: Introduction." *Globalizations* 3.3 (2006): 283–295.

"Q&A: 'Terror' Detainee Release." British Broadcasting Corporation (21 Sept. 2004). BBC News Online: www.news.bbc.co.uk/2/hi/uk_news/politics/3676750.stm.

"Q&A: Terror Laws Explained." British Broadcasting Corporation (25 Jan. 2005). BBC News Online: www.news.bbc.co.uk/2/hi/uk_news/3683244.stm.

Qassim, Abu Bakker. "The View From Guantánamo." *New York Times* 155.53705 (2006): 15.

Quirk, Matthew. "Calendar." *Atlantic* (10727825) 298.2 (2006): 17.

Quiroga, José. *Cuban Palimpsests.* Minneapolis: University of Minnesota Press, 2005.

Quiroga, José. *Tropics of Desire: Interventions from Queer Latino America.* New York: New York University Press, 2000.

Quiroga, José. "Fleshing Out Virgilio Pinera from the Cuban Closet." *¿Entiendes? Queer Readings, Hispanic Writings.* Ed. Emilie L. Bergmann and Paul Julian Smith. Durham, NC: Duke University Press, 1995. 167–180.

Radway, Janice. "What's in a Name? Presidential Address to the American Studies Association, 20 November, 1998." *American Quarterly* 51.1 (1999): 1–32.

Raj-Hashim, Rita. "A Review of Migration and Labour Policies." *The Trade in Domestic Workers: Causes, Mechanisms, and Consequences of International Migration.* Kuala Lumpur: APDC; Atlantic Highlands, NJ: Zed Books, 1994. 119–134.

Rajagopal, Balakrishnan. "Limits of Law in Counter-Hegemonic Globalization: The Indian Supreme Court and the Narmada Valley Struggle." *Law and Globalization from Below: Towards a Cosmopolitan Legality.* Ed. Boaventura de Sousa Santos and César A. Rodríguez-Garavito. Cambridge: Cambridge University Press, 2005. 183–217.

Ralston, Jeannie. "09360: No Man's Land." *National Geographic* 207.4 (2005): 122–132.

Ramet, Sabrina P. *Balkan Babel: The Disintegration of Yugoslavia from the Death of Tito to the Fall of Miloševi .* Cambridge, MA: Westview Press, 2002.

Randazzo, Timothy. "Social and Legal Barriers: Sexual Orientation and Asylum in the United States." *Queer Migrations: Sexuality, US Citizenship, and Border Crossings.* Ed. Eithne Luibhéid and Lionel Cantú Jr. Minneapolis: University of Minnesota Press, 2005. 30–60.

Ransom, David. "The Poverty of Aid." *New Internationalist* (November 1996): 7–10.

Rao, Brinda. *Dry Wells and "Deserted" Women: Gender, Ecology and Agency in Rural India*. New Delhi: Indian Social Institute, 1996.

Rasul v. Bush, No. 03–334 (2004).

Ratner, Michael. "The War on Terrorism: The Guantanamo Prisoners, Military Commissions, and Torture." Center for Constitutional Rights. Date posted: January 14, 2003. Date accessed: May 23, 2004. www.ccr-ny.org/v2/viewpoints/viewpoint.asp?ObjID=oCjCc05Q9n&Content=142.

Ratner, Michael. "The War on Terrorism: The Guantanamo Prisoners, Military Commissions, and Torture." *Lost Liberties: Ashcroft and the Assault on Personal Freedom*. Ed. Cynthia Brown. New York: New Press, 2003. 132–150.

Rauch, Jonathan. "Guantanamo's Problem Isn't in Cuba: It's in Washington." *National Journal* 37.28 (2005): 2175–2176.

"Reaffirming the Rule of Law." *New York Times* 29 June 2004: A26+.

Reanne, Frank. "International Migration and Infant Health in Mexico." *Journal of Immigrant Health* 7.1 (2005): 11–22.

"Recruitment Agencies are Abusing and Exploiting Nurses, says ICN." *British Journal of Nursing (BJN)* 11.7 (2002): 417.

Redgrave, Corin. "Does Blunkett Back the Law?" *New Statesman* 133.4680 (2004): 23.

Regmi, Gopal, and Clem Tisdell. "Remitting Behaviour of Nepalese Rural-to-Urban Migrants: Implications for Theory and Policy." *Journal of Development Studies* 38.3 (2002): 76.

Reilly, Patrick. "Importing Controversy." *Modern Healthcare* 33.13 (2003): 20.

Rekart, Michael L. "Sex-Work Harm Reduction." *The Lancet* 366.9503 (2005): 2123–2134.

Remennick, Larissa. "Retired and Making a Fresh Start: Older Russian Immigrants Discuss their Adjustment in Israel." *International Migration* 41.5 (2003): 153–175.

Rempel, Henry, and Richard A. Lobdell. "The Role of Urban-to-Rural Remittances in Rural Development." *Journal of Development Studies* 14.3 (1978): 324.

Renda, Mary. *Taking Haiti: Military Occupation and the Culture of US Imperialism, 1915–1940*. Chapel Hill: University of North Carolina Press, 2001.

"Review of Guantánamo." *New York Times* 153.52890 (2004): A10.

Reynolds, Paul. "Al-Qaeda Suspected in Kenya Attacks." British Broadcasting Corporation (28 Oct. 2002). BBC News Online: www.news.bbc.co.uk/2/hi/africa/2523737.stm.

Rhodes, Sybil D. "The Comparative Politics of Formal and De Facto Multiple Citizenships." *Conference Papers – American Political Science Association* (2003): 1–13.

Ricardo, Roger. *Guantánamo: The Bay of Discord*. Trans. Mary Todd. Melbourne: Ocean Press, 1994.

Richards, Chris. "X-rays of Guantanamo Bay." *New Internationalist* (2003): 7.

Richardson, Allan. "Romantic Voodoo: Obeah and British Culture, 1797–1807." *Sacred Possessions: Vodou, Santería, Obeah, and the Caribbean*. Ed. Fernández Olmos and Paravisini-Gebert. New Brunswick, NJ: Rutgers University Press, 1997. 171–194.

Richardson, Laurie, and Jean-Roland Chery. *Feeding Dependency, Starving Democracy: USAID Policies in Haiti*. Boston: Grassroots International, 1997.

Ridet, Philippe. "M. Sarkozy ne veut pas entendre parler de 'l'anniversaire' des émeutes." *Le Monde* (26 Oct. 2006). www.lemonde.fr/web/article/0,1–0,36–827822,0.html.

Ridgeway, James. *It's All for Sale: The Control of Global Resources*. Durham, NC: Duke University Press, 2004.

Riding, Alan. "On a London Stage, a Hearing for Guantánamo Detainees." *New York Times* 153.52881 (2004): E3.

Ripley, Amanda, et al. "The Rules of Interrogation." *Time* 163.20 (2004): 44–46.

Risen, James. "35 Guantánamo Detainees Are Given to Pakistan." *New York Times* 154.52977 (2004): 35.

Risen, James, and Tim Golden. "Three Detainees Kill Themselves at Guantànamo Prison." *New York Times* 155.53607 (2006): 37.

Risen, James, and Tim Golden. "Three Prisoners Commit Suicide at Guantánamo." *New York Times* (11 June 2006): A1, A24.

Ro'i, Yaacov, ed. *Jews and Jewish life in Russia and the Soviet Union.* Ilford, UK: Frank Cass, 1995.

Roach, Joseph. *Cities of the Dead: Circum-Atlantic Performance.* New York: Columbia University Press, 1996.

Robbins, Bruce. *Feeling Global: Internationalism in Distress.* New York: New York University Press, 1999.

Robbins, Bruce. "Some Versions of US Internationalism." *Social Text* 45 (1995): 97–123.

Robbins, Bruce, and Pheng Cheah, eds. *Cosmopolitics: Thinking and Feeling Beyond the Nation.* Minneapolis: University of Minnesota Press, 1998.

Robbins, Jon. "Liberty Hell." *Lawyer* 19.27 (2005): 20.

Roberts, Adam. "The Changing Faces of Terrorism." British Broadcasting Corporation. BBC News Online: www.bbc.co.uk/history/recent/sept_11/changing_faces_print.html.

Roberts, Kenneth D., and Michael D. S. Morris. "Fortune, Risk, and Remittances: An Application of Option Theory to Participation in Village-Based Migration Networks." *International Migration Review* 37.4 (2003): 1252–1281.

Robinson, Jane J. A. "Editorial." *International Nursing Review* (1 Dec. 2005): 243+.

Robinson, Kathryn. "International Labour Migration of Asian Women." *Asian Studies Review* 24.2 (2000): 269.

Robinson, William I. "(Mal)Development in Central America: Globalization and Social Change." *Development & Change* 29.3 (1998): 467.

Rodriguez, Edgard R., and Erwin R. Tiongson. "Temporary Migration Overseas and Household Labor Supply: Evidence from Urban Philippines." *International Migration Review* 35.3 (2001): 709–725.

Rodríguez, Juana María. *Queer Latinidad: Identity Practices, Discursive Spaces.* New York: New York University Press, 2003.

Rodriguez, Olga R. Associated Press, "Mexico Angered by Border Fence." *Cincinnati Enquirer* (6 Oct. 2006): A17.

Rogaly, Ben, and Abdur Rafique. "Struggling to Save Cash: Seasonal Migration and Vulnerability in West Bengal, India." *Development & Change* 34.4 (2003): 659.

Romero, Mary. *Maid in the USA.* New York: Routledge, 1992.

Roosevelt III, Kermit. "Application of the Constitution to Guantanamo Bay." *University of Pennsylvania Law Review* 153.6 (2005): 2017–2071.

Rosaldo, Renato. *Culture and Truth: The Remaking of Social Analysis.* Boston: Beacon Press, 1989.

Rosales, Francisco Arturo. *¡Pobre Raza! Violence, Justice, and Mobilization among México Lindo Immigrants, 1900–1936.* Austin: University of Texas Press, 1999.

Rosello, Mireille. *France and the Maghreb: Performative Encounters.* Gainesville: University of Florida Press, 2005.

Rosello, Mireille. "Interpreting Immigration Laws: 'Crimes of Homosexuality' or 'Crimes Against Hospitality.'" *Diaspora* 8.3 (1999): 209–224.

Rosello, Mireille. "The National Sexual: From the Fear of Ghettos to the Banalization of Queer Practices." *Articulations of Difference: Gender Studies and Writing in French.* Ed. Dominique D. Fisher and Lawrence R. Schehr. Stanford: Stanford University Press, 1997. 246–271.

Rosello, Mireille. "'Get out of Here!': Modern Queer Languages in the 1990s." *Canadian Review of Comparative Literature/Revue Canadienne de Littérature Comparée* 21.1–2 (March 1994): 149–168.

Rosen, Fred, and Deidre McFadyen, eds. *Free Trade and Economic Restructuring in Latin America: A NACLA Reader.* New York: Monthly Review Press, 1995.

Rosen, Jeffrey. "Privacy Pleas." *New Republic* 228.20 (2003): 19.

Rosenberg, Debra. "Judging the Percentages." *Newsweek* 144.2 (2004): 10.

Rosenfeld, Harvey. *Diary of a Dirty Little War: The Spanish-American War of 1898.* Westport, CT: Praeger, 2000.

Ross, S. J., D. Polsky, and J. Sochalski. "Nursing Shortages and International Nurse Migration." *International Nursing Review* 52.4 (2005): 253–262.

Roulleau-Berger, Laurence, ed. *Youth and Work in the Post-Industrial City of North America and Europe.* Leiden: Brill, 2003.

Rowe, John Carlos. *Literary Culture and US Imperialism: From the Revolution to World War II.* Oxford: Oxford University Press, 2000.

Roy, Arundhati. *The Cost of Living.* New York: Modern Library, 1999.

Roy, Arundhati. *Power Politics.* Boston: South End Press, 2001.

Rubin, Barry, and Judith Colp Rubin, eds. *Hating America: A History.* Oxford: Oxford University Press, 2004.

Ruggiero, Kristin. *The Jewish Diaspora in Latin America and the Caribbean: Fragments of Memory.* Brighton: Sussex Academic Press, 2005.

Rumsfeld v. Padilla, No. 03–1027 (2004).

"Rumsfeld Favors Repatriating Detainees." *New York Times* 154.53241 (2005): A3.

Russell, Jim. "Rethinking Post-National Citizenship: The Relationship between State Territory and International Human Rights Law." *Space & Polity* 9.1 (2005): 29–39.

Rutter, Terri. "Job Discontent Fuels Aggressive Recruitment of Nurses." *Bulletin of the World Health Organization* 79.12 (2001): 1171.

Ryan, Lyndall. "Books." *Australian Historical Studies* 28.109 (1997): 204.

Sabatier, Colette. "La Mère et son bébé: variations culturelles analyse critique de la littérature." *International Journal of Psychology* 21.4/5 (1986): 513.

Sachar, Howard Morley. *A History of Israel From the Rise of Zionism to Our Time.* New York : Knopf, 1976.

Sadowski-Smith, Claudia. *Globalization on the Line: Culture, Capital, and Citizenship at US Borders.* New York: Palgrave Macmillan, 2002.

Safran, William. "Diasporas in Modern Societies: Myths of Homeland and Return." *Diaspora* 1.1 (1991): 83–89.

Said, Edward W. "Preface to the Twenty-fifth Anniversary Edition." *Orientalism.* New York: Random House, 2003.

Saikia, Sayeeda Yasmin. *Fragmented Memories: Struggling to be Tai-Ahom in India.* Durham, NC: Duke University Press, 2004.

Salvage, Jane. "International Champion." *Nursing Standard* 20.19 (2006): 26.

Salvage, Jane. "Workers of the World." *Nursing Standard* 21.5 (2006): 18–19.

San Juan Jr., E. *After Postcolonialism: Remapping Philippines-United States Confrontations.* Lanham, MD: Rowman & Littlefield, 2000.

San Juan Jr., E. *Beyond Postcolonial Theory*. New York: St. Martin's Press, 1998.

Sana, Mariano, and Douglas S. Massey. "Household Composition, Family Migration, and Community Context: Migrant Remittances in Four Countries." *Social Science Quarterly* 86.2 (2005): 509–528.

Sanchez-Trujillo v. INS, 801 F. 2d. 1571 (9th Cir. 1986).

Sanders, Teela. *Sex Work: A Risky Business*. Cullompton, UK: Willan Publishing, 2005.

Sanghera, Jyoti. "Unpacking the Trafficking Discourse." *Trafficking and Prostitution Reconsidered: New Perspectives on Migration, Sex Work, and Human Rights*. Ed. Kamala Kempadoo, Jyoti Sanghera, and Bandana Pattanaik. Boulder: Paradigm Publishers, 2005. 3–24.

Sarat, Austin, Lawrence Douglas, and Martha Merrill Umphrey, eds. *The Place of Law*. Ann Arbor: University of Michigan Press, 2003.

Sarausad, Mary Rose Geraldine A. "Struggles from Within: Migrant Women in Southeast Asia." *Development* 49.1 (2006): 134–136.

Sardar Sarovar Narmada Nigam Ltd. Website: www.sardarsarovardam.org.

Sassen, Saskia. "Global Cities and Survival Circuits." *Global Woman: Nannies, Maids, and Sex Workers in the New Economy*. Ed. Barbara Ehrenreich and Arlie Russell Hochschild. New York: Metropolitan Books, Henry Holt, 2002. 254–274.

Sassen, Saskia, ed. *Global Networks, Linked Cities*. New York: Routledge, 2002.

Sassen, Saskia. *Cities in a World Economy*. Thousand Oaks, CA: Pine Forge Press, 2000.

Sassen, Saskia. *Guests and Aliens*. New York: New Press, 1999.

Sassen, Saskia. *Globalization and Its Discontents: Essays on the New Mobility of People and Money*. New York: New Press, 1998.

Sassen, Saskia. *Losing Control? Sovereignty in an Age of Globalization*. New York: Columbia University Press, 1996.

Sassen, Saskia. *The Global City: New York, London, Tokyo*. Princeton: Princeton University Press, 1991, 2001.

Sassen, Saskia. *The Mobility of Labor and Capital: A Study in International Investment and Labor Flow*. Cambridge: Cambridge University Press, 1988.

Saunders, Penelope. "Traffic Violations." *Journal of Interpersonal Violence* 20.3 (2005): 343–360.

Savage, Luiza C. "Prisoners with No Country." *Maclean's* 119.13 (2006): 28–29.

Sayyid, S. "Crusades and Jihads in Postcolonial Times." British Broadcasting Corporation. BBC News Online: www.bbc.co.uk/history/recent/sept_11/west_print.html.

Schechter, Patricia A. "Empire of Care: Nursing and Migration in Filipino American History." *Pacific Historical Review* 74.1 (2005): 142–143.

Schell, Jonathan. "Healing the Law." *Nation* 279.4 (2004): 12–42.

Schmertz, Jr., John R., and Mike Meier. "*Habeas Corpus*." *International Law Update* 9 (2003): 56.

Schmidt, Hans. *The United States Occupation of Haiti, 1915–1934*. New Brunswick, NJ: Rutgers University Press, 1971.

Schmitt, Eric. "Senate Approves Limiting Rights of US Detainees." *New York Times* 155.53395 (2005): A1–A21.

Schmitt, Eric, and Tim Golden. "Lawmakers Back Use of Evidence Coerced From Detainees." *New York Times* 155.53431 (2005): A21.

Schneider, Daniella. "Human Rights Issues in Guantanamo Bay." *Journal of Criminal Law* 68.5 (2004): 423–439.

Schrieder, Gertrud, and Beatrice Knerr. "Labour Migration as a Social Security Mechanism for Smallholder Households in Sub-Saharan Africa: The Case of Cameroon." *Oxford Development Studies* 28.2 (2000): 223–236.

Schulhofer, Stephen J. "Does the Treatment of Prisoners at the Detention Facility in Guantánamo Bay Violate International Law? Pro." *International Debates* 4.4 (2006): 110–122.

Schulte, Axel, and Dietrich Tränhardt, eds. *International Migration and Liberal Democracies: Yearbook Migration 1999/2000 = Internationale Migration und Freiheitliche Demokratien: Jahrbuch Migration 1999/2000.* Germany: Lit; London: Global, 2000.

Schumann, Christopher M. "Bring It On: The Supreme Court Opens the Floodgates with *Rasul v. Bush*." *Air Force Law Review* 55 (2004): 349–370.

Schwirian, Kent P., and Patricia M. Schwirian. "Neighboring, Residential Satisfaction, and Psychological Well-Being in Urban Elders." *Journal of Community Psychology* 21.4 (1993): 285–299.

Sciolino, Elaine. "Spanish Judge Calls for Closing US Prison at Guantánamo." *New York Times* (4 June 2006): A16.

Sciolino, Elaine. "4 Detainees Are Returned to France After 2 Years at Guantánamo." *New York Times* 153.52924 (2004): A5.

Sciolino, Elaine, and Ariane Bernard. "Anger Festering in French Areas Scarred in Riots." *New York Times* (21 Oct. 2006): A1, A8.

Scott, Allen J., ed. *Global City-Regions: Trends, Theory, Policy*. Oxford: Oxford University Press, 2001.

Scott, James C. *Domination and the Arts of Resistance: Hidden Transcipts*. New Haven: Yale University Press, 1990.

Scott, James C. *Weapons of the Weak: Everyday Forms of Peasant Resistance*. New Haven: Yale University Press, 1985.

Scrambler, Graham, and Annette Scrambler. *Rethinking Prostitution: Purchasing Sex in the 1990s*. New York: Routledge, 1997.

Scully, Megan. "House Committee Begins Work On Military Tribunal Issue." *Congress Daily* (2006): 9.

Scully, Megan, and John Stanton. "Senate Orders Iraq Progress Reports, Not Withdrawal Plans." *Congress Daily* (2005): 3–4.

Scully, Megan, Jill Smallen, and Charlie Mitchell. "Review of Detainee Policies Begins." *National Journal* 38.28 (2006): 49.

Scully, Megan, Jill Smallen, and Charlie Mitchell. "Defense Bill Calls for Reports on Iraq." *National Journal* 37.47/48 (2005): 3638.

Secure Fence Act of 2006 (H.R. 6061). Library of Congress. www.congress.gov/cgi-bin/bdquery/z?d109:H.R.6061:.

"Security Investigators Arrive at Guantánamo." *New York Times* 152.52624 (2003): A26.

Seddon, David, Jagannath Adhikari, and Ganesh Gurung. "Foreign Labor Migration and the Remittance Economy of Nepal." *Critical Asian Studies* 34.1 (2002): 19–40.

Seelye, Katharine Q., et al. "Newsweek Says It Is Retracting Koran Report (Cover story)." *New York Times* 154.53217 (2005): A1–A18.

Seelye, Katharine Q. "Red Cross Reported Koran Abuses." *New York Times* 154.53220 (2005): A22.

Seelye, Katharine Q. "Detainees Are Not POWs, Cheney and Rumsfeld Declare." *New York Times* 151.52012 (2002): A6.

Seelye, Katharine Q. "Moscow, Seeking Extradition, Says 3 Detainees Are Russian." *New York Times* 151.52077 (2002): A13.

Seelye, Katharine Q. "Rumsfeld Defends Treatments by US of Cuba Detainees (Cover story)." *New York Times* 151.52007 (2002): A1.

Seelye, Katharine Q. "US to Hold Taliban Detainees in 'the Least Worst Place'." *New York Times* 151.51981 (2001): B6.

Seelye, Katherine Q., and Steven Erlanger. "US Suspends the Transport of Terror Suspects to Cuba (Cover story)." *New York Times* 151.52008 (2002): A1.

Selsky, Andrew. Associated Press. "Guantanamo Criticism Renewed." *Cincinnati Enquirer* (12 June 2006): A2.

Semyonov, Moshe, and Anastasia Gorodzeisky. "Labor Migration, Remittances and Household Income: A Comparison between Filipino and Filipina Overseas Workers." *International Migration Review* 39.1 (2005): 45–68.

Sen, Gita. "National Development and Local Environmental Action – The Case of the River Narmada." *The North, the South, and the Environment: Ecological Constraints and Global Economy.* Ed. V. Bhaskar and Andrew Glyn. New York: St. Martin's Press, 1995. 184–200.

"Sex Trafficking Most Profitable International Illegal Trade." *Women's International Network News* 26.4 (2000): 75.

Seymour, Richard. "Guantanamo Pressure Increases." *Middle East* (2006): 26–28.

Shacochis, Bob. *The Immaculate Invasion.* New York: Viking, 1999.

Shain, Yossi. "The Mexican-American Diaspora's Impact on Mexico." *Political Science Quarterly* 114.4 (Winter 1999/2000): 661.

Shane, Scott. "Seeking An Exit Strategy for Guantánamo." *New York Times* 155.53614 (2006): 1–4.

Shanker, Thom. "Pentagon Plans To Tell Names Of Detainees." *New York Times* 150.53502 (2006): 20.

Sharp, David. Associated Press, "US Plans to Secure Border with Canada – Soon as It Finds It." *Cincinnati Enquirer* (1 Oct. 2006): A4.

Sheffer, Gabriel. *Diaspora Politics: At Home Abroad.* Cambridge: Cambridge University Press, 2003.

Shenon, Philip. "Britain Defends US Treatment of Detainees at Guantánamo." *New York Times* 151.52006 (2002): A12.

Sherwood, Carlton. "Gitmo Prisoners Are Where They Belong." *Human Events* 61.25 (2005): 6.

Shilomowitz, Ralph. "Reviews of Books: Africa, Asia, and Australia." *Journal of Economic History* 58.1 (1998): 257.

Siddique, M. A. B., ed. *International Migration into the 21st Century: Essays in Honor of Reginald Appleyard.* Northampton, MA: Edward Elgar, 2001.

Sikes, Alan. "Social Protest and the Performance of Gay Identity." *UnderCurrent.* www.web.archive.org/web/20021230200816/http://www.uoregon.edu/~ucurrent/uc5/5-sikes.html.

Sikod, Fondo, and Gérard Tchouassi. "Diaspora Remittances and the Financing of Basic Social Services and Infrastructure in Francophone Africa South of the Sahara." *Perspectives on Global Development & Technology* 5.3 (2006): 239–255.

Silliman, Jael. "Gender Silences in the Narmada Valley." *Eye to Eye: Women Practising Development Across Cultures.* Ed. Susan Perry and Celeste Schenck. New York: Zed Books, 2001. 71–88.

Silverstein, Merril, Zhen Cong, and Shuzhuo Li. "Intergenerational Transfers and Living Arrangements of Older People in Rural China: Consequences for Psychological Well-Being." *Journals of Gerontology Series B: Psychological Sciences & Social Sciences* 61B.5 (2006): S256–S266.

Silvey, Rachel. "Consuming the Transnational Family: Indonesian Migrant Domestic Workers to Saudi Arabia." *Global Networks* 6.1 (2006): 23–40.

Silvey, Rachel. "Transnational Migration and the Gender Politics of Scale: Indonesian Domestic Workers in Saudi Arabia." *Singapore Journal of Tropical Geography* 25.2 (2004): 141–155.

Simich, Laura, Morton Beiser, and Farah N. Mawani. "Social Support and the Significance of Shared Experience in Refugee Migration and Resettlement." *Western Journal of Nursing Research* 25.7 (2003): 872–891.

Simmonds, Roger, and Gary Hack, eds. *Global City Regions: Their Emerging Forms*. New York: Spon, 2000.

Simpson, Glenn R., and Charles Forelle. "A Third Guantanamo Bay Worker Is Arrested on Suspicion of Spying." *Wall Street Journal – Eastern Edition* 242.65 (2003): A3.

Simpson, Roy L. "Surviving a Client/Server Migration." *Nursing Management* 26.10 (1995): 47–49.

Sinclair, M. Thea. *Gender, Work and Tourism*. New York: Routledge, 1997.

Sinfield, Alan. "Diaspora and Hybridity: Queer Identities and the Ethnicity Model." *Textual Practice* 10.2 (1996): 271–293.

Singh, Jerome A., et al. "The Ethics of Nurse Poaching from the Developing World." *Nursing Ethics* 10.6 (2003): 666–670.

Skeet, Muriel. "Physician and Nurse Migration (Book)." *Journal of Advanced Nursing* 5.5 (1980): 553–554.

Skeldon, Ronald. "Trafficking: A Perspective from Asia." *International Migration* 38.5 (2000).

Skrobanek, Siriporn, Natya Boonpakdee, and Chutima Jantateero, eds. *The Traffic in Women: Human Realities of the International Sex Trade*. New York: Zed Books, 1997.

Sloss, David L., and David D. Caron. "Availability of US Courts to Detainees at Guantánamo Bay Naval Base – Reach of *habeus corpus* – Executive Power in War on Terror." *American Journal of International Law* 98.4 (2004): 788–798.

Smith, Andrea L., ed. *Europe's Invisible Migrants*. Amsterdam: Amsterdam University Press, 2003.

Smith, Clive Stafford. "Gitmo's Hunger Strikers." *Nation* 281.12 (2005): 8–9.

Smith, Clive Stafford. "Inside Guantanamo (Cover story)." *New Statesman* 134.4767 (2005): 14–17.

Smith, Craig S. "Rioting by Immigrants Embroils Paris Suburbs." *New York Times* (5 Nov. 2005): A1.

Smith, Craig S. "Riots and Violence Spread from Paris to Other French Cities." *New York Times* (6 Nov. 2005): A3.

Smith, Craig S. "6 Former Guantánamo Detainees on Trial in Paris." *New York Times* (4 July 2006): A8.

Smith, Craig S. "Furor Over a French Immigration Crackdown." *New York Times* (8 July 2006): A6.

Smith, Jennie M. *When the Hands Are Many: Community Organization and Social Change in Rural Haiti*. Ithaca: Cornell University Press, 2001.

Smith, Larry, and Steven T. Taylor. "How to Make a Momentous Supreme Court Decision Mean Something." *Of Counsel* 24.8 (2005): 11–14.

Smith, Paul J., ed. *Human Smuggling: Chinese Migrant Trafficking to America's Immigration Tradition*. Washington, DC: Center for International and Strategic Studies, 1997.

Solomon, M. Scott. "Migrant Domestic Workers and Globalization: Bridging Gender, Class, and Critical IPE." *Conference Papers – International Studies Association* (2004): 1–30.

Sonnett, Neal R. "Guantanamo Still a Legal Black Hole." *Human Rights: Journal of the Section of Individual Rights & Responsibilities* 33.1 (2006): 8–9.

"Southern Cross." *Economist* 377.8454 (2005): 13–15.

Spellman, W. M. *The Global Community: Migration and the Making of the Modern World.* Stroud: Sutton, 2002.

Spencer, Ian R. G. *British Immigration Policy since 1939.* New York: Routledge, 1997.

Spencer, Sarah. *The Politics of Migration: Managing Opportunity, Conflict and Change.* Oxford: Blackwell, 2003.

Spolsky, Bernard, and Elana Shohamy. *The Languages of Israel: Policy, Ideology and Practice.* Buffalo: Multilingual Matters, 1999.

Sriskandarajah, Dhananjayan. "The Migration-Development Nexus: Sri Lanka Case Study." *International Migration* 40.5 (2002): 283.

Stalker, Peter. *The No-Nonsense Guide to International Migration.* Oxford: Verso, 2001.

Stark, Oded. "On the Role of Urban-to-Rural Remittances in Rural Development." *Journal of Development Studies* 16.3 (1980): 369.

Steen, R., et al. "Pursuing Scale and Quality in STI Interventions with Sex Workers: Initial Results from Avahan India AIDS Initiative." *Sexually Transmitted Infections* 82.5 (2006): 381–385.

Stein, Lisa. "The Week." *US News & World Report* 138.21 (2005): 14–17.

Stein, Lisa. "Spies among Them?" *US News & World Report* 135.11 (2003): 16.

Stein, Lisa. "Kidnapped." *US News & World Report* 132.4 (2002): 14.

Stephen, Andrew. "Torturers? Who, Us??" *New Statesman* 134.4767 (2005): 18–19.

Stephen, Andrew. "Donald Rumsfeld and Vice-President Cheney Appear a Sorry Twosome, Unable to Grasp Unpalatable Realities that are Staring Them in the Face." *New Statesman* 133.4688 (2004): 13–14.

Stewart, M. J., et al. "Immigrant Women Family Caregivers in Canada: Implications for Policies and Programmes in Health and Social Sectors." *Health & Social Care in the Community* 14.4 (2006): 329–340.

Stiglitz, Joseph E. *Globalization and Its Discontents.* New York: W. W. Norton, 2002.

Stilwell, Barbara. "Nurses on the Move: Migration and the Global Health Care Economy." *International Nursing Review* 53.1 (2006): 12.

Stilwell, Barbara, et al. "Migration of Health-Care Workers from Developing Countries: Strategic Approaches to Its Management." *Bulletin of the World Health Organization* 82.8 (2004): 595–600.

Stodolska, Monika, and Carla A. Santos. "'You Must Think of *Familia*': The Everyday Lives of Mexican Migrants in Destination Communities." *Social & Cultural Geography* 7.4 (2006): 627–647.

Stolberg, Sheryl Gay. "Justices Tacitly Backed Use of Guantánamo, Bush Says." *New York Times* (8 July 2006): A12.

Stolberg, Sheryl Gay. "Seeks Tribunals (Cover story)." *New York Times* 155.53695 (2006): A1–A20.

Stoller, Eleanor Palo, and Adam T. Perzynski. "The Impact of Ethnic Involvement and Migration Patterns on Long-Term Care Plans Among Retired Sunbelt Migrants: Plants for Nursing Home Placement." *Journals of Gerontology Series B: Psychological Sciences & Social Sciences* 58B.6 (2003): S369–S376.

Stone, Alan A. "Doctors and Torture (Cover story)." *Psychiatric Times* 22.1 (2006): 1–8.

Stovall, Tyler. *The Rise of the Paris Red Belt.* Berkeley: University of California Press, 1990.

Stovall, Tyler, and Georges van den Abbeele, eds. *French Civilization and Its Discontents: Nationalism, Colonialism, Race*. Lanham, MD: Lexington Books, 2003.

Strauss, Herbert A. *Hostages of Modernization: Studies on Modern Antisemitism, 1870–1933*. New York: Walter de Gruyter, 1993.

Suárez-Orozco, Marcelo M., Carola Suárez-Orozco, and Desirée Baolian Qin, eds. *The New Immigration: An Interdisciplinary Reader*. New York: Routledge, 2005.

Summary of H.R. 6061: www.gop.gov/Committeecentral/bills/hr6061.asp.

Surin, Kenneth. "Hostage to an Unaccountable Planetary Executive: The Flawed 'Washington Consensus' and Two *World Bank Reports*." *World Bank Literature*. Ed. Amitava Kumar. Minneapolis: University of Minnesota Press, 2003. 128–139.

Surtees, Rebecca. "Female Migration and Trafficking in Women: The Indonesian Context." *Development* 46.3 (2003): 99–106.

Suskind, Ron. "The Unofficial Story of the al-Qaeda 14." *Time* 168.12 (2006): 34–35.

Süssmuth, Rita, and Werner Weidenfeld, eds. *Managing Integration: The European Union's Responsibilities towards Immigrants*. Washington, DC: Bertelsmann Stiftung, Migration Policy Institute, 2005.

Swarns, Rachel L. "Senate Moves Toward Action on Border Fence." *New York Times* (29 Sept. 2006): A18.

Swarns, Rachel L. "Terror Laws Cut Resettlement of Refugees." *New York Times* (28 Sept. 2006): A21.

Syson, Sue. "Life History and Zimbabwean Nursing Student: 'Global Boarder'." *Management in Education* 19.1 (2005): 8–11.

Tabak, Faruk, and Michaeline A. Crichlow, eds. *Informalization: Process and Structure*. Baltimore: Johns Hopkins University Press, 2000.

Takhar, Opinderjit Kaur. *Sikh Identity: An Exploration of Groups among Sikhs*. Aldershot: Ashgate, 2005.

"Tale of 5 Muslims: Out of Guantanamo And Into Limbo (Cover story)." *Wall Street Journal – Eastern Edition* 247.128 (2006): A1–A12.

Tan, Michael L. "Walking the Tightrope: Sexual Risk and Male Sex Work in the Philippines." *Men Who Sell Sex: International Perspectives on Male Prostitution and HIV/AIDS*. Ed. Peter Aggleton. Philadelphia: Temple University Press, 1999. 241–262.

Taranto, James. "Read and Despair." *American Spectator* 39.9 (2006): 46–47.

Taylor, Andrew. Associated Press. "Congress Pushes Security Bills." *Cincinnati Enquirer* (30 Sept. 2006).

Taylor, J. Edward. "The New Economics of Labour Migration and the Role of Remittances in the Migration Process." *International Migration* 37.1 (1999): 63.

Taylor Jr., Stuart. "Falsehoods About Guantanamo." *National Journal* 38.5 (2006): 13–14.

Taylor Jr., Stuart. "'Enemy Combatants': Inching Toward Due Process." *National Journal* 36.9 (2004): 599–600.

Taylor Jr., Stuart. "Guantanamo: Why the President is Courting Defeat." *National Journal* 36.17 (2004): 1233–1234.

Taylor Jr., Stuart. "Guantanamo: A Betrayal of What America Stands For." *National Journal* 35.30 (2003): 2399.

Taylor Jr., Stuart. "Al Qaeda Detainees: Don't Prosecute, Don't Release." *National Journal* 34.17 (2002): 1203.

Tazreiter, Claudia. *Asylum Seekers and the State: The Politics of Protection in a Security-Conscious World*. Aldershot: Ashgate, 2004.

"Technology Worker Visas at Centre of Industry Debate." *Migration World Magazine* 26.4 (1998): 10.

Terrell, John Edward, ed. *Archaeology, Language, and History: Essays on Culture and Ethnicity.* Westport, CT: Bergin & Garvey, 2001.

"Terror Detention Law Must Go." British Broadcasting Corporation (4 April 2004). BBC News Online: www.news.bbc.co.uk/2/hi/uk_news/politics/3534274.stm.

"Terror Laws Come Under Spotlight." British Broadcasting Corporation (18 Dec. 2005). BBC News Online: www.news.bbc.co.uk/go/pr/fr/-/2/hi/uk_news/politics/3329423.stm.

"Terror Suspect Freed from UK Jail." British Broadcasting Corporation (2 Feb. 2005). BBC News Online: www.news.bbc.co.uk/go/pr/fr/-/2/hi/uk_news/4226097.stm.

"Terror Suspects' Appeal Rejected." British Broadcasting Corporation (11 Aug. 2004). BBC News Online: www.news.bbc.co.uk/go/pr/fr/-/2/hi/uk_news/politics/3553978.stm.

Testas, Abdelaziz. "Maghreb-EU Migration." *Mediterranean Politics* 6.3 (2001): 64.

Thai, Hung Cam. "Clashing Dreams: Highly Educated Overseas Brides and Low Wage US Husbands." *Global Woman: Nannies, Maids, and Sex Workers in the New Economy.* Ed. Barbara Ehrenreich and Arlie Russell Hochschild. New York: Metropolitan Books, Henry Holt, 2002. 230–253.

"Thailand: New Information on Traffic in Women." *Women's International Network News* 23.1 (1997): 59.

Thapan, Meenakshi, ed. *Transnational Migration and the Politics of Identity.* Thousand Oaks, CA: Sage, 2005.

"The American Prison Camp." *New York Times* 153.52638 (2003): A28.

"The Bali Bombers' Network of Terror." British Broadcasting Corporation. BBC News Online: www.news.bbc.co.uk/2/hi/asia-pacific/2499193.stm.

"The Cost of Doing Your Duty." *New York Times* (11 Oct. 2006): A26+.

"The Court and Guantánamo." *New York Times* 153.52824 (2004): A22.

"The Court Goes to War." *National Review* 58.14 (2006): 16.

"The Four Hijacks." British Broadcasting Corporation. BBC News Online: www.news.bbc.co.uk/2/shared/spl/hi/guides/456900/456983/html/default.stm.

"The Imperial Presidency at Work." *New York Times* 155.53460 (2006): 11.

"The Political Scene." *Country Report. United States* (2003): 16–18.

"The President's News Conference With Prime Minister Tony Blair of the United Kingdom in London." *Weekly Compilation of Presidential Documents* 39.47 (2003): 1652–1658.

"The Silence of the Doctors." *Nation* 281.22 (2005): 26–32.

"The World Needs Urgent Action on a Huge Scale: A Conversation with Dr Jean Yan." *International Nursing Review* 53.2 (2006): 88–89.

Thieme, John. *Post-Colonial Studies: The Essential Glossary.* London: Arnold; Oxford: Oxford University Press, 2003.

Thieme, Susan, and Simone Wyss. "Migration Patterns and Remittance Transfer in Nepal: A Case Study of Sainik Basti in Western Nepal." *International Migration* 43.5 (2005): 59–98.

Thomas, Evan, et al. "How a Fire Broke Out." *Newsweek* 145.21 (2005): 32–34.

Thomas, Keith. *Changing Conceptions of National Biography.* Cambridge: Cambridge University Press, 2005.

Thomas, P. "The International Migration of Indian Nurses." *International Nursing Review* 53.4 (2006): 277–283.

Thomas-Hope, Elizabeth. "Return Migration to Jamaica and Its Development Potential." *International Migration* 37.1 (1999): 183.

Thornburgh, Nathan, et al. "Gitmo. How to Fix It." *Time* 168.2 (2006): 23–24.

"Three Teenagers Are Released From Guantánamo and Sent Home." *New York Times* 153.52744 (2004): A21.

"Timeline: Al-Qaeda." British Broadcasting Corporation. BBC News Online: www. newsvote.bbc.co.uk/mpapps/pagetools/print/news.bbc.co.uk/1/hi/world/3618762.stm.

Todd, Emmanuel. *After the Empire: The Breakdown of the American Order.* New York: Columbia University Press, 2003.

Tölölyan, Khachig. "The Nation-State and Its Others: In Lieu of a Preface." *Diaspora* 1.1 (1991): 3–7.

Tomasi, Silvano M. "Migrants and Refugees in the Horn of Africa." *Migration World Magazine* 27.5 (1999): 36.

Tong, Benson. *The Chinese Americans.* Boulder: University Press of Colorado, 2003.

"Too Many Arrests, Too Few Charges?" British Broadcasting Corporation (2 April 2004). BBC News Online: www.news.bbc.co.uk/go/pr/fr/-/2/hi/uk_news/magazine/3590753. stm.

Torres, Rodolfo D., Louis F. Mirón, and Jonathan Xavier Inda, eds. *Race, Identity, and Citizenship: A Reader.* Oxford: Blackwell, 1999.

Tram, Peter. "Ministry to Thai Workers Overseas." *Migration World Magazine* 29.4 (2001): 29.

"Treat, Train and Retain Nurses in Africa." *Australian Nursing Journal* 14.4 (2006): 14.

Trebilcock, Michael J., and Matthew Sudak. "The Political Economy of Emigration and Immigration." *New York University Law Review* 81.1 (2006): 234–293.

Trends in International Migration: Continuous Reporting System on Migration. Annual Report 2002 Edition. Organisation for Economic Co-Operation and Development. Paris: OECD, 2003.

Trends in International Migration: Continuous Reporting System on Migration. Annual Report 2001 Edition. Organisation for Economic Co-Operation and Development. Paris: OECD, 2002.

Trends in International Migration: Continuous Reporting System on Migration. Annual Report 2000 Edition. Organisation for Economic Co-Operation and Development. Paris: OECD, 2001.

"Trials and Tribulations." *Economist* 372.8390 (2004): 27–28.

Trouillot, Michel-Rolph. "Haiti's Nightmare and the Lessons of History." *Haiti: Dangerous Crossroads.* Ed. North American Congress on Latin America (NACLA). Boston: South End Press, 1995. 121–132.

Trouillot, Michel-Rolph. *Silencing the Past: Power and the Production of History.* Boston: Beacon Press, 1995.

Trouillot, Michel-Rolph. *Haiti: State Against Nation – The Origins and Legacy of Duvalierism.* New York: Monthly Review Press, 1990.

Trueba, Enrique (Henry) T. *The New Americans: Immigrants and Transnationals at Work.* Lanham, MD: Rowman & Littlefield, 2004.

Truong, Thanh-Dam. *Sex, Money and Morality: Prostitution and Tourism in Southeast Asia.* London: Zed Books, 1990.

Tsai, Shih-Shan Henry. *The Chinese Experience in America.* Bloomington: Indiana University Press, 1986.

Turnbow, Kate. "US Senate Address Secure Fence Act." *The Capital Journal* (21 Sept. 2006). www.capjournal.com.

"Twenty-Three Detainees Attempted Suicide In Protest at Base, Military Says." *New York Times* 154.53105 (2005): A12.

Tyler, Patrick E. "Ex-Guantánamo Detainee Charges Beating." *New York Times* 153.52786 (2004): A10.

Tyner, James A. "The Web-based Recruitment of Female Foreign Domestic Workers in Asia." *Singapore Journal of Tropical Geography* 20.2 (1999).

Udall, Lori. "The International Narmada Campaign: A Case of Sustained Advocacy." *Toward Sustainable Development? Struggling over India's Narmada River.* Ed. William F. Fisher. Armonk, NY: M. E. Sharpe, 1995. 201–230.

"Une Saint-Sylvestre sous haute surveillance." *Le Monde* (31 Dec. 2005).

"United and Strengthening America by Providing Appropriate Tools Required to Intercept and Obstruct Terrorism" (USA PATRIOT). Public Law 107–56 (2001).

United Nations Department of Economic and Social Affairs. "Summary of the Report of the Global Commission on International Migration" (2005). www.gcim.org.

United Nations High Commissioner for Refugees (UNHCR). *The State of the World's Refugees: Fifty Years of Humanitiarian Action.* Oxford: Oxford University Press, 2000.

United Nations High Commissioner for Refugees (UNHCR). www.unhcr.ch/cgi-bin/texis/vtx/news/opendoc.htm?tbl=NEWS&id=4395c3354.

"United Nations Human Rights Commission Report Analysis of the Rights of Guantánamo Bay Detainees." *International Debates* 4.4 (2006): 104–105.

United States Agency for International Development (USAID). *Haiti: USAID Monitoring Report/Rapport de Suivi d'USAID 3–6.* Port-au-Prince, Haïti: USAID, 1995–6.

United States Agency for International Development (USAID). *USAID/Haiti Recovery Program (October Briefing Book).* Port-au-Prince, Haïti: USAID, 1994.

United States. Central Intelligence Agency. *Cuba.* Washington, DC: Central Intelligence Agency, 1992. [GOVT. DOC# PrEx 3.10/4:C 89/6 and GOVT. DOC# PREX 3.10/4:C 89/7].

Upton, John. "In the Streets of Londonistan." *London Review of Books* 26.2 (22 Jan. 2004) www.lrb.co.uk/v26/n02/print/upto01.html.

Urbach, Roger, Orlando Nuñez, and Boris Kagarlitsky, eds. *Globalization and Its Discontents: The Rise of Postmodern Socialisms.* Chicago: Pluto Press, 1997.

"US Dollars Sent South Now Fuel Salvador Economy." *Migration World Magazine* 24.3 (1996): 7.

"US Military Commission Trials to Resume, Additional Proceedings to Begin." *American Journal of International Law* 99.4 (2005): 898–899.

"US Releases 14 Saudis at Guantánamo Bay." *New York Times* (25 June 2006): A16.

"US Remembers 9/11 Five Years On." British Broadcasting Corporation. BBC News Online: www.newsvote.bbc.co.uk/mpapps/pagetools/print/news.bbc.co.uk/2/hi/americas/5333646.stm.

"US Reveals the Identities Of Guantánamo Detainees." *New York Times* 155.53508 (2006): A9.

Valladares, Armando. "Castro Outfoxes Clinton – and Guantanamo's Detainees Pay." *Wall Street Journal – Eastern Edition* 225.19 (1995): A11.

van Dalen, Hendrik P., George Groenewold, and Tineke Fokkema. "The Effect of Remittances on Emigration Intentions in Egypt, Morocco, and Turkey." *Population Studies* 59.3 (2005): 375–392.

Van Eyck, Kim. "Women, Workers, and Migrants in the Globalized Public Health Sector: Debate at the 2004 International Labour Conference." *Development in Practice* 15.5 (2005): 701–709.

van Selm, Joanne, ed. *Kosovo's Refugees in the European Union.* London: Continuum, 2000.

van Selm, Joanne. *Refugee Protection in Europe: Lessons of the Yugoslav Crisis.* The Hague: Kluwer Law International, 1998.

Vanita, Ruth, ed. *Queering India: Same-Sex Love and Eroticism in Indian Culture and Society*. New York: Routledge, 2002.

VanWey, Leah K., Catherine M. Tucker, and Eileen Diaz McConnell. "Community Organization, Migration, and Remittances in Oaxaca." *Latin American Research Review* 40.1 (2005): 83–107.

Vargas, Zaragosa, ed. *Major Problems in Mexican American History: Documents and Essays*. Boston: Houghton Mifflin, 2005.

Vertovec, Steven, ed. *Migration and Social Cohesion*. Northampton, MA: Edward Elgar, 1999.

"Viewpoints: The World since 9/11." British Broadcasting Corporation. BBC News Online: www.newsvote.bbc.co.uk/mpapps/pagetools/print/news.bbc.co.uk/2/hi/americas/5317612.stm.

Vink, Maarten. *Limits of European Citizenship: European Integration and Domestic Immigration Policies*. Basingstoke: Palgrave Macmillan, 2005.

Volpp, Leti. "The Legal Mapping of US Immigration, 1965–1996." *Crossing into America: The New Literature of Immigration*. Ed. Louis Mendoza and S. Shankar. New York: New Press, 2003. 257–269.

Volpp, Leti. "The Citizen and the Terrorist." *UCLA Law Review* 49 (June 2002).

"Vote, Sweet Vote." *Economist* 371.8381 (2004): 40.

Wagle, Sobodh. "The Long March for Livelihoods: Struggle Against the Narmada Dam in India." *Environmental Justice: Discourses in International Political Economy*. Ed. John Byrne, Leigh Glover, and Cecilia Martinez. New Brunswick, NJ: Transaction Publishers, 2002. 71–96.

Waldinger, Roger, ed. *Strangers at the Gates: New Immigrants in Urban America*. Berkeley: University of California Press, 2001.

Waldman, Amy. "Guantánamo And Jailers: Mixed Review By Detainees." *New York Times* 153.52791 (2004): A6.

Waller, Marguerite, and Sylvia Marcos, ed. *Dialogue and Difference: Feminisms Challenge Globalization*. Basingstoke: Palgrave Macmillan, 2005.

Wallerstein, Immanuel. *The Decline of American Power*. New York: New Press, 2003.

Wallman, Sandra. "Global Threats, Local Options, Personal Risk: Dimensions of Migrant Sex Work in Europe." *Health, Risk & Society* 3.1 (2001): 75–87.

Walters, William H. "Place Characteristics and Later-Life Migration." *Research on Aging* 24.2 (2002): 243.

"War on Terrorism Detainee Mission." www.www.nsgtmo.navy.mil.

Ward, C., and I. Styles. "Culturing Settlement Using Pre- and Post-Migration Strategies." *Journal of Psychiatric & Mental Health Nursing* 12.4 (2005): 423–430.

Ward, H., and S. Day. "Have Changes in the Sex Industry Increased STI Risk?" *Sexually Transmitted Infections* 79 (2003): A26.

Ward, Kathryn, ed. *Women Workers and Global Restructuring*. Ithaca: ILR Press, 1990.

Ware, Helen. "Demography, Migration and Conflict in the Pacific." *Journal of Peace Research* 42.4 (2005): 435–454.

Warner, Michael. *The Trouble With Normal: Sex, Politics, and the Ethics of Queer Life*. Cambridge, MA: Harvard University Press, 2000.

Warner, Michael. *The Trouble with Normal: Sex, Politics and the Ethics of Queer Life*. New York: Free Press, 1999.

Warner, Michael, ed. *Fear of a Queer Planet: Queer Politics and Social Theory*. Minneapolis: University of Minnesota Press, 1993.

Warner, Michael. Special section on "Fear of a Queer Planet." *Social Text* 9.4 (1991): 3–56.

"Warning of Threat." *Beijing Review* 47.34 (2004): 6.

Watney, Simon. "AIDS and the Politics of Queer Diaspora." *Negotiating Lesbian and Gay Subjects.* Ed. Monica Dorenkamp and Richard Henke. New York: Routledge, 1995.

Watts, Charlotte, and Cathy Zimmerman. "Violence against Women: Global Scope and Magnitude." *The Lancet* 359.9313 (April 6, 2002): 1232–1237.

Watts, Julie R. *Immigration Policy and the Challenge of Globalization: Unions and Employers in Unlikely Alliance.* Ithaca: Cornell University Press; London: ILR Press, 2002.

Weber, Cynthia. *Faking It: US Hegemony in a "Post-Phallic" Era.* Minneapolis: University of Minnesota Press, 1999.

Weber, Robin. "Don't Mess with Texas." *Dermatology Nursing* 17.3 (2005): 212.

Wegener, Phillip E. "Soldierboys for Peace: Cognitive Mapping, Space, and Science Fiction as World Bank Literature." *World Bank Literature.* Minneapolis: University of Minnesota Press, 2003. 280–296.

Weil, Patrick. "Towards a Coherent Policy of Co-Development." *International Migration* 40.3 (2002): 41.

Weiner, Tim. "Haitian Ex-Paramilitary Leader Confirms CIA Relationship." *New York Times* (3 Dec. 1995): A6.

Weiner, Tim. "Key Haiti Leaders Said to Have Been in the CIA's Pay." *New York Times* (1 Nov. 1993): A1.

Welch, Michael. *Detained: Immigration Laws and the Expanding INS Jail Complex.* Philadelphia: Temple University Press, 2002.

West, Bing. "America as Jailer." *National Review* 58.13 (2006): 27–29.

Westwood, Sallie, and Annie Phizacklea. "The Politics of Belonging – Sex Work, Domestic Work: Transnational Household Strategies." *Trans-nationalism and the Politics of Belonging.* New York: Routledge, 2000. 120–145.

Westwood, Sallie, and Annie Phizacklea. *Trans-nationalism and the Politics of Belonging.* New York: Routledge, 2000.

Whalen, Carmen Teresa, and Víctor Vázquez-Hernández, eds. *The Puerto Rican Diaspora: Historical Perspectives.* Philadelphia: Temple University Press, 2005.

"What Bush Can Do, and What He Can't." *Economist* 380.8485 (2006): 28–29.

"What Now?" *Economist* 370.8364 (2004): 53–54.

White, Caroline. "British Doctors Call for Independent Scrutiny of Guantanamo Bay Detainees." *BMJ: British Medical Journal* 333.7569 (2006): 617.

"Who's Who in Al-Qaeda." British Broadcasting Corporation. BBC News Online: www.newsvote.bbc.co.uk/mpapps/pagetools/print/news.bbc.co.uk/2/hi/middle_east/2780525.stm.

Widgren, Jonas, and Philip Martin. "Managing Migration: The Role of Economic Instruments." *International Migration* 40.5 (2002): 213.

Wilke, Christiane. "War v. Justice: Terrorism Cases, Enemy Combatants, and Political Justice in US Courts." *Politics & Society* 33.4 (2005): 637–669.

Wilks, Michael. "Guantanamo: A Call for Action." *BMJ: British Medical Journal* 332.7541 (2006): 560–561.

Williams, Allan M., Vladimir Baláž, and Daniel Kollar. "Coming and Going in Slovakia: International Labour Mobility in the Central European 'Buffer Zone'." *Environment & Planning A* 33.6 (2001): 1101.

Williams, Allan M., Vladimir Baláž, and Claire Wallace. "International Labour Mobility and Uneven Regional Development in Europe." *European Urban & Regional Studies* 11.1 (2004): 27–46.

Williams, Eric. *Capitalism and Slavery: The Caribbean.* London: Penguin, 1964.

Willis, Katie, and Brenda Yeoh. *Gender and Migration.* Northampton, MA: Edward Elgar, 2000.

Wilson, Ellen K., and Chris McQuiston. "Motivations for Pregnancy Planning Among Mexican Immigrant Women in North Carolina." *Maternal & Child Health Journal* 10.3 (2006): 311–320.

Winkelmann-Gleed, Andrea, and Janet Seeley. "Strangers in a British World? Integration of International Nurses." *British Journal of Nursing* 14.18 (2005): 954–961.

Wolff, Richard, et al. *Possible Urban Worlds: Urban Strategies at the end of the 20th Century.* Boston: Birkhäuser, 1998.

Wolffe, Richard, Holly Bailey, and John Barry. "No More Happy Talk." *Newsweek* 145.26 (2005): 30.

Woollacott, Angela. "Imperial Dis/connections: Recent Work in Australian History." *Journal of British Studies* 38.1 (1999): 119.

"World." *Australian Nursing Journal* 13.2 (2005): 25.

World Bank. *World Development Report 1999/2000: Entering the 21st Century.* Oxford: Oxford University Press, 2000.

World Bank. "Haiti and the Heavily Indebted Poor Countries Debt Relief Initiative." www.lnweb18.worldbank.org/External/lac/lac.nsf/Countries/Haiti/4939BA8C8760 F114852569960056D48 . . . . Date posted: November 2000. Date accessed: August 9, 2002.

World Bank. "Draft of Haiti: The Challenges of Poverty Reduction." Washington, DC: World Bank, 1997.

World Bank. *World Development Report 1997: The State in a Changing World.* Oxford: Oxford University Press, 1997.

"World Bank Literature" (online book abstract published by press). University of Minnesota Press. www.upress.umn.edu/Books/K/kumar_world.html>. Date accessed: August 6, 2002.

Yadan, Kiran. "In Troubled Waters." *Financial Express* (April 23, 2006). Sardar Sarovar Narmada Nigam Ltd. Website: www.sardarsarovardam.org/news/news181.htm.

Yea, Sallie. "Runaway Brides: Anxieties of Identity among Trafficked Filipina Entertainers in South Korea." *Singapore Journal of Tropical Geography* 25.2 (2004): 180–197.

Yeates, Nicola. "A Dialogue with 'Global Care Chain' Analysis: Nurse Migration in the Irish Context." *Feminist Review* (2004): 79–95.

Yeoh, Brenda S. A., Shirlena Huang, and Joaquin Gonzalez III. "Migrant Female Domestic Workers: Debating the Economic, Social and Political Impacts in Singapore." *International Migration Review* 33.1 (1999): 114–136.

Yin, Tung. "Ending the War on Terrorism One Terrorist at a Time: A Noncriminal Detention Model for Holding and Releasing Guantanamo Bay Detainees." *Harvard Journal of Law & Public Policy* 29.1 (2005): 149–212.

Young, Joseph A. and Jana Evans Braziel, eds. *Race and the Foundations of Knowledges: Cultural Amnesia in the Academy.* Urbana-Champagne: University of Illinois Press, 2006.

Young, Robert J. C. *Postcolonialism: An Historical Introduction.* Oxford: Blackwell, 2001.

Young, Robert J. C. *Colonial Desire: Hybridity in Theory, Culture and Race.* New York: Routledge, 1995.

Young, Robert J. C. *White Mythologies: Writing History and the West.* New York: Routledge, 1990.

Yu Xu, and Jianhui Zhang. "One Size Doesn't Fit All: Ethics of International Nurse Recruitment from the Conceptual Framework of Stakeholder Interests." *Nursing Ethics* 12.6 (2005): 571–581.

Zachariah, K. C., E. T. Mathew, and S. Irudaya Rajan. "Impact of Migration on Kerala's Economy and Society." *International Migration* 39.1 (2001).

Zachariah, K. C., E. T. Mathew, and S. Irudaya Rajan. "Social, Economic and Demographic Consequences of Migration on Kerala." *International Migration* 39.2 (2001).

Zachariah, K. C., B. A. Prakash, and S. Irudaya Rajan. "The Impact of Immigration Policy on Indian Contract Migrants: The Case of the United Arab Emirates." *International Migration* 41.4 (2003): 161.

Zagorin, Adam, and Brian Bennett. "One Life Inside Gitmo." *Time* 167.11 (2006): 20–23.

Zarembka, Joy M. "America's Dirty Work: Migrant Maids and Modern-Day Slavery." *Global Woman: Nannies, Maids, and Sex Workers in the New Economy.* Ed. Barbara Ehrenreich and Arlie Russell Hochschild. New York: Metropolitan Books, Henry Holt, 2002. 142–153.

Zenaida, Agnes. "Family, Child Labour and Migration: Child Domestic Workers in Metro Manila." *Childhood* 6.1 (1999): 57.

Zernike, Kate. "Senate Approves Broad New Rules to Try Detainees." *New York Times* (29 Sept. 2006): A1, A20.

Zernike, Kate. "Newly Released Reports Show Early Concern on Prison Abuse." *New York Times* 154.53086 (2005): A1–A24.

Zolberg, Aristide R., and Peter M. Benda, eds. *Global Migrants, Global Refugees: Problems and Solutions.* New York: Berghahn Books, 2001.

Zolberg, Aristide R., Astri Surhke, and Sergio Aguayo, eds. *Escape from Violence: Conflict and the Refugee Crisis in the Developing World.* Oxford: Oxford University Press, 1989.

Index